Miracle-Gro® Complete Guide to Perennials

Meredith® Books
Des Moines, Iowa

D0514635

Miracle-Gro Complete Guide to Perennials
Editor: Marilyn Rogers
Contributing Editor: Megan McConnell Hughes
Contributing Writer: Scott Aker, Laura Deeter
Contributing Designer: Greg Nettles/Squarecrow Creative Group
Copy Chief: Terri Fredrickson
Copy Editor: Kevin Cox
Publishing Operations Manager: Karen Schirm
Senior Editor, Asset and Information Management: Phillip Morgan
Edit and Design Production Coordinator: Mary Lee Gavin
Art and Editorial Sourcing Coordinator: Jackie Swartz
Editorial Assistant/Photo Researcher: Susan Ferguson
Book Production Managers: Pam Kvitne, Marjorie J. Schenkelberg,
  Mark Weaver
Imaging Center Operator: David Swain
Contributing Copy Editors: Susan Lang
Contributing Proofreaders: Jodie Littleton, Stephanie Petersen
Contributing Map Illustrator: Jana Fothergill
Contributing Indexer: Richard Evans
Other Contributors: Janet Anderson, Kate Carter Frederick

Meredith® Books
Editor in Chief: Gregory H. Kayko
Executive Director, Design: Matt Strelecki
Managing Editor: Amy Tincher-Durik
Executive Editor: Benjamin W. Allen
Senior Associate Design Director: Tom Wegner
Marketing Product Manager: Brent Wiersma

Executive Director, Marketing and New Business: Kevin Kacere
Director, Marketing and Publicity: Amy Nichols
Executive Director, Sales: Ken Zagor
Director, Operations: George A. Susral
Director, Production: Douglas M. Johnston
Business Director: Janice Croat

Senior Vice President: Karla Jeffries
Vice President and General Manager: Douglas J. Guendel

Meredith Publishing Group
President: Jack Griffin
Executive Vice President: Doug Olson

Meredith Corporation
Chairman of the Board: William T. Kerr
President and Chief Executive Officer: Stephen M. Lacy

In Memoriam: E.T. Meredith III (1933–2003)

Photographers
Photographers credited may retain copyright © to the listed
photographs. L=Left, R=Right, C=Center, B=Bottom, T=Top

William Adams: 100TL, 146BL; Mike Bolton/Garden Picture
Library/PhotoLibrary: 229L; Kathy Cafazzo/Peoria Gardens, Inc:
242BR; David Cavagnaro: 55TRC, 68TR, 144BR, 180BR, 188R,
237R, 245TR, 246TL; Jay Cossey: 141BL; Margery Daughtrey/
Cornell University: 149BR; Catriona Tudor Erler: 71TCCR,
184R, 189BL; Derek Fell: 101TCR, 242CR; Judy Fetzer/New York
Botanical Garden/Bugwood.org: 152TR; Garden Picture Library/
PhotoLibrary: 193TL, 207BL, 216BL; John Glover/Positive
Images: 48L; Saxon Holt: 108, 109B, 109T, 190BL, 225TR; Iowa
State University/Plant & Insect Diagnostic Clinic: 151TR.
151BR; Bill Johnson: 141TCL, 141TC, 141BLC, 143TL, 143BL,
145TL, 246BL, 246TR; Michael Krot: 141TR; Rosemary
Kautzky: 27BLC, 47BR, 215L, 247BL; David Liebman: 141BCR;
Kathy Martin: 101BCR; Montanabw/Wikipedia Commons
Images: 100BR; J. Paul Moore: 193BL; Jerry Pavia: 162BL, 212BL,
227L, 242TR; Rich Pomerantz: 47BC; Graham Rice/
GardenPhotos.com: 150TR; Joseph G. Strauch Jr.: 142TL, 142R,
143BR, 144TL, 150BR; Michael Thompson: 18BL, 18BC, 18BR,
149TR, 216BR, 217BL; Mary Walters/Image Botanica: 19BL,
207TR, 210BL, 228BR.

Cover Photographer: David McDonald

All of us at Meredith® Books are dedicated to providing
you with the information and ideas you need to enhance your
home and garden. We welcome your comments and suggestions
about this book. Write to us at:
  Meredith Corporation
  Meredith Gardening Books
  1716 Locust St.
  Des Moines, IA 50309–3023

If you would like more information on other Miracle-Gro
products, call 800/225-2883 or visit us at: www.miraclegrow.com

Note to the Readers: Due to differing conditions, tools,
and individual skills, Meredith Corporation assumes no
responsibility for any damages, injuries suffered, or losses
incurred as a result of following the information published
in this book. Before beginning any project, review the
instructions carefully, and if any doubts or questions
remain, consult local experts or authorities. Because codes
and regulations vary greatly, you always should check
with authorities to ensure that your project complies
with all applicable local codes and regulations. Always
read and observe all of the safety precautions provided
by manufacturers of any tools, equipment, or supplies,
and follow all accepted safety procedures.

Contents

Perennial promises

▲ Perennials provide long-lasting decoration for your backyard hideaway. Use them in large beds taking up most of your landscape or spot them in here and there among the shrubs and other plantings in your yard. However you use them, perennials light the spark that sets your home apart from all the others in your neighborhood.

You can count on perennials. Whether you are looking for stalwart plants to stand up to the rigors of a hot, dry site or wish to create a color-rich border of blossoms that put on a show that starts in early spring, perennials are up to the challenge. Is your landscape plagued by wet clay soil that seems to foster little plant life? Many perennials thrive in wet sites. Want to add some spark to the planting area around your patio? Perennials will add a punch of pizzazz.

Brimming with color, texture, and an ample dose of tenacity, perennials make many promises and they deliver, first with come-again flowers and foliage. When planted in the proper site and properly cared for, perennials return year-after-year. Thanks to their way of sending up new foliage, blooming, and retreating back to the earth, perennials promise constant landscape change.

At the same time, perennials guarantee predictability. Every year at about the same time they unfurl new leaves and send up flower stalks. You'll come to know that when common salvia begins to bloom in late spring, common yarrow will follow suit in a few days.

Perennials are great growers. Some flourish in the desert Southwest, and others grow with gusto in the Northern Plains states. Many thrive in the heat and humidity of the Southeast while others happily reside in upper elevations where the climate is cooler and drier.

When thoughtfully selected and properly

◄ The chapter Good Garden Design explains how to create gorgeous plant combinations based on plant shape, foliage textures and colors, as well as on flowers. Plant combinations are the basis for any garden of any size.

planted, perennials promise to come back again and again to dress up your garden.

Growing knowledge

Just as you can count on perennials to work hard in your landscape, you can depend on this book to be your one-stop source for all your questions about perennials. Arranged in a quick-read, information-packed format, the following pages boast at-a-glance sidebars, tip boxes, and charts to inform and inspire your perennial planting. You'll find step-by-step directions and pictures to guide you as you design and create your garden, plant perennials, and diagnose problems.

Chapter 1 introduces you to perennials and the many ways in which you can put them to work in your yard. It helps you sort out why you want to grow perennials so that you are better able to select plants and know that they'll be up to the job you have for them.

If you have ever been overwhelmed by the vast selection at your local garden center, you know the challenge involved in choosing perennials for your landscape. In Chapter 2, you'll find tips on selecting

perennials based on climate, soil type, water availability, maintenance requirements, and many other factors. Choosing the right perennials for your landscape ensures that the promises of perennials are fulfilled.

Chapter 3 introduces you to the principles of garden design. It breaks the sometimes daunting task of envisioning and planning a garden into manageable steps. The result is a cohesive landscape design that offers up many planting possibilities.

For planting tips, turn to Chapter 4, for quick and easy techniques that ensure your perennials get off to a good start and are equipped to thrive for many years.

Chapter 5 is all about taking care of perennials. Two common terms in perennial gardening—deadheading and dividing—are demystified with step-by-step photos, quick reference charts, and straightforward advice. The chapter also covers annual maintenance and provides tips for keeping garden chores to a minimum so you can maximize your time enjoying the plants.

A well-tended perennial patch rarely encounters serious pest problems, but if the need for pest control

arises, you'll be ready with the troubleshooting tips in Chapter 6. You'll find lots of photos of the pests and diseases commonly affecting perennials and a plethora of remedies to end them.

Explore the encyclopedia

General knowledge about how to grow perennials is invaluable, but often you'll find yourself with a question about a specific plant. Turn to Chapter 7, the encyclopedia, for plant-specific answers. Here you'll find detailed descriptions of more than 400 perennials of all shapes and sizes, including plants for every growing region in North America. You'll find information on blooming perennials for sun and shade, vines suitable for perennial gardens, foliage plants, ornamental grasses, and much more.

The entries are organized by common name for easy reference. Each entry displays at least one photograph of the perennial and includes a detailed description of the plant and its growing habit as well as information on recommended cultivars and related species.

In addition, you'll find tips for integrating the plant into your landscape, suggestions for companion plants, and a rundown of annual maintenance needs.

All of the plants mentioned in Chapters 1 through 6 are in the encyclopedia section. If you find an intriguing plant in an early chapter, flip to the encyclopedia to learn more about it. You might decide

it's a great fit for your perennial garden.

Dig in

Part of the joy of gardening is the opportunity to explore new plants, techniques, and garden theories. Whether you're planting perennials for the first time or you've been at it for years, there is always something new to learn. So go for it! Create a beautiful perennial garden, grow new plant varieties, and try your hand at deadheading and dividing. Use this book as your guide and you're sure to embrace the joy of growing perennials. That's a promise!

▼ Perennials create a changing scene throughout the year. The earliest, Lenten roses, can be found blooming under the snow. Whenever spring arrives in your region, you'll find sprouts such as this emerging variegated solomon's seal popping up daily to awaken your senses.

Why grow perennials?

The longevity of perennials is the chief reason why many people choose them for their beds and borders. Although most perennials don't have the potential to live as long as, say, an oak tree, they live longer than annuals, which need to be planted every year.

Plant a garden of perennials and every year watch them unfurl new foliage and flowers. With proper care, many perennials can easily live 15 years or more. Peony, a fragrant spring-blooming perennial, is known to live 100 years or more.

Most perennials need to be divided many times over their lifetime. You can easily multiply your collection and share the excess with neighbors and friends.

Constant change

Perennials are quick change artists, at some times, almost changing daily. As an example, astilbe's foliage emerges as deep red stems in spring. Then the tiny green leaflets unfurl, doubling in size almost daily. The flower buds start out as tight, dense clusters, shooting above the foliage, and finally opening as feathery flowers. During this time, the whole plant changes in appearance from a rounded mound to a broad, flat clump of foliage from which tall wands of colorful flowers emerge.

Perhaps the most striking change in the perennial garden is evident in ornamental grasses. Some grasses are capable of going from a dormant mound to 18 feet tall in a season. Throughout the growing season ornamental grasses offer weekly changes as they progress from small tufts of green, to arching blades swaying in the breeze to stalks of dramatic seedheads in fall.

Keep this evolving nature in mind when designing with perennials. A plant with eyecatching summer flowers might also boast bold seedheads that last into winter. Plant it where you need a burst of color in summer and structural interest in winter.

Year-round interest

In addition to featuring individual plants that change during the season, a perennial garden provides a progression of flowering. Consider a shade garden. In late winter, Lenten rose flowers put on a show followed by the spring blossoms of barrenwort, and then come lungwort and columbine and other spring bloomers.

Late spring brings amsonia, violet, bleeding heart, and astilbe. Summer displays include coral bells, yellow corydalis and an

▲ You can count on perennials to provide interest from spring to fall. Some, such as hybrid anemones and chrysanthemums, begin blooming in late summer to early fall. Others are winding down the season but still offer colorful foliage or ripening seed heads, like this miscanthus, an ornamental grass.

▼ Woodland phlox, fringed bleeding heart, lady's mantle, and tulips welcome spring.

incredible array of hosta varieties with colorful foliage, and some with fragrant flowers from which wafts an amazing perfume.

Just when you think the end of the season is near, along comes rose turtlehead, toad lily, and Japanese anemone. And that's only in the shade garden.

By combining herbaceous perennials with bulbs, annuals, and grasses, even a garden in the upper Midwest can have something in bloom from March through November. In warm climates a garden can feature a year-long display of subtropical delights.

In every region seedheads, colorful stems, and evergreen foliage carry the garden through times when plants are out of bloom. Winter might be a down time in cold climates, summer a down time in the hottest areas, but with thoughtful planning in the design phases, any gardener can create a perennial garden to enjoy every day of the year.

Trouble-free growers

Most perennials tolerate insects and diseases, even though they're not immune to problems. For example phlox regularly gets powdery mildew, and even the

◀ Yellow lady's mantle, blue salvia, and pink astilbe bloom in early summer. Pink snapdragons (foreground), which are annuals, round out this garden.

resistant types occasionally have a small amount of the disease on their foliage. However powdery mildew rarely kills phlox—or any other perennial—and simply thinning the plant helps lower the incidence of the disease. Slugs and snails can riddle hosta leaves, but they rarely kill plants.

Don't let problems dissuade you from using perennials. The vast majority are well behaved and long lived. Serious ailments rarely crop up in most gardens, and simple changes, such as switching species or varieties, usually cures the problem.

▲ Many perennials, including the snow-capped showy sedum and ornamental grasses in this garden, add structure and color to the winter landscape.

A YEAR-ROUND PERENNIAL GARDEN

There is no need to tuck the garden in for a long winter nap if you live in a cold-winter climate, or for a summer siesta if you're in a hot spot. Call on intriguing perennial foliage, seedheads, and plant forms to add a spark of interest to the landscape when blooms are few. Here's a roundup of some of the best plants for bridging the flower gap.

PLANTS FOR WINTER AND FALL INTEREST IN COLD-CLIMATE GARDENS

Arkansas amsonia: brilliant yellow fall color
Astilbe: feathery seedheads
'Autumn Joy' stonecrop: great seedheads all winter long
Butterfly weed: long-lasting seedheads
Geranium: red fall color
Hen-and-chicks: evergreen foliage
Lamb's ears: silvery foliage
Ornamental grasses: many maintain a pleasing upright form until early spring
Pink: evergreen foliage
Purple coneflower: bold seedheads
Siberian iris: yellow fall color
Thrift: evergreen foliage

PLANTS FOR SUMMER INTEREST IN HOT-CLIMATE GARDENS

Agapanthus: deep blue flowers all summer
Centranthus: iridescent reddish pink flowers and gray-green foliage
Coreopsis: bright yellow blossoms for much of the summer
Liriope: evergreen foliage
New Zealand flax: variegated foliage in shades of red, pink, cream, yellow, and green
Texas hyssop: raspberry-red flowers top 3-foot-tall plants
Firecracker penstemon: Bright scarlet tubular flowers attract hummingbirds
Autumn and blue anise sages: masses of brilliantly colored blooms

Geranium in fall

Agapanthus in summer

Why grow perennials? *(continued)*

▶ Many perennials are available to create colorful water-thrifty gardens in arid and other regions.

▲ If you have problems with water standing in your yard for long periods after a rain, try filling it with perennials such as yellow and blue flag irises, rodgersia, and Japanese primrose.

Solutions for tough spots

Is there a challenging garden area in your landscape? Perhaps you have a slope that is too steep to safely mow or a very shady spot where grass won't grow.

Maybe there is a wet spot in your yard and all the shrubs you've tried to grow in it have died. Or you might live in a community where water is at a premium and water restrictions enforced.

Perennials triumph in all kinds of planting situations. You'll find perennials for sites with standing water and ones for very hot, dry spots, for windy exposed sites, and for deep shade. There are perennials that thrive in poor soil as well as fertile, or that prefer alkaline or acid soil.

You will find flowering evergreen groundcovers that can take over your hillside, eliminating your need to mow while holding the soil in place. Shade-loving groundcovers will flourish where grass won't.

In a low, poorly drained spot where water collects after every rain, create a bog or rain garden filled with water-loving perennials.

The south side of your house, where it's always hot, dry, and sunny, is the perfect spot for native plants, fully adapted to such sites.

Where water restrictions are a constant, a xeriscape (water conserving garden) is a good solution. A surprising number of perennials thrive with little water.

Perennials present solutions to many other landscape problems; see the chart on page 11 for colorful, texture-rich plants for your tough spot.

Landscape solutions

Perennials also fill nearly any landscape role. They help control runoff with their roots by slowing the water flow long enough for it to soak in. Use them on hillsides to control erosion.

◀ Use perennials to hold the soil on a slope and avoid the safety issues of mowing such a steep grade.

▲ Colorful hostas, Japanese painted fern, and white-flowering astilbe take the blah out of a shady corner.

Many perennials make fantastic groundcovers that can be used as a lawn replacement in small areas, such as courtyards. A thyme lawn, for example, will never need mowing, will have pretty pink flowers in summer, and—if you choose the right species—will remain green even in winter. Many low-growing perennials will even handle foot traffic.

PERENNIALS FOR SPECIALTY GARDENS

FRAGRANCE
Catmint
False solomon's seal
'Fragrant Angel' coneflower
Hyssop
Iris
Lavender
Lily
Pinks
Thyme

CUT FLOWERS
Astilbe
Baby's breath
Delphinium
Foxglove
Gayfeather
Ornamental grasses
Phlox
Shasta daisy
Torch lily
Yarrow

ATTRACT WILDLIFE
Avens
Bee balm
Bellflower
Butterfly weed
Cardinal flower
Columbine
Lupine
Sea holly
Thrift

XERISCAPE
Baby's breath
Daylily
Evening primrose
Lamb's-ears
Lavender cotton
Miscanthus
Mountain bluet
Mullein
Penstemon
Sedum
Yarrow

▼ Butterfly milkweed is a favorite nectar source for monarchs and many other butterflies.

PERENNIAL SOLUTIONS

Plant	Notable characteristic
WET SOILS	
Cardinal flower	Brilliant red flowers in late summer
Joe-pye weed	Large mauve blooms; up to 6 feet tall when in bloom
New York ironweed	Dark purple to red violet flowers on 7-foot-stems in late summer
Rodgersia	Coarse texture, flower plumes in spring or summer
Sweet flag	Long-lasting swordlike foliage
DRY SOILS	
Blue fescue	Ornamental grass with bluish green foliage
Catmint	Fragrant foliage and purple flowers in early summer
False indigo	Pealike purple flowers in late spring followed by attractive seedpods
Liriope	Dark green grasslike foliage
Penstemon	Bright flower colors, upright shape
White gaura	Airy white flower stalks from midsummer to fall
Yucca	Rounded clump of upright foliage
SHADE	
Astilbe	Long-lasting flower stalks in summer
Foam flower	White or light pink flowers in spring
Hardy begonia	Heart-shape foliage; pink flowers in fall
Hosta	Grown for foliage; many cultivars
Lenten rose	Coarse-textured foliage; blooms in late winter to early spring
Lungwort	Early spring flowers and variegated foliage
Old-fashioned bleeding heart	Heart-shape pink flowers in early summer
Toad lily	Orchidlike flowers in late summer to fall
Yellow waxbells	Maplelike foliage and yellow flowers in late summer to early fall

Plant	Notable characteristic
ALKALINE SOIL	
Coral bells	Many cultivars with colorful foliage
Creeping baby's breath	White flowers in summer
Geranium	Spring or summer flowers depending on species; foliage of many turns red in fall
Japanese anemone	Late summer or fall flowers
Pincushion flower	Bluish purple flowers on wiry stems
Pinks	White, pink, or red flowers in spring and summer; evergreen foliage
ACID SOIL	
Bear's breeches	Tall flower spikes in late spring to early summer and texture-rich foliage
Cinnamon fern	Reddish brown fronds in center of plant
Fringed bleeding heart	Finely cut foliage; flowers all summer
Gayfeather	Purple or white flower spikes in summer
Heart-leaf bergenia	Shiny evergreen foliage
Japanese iris	Showy flowers in late spring or summer
Lenten rose	Flowers in late winter
FULL SUN	
Coreopsis	Yellow flowers all summer
Hollyhock	Summer flowers on tall spikes
Maltese cross	Silver foliage and magenta flowers in early summer
Oriental poppy	Flowers with paperlike petals in late spring and early summer
Penstemon	White, pink, red, blue, lilac, purple, or yellow flowers all summer
Peony	Large, fragrant flowers in late spring
Mountain bluet	Blue to violet flowers in midspring to early summer
Tree mallow	Shrublike perennial with white, pink, or purple-pink flowers

▲ Meadow rue, foxtail lily *(Eremurus* spp.), and bishop's goutweed *(Aegopodium podagraria* 'Variegata') make a nontraditional foundation planting.

▲ Red-flowered coral bells combine with several types of thyme and lamb's-ears to form a texture- and color-rich groundcover.

Just like trees and shrubs, perennials are invaluable to landscape designs. Use them as focal points and in foundation plantings. Grow perennials in containers or plant them in masses to unify your landscape plan.

Perennials are outstanding choices for foundation plantings. In many regions, foundation plantings consist of a row of evergreens in front of the house. This row of uninspiring plants does a poor job of accomplishing its mission, which is to direct attention away from sore spots.

Mixing plants

Gardeners tend to put herbs in an herb garden, annuals in an annual garden, vegetables in a vegetable garden, and perennials in a perennial garden. Although that arrangement simplifies some tasks, such as harvesting and pest control, it robs you of the possibilities for making intriguing design combinations and finding solutions to any problems that plague your landscape.

Try something new: Mingle perennials with all the different types of landscape plants for noteworthy, unexpected results. For example in a foundation planting, try making small groupings that include an evergreen shrub, a deciduous shrub or two, and a few perennials.

Don't worry about changing your entire foundation planting area all at once; making just a few small changes can increase the visual appeal of your home. By adding perennials into the mix, you can have a foundation planting with dramatic appeal all season long. The evergreens will provide texture and interest all year, especially in winter; the deciduous shrubs provide flowers in spring, summer or fall, and fall color; and the perennials will add punch in summer.

Perennials for structure

Many homeowners plant a small tree at the corner of their house as a structural focal point for the foundation planting. Usually that small tree grows into a much larger tree than expected and starts to cause problems with its roots growing into pipes and its branches rapping against windows and walls.

You can use perennials as tree substitutes in a

THE GROWING GARDEN

Plants, just like people, develop and change as they age. A garden in infancy is filled with small "cute" plants with lots of space between them. It can be hard to visualize what the garden will look like in two, three or five years, even for someone who knows that their 'Sum and Substance' hosta can grow 7 to 8 feet across.

In an adolescent garden plants may be lazy (overly floppy), moody (quit blooming), bullying (spreading aggressively) or obstinate (simply refusing to grow at all).

The middle-aged garden is a time when many species suffer from "middle age spread." They start growing and growing and taking up more and more space in the garden.

They also start to lose their youthful good looks and perhaps they may no longer bloom well, or the plant may develop a hole in its center. Plants grown for their colorful stems or foliage can start to fade as they enter middle age.

What can be middle age for one plant is old age for another, and you might find that certain plants simply quit coming up.

As your plants age so does your garden, and each stage has different needs.

▲ If you have no extra ground in which to plant a garden or you want to expand your horizons, try growing perennials in containers. The portability of containers lets you bring species that are not hardy in your region inside for the winter.

foundation planting. Many have the size and structure to take on the role without the wide ranging roots and branches of a tree. Some even provide structure throughout the year, not just in summer.

In containers

Perennials add color, texture, structure, and all their other characteristics to a container planting, extending the interest and generating a wider range of possibilities. Campanula, black-eyed susan, purple coneflowers, and stonecrops are all excellent container plants and can readily provide

architecture, height, and texture to any container planting.

Showcase a theme

Having a theme will help you make smart plant selections and will give you good ideas as you start your garden's design. The diverse world of perennial plants offers many possibilities for garden themes. For example, you might be interested in Biblical, Shakespearean, or butterfly gardens. Not all themes need to be so specialized. Build a theme on your needs. For example, if you're home only at night to enjoy a garden, consider

▲ Perennials create a welcoming entry to a home. Yellow yarrow, blue oat grass, and blue salvia planted near the sidewalk and red centranthus in the background greet visitors and walkers as they pass by this home.

planting a moon garden filled with white or pastel flowers.

Some people collect a specific perennial and its many varieties and build their garden around the collection. With so many perennials to

choose from, a collection-themed garden is almost always unique. You can learn more about your favorite perennials through plant societies and reputable online sources.

GROW A BACKBONE

Structure comes from the plants that have a garden presence all year; they're the garden's backbone. Trees and shrubs are structural plants, but not the only ones. Many perennials have enough presence to provide the structure a garden needs.

Plant name	Notable trait	Zones
Asters	Depending on the species, plants form dense 2- to 5-foot-tall mounds	4–9
Feather reed grass	Columnar form and seedheads that stand upright for most of the winter	5–9
Heart-leaf bergenia	Stiff, round, cabbagelike evergreen foliage	4–10
Lavender	Silver leaves persist through winter	5–8
Liriope	Evergreen groundcover	6–10
Purple coneflower	Seedheads are sturdy and last most of the winter	3–8
Russian sage	Silvery stems all year	3–9
Sedum	Upright cultivars have long-lasting stems, leaves, and seedheads that persist all winter	3–9
Yarrow	Ferny, semievergreen foliage	3–10
Yucca	Rounded mound of stiff, sharp leaves	4–11

Perennial challenges

◀ Your work in a garden is never done. Even if your garden is a third the size of this one, you'll need to spend time weeding and deadheading every week. The larger the garden the more time you'll spend in it. Of course, most gardeners enjoy the work and consider the time well spent.

You might be asking yourself, "Where do I start?" Perennials can be challenging even for veteran gardeners, but they're also a delight. You never stop learning when you work with perennials—and you'll always find a new plant, a new technique, or a new way of combining plants to spark your creative spirit.

Short flowering window

Some people consider the limited flowering time for each individual species to be a shortcoming. Most perennials flower for two to four weeks, and a garden planted exclusively with perennials often experiences a lull in flowering as the seasons change. In addition, few perennials bloom from late spring to early summer or from late summer to early fall. Annuals such as impatiens and petunias, on the other hand, are blanketed with blossoms from late spring until frost.

You can add a few annuals to the perennial garden to enjoy blooms all season long. Or you can consider perennials' short flowering time to be a challenge. And your task is to bring together a group of plants that will provide blooms from spring to fall.

A garden filled with annuals will have a consistent look throughout the growing season, but a perennial garden changes every couple of weeks. For example, purple moss phlox may blanket the ground in spring. Then coreopsis, blanket flower, black-eyed susan, and daylily send up blossoms in summer. And asters, many ornamental

The previous pages describe the many reasons to grow perennials. With all their laudable traits, perennials may seem to have no shortcomings.

While it is true these long-lived plants can be used to great advantage in any garden situation, they do present a few challenges.

The biggest hurdle is probably the reason you are reading this book—growing perennials requires a little knowledge. There are hundreds of species of perennials and many plant-specific care techniques.

◀ Deadheading is the most frequent task required in a perennial garden. Removing spent flowers tidies the garden as well as spurs most perennials to start a second round of blooming. Many perennials will bloom all summer if deadheaded routinely.

grasses, and sedums decorate the landscape in fall. A perennial garden changes constantly, and there is always something new for you to enjoy.

Provide ample space

The constantly changing nature of a perennial garden requires plenty of planting space. The individual plants need space to grow, expand, and mature. You'll also want to allocate enough space that you can grow a diverse group of plants.

While three annuals is enough to provide color all summer, you might need 15 to 18 perennials to ensure a colorful show from spring to fall and that can add to your work load. Be aware though, a bigger garden means more garden chores.

Although perennials require lots of space to grow in a garden, when grown in a pot they take no more space than annuals. For a texture-rich display in a container garden, pair perennials with annuals and shrubs.

Plant on!

Don't let these challenges dissuade you from growing perennials. One of their best characteristics is that they are generally forgiving.

If you don't have time to divide a plant in spring or forget to deadhead after the first flush of blooms, it's usually not a problem. The stalwart plants will grow on, maybe just a little slower.

▲ Dividing plants may seem like a mysterious process that gardeners do to torment their perennials. It's actually beneficial to the plants, removing dead and weak material that can undermine their health. The only difficulty is remembering how often you need to divide certain perennials.

THREE PERENNIAL MYTHS

PERENNIALS ARE NO-MAINTENANCE

Anyone who has grown a garden, even ones filled with plants such as 'Autumn Joy' sedum touted to require no maintenance, knows that there is no such thing as a "no-maintenance" perennial garden. All plants require watering, must be cut back either at the end of the season or the next spring, need occasional fertilizing, or may require staking, deadheading, or dividing. Even silk flowers need dusting!

However, you can strive for a lower maintenance garden by choosing plants that require less deadheading, no staking, or less water and fertilizer than others.

A PERENNIAL GARDEN ONLY LOOKS GOOD WHEN PLANTED IN THE ENGLISH BORDER STYLE

English gardens have been around for hundreds of years, and the gardens of Gertrude Jekyll, Edwin Lutyens, and Vita Sackville-West are gorgeous and worthy of admiration if not imitation. The highly variable climates of North America, however, do not always lend themselves to a classic English border. You're better off finding the style of garden that suits your lifestyle and taste.

In reality there are as many garden styles and tastes as there are gardeners. The general rules, tips, and techniques discussed in chapter 3 will help you decide what design and style suits you best.

PERENNIALS ARE NOTHING BUT FANCY WEEDS

A simple definition of a weed is a plant that is out of place. Any plant—perennial, annual, shrub, or grass—that is growing where it shouldn't can be classified as a weed.

Although some perennials display questionable behavior—spreading by runners or setting copious amounts of seed, most perennials on the market today are bred to be well-mannered plants.

Breeders are slowly domesticating the most popular perennials so that they are better behaved and are less likely to wreak havoc in your garden. For gardeners that means less work, and less chance that a single plant will take over the garden.

▲ Once all the work is done, you have the reward of a relaxing spot in which to pull up a chair and watch the birds and butterflies flitting from flower to flower or seed head to seed head and know that you made it happen.

Selecting perennials

▲ When planning your first perennial garden, be aware that it will change over the years. Trees grow, creating more shade. Your tastes change. Some plants die for no apparent reason, giving you the opportunity to try new plants. It's all part of the excitement of gardening with perennials.

Whether you are new to gardening or consider yourself an old hand, the number of choices you have with perennials may leave you staggering. Novice gardeners can be overwhelmed by the many different species—and make mistakes with their choices—while seasoned gardeners find it hard to keep up with all the new varieties on the market every year.

With so many perennials and so many colors, bloom times, and flower types to choose from, it makes a trip to the garden center so exciting.

If you're just starting a perennial garden, take time to plan carefully and research all the perennials you would like to use. Because perennials are a long-term investment, spending time up front pinpointing which ones best fit your needs and the constraints of your climate, soil, and other factors will ensure you make fewer mistakes. The factors in choosing perennials are the same as those for choosing annuals or vegetables, but the diversity of perennials gives you more to think about.

Remember, too, most perennial gardens are always works in progress, even gardenswplanted decades ago. Conditions in your garden may change as trees mature and cast more shade, or you may want to try a new hybrid version of an old standby.

You may start with a concept or theme guided by your favorite colors or the part of the growing season in which you want perennials to bloom, but several years down the road you are likely to have replaced some plants that didn't completely satisfy you. You'll almost certainly be dividing and spreading others that have been star performers and trying new plants you've never grown before. Part of the fun of growing perennials is the

WHAT'S YOUR ZONE?

▲ Magazines, books, and catalogs are among your best information sources for learning about new perennials on the market.

Plants have varying degrees of cold and heat hardiness. For example hybrid peonies are very cold hardy and thrive where winter temperatures dip to -40°F but languish in subtropical regions of the Southeast. Hardy begonia, on the other hand, does not survive winter temperatures below zero but happily grows in high summer temperatures.

A system for ranking plants on heat hardiness is still under development, but for cold hardiness, you can turn to the USDA Hardiness Zone Map, developed by the United States Department of Agriculture. On this map, North America is divided into 11 zones based on average minimum temperatures. Plants are assigned to one of these hardiness zones based on the coldest temperature they survive. To determine your hardiness zone, flip to the map on page 255.

Look for plant hardiness zone ratings on plant tags and in plant descriptions online and in catalogs. Ratings are often given as a range of zones, for example, Zones 3 to 8. In general, the plant will survive winter in the coldest zone as well as tolerate summer heat in the warmest one. However, because water availability and humidity affect heat rankings, the warmer hardiness zone is not always accurate. A plant rated to Zone 8 in the South may grow in Zone 10 or 11 in the Southwest.

Because temperatures have been trending upward in the last decade, you might be able to grow plants not rated as hardy in your region. However, protect them in winter, just in case.

▲ Check out local public and private gardens to help identify your style as well as learn about which plants grow best in your region.

opportunity to select new plants and to improve your garden year after year.

Getting started

Some experts insist that the first step in selecting plants for a garden is to consider the site factors that limit plant growth. However, perhaps it's better, and more fun, to start by getting to know your personal preferences. This is what makes your perennial garden your own.

Thumb through catalogs and circle plants that catch your eye. Check out books on garden design and take notes on what appeals to you and what doesn't. Browse the encyclopedia at the back of this book and flag the plants that attract your interest.

Visit public gardens and jot down the names and attributes of the perennials you find most appealing. If people in your neighborhood garden, take a walk and make notes about plants and

designs that inspire you. Chat with your neighbors and learn more about the plants that grow well for them.

As time goes on you will discover which colors, growth habits, and foliage textures appeal to you the most. You may like the wild prairie look of masses of perennials growing among ornamental grasses, or the romanticism of the cottage garden. The

bold combination of orange and blue flowers may fit your personality, or you might prefer the subtle play of soft pink and white in a garden. You might even find you're more interested in foliage and texture than you are in flower color.

Once your desires are firmly in mind, then begin to think about the limiting factors in your garden.

Select plants for light conditions

▲ Making a light map will help you identify the best planting spots for your perennials.

The amount of sun your garden receives plays a big role in your choice of perennials. Even though in most climates, the majority of perennials do best with at least six hours of sunlight, there are so many perennials to choose from that you can have a bright and dynamic garden in all but the deepest shade, wherever you live.

Take the time to notice how sun and shade patterns change throughout the day. Soft morning sun is different from blazing afternoon sun. The dappled shade of a tree is different from the dense shade cast by your home, a privacy fence, or a garden shed. And shade patterns of trees are much different in spring than in midsummer.

Your impression of how much light your garden receives is likely inaccurate and may be based on the times of day when you tend

to be outdoors. It's important to take a more scientific approach to map the light conditions in your garden.

Make a light map

You can get a better idea of the patterns by making a light map. Trace a copy of the plat, survey map, or a plan of your property on several pieces of tracing paper. Every two hours throughout the day, starting an hour or so after sunrise and continuing to an hour before dusk, observe the shade patterns in your yard and mark them on one copy of the plan. Use a pencil to apply the shading technique that you may have learned in high school art class, pressing hard for deep shade and lightly for light shade.

When you lay these pieces of tracing paper over each other, you get a fairly accurate composite of how much shade or sun you are dealing with in various parts of your yard. The composite is even easier to see if you place the stack of shaded papers on a light box.

Put another copy of your map over the stacked copies and make a final composite drawing. Write notes on the copy about the degree of shade in each area and whether it is shaded in the morning or in the afternoon. Also mark the location of young trees. As they grow

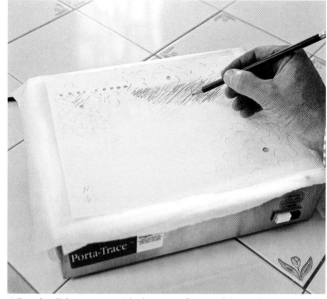

▲ To make a light map, start with a base map of your yard. Lay tracing paper over it, then beginning in the morning, mark shady areas of your yard on the tracing paper. Check the yard every two hours, marking the shady areas on a new sheet of paper. When done, you'll have a complete picture of the shade patterns in your yard.

they will cast more shade, and you'll want to avoid planting perennials that require sunlight and do not transplant well near them. You'll end up with a drawing that roughly divides your property into areas of full sun, light shade, partial shade, and consistent shade.

There are no absolutes for determining just how much light each perennial needs. Catalog descriptions, signs at the garden center, and plant tags don't split hairs when it comes to light conditions, and perennials are usually quite adaptable within these

broad categories of sunlight exposure, as long as their other needs are met.

The real question is whether they will function as ornamentally as you intend. A young oriental poppy, which is labeled for full sun, can function just fine if it receives a half day of sun, but an old clump might produce only a few weak, undersized flowers. If your yard is shady, pay special attention to plants' foliage, because you may have to rely on beautiful foliage instead of flowers. In both shady or sunny gardens, choose plants with staggered

▲ A dense hedge on the east prevents sunlight from reaching this section of the yard before 8 a.m. The area seems mostly shady, but it's actually sunny.

▲ By noon the sun shines bright; a shed on the northwest blocks it from hitting portions of the area. The tree casts some shade, dappling the ground below.

▲ As the sun moves across the sky, the area becomes sunnier until about 3 or 4 p.m. By 6:30 p.m. long shadows stretch across it.

bloom times and bright colors to increase the impact.

► Walls and structures create a consistent dense pattern of shade.

Consider your region

Plants' need for sun and shade varies in different regions. For example, in the coastal Pacific Northwest, the constant clouds prevent plants from receiving optimal amounts of light and keeps temperatures low, often too low for the best growth of sun- and heat-loving perennials. Under a canopy of evergreens, light levels are so low that some shade plants may have trouble growing.

In the Deep South the combination of heat and humidity takes a toll on plants. Many sun-loving perennials won't survive without shade to cool them in the afternoon, and nothing can keep some shade plants alive. Where summers are cool, these same shade plants often do well in full sun.

Gaining sunlight

If your garden is too shady, you may be able to improve light conditions by thinning the tree's canopy or limbing it up (removing a few lower limbs). Limbing lets in light under the canopy, especially when the sun's angle is low. Thinning allows more light to pass through the canopy throughout the day. You might also consider removing trees, if your property is crowded. More light will reach your garden and the health of the remaining trees may also improve.

GREAT FLOWERS AND FOLIAGE FOR SHADE

These perennials bloom well in light shade to full shade. In the deepest shade, such as that found on the north side of a wall or under the canopy of a maple or beech tree, they bloom less but their foliage is attractive enough to make them worthwhile.

Plant	Notable characteristics	Growing notes	Zones
Black snakeroot	Fragrant white flowers in mid- to late summer	Moist soil rich in organic matter	3–8
Celandine poppy	Yellow flowers in mid to late spring	If soil is kept moist, foliage will persist until fall	4–9
Foam flower	Groundcover with white or pink flower spikes in midspring; evergreen in warm climates	Spreads but easy to contain	3–8
Heart-leaf bergenia	Shiny evergreen foliage and deer resistant	Well-drained soil rich in organic matter	4–8
Hosta	Grown for attractive foliage, which may be green, blue, yellow, or variegated	Moist well-drained soil rich in organic matter	3–8
Lungwort	Large white-splattered deep green leaves	Well-drained soil rich in organic matter	4–8
Red barrenwort	Graceful groundcover with reddish spring foliage and red-and-yellow flowers in spring	Excellent drought tolerance; good choice for under a tree	4–8
Rose turtlehead	Upright plant with pink flower spikes in late summer to fall	Moist well-drained soil rich in organic matter	4–8
Woodland phlox	Groundcover with purplish blue or white flowers in midspring	Moist well-drained soil	4–9

Black snakeroot

Celandine poppy

Foam flower

Heart-leaf bergenia

Hosta

Lungwort

Red barrenwort

Rose turtlehead

Woodland phlox

SELECTING PERENNIALS | **19**

Select plants for soil conditions

▲ Wherever water stands on the soil surface, you will need to pay special attention to plant selection. Soil that is poorly drained contains little oxygen, and roots essentially suffocate. This garden is an extreme case, but any slow-draining soil is problematic.

▲ Primroses and sedges thrive in wet situations as do numerous other perennials. However, because your plant choice is considerably limited in wet sites, you might prefer to work on improving drainage.

Soil conditions are the next factor to consider when selecting plants. Take into account the soil's ability to drain and to hold nutrients. Most perennials need soil that drains freely and supplies nutrients. Only wetland species, which naturally grow in bogs, around the margins of ponds, and along streams tolerate soil that is saturated for long periods. Where drainage is excessive plants must tolerate dry conditions.

Drainage

Water moves through well-drained soil with ease. It does not puddle or pool on the surface for extended periods, nor does it run out of the soil so fast that it leaves plants gasping for water. One way to learn whether your soil is well drained is to grab a handful a few days after a soaking rain. If it is well drained it should crumble slightly.

Saturated soil is often an indicator of an impervious layer in the soil. Water may flow downward through the pores in the upper levels of the soil but is forced to move sideways when it encounters a layer of clay or solid rock.

Soil compaction also leads to waterlogging because it eliminates many of the pores in the soil that act as conduits for water to flow through. Soil compaction is a common problem around newly constructed homes as well as in areas getting repeated foot traffic, such as a garden path or play area.

Many people think that if their garden is sloped, the soil will be well drained. That's not necessarily true. Soil on a steep slope may have excellent surface drainage but poor internal drainage. Internal drainage refers to how well water moves downward through the layers of soil by the force of gravity. On a slope, water may be running off rather than soaking in. By definition surface drainage is not an issue if the soil has good internal drainage. If internal drainage is poor and most of the water is running off, then plants are in trouble.

Beware of excessive drainage

Although it may seem that nearly all perennials want good drainage, it is possible to give them too much of a good thing. Soils in coastal plain areas near the beach are nearly all-sand with varying levels of organic matter. These soils are excessively well drained, and any rain that falls on them tends to drain very rapidly.

If working with excessively drained soil, you may have to limit your plant selection to perennials that tolerate dry conditions or plan to irrigate the garden once or twice a week or more often if rainfall is lacking.

Soil components

The components making up the soil affect both drainage and fertility. The best soil for

▶ If your soil is sandy or rocky and excessively drained, you will need to select plants that tolerate dry soil. That does not mean you must grow cactus. Autumn sage, perennial salvia, artemisia, and many ornamental grasses do well in excessively drained soil.

GREAT PERENNIALS FOR WATERLOGGED SOIL

Moisture-loving perennials can turn an ugly muddy spot into a colorful focal point. These plants are excellent choices for bogs and rain gardens. Combine them with sedges and bulrushes. Generally plants that tolerate wet areas need more than half a day of sun.

Plant	Notable characteristics	Growing notes	Zones
Cardinal flower	Bright red flowers in late summer attract hummingbirds	Full sun or part shade	3–9
Helenium	Colorful daisies in autumnal colors	Full sun	3–8
Japanese iris	Blue, purple, pink, or white flowers in late spring or summer	Full sun or part shade and soil rich in organic matter	5–8
Joe-pye weed	Pink flowers in late summer on 6-foot-tall stems	Full sun or part shade	3–7
Ligularia	Yellow flowers on tall stalks in mid- to late summer; large leaves for textural accent	Part shade to full shade	4–6
Queen-of-the-prairie	Fragrant pink flowers on 4- to 6-foot-tall stems	Full sun or part shade	3–9
Hardy hibiscus	Massive, tropical looking red, white, or pink flowers in mid- to late summer	Full sun and soil rich in organic matter	5–9
Siberian iris	Blooms in early summer; many flower colors available	Full sun or part shade	3–9
Swamp milkweed	Fragrant pink flowers on 5-foot-tall stems in summer	Full sun	4–9

Cardinal flower

Hardy hibiscus

Helenium

Japanese iris

Joe-pye weed

Ligularia

Queen-of-the-prairie

Siberian iris

Swamp milkweed

Select plants for soil conditions *(continued)*

▲ Sandy soil is coarse textured, well-drained, and easy to work. It tends to be drier and less fertile than clay and loam.

▲ Loam is a mix of sand, clay, and organic matter that is loose, well-drained yet moisture retentive, fertile, and easy to work.

▲ Clay soil holds plenty of moisture and is highly fertile. However, it is a tight, sticky soil that can be stingy with its water and difficult to work.

▲ A sediment test helps you learn your soil type. Place a handful of soil in a jar and shake. The different particles settle out in order of their weight.

growing perennials is loam—made up of clay, sand, and silt particles, and an ample amount of organic matter. Most garden soils are not this perfect mix of materials, which occasionally makes for challenging growing conditions.

Soils with a high clay content retain nutrients well but tend to be poorly drained. Because the spaces between individual clay particles are so small, it takes a long time for water to percolate down through the soil. In periods of frequent rainfall, this can easily translate into long periods of saturation, when all pore spaces in the soil are filled with water, leaving no room for oxygen. Depriving plants of oxygen kills them if their roots are not equipped to grow in waterlogged soil. If you don't relish the idea of modifying soil conditions to improve drainage, select perennials that naturally grow in wetlands.

Silt particles are smaller than grains of sand but larger than clay particles and are more irregular in shape. Soils with a high silt content tend to drain freely and hold nutrients well.

Soils containing a great deal of sand don't hold nutrients but they drain quickly—sometimes too quickly, creating excessively dry soil.

Some soils, such as those in areas once dominated by grassland, naturally contain a lot of organic matter. These soils tend to retain nutrients and moisture well, and the organic matter keeps the soil open and loose, even if the clay content is high. If the soil contains a lot of sand, the organic matter helps it to retain moisture and nutrients, making for better plant growth.

Plants to match the soil

You can work with the soil to improve drainage and fertility by adding organic matter or by making more drastic changes. Or you can choose plants that will grow in the conditions your soil provides. You'll find more detailed information on preparing soil for planting perennials in chapter 4.

If instead you prefer to select plants that thrive in your soil conditions, there are many wonderful plants that can be grown in almost any type of soil and drainage situation. But first you need to carefully analyze the conditions to see just what you have to offer.

You can do a preliminary analysis by grabbing a handful of moist soil and feeling it. If it is sticky and can be formed into a tight ball, you have clay soil. If too dry to form a ball, clay soil breaks into large, dense chunks. Sandy soil feels gritty and won't hold together, wet or dry. Silty soil feels silky when wet and powdery when dry. Moist loam forms a ball, but the ball readily breaks apart. The soil does not feel gritty, but its individual particles are large and easy to see. Drier loam also breaks into chunks, but the chunks are smaller and less dense than those of clay.

For a better idea of soil type, do a sediment test. Place a handful in a jar with 1 tablespoon of dishwasher soap. Fill the jar with water, shake, then let it sit. The components will settle out in this order: sand, silt, organic matter, and clay. The larger particles—sand, silt, organic matter—will settle fairly rapidly, in a few hours to a few days. Clay can take a week or more to settle.

Once the water is clear and you see distinct layers, measure the height of the total soil and of each layer. Divide the height of each layer by the total height to learn which component dominates your soil.

Other soil factors

Other soil factors you need to consider when selecting plants are pH—whether the soil is acid or alkaline—and salts. The most accurate reading of pH and salts is learned by sending a sample of soil to a laboratory for testing. The lab will also be able to tell you about the fertility of your soil.

▲ Adding organic matter helps improve both sandy and clay soil. Earthworms are a good sign that the soil is fertile and well drained.

Plants for the soil

You will find information about the best soil conditions for each perennial in the encyclopedia. If you have sandy soil, look at the entries for plants that need excellent drainage. Check the entries for ones needing well-drained soil if soil is loam to sandy loam. Plants that do best in poor soil want soil that is infertile. Average fertility means the plant grows in any reasonably fertile soil. Gritty soils are great for alpine plants, which require good drainage, and for plants that thrive in arid conditions. Both wet soil and clay soil contain little oxygen, and so plants that do well in wet situations often do well in clay soil. However, clay soil may be too dry for water-loving plants. Numerous plants thrive in acid soils, just as many others do better in alkaline soil.

SPECIALIZED STRUCTURES

Hairs create a humid zone above leaves, which helps slow water loss from the plant. The silver color reflects light and helps keep plants cool.

Plants that adapted to growing in adverse conditions—dry sandy soil, a bog, or dense shade—are often equipped with features that help them thrive.

For example sedums have thick fleshy succulent leaves that store water. The water comes in handy because sedums grow best in very well-drained soil that is often dry. During droughty periods the

Succulent leaves store water, which plants, such as this sedum and other desert plants, draw on during periods of drought.

plants tap into this water reserve in their leaves.

Plants with silver foliage, such as artemisia and lamb's-ears, are adapted to hot, dry areas. The silver leaves reflect light, keeping the plant cool and allowing it to survive in arid conditions. The silver color may come from wax or hairs, both of which keep the plant from losing water.

Large leaves, such as those of this hosta, help plants take in light when sunlight is at a premium in shady situations.

Specialized structures are not limited to plants that grow in hot, dry climates. Plants that thrive in shade—hosta for example—often have large dark green leaves. The large leaves help plants maximize the amount of light they can absorb. The dark green results from an accumulation of chlorophyll, which turns light into energy.

Consider your gardening habits

▲ When you are only home during the evening or only able to spend time in your garden at dusk, fragrant plants such as lavender provide sensory appeal. Blue flowers stand out in dim light.

▲ Low-maintenance perennials such as goldenrod, sedum, black-eyed susan , and ornamental grasses keep your garden from being a chore.

Don't forget to think about your own habits and patterns of life when deciding what to plant. If you usually go away for a month in the heat of summer, you might miss the blooms of cardinal flower, black-eyed susan, and purple coneflower. Because you won't be there to enjoy them, instead focus on perennials that bloom in spring or fall, or whenever you are home. If you entertain in the evening or have a long commute, consider perennials with white or pastel flowers that are open all night. White-flowered varieties of hostas, Oriental poppies, hollyhocks, and iris will allow you to enjoy your garden even if you can't get to it before dusk.

Think about time

Be honest about the amount of time that you can commit to your perennial garden. If you can spend only a few hours maintaining it every few months, look for perennials that smother and shade developing weeds, don't require staking, need little water, and seldom have pest or disease problems.

You can quickly decide on some perennials by taking a walk around your neighborhood in various seasons of the year. Pay attention to the yards that are not as well cared for as most, and note the perennials that are growing well in them.

You may get to know your neighbors better, and some may even offer you divisions of their hardy and self-sufficient perennials.

You can also get ideas at public parks and commercial areas that receive only minimal care. These are often the best places to learn about the newest developments in ironclad perennials that tolerate a lot of abuse.

◀ Deer feeding can devastate a garden. Where their population is high, choose perennials known to not attract them but be aware that when hungry, deer will eat anything.

▼ Rabbits tend to show up just when flower buds are ready to open.

If you like to spend every free moment in the garden, you can choose perennials that may require a bit more care but promise multiple seasons of interest. Lungwort, for example, has lovely spring flowers, and its spotted or silvery leaves are attractive all summer. Arkansas amsonia has lovely blue spring flowers, and its foliage turns golden yellow in autumn. The foliage of pinks provides a cool blue-gray texture in the garden even after the last flower has faded. And the seedpods of false indigo are interesting long after the spires of blue flowers fade.

A visit to your local public garden or arboretum will net some ideas for perennials to try in your own garden. Public gardens often test the latest varieties on the market.

Seasoned gardeners who want a new challenge may decide to take their gardening in an entirely new direction by exploring alpine plants, terrestrial orchids, or bog garden plants. All have exacting requirements and need frequent tending. Their novelty and beauty are worth the careful planning and effort that is needed to grow them well.

PERENNIALS THAT SHRUG OFF RABBITS AND DEER

Gardening alongside rabbits and deer can be a frustrating challenge. If these animals are prevalent in your area, you will want to be careful to plant only the perennials that they are least likely to eat. You can put barriers in place to keep the creatures in check, or treat plants with repellents that discourage them from munching, but the barriers are often unsightly and the repellents must be reapplied frequently. It is much easier to simply grow plants that are least likely to be eaten.

Plant	Growing notes	Zone
Amsonia	Full sun to part shade; moist, well-drained soil	3–9
Anemone	Part shade to full sun; moist soil high in organic matter	5–8
Artemisia	Full sun; well-drained soil with low fertility	3–7
Astilbe	Part to full shade; moist, well-drained soil	4–8
Bear's breeches	Full sun to part shade; well-drained soil	5–10
Bee balm	Full sun to part shade; moist, well-drained soil	3–9
Black-eyed susan	Full sun; well-drained soil	3–8
Blanket flower	Full sun; well-drained soil high in organic matter	3–8
Blazing star	Full sun; rich, moist soil	3–9
Bleeding heart	Part to full shade; rich, moist, well-drained soil	3–8
Bugbane	Sun to shade; well-drained fertile soil	4–8
Butterfly weed	Full sun; well-drained soil with low fertility	4–9
Catmint	Full sun to part shade; well-drained soil	4–7
Coral bells	Full sun to part shade; moist, rich soil	3–8
Coreopsis	Full sun; moist, well-drained soil	4–9
Cushion spurge	Full sun to part shade; well-drained soil	4–9
Evening primrose	Full sun; well-drained average soil	4–9
False indigo	Full sun to part shade; well-drained soil with low fertility	3–8
Gas plant	Full sun to part shade; moist, well-drained fertile soil	3–8
Globe thistle	Full sun; well-drained fertile soil	4–9
Goldenrod	Full sun to part shade; well-drained soil	4–9
Joe-pye weed	Full sun to part shade; moist, well-drained, fertile soil	3–7
Lenten rose	Part to full shade; well-drained rich soil	4–9
Monkshood	Part shade to full sun; moist fertile soil	3–7
Oriental poppy	Full sun; moist, well-drained soil rich in organic matter	3–7
Pincushion flower	Full sun; fertile, well-drained soil rich in organic matter	5–8
Pinks	Full sun or part shade; well-drained, fertile soil	3–10
Purple coneflower	Full sun; average garden soil	3–9
Queen-of-the-meadow	Full sun to part shade; well-drained to wet soil	3–9
Yarrow	Full sun; well-drained soil	3–10
Yellow foxglove	Part shade; average garden soil	3–8
Yellow waxbells	Part shade to shade; moist well-drained acid soil	5–9

Select plants for your space

In the past, when lot sizes were larger many gardeners did not have to be overly concerned with space when choosing perennials. They had the option of arranging perennials along a property line, beside a fence at the back of the yard, or next to a large vegetable garden.

Today's homes generally are built on smaller lots, and the portion taken up by the house, garage, shed, and driveway is larger, leaving gardeners with little space for planting. And many gardeners live in townhomes with very small yards. If your planting area is modest, you'll have to consider the mature size of perennials when planning your garden.

It's not surprising that the trend has been to plant smaller, more compact perennials that have a large visual impact in relation to the space they need. A small perennial garden may be easier to tend and less time consuming than a large perennial border, and a smaller garden requires smaller plants if it is to incorporate the same richness and diversity of a traditional perennial border.

Contain your perennials

Even those who garden on a deck or balcony can plant perennials. Few plants are better suited to containers, and perennials can supply color and texture at times of the year that other container plants cannot.

The sophisticated spring perennial garden counts on perennials like pinks, coral bells, and basket-of-gold to provide interest when spring-planted annuals have not yet hit their stride.

In milder climates early spring bloomers may actually bloom in winter, and summer and fall bloomers may rebloom in winter. In any region, perennials can carry the container through the winter with its foliage.

▲ In a small yard, you might decide to eliminate the grass. Carving planting beds out of paved areas provides a yard suitable to entertaining and to gardening.

▲ Where space is at a premium or you have no garden space, consider planting perennials in a container. Balloon flower, spike speedwell, and false indigo combine with begonia and dusty miller in this mixed planting.

▲ Compact plants that are both short and nonspreading such as 'Red Fox' or 'Heidikind' spike speedwell are excellent choices for growing in small gardens and in containers.

When choosing perennials for containers, it is important to select species that are at least one zone hardier than the USDA Hardiness Zone you live in because the volume of soil in the container is too small to buffer the roots from air temperature extremes.

You can protect containers with bats of insulation or

▼ Even if you have plenty of space, a container filled with perennials such as purple coneflower can create a long-blooming accent among the other plants in your garden.

straw bales. You can even use an electric heating tape on the bottom of your large containers to moderate the worst of the winter cold. Because none of these options are very aesthetic, hide the plants behind a shed or store them in an unheated garage.

Get organized

When thinking about all these layers of information, it may be helpful to make a card for each area that you want to plant in perennials. When you are thumbing through catalogs and references, use the card to remind you to check for adaptability to the parameters you have written down that are not based on your preferences—things like maximum mature size your garden can accommodate, the light conditions, drainage and other soil factors, and the need for the plant to resist deer and rabbit feeding.

This may help you zero in quickly on a short list of possibilities so you can get to the fun of picking the colors, textures, and bloom times that you want. Always come back to your preferences. The perfect perennials for your conditions are not the right perennials for you if you dislike the flower color or the foliage looks weedy to you.

Have fun

Finally don't forget to try something new or even break the rules with a few plants. Perennials are diverse and adaptable. You can always choose perennials that are fail-safe and easy to plant, but also try plants that are new to you or to the market.

If you are tending an existing perennial bed, periodically plant something new. Unlike the trees, lawn, and deck, perennials provide a dynamic and ever-changing element to your landscape. They are the spice and seasoning that give your yard a subtly different flavor from season to season and from year to year.

GREAT PERENNIALS FOR CONTAINERS

Many perennials that flourish in the ground will grow just as well and look just as good in a container. Remember for the easiest overwintering, select perennials that are hardy to at least one zone colder than your own. For example, if you garden in Zone 5, select perennials for containers that are hardy to Zone 4 or even Zone 3.

Plant	Notable characteristics	Growing notes	Zone
Bellflower	Clusters of violet or white flowers in late spring to midsummer	Full sun to part shade; well-drained soil	3–8
Black-eyed susan	Yellow daisylike flowers in summer	Full sun; well-drained soil	4–9
Coral bells	Evergreen to semievergreen green, purple, gold, bronze, or variegated foliage	Full sun to part shade; well-drained soil that is rich in organic matter	3–8
Coreopsis	Yellow daisy-like flowers in early to midsummer	Full sun; moist soil	4–9
Hosta	Grown for attractive foliage available in many variegations	Part to full shade; moist soil with lots of organic matter	3–8
New Zealand flax	Variegated or solid foliage in shades of green, cream, yellow, rust, orange, or red	Full sun; fertile soil	8–11
Penstemon	Pink and red bell-shape flowers in summer	Full sun to part shade; moist, well-drained soil	2–8
Pinks	Fragrant pink, white, and red carnationlike flowers in late spring to early summer and evergreen foliage	Full sun; well-drained soil	3–10
Sedum	Succulent plant with year-round interest; many varieties available	Full sun; well-drained soil	3–9

Bellflower

Black-eyed susan

Coral bells

Coreopsis

Hostas

New Zealand flax

Penstemon

Pinks

Sedum

About plant names

▲ Purple coneflower is sometimes simply referred to as coneflower. That can create problems for people who call black-eyed susan, which is *Rudbeckia,* coneflower. To communicate clearly, you have to know the botanical names of plants.

One of the greatest challenges of choosing and buying perennials is sorting out their names. Knowing the correct name of a plant is important, if you want to be sure you are getting the same plant that you admired in your local public garden or found in the encyclopedia of this book.

Hundreds of species of plants can be grown in the perennial garden, and some species, like daylily, have been intensively bred and selected to the point where there are thousands of named varieties.

The most important thing to know is that plants have two types of names: a botanical name and a common name. (Plants new to the market may lack a common name since they're not yet well known.)

Most people prefer to use a common name for a plant. Common names are popular names that are easy to pronounce. But with the hundreds of species on the market, you can get into trouble relying solely on common names.

Common names

Common names are fluid and may change from place to place. For example, you may know the grassy plant with tall flame-red and yellow flower spikes as torch lily, but your neighbor may call it red hot poker.

Also, one common name may refer to several plants. For instance, fringed sage and white sage are also called artemisia. They are nothing like the many salvia plants, which are also called sage.

Although common names are used informally in conversation and are often poetic, they can be very confusing.

▲ Species purple coneflower, *Echinacea purpurea,* is a 1 to 3-foot-tall plant with unscented pinkish purple flowers and a brown center cone.

▲ Breeders have crossed *Echinacea purpurea* with *E. tennesseensis* or *E. paradoxa* to create purple coneflowers in shades of orange or yellow, such as 'Harvest Moon'.

▲ 'Razzmatazz' is a cultivar of purple coneflower. Its main difference from the species is the double pink flowers lacking a cone. Other cultivars bloom in different colors, have larger or taller cones, broader petals, or petals that curl back.

▲ Some of these hybrids have been trademarked. For example, this Orange Meadowbrite is the cultivar 'Art's Pride'.

FESTIVAL GRASS™

Cordyline 'JURred'

P.P. #14,224. All propagation, except under licence, is prohibited by law.

Glossy ruby/burgundy foliage

Festival Grass™ is a compact, clump-forming Cordyline, with shiny ruby/burgundy strappy foliage that cascades into a round ball shape. It has large sprays of fragrant small, showy, star-shaped blush pink flowers in late spring & summer. Festival Grass™ is ideal planted either singly in pots or as a stunning color highlight with other plants in gardens and landscapes.

Key Facts & Growing Guide

Hardy in Zones 8b-11

Full Sun to part shade

Plant 24" apart

Grows to 24-36" high & up to 48" wide

Select a container 15-18" wide

Grows well in most soil types

Use 'Slow Release' fertilizer in spring

Protect from severe frosts

In frost prone areas, grow in pots and move indoors over winter and keep plant moist.

◀ On plant tags, cultivar names are enclosed in single quotes; trademark names carry a register or trademark symbol. For example, Festival Grass™ is the cultivar 'JURred'. USPPAF means that the plant is patent protected and cannot be propagated by others.

HIBISCUS
'Brandy Punch'
USPPAF
"Marsh Mallow"

Heuchera
'Georgia Peach'
Alum root

PLANT NAMES AT A GLANCE

Cultivar name. The cultivar name is assigned by the plant breeder. Popular cultivars are commonly referred to by their cultivar names in nurseries and garden centers.

Rudbeckia fulgida 'Goldsturm'

Genus name. The first word in a plant's botanical name is the genus. Think of this as a surname. There are several members of the *Rudbeckia* plant family.

Specific epithet. The second word in a botanical name is the specific epithet. This identifies the plant specifically, separating it from all other plants in the genus.

Species. Together the genus name and the specific epithet forms the species name and positively identify a plant.

'Goldsturm' black-eyed susan

Common name. The common name fluctuates. One person might call this plant black-eyed susan while another calls it coneflower.

Botanical names

More often now, you will find botanical names on plant labels, in catalogs, and garden books to cut through the confusion. The concept of a botanical name is simple. The genus—first part of the name—can be thought of as a surname. It is always capitalized. Usually several related plants share this name, but often only a few in the group are widely grown in perennial gardens.

The specific epithet—the second part of the name, which is never capitalized—pinpoints a particular plant in a genus. Together, the two names form the botanical name and identify the plant species, which is defined as a population of plants that interbreed freely with each other and have similar characteristics.

For example, *Geranium sanguineum* is the botanical name for bloody cranesbill. The species grows 1½ feet tall and bears bright magenta flowers, but some are 6 inches tall with light pink blooms. These naturally occurring variants have a variety name to distinguish them, *Geranium sanguineum striatum*.

If the variant is peculiar to a region but not a distinct species, it may have a subspecies name. *Pulmonaria longifolia cevennensis* is the botanical name for a lungwort that has wider flowers than the species; it occurs in a region of France.

Plant cultivars and crosses

Horticulturists leave their mark on botanical names too. Plants may be hybridized and selected to get the best plants with the largest, most colorful flowers. These plants are given a cultivar name that is always enclosed in single quotes. The term "cultivar" is a contraction of the term cultivated variety. Cultivars can be propagated by division or cuttings to produce more plants that are identical to the selected plant.

An example of a cultivar is *Paeonia lactiflora* 'Sarah Bernhardt'. Some perennials, including peonies, daylilies, and chrysanthemums, have thousands of distinct-named cultivars.

Breeders may even cross species to produce hybrids. The symbol × between the genus name and the specific epithet name indicates the plant is a hybrid, for example is Frikart's aster, *Aster ×frikartii*. If a lot of different species were used to create the hybrid, contributed to a breeding program are many, or the breeding history is unknown, the genus name may be used alone without a species name being given, as long as a cultivar name is also used, for example, *Coreopsis* 'Creme Brulee'.

More recently breeders have begun to apply trademark names to perennials. They give the plants a cultivar name that may be rather odd, along with a catchy trademark name for use in all promotional materials. An example is *Echinacea* 'CBG Cone3', better known as Mango Meadowbrite™.

Names change

Taxonomists are constantly studying the relationships between plants, and they sometimes reclassify plants, moving them to a different genus or giving them a new botanical name. Garden chrysanthemums had the genus name of *Chrysanthemum*. Then, for a time its name changed to *Dendranthema*, but in 1999 taxonomists reclassified it as *Chrysanthemum*. With the advent of DNA testing, the changes have become more frequent. The constant changing is hard on nursery staff; some quickly change the name on their plant tags and signs, while others don't. Advice for the gardener: If you can't find what you want, ask.

Sources for perennials

◀ Many perennials can be started by seed in a greenhouse or in your home under lights. Generally, only straight species are available by seed.

Perennials typically take longer to germinate than annuals, but you'll get scores of plants at a fraction of the cost of potted specimens from your local nursery.

If you have a greenhouse, conservatory, or a table set up with grow lights, you can grow varieties available from specialty seed catalogs that you can't find at your local nursery or garden center. You might even have some extra seedlings that you can share or trade with gardening friends.

The seeds of many species of perennials, such as Lenten rose and peony, do not germinate until they have gone through a cold period. It's easy enough to germinate these seeds by sowing them on some moist potting soil, securing them in a zip-lock plastic bag, and placing them in the crisper compartment of your refrigerator. After three or four months of cold, they germinate like other seeds. Other seeds, such as those of lupines, have a very hard seed coat that must be nicked or filed before they will germinate.

What is the best source for perennials? There's no simple answer. Some gardeners on a limited budget might collect divisions of bleeding heart, iris, peony, and a host of other plants from neighbors and relatives to create a stunning garden with no investment other than labor.

A garden created from shared plants can be charming and carry a lot of sentiment for the gardener.

Unfortunately casual sharing of plants may cause diseases, weeds, and insect pests to spread from one garden to another. Inspect divisions carefully before planting them in your garden and monitor them in their first season so you can deal with any problems before they have the chance to spread.

Do some research into the invasive potential of the shared plants you receive— some perennials are so aggressive that they crowd out other plants. You may be wise to resist the urge to plant your garden with great numbers of freebies. After all if they are survivors and multiply easily, you will possibly have more of these perennials than you can handle in a few years.

Start from seed

Some perennials can be grown from seeds. Short-lived perennials tend to be the best candidates. Perennials with daisy-type flowers—for example, black-eyed susan, and Shasta daisy— are relatively easy to grow from seed, as are yarrow, lupine, blanket flower, hollyhock, and columbine. If you happen to have the right soil and climate conditions, they may seed themselves freely in your garden.

Start with plants

Most gardeners prefer to buy perennials as plants than to grow them from seed. They like to shop for plants locally from their favorite garden center, big box home store, or to order plants online or from mail-order nurseries.

All of these sources provide perennials that are uniform, usually free of pests and diseases, and ready to plant. Each source has advantages and disadvantages, and if you

◀ Perennials can be bought locally or by mail order. Local nurseries provide larger plants or plants in a wider range of sizes and let you check the plant before buying. Mail order sources typically offer more plant choices.

GREAT PERENNIALS FROM SEED

The following perennials are relatively easy to start from seed. You can sow them directly in the garden in well-prepared soil, or you can start them indoors under lights or in a greenhouse. All sprout fairly quickly and transplant easily. If started early enough and grown in good conditions, they may even bloom in their first season.

Plant	When to sow	Planting depth	Days to germination	Transplanting notes
Black-eyed susan	Indoors: 6–8 weeks before last frost Outdoors: 2 weeks before last frost	Surface	5–21	After last frost; full sun
Columbine	Indoors: 6–8 weeks before last frost; sow in plant flats; refrigerate for 2 to 3 weeks, then move to a sunny window	Surface	30–90	After last frost; full sun to part shade
Coreopsis	Indoors: 8–10 weeks before last frost Outdoors: after last frost or fall	Surface	5–25	After last frost; full sun
Delphinium	Indoors: 8–10 weeks before last frost Outdoors: in early spring or early fall	Just cover	14–28	In early spring when soil is still cool; full sun or part shade
Hollyhock	Indoors: in peat pots 6–8 weeks before last frost Outdoors: after last frost	Surface	10–14	After last frost; full sun
Lupine	Indoors: plant in peat pots 6–8 weeks before last frost Outdoors: early spring when soil is still cool	$1/8$"	14–60; for best germination soak seeds in warm water overnight	After last frost; full sun to part shade
Oriental poppy	Indoors: in peat pots 6–8 weeks before last frost Outdoors: in early spring when soil is still cool	Just cover	10–30	After last frost; full sun
Penstemon	Indoors: 6–8 weeks before last frost Outdoors: early spring	Just cover	15–20	After last frost; full sun
Pinks	Indoors: 10–12 weeks before last frost Outdoors: early spring	Just cover	14–21	In early spring when soil is still cool and frost is possible; full sun
Purple coneflower	Indoors: 10–12 weeks before last frost Outdoors: early spring	$1/8$"	10–21	In early spring when soil is still cool and frost is possible; full sun
Shasta daisy	Indoors: 6–8 weeks before last frost Outdoors: early spring	Surface	7–28	After last frost; full sun or part shade
Torch lily	Indoors: in peat pots 6–8 weeks before last frost Outdoors: early spring	$1/4$"	10–30	After last frost; full sun or part shade
Yarrow	Indoors: 10–12 weeks before last frost Outdoors: early spring	Surface	10–100	In early spring when soil is still cool and frost is possible; full sun

Black-eyed susan

Columbine

Coreopsis

Delphinium

Hollyhock

Lupine

Oriental poppy

Penstemon

Pinks

Purple coneflower

Shasta daisy

Torch lily

Yarrow

Sources for perennials *(continued)*

▲ Most local nurseries are a terrific resource of information on the plants you are thinking about buying. The staff can tell you about the success rates of specific perennials as well as help you find local designers and landscapers if you don't feel like designing and planting the garden on your own.

grow a lot of perennials, you will soon learn what plants to buy from which source.

Shop mail or online

Mail order gives you a huge variety of plants to choose from without leaving your home. If you live far from a major garden center, mail order and online purchasing may be the only practical way to get some of the perennials you want to try.

If you're a fan of iris, daylilies, peonies, or one of the other perennials for which there are thousands of varieties, mail order is the only way you can possibly experience the full breadth of flower types and colors available. Even if you live in an area with lots of nurseries, you're unlikely to find all those choices locally.

Perennials with fleshy roots, such peony, iris, and daylilies, are naturally adapted to shipping by mail order. In fact there is little if any advantage to buying the plants in pots. Perennials with very fine root systems that are more fragile or dry out easily may not take well to shipping unless they are potted in soil.

Many mail order firms do a good job of sending perennials growing in pots, and although you may end up paying substantial shipping fees, a specialty nursery may be the only source for a certain plant that you want. Many mail order nurseries have good refund or replacement policies.

When you order be clear about any preference you have for back-ordering or substitutions, if those options are offered. And although it may seem obvious, make sure that someone will pick up and care for the shipment if you happen to be on vacation when the box arrives at your doorstep. The plants inside may perish before you return.

One of the major disadvantages in shopping online or from a catalog is the fact that you can't touch or see the plants you are buying. You have to trust that the color of the flowers or leaves will be as depicted. All too often catalog images are retouched and enhanced to give them more appeal. Catalog and online images

◀ Check plant roots before buying, especially when shopping at home centers. Roots should fill the pot and be white and healthy looking.

that don't appear posed or contrived often means the plants you receive will be the right color, although these days, hardly any supplier can resist using its photo editing software.

Shop at garden centers

Shopping at your local garden center gives you a chance to see the plants firsthand before making a purchase. Garden centers often rotate their displays of perennials over the season, showcasing the plants that are in bloom. It's easy to fall into the trap of buying these blooming perennials when you visit your favorite nursery and overlooking some other possibilities that deserve your consideration.

If you shop at a nursery only on Memorial Day weekend, and you buy only plants that are in bloom, your garden will be a riot of color in late May and early June but dull much of the rest of the season. To create instant impact in your perennial garden, buy plants that are just coming into bloom rather than ones that are at or slightly past their peak.

Select healthy plants

You may wonder how to select the best plant of a given variety from all those available. It's tempting to judge plants only by their top growth, and it is certainly a good idea to choose a plant that is free of any sign of insect or disease damage.

Also take a good close look at the soil to see if any weeds are growing in the pot. Weeds often are a sign that the plant may have been carried over from the previous year's stock. The plant may still be healthy, but it may have been stressed during its long stay in the pot.

Most important: Try to take a look at the roots. If the plants are inexpensive and they look uniformly healthy, you might be able to judge the roots by checking the drain holes of the pots. Healthy roots poking out of them are a good sign.

If you are investing a lot of money and the group of plants doesn't seem uniform, ask to knock one of the plants out of the pot to inspect the roots. Roots should be white, ivory, or tan, and should exhibit signs of active growth. If roots are shriveled, slimy, or mushy, the plant may be suffering from root rot. If you check several of the plants and cannot find one that seems healthy, keep the plant on your shopping list and buy it another time.

The size of the container is often a consideration, both in expense and transporting plants to your home. A bigger pot doesn't necessarily mean a larger plant. For example, peonies are sometimes moved into large pots in spring after being held bareroot in refrigerated storage all winter. Usually they are planted in 1- or 2-gallon pots because the thick roots will not fit in a smaller pot. Nurseries also buy other perennials as small plants, known as liners, in spring and pot them into 1-gallon containers.

When you buy these plants, they may only have a few weeks' growth on them and offer no advantage over buying a bare-root plant by mail order. To learn whether a plant is well rooted, tip it over and check the roots.

Your local garden center offers an advantage for buying plants such as pinks, penstemon, thrift, and purple coneflower that languish if they are in the dark for even a short period of time.

Shop at a home center

Home centers and big box retailers typically offer a limited selection of perennials, but what they do offer tends to be easy to grow in many regions.

The prices are usually much lower than mail order or garden center prices, and the product tends to be very uniform since it is grown to exacting specifications in large state-of-the-art facilities. These stores move plants quickly in the door and out, and the plants may receive

▲ Perennials are typically available in 1-gallon containers and in 4- to 6-inch containers. Many mail-order sources sell perennials bare-root to save shipping costs. Large plants create a "finished" garden, but smaller ones quickly catch up. As long as they are handled correctly, bare-root plants often provide results equal to those of large plants and catch up in size within a year.

little care in the way of watering, feeding, and temperature control.

Buy plants from these vendors as soon as possible after they are delivered to the store. The plants may be stressed if store employees are too busy to water as needed and the weather is hot and dry. Some potted perennial wholesalers are now selling on consignment through big box stores and may have staff that visit stores to care for the plants.

Shopping at a home center usually offers an inexpensive way to delve into perennial gardening without a major outlay of funds up front. If you need a large number of perennials to start your garden, big box retailers are a good option, and your dollar will have more impact.

It is very important to do your research since these stores sometimes sell plants that aren't really adapted for your local climate.

Buy for all seasons

No matter where you buy your plants, don't limit your choices to ones that bloom in a single season, unless that is

the only time when you are at your home to enjoy the plants. It's true you are unlikely to get excited about species that aren't at their prime in the season you are shopping. But some perennials, such as butterfly weed, are slow to emerge in spring. If you aren't looking for plants that offer a wide range of bloom times, you might miss it entirely.

Shopping throughout the summer can help you find perennials for summer-long blooms. Spreading out your shopping can save you money as well. Most garden centers and big box retailers reduce prices at the end of spring, and you can often get plants for half price. Unlike annuals, trees, and shrubs, perennials may be able to survive the neglect they experience on the shelf and go on to grow well in your garden, as long as their roots are intact and healthy.

Even online sources and mail order catalogs offer sales to clear inventory. Because of the immediate nature of their sales, many online nurseries offer very good prices near the end of the shipping season.

Good garden design

▲ An effective garden design consists of line, form, texture, and color arranged so all the elements come together to enhance each other.

Garden design follows the same guidelines as any other art form. Whether designing your garden, decorating your home, making a floral design, or creating a sculpture or painting, you rely on the same elements: line, form, texture, and color.

These design components are nothing more than the color, size, shape, texture, and configuration of all the "stuff" that makes up a garden. Gardeners tend to concentrate only on the plants, but the "stuff" of a garden is far more than just the plants. The bed, the plants, any ornaments, the walkways, and even the mulch all have line, form, texture, and color.

In addition each part contributes to the overall picture. The plants are in the bed, which has a particular shape and may be covered with mulch, which also has certain characteristics. If the bed is large, it may have a pathway running through it, for access and maintenance.

A garden designer must keep in mind the elements of each piece as well as those of the overall garden. To effectively manipulate the various elements you must know what each element is and understand how it works.

The easiest way to proceed is to look at each element separately and then bring them together so you can put what you've learned into practice.

Line and form

▲ The sharply cut edge of this garden draws a distinct line of meandering curves. Hostas draped over the edge soften the line.

▲ A path creates a zigzag line through an informal garden. Pink flowers along the path enhance the line.

Line comes from the contours—shape or outline—of the beds, pathways, plants, containers, ornaments, structures, and all other objects in a garden. In addition, the silhouettes and shadows of all the objects create line.

Form is similar to line, but it incorporates the three-dimensional aspect of objects. It is the mass and volume of the plants and other objects in a garden.

Line

The beds might have curving lines; it may be kidney-shape, circular, or oval. It can have many curves or just a few.

Or the beds might have straight lines and be square, rectangular, triangular, or some other angular geometric shape. Pathways might meander or be straight. Plants may be upright, round, flattened, or shaped like a fountain. They may have a stiff or a lax appearance. Lines of objects are just as varied.

Put line to work

You can use line to set a mood or create the feeling of distance or intimacy. Line helps draw the eye toward or away from a feature in the yard. How? It can focus the eye toward an object in the

▲ Upright plants and upright columns draw your attention skyward.

▲ To see how line can bring intimacy or expanse to your yard, look out a window and mentally locate three points in your yard. Point one is the frame of the window. Point two is the far end of your yard. Set the third point halfway between the first two. To shrink the space, as here, put your garden, or a focal point, at number three. To enlarge the space, place it at point two.

▲ A focal point at the end of a line draws your eye and enlarges the space. This garden is composed of lines created mainly by plants with solid forms.

▲ A mix of perennials with different forms and shapes creates a rich diverse picture packed with interest and excitement.

distance through the manipulation of perspective.

As an exercise stand in your kitchen, living room, family room, or any room with a good-size window. Notice that the window creates a frame around the scene. The edges of the window are point one on a line.

Next focus your attention to the end of the yard, point two on the line, which is still framed by the window. Pick a point somewhere in between the first two points, and that becomes point three.

If you want to shrink the size of your yard, mentally place an ornamental tree, a piece of artwork, or a garden at point three. Notice how the space seems to move toward the window. With the

leading edge of your garden at point three, you create the appearance of intimacy.

If you need to enlarge the space, place the tree or artwork at point two. This distant focal point attracts your eye and so the area seems larger.

Combining plants with contrasting silhouettes creates excitement and interest. How you use line in the landscape also influences the formality of your space. (See "Set the Mood" box on page 37.)

Testing line

Lines should flow smoothly in the garden. Sharp breaks and corners can create a feeling of unrest, especially in an informal garden. How do

you know if your line flows smoothly? Use a garden hose to outline a potential garden bed, then check it out from a distance—perhaps from an upstairs window or from across the street. You will get a good idea of the flow of the line from various angles. Your eye should travel the line easily and not be distracted.

If this technique doesn't work for you, get out your lawn mower and push (or drive) it along the hose. If you can't easily mow around the hose, your line doesn't flow well, and it will make caring for your lawn difficult once you plant the bed as well.

Form

Because form is so similar to line, it can be difficult to

think about when you're putting plants together, even though everything in the world is three-dimensional. A plant that grows 2 feet tall and spreads out 2 feet on all sides has a sort of boxy form, although it's outline or shape may be rounded. A plant that has a low, broad rosette of leaves at its base and a flower stem that rises several feet above the leaves is triangular in outline, but somewhat conical in form.

Most garden plans leave out the three-dimensional aspect of a garden. Usually seen from above, known as bird's-eye view, you get width and depth, but not height. If someone draws a plan from the front, you see the height and width, but not the depth of the garden.

▲ Yellow-flowered goldenrod has an open form while the hosta below it is solid in form. The line of goldenrod is upright during the summer and becomes arching to fountainlike to flat-topped, depending on the species, when plants are in bloom.

▲ Aster has a dense solid form and a rounded outline throughout the growing season. When plants are in bloom, they become even more dense. The three-dimensional form is like a rounded cushion or ottoman.

If you have trouble visualizing a garden in three dimensions, try this: Gather various size yarn pom-poms and pieces of green craft foam. Use the pom-poms for mounded plants; cut the foam into other shapes, and set the pom-poms and foam on a birds-eye view plan. This will give you an idea of the form of the plants and the garden although not a completely accurate one.

SET THE MOOD

How you use line in the garden lends the space a formal, structured feeling or an informal, relaxed atmosphere. Straight lines, square corners, and geometric shapes give a garden a formal appearance, and curving lines make a garden informal.

Remember that line is present throughout the garden. Everything from bed edges to pathways to garden art is part of the element of line. The outline or silhouette of plants also constitutes line, as does their shadows.

The most pleasing garden designs often combine a mix of straight and curving lines. Include more straight lines or more curving lines depending on the feeling you want to create. For example in a formal landscape, plant straight-edged beds with mounded, billowing plants. Lead visitors through an informal garden on straight paths.

Straight edges on beds and well-manicured plants with solid forms create a formal mood.

Curved lines, open forms, and plants that break up a straight line contribute an informal mood.

Computer design software can supply you with a bird's eye view as well as an image of the finished garden. Be careful though: Most consumer products are limited in plant palette and often show plants only in flower, which gives a false sense of what your garden will look like.

Apply form to plants

A plant has a solid form if you can't see through it; if you can, it has an open form. For example, the broad leaves of hosta give the plant a solid form, while astilbe's ferny see-through foliage gives this airy plant an open form.

Combinations of solid and open forms generate interest and contrast in a garden. The forms of perennials, like those of trees and shrubs, change from season to season, creating another layer of interest in a garden. A solid plant such as hosta takes on an open appearance when it is in bloom. An ornamental grass that has feathery plumes in late summer, acquire an open form.

STRIKING FORM COMBOS

The forms in a combination of dense showy sedum and airy Russian sage contrast nicely.

Use form to add spark and interest to your garden. Place open forms near solid ones and use plants that change form dramatically. Try these contrasting plant combinations.
● Grow open astilbe next to solid rose turtlehead in a shady spot.
● Plant dwarf goatsbeard next to lungwort for dichotomy of form and line.
● Combine bear's breeches, with its very large leaves, and the smaller-leaved purple coneflower. These two plants not only have dramatically different foliage, but different flowering form as well. The bear's breeches will flower with a large spike, contrasting with the flattened shape of the coneflowers.
● For a dramatic contrast, pair the lacy wands and purple flowers of Russian sage with the bold yellow daisies and large flower cones of black-eyed susan.

Texture

▲ Small, thin leaflets and shiny surfaces create the sense of fine texture. Although the leaves of the fern are larger than those of the European ginger (*Asarum europaeum*), it is finer textured than the ginger.

▲ All objects and plants in a garden contribute texture to the garden, from the regular pattern of the brick (medium texture), the rough surface of the gravel mulch (finer textured than the brick), the solid fountain (coarse) as well as the plants.

Texture is most commonly associated with the touch or feel of an object's surface. However texture has a different meaning in garden design because plants are three dimensional and are arranged in the landscape so people can enjoy their visual beauty as opposed to their tactile beauty. In garden design, then, texture is the overall visual appearance of the components of the garden.

Texture results from the plant's leaf or flower size, from the appearance of the surfaces of the plant, and from the shapes of the leaves and flowers.

Garden texture may be described as "fine," "coarse," "bold," "smooth," "rough," or "soft." Essentially, though there are three textures, fine, medium, and coarse.

A plant is said to be fine textured if it has small or slender leaves or flowers, or finely divided leaves, or shiny surfaces. Coarse-textured plants have large leaves and flowers, large teeth on the leaves, or rough surfaces. Medium texture falls anywhere in between fine and coarse textures.

Texture isn't always clear-cut; instead, it's relative. A plant that you think is fine textured may look medium or even fine textured next to another plant. If you are unsure about the texture of your plants, don't panic. If you simply combine a plant with large leaves with one that has small leaves you will create contrast.

Because the labels are often similar and are used interchangeably, you may have a hard time understanding whether someone is talking about texture or form when you're starting out. In general, when people are talking about an open plant, it will have fine texture. A coarse-textured plant is more solid in form, and people will use the term bold when talking about plants with coarse texture and ones with a strong form.

Design with texture

Often gardens are designed with an emphasis on flower color. A perennial's flowers add zip to the garden for a couple of weeks, but its texture is present from spring to fall—and sometimes through winter. When you consider texture as you make plant combinations, your space will be eye catching for

◀ The small thin leaves of an ornamental grass have the finest texture in this grouping. The Japanese maple has deeply cut foliage and is usually considered fine in texture, but against the grass, it is medium textured.

▼ Yellow corydalis with its finely divided leaves and small blooms is considered a fine-textured plant, although it's leaflets and flowers are more medium in size. It is also one of the few plants that will bloom in shade all summer.

▲ Large leaves with large teeth on their edges create the coarse texture of 'Ace of Spades' ornamental rhubarb *(Rheum)*. The nearby green heart-leaf brunnera seems fine textured in comparison, although in most instances it is coarse.

▲ A crinkled surface makes a leaf appear coarse textured.

the entire growing season.

For example pair a plant with small, fine-textured foliage, such as 'Moonbeam' coreopsis, with a plant bearing larger, coarse-textured leaves, such as purple coneflower, to create contrast and excitement. Whereas opposing textures enliven a space, a group of plants with similar texture will foster a sense of calm.

A plant in flower often has a different texture than it does when not in bloom.

PLANT TEXTURES

FINE-TEXTURED PERENNIALS
Amsonia
Lady's mantle in bloom
Lavender
Maidenhair fern
Silver mound artemisia
Thrift
White gaura

MEDIUM-TEXTURED PERENNIALS
Anise hyssop
Blue false indigo
Blue star
Butterfly weed
Goldenrod
Lady's mantle in leaf
Siberian iris

COARSE-TEXTURED PERENNIALS
Bear's breeches
Bigleaf ligularia
Heart-leaf bergenia
Heart-leaf brunnera
Hollyhock
Hosta

For example the foliage of pincushion flower forms a dense mat that remains low to the ground. Later in summer the foliage is topped by wands of flat flowers that wave gracefully in the slightest breeze. The blooms create such an open, airy appearance that any flowers behind them are noticeable through the wispy stems.

Texture is tops in shade

Few shade plants bloom during the summer, so shade gardens can be nothing but a mass of green. To keep the garden interesting during this drought of flower power,

▲ The solid form—and coarse texture—of the birdhouse behind fine-textured grasses and flowers creates an "end" to a section of a garden

use foliage texture to create interest. You can do this simply by planting perennials with contrasting textures side by side.

Ferns are rich in texture and are an excellent choice for the shade garden. Most ferns are fine textured, but because the degree of fineness depends on the species, they can be paired with coarse-textured plants such as hosta and yellow waxbells or with fine-textured plants such as sedge and toad lily.

Define space with texture

As with line, you can use texture to manipulate space. Fine-textured plants often are

almost translucent, giving the impression that you can see everything behind them. Use them to make a garden seem larger. Or plant them at the back of your garden; the garden will seem to stretch into infinity.

The reverse is also true. You can make a garden appear smaller by selecting coarse-textured plants. Place them at the back of the garden; because they standout the back of the garden will seem closer. Plants with large leaves can also act as walls, enclosing a space to form a garden room.

For gardens that are viewed from afar, coarse textured plants are better than fine textured ones because they are easier to see.

▲ Deeply cut rough-surfaced leaves with sharp prickles on their edges, along with spiny flowers, add up to coarse texture in globe thistle.

Balance

The last few pages explored the characteristics of garden objects. Now you'll learn to combine design elements as you arrange plants, garden art, and hardscaping into a composition. (Hardscaping is the hard, nonliving objects in your garden, such as paving, a deck or patio, or fence.)

Five simple garden design principles—balance, rhythm, scale, variety, and repetition—will help you create a cohesive, eye-pleasing garden.

Manipulate these design principles effectively and usually the design elements (line, form, texture, and color) will fall into place. Some gardeners prefer to concentrate on the elements, which often then means that the principles fall into place. Whichever you choose, the bottom line is: Once you have a working knowledge of design elements and design principles, you can really work some magic into your garden.

The next few pages cover the principles, or rules, for garden design. The best thing about rules is that they are made to be broken. Once you fully understand how all the principles work together, don't be afraid to go your own way once in a while. By making things a bit off balance, out of scale, or with an unusual rhythm, professional designers create stunning gardens. Then instead of just the elements or principles falling into place, the plan for the entire garden seems to simply fall in place. You'll know this kind of garden when you see it.

But don't get ahead of yourself. Start with the rules and then learn to break them. Only then will you be ready to follow a path and

▲ Balance greatly influences garden style. Symmetrical designs with straight lines and equal sides create formal compositions. Designers even call symmetrical compositions formal balance.

◀ Asymmetrical—or informal—balance can result in wild-and-woolly gardens. And yet, when you look closely, you can see that there's a well-planned aspect to the wildness.

occasionally be able to veer off. Until then, have fun with your designs as you learn.

Balance defined

The formal definition is a good place to start: Balance is a general equilibrium between all parts and sides of a composition. In garden design, it refers to the visual weight of plants and objects in the garden when seen from a particular viewpoint. A balanced composition creates a feeling of stability and harmony and contributes to the garden's unity.

Balance works like an old-fashioned scale with a central pivot holding a horizontal arm that has plates at each end. When balanced, the scale's plants hold equal amounts of weight. A garden is balanced when its visual weight appears to be equally distributed. Because plants grow and gardens are always in flux, balance is dynamic—changing over time and from each point of view.

One way to visualize balance is to think about the terms "symmetrical" and "asymmetrical." Consider the human body. It is more or less symmetrical—or the same—from left to right but not from top to bottom or front to back; in that direction, people are asymmetrical.

Although most things in nature display some kind of symmetry, few are perfectly symmetrical. Many studies show that symmetry is pleasing to humans, which is why people are often drawn symmetrical garden designs.

Asymmetrical is not the same as being out of balance; it's just not the same. For example try this simple exercise: Stand on one foot. Why didn't you fall over? Because you shifted your weight to remain balanced. You were no longer symmetrical; you were asymmetrical, but still balanced.

Here's another example of balance in action. Think about arranging furniture. You have all your living room furniture sitting on the

▶ When you draw a line through the middle of this garden, you see that the bright chartreuse hosta stands out and balances the other side of the garden, which is primarily dark green. The garden is asymmetrical but balanced.

moving truck and need to arrange it in a new living room. You have a couch, two chairs, a coffee table, an end table, and a piano. It's unlikely you would place all the furniture on one side of the room and leave the rest empty. People naturally arrange the furniture to create balance in a room.

Balance in the garden

Achieving balance in the garden is also something you do naturally. Imagine that you are planning a garden and want to include your favorite plant phlox, which can grow 4 to 6 feet tall and wide (as well as deep).

You decide to place the phlox on the left side of the garden. How do you balance it on the right? If you have a formal garden, you might place another phlox on the right. Or you can put a different plant but one that

has the same volume as the phlox, such as bear's breeches or bee balm, on the other side. You could also use a

grouping of smaller plants, such as coreopsis, to balance the phlox. Both solutions create balance in the garden.

▲ Here, the nearly matching plants on either side of the center point of this garden create symmetrical balance.

Repetition and variety

▲ Clumps of blue oat grass strategically draw visitors to the front door, as does the path with its alternating stripes of brick and aggregate concrete.

◄ Black planters, black-and-white tiles, and black walls create a strong repetitive pattern. Tall tree ferns in each planter soften the look. White tiles create variety. This is an extreme example of repetition that would be monotonous if it wasn't so striking.

Two principles are what prevent a garden from becoming boring: repetition and variety.

Repetition

Essential to good design, repetition helps your eye flow through the garden and is the glue that holds the landscape together. It allows the observer to realize that this is a garden scene and not simply a collection of plants on display. Repetition is especially effective at tying together several small gardens that are spread across a yard.

But the urge to try new plants of all shapes and sizes can make repetition a tough principle for some gardeners to embrace.

A garden room

To further understand the power of repetition, take a cue from interior design. When you paint your living room, you don't usually paint each wall a different color.

Painting all walls in one room the same color—which most people say is pleasing—is repetition in action. The wall color provides cohesion to the room. An interior designer might repeat the wall color in other parts of room decor, such as in the window treatments or accessories. They may even carry the color down the hall to another room.

Think of your garden as a room and repeat key elements. You can repeat colors, shapes, textures, and plants. Many garden designers have favorite plants, which often show up in their designs. If bee balm is your favorite, use it throughout your garden for a sense of harmony and balance and to add consistent long-lasting color, form, line, and texture.

What if you have a small yard and simply don't have enough space for a garden to repeat several plants over and over? Let a patio, a walkway, a fence, or even the side of your house help. For example, brick in the patio can repeat a color or pattern elsewhere in the garden. You can choose plants based on the color of your house or paint one wall to coordinate with the plants.

Variety

Repetition and variety are opposite design principles that work hand-in-hand to create a "wow" factor in a garden—something that stops you in your tracks and makes you walk over to get a closer look.

Certain individual plants can provide that factor by

► In this garden the repeating round shapes, green foliage, pink flowers, and same size plants has become monotonous. Even though the grass in the urn is taller, it carries the same line and does not break up the space.

virtue of their color, size, texture, or uniqueness, but to get the maximum effect from the plant, you'll have to carefully combine it with other plants.

Imagine a garden planted with just one type of plant. Pick your favorite or choose one of the really showy perennials, such as coreopsis, daylily, or purple coneflower. If you had a garden of just daylilies it would look fantastic for a few weeks, but then what? Say you really know the daylily cultivars and are able to stretch the bloom time from early to midsummer. That is more interesting, but is it enough to keep you interested in your garden all summer? Only if you are a daylily fanatic.

Variety in action

Think about variety in terms of decorating your home and whether you'd actually paint all four walls of a room the same color. Although most people probably say they'd use the same color on all walls, others might paint one wall a different color, or wallpaper one wall, or paint the lower third of the walls a different color for variety.

You probably wouldn't pick colors that were dramatically different. The wallpaper would pick up the paint color or the color of the lower part of the wall would blend well with the main color, but still the room would have variety.

The same can be said of gardening. If your favorite plant is daylily, place something nearby that is a different color, texture, shape, or size but that complements the daylily. If you want to showcase a favorite hosta, plant a fern next to it. The fern and hosta might both be green, but their differing textures

introduce variety. Because the fern is finer textured, it plays second fiddle to the hosta so the hosta stands out.

Variety in the garden

You probably already do things to create variety. In fact variety is probably the easiest design principle for gardeners to understand. Gardeners love plants so much that gathering a bunch of plants for their garden is easy. Inanimate objects such as mulch, a paver patio, or a wood gazebo also add a variety with their textures and colors.

Some of the design tips for creating interesting textural combinations will generate variety in your garden. Put a plant with large, bold leaves next to one with smaller more delicate leaves for contrast and interest.

Using different colors, textures, and heights are all ways to create variety in a garden. When you go to the garden center, look at the sizes and shapes of flowers and not just the colors. Then consider the foliage. Doing this forces you to think about design and not just the plant.

Imagine a shopping cart holding 'Moonbeam' coreopsis, blue fescue, Russian sage, and fernleaf yarrow. All have fine texture. The blue fescue and Russian sage have spiky leaves or flowers. How can you add the "wow" to this group of plants? Put bear's breeches or hardy hibiscus in the cart for

contrasting foliage.

Dramatic changes make you stop and take notice. It is not a feeling of unrest of interplay. The plants, garden art, hardscape material, and containers play off each other, working together to create a more intriguing scene than they could on their own.

▼ Showy sedum and a few short perennials with a flat form are the main players making up this garden. The butterfly bush, ornamental grass, and sculpture, punctuate the design, preventing it from becoming monotonous.

Rhythm and scale

The way to generate movement and flow in a garden is to introduce rhythm. Rhythm is defined as the changes in patterns that you encounter throughout the garden.

To understand this definition, look at this series of shapes △◇△◇△◇△. For a pattern to develop, you need to repeat shapes, such as the combination of the diamond and the triangle. A diamond and a triangle are different (think variety), but if used over and over (think repetition) they begin to create a pattern.

To be effective rhythm involves more than repeating

▼ Even formally balanced gardens have rhythm. The plants are repeated throughout the garden but are placed in different positions in each grid, creating an unexpected pattern.

▲ This planting draws a zigzag that leads your eye from top to bottom. Its rhythm creates the movement of your eyes through the composition.

▲ Stepping stones curving through a sea of thyme create a rhythm that moves your eyes and your feet down the path.

just two shapes or plants over and over. It needs punctuation, or something to accent the pattern.

Think about your favorite style of music. Maybe it is rock, classical, ragtime, swing, jazz, blues, or Latin. Whichever you prefer, you can recognize its beat. The pattern of the beat is the rhythm that takes the tune from start to finish.

Rhythm in a garden embraces the same definition. It is repetition of a pattern that creates movement from the beginning to the end of the garden. Obviously the plants aren't moving; it's the eyes of the person viewing the garden that moves.

Give your garden rhythm

Look for ways to create flow and movement in the garden. Examples of rhythm include a curved pathway, a plant placed to partially block another plant, a series of two or three plants repeated in several places to tie different parts of the garden together.

Some of the things you do naturally in a garden create rhythm. For example, you put short plants in front and large plants in the back. The most obvious reason for doing this is so you can see all the plants. But in order to view all the plants, you have to look down to see the smaller ones and rise to see the bigger plants. Doing this, you have just generated movement, which is rhythm.

Using plants that sway in the breeze also creates rhythm. Ornamental grasses generate rhythm year-round. In spring the small tufts of

◀ A series of flowing grasses seem to pull you down the garden path.

Rhythm & scale *(continued)*

◄ The birdhouse on its thick wooden column is in scale with the large leaved plants and dark colors of this garden. A smaller birdhouse would seem puny.

An example of poor use of scale is a large perennial grass planted along the foundation of a home. Some grasses grow 20 feet tall and 10 feet across. The plant can quickly overwhelm a single-story house, making the dwelling appear swamped. A grass that grows no more than a third of the height of the house will look better because it is in scale with the house.

Achieve good-looking scale in your perennial beds by abiding by this rule: The tallest plant should be one-half the width of the bed. For example, if your planting bed is 6 feet wide, the tallest plant should be about 3 feet tall.

foliage flutter in the breeze. The straplike leaves sway back and forth in summer, and the feathery plumes dance above the foliage in late summer and fall.

Walkways can introduce rhythm into the garden. A curved pathway might mask views of the garden beyond the curve, forcing the observer to move to see the rest of the garden. Paving materials also create rhythm. For example, alternating colors or bars in the paving draws you along the path. Mulch blanketing the path has no rhythm, but arranging a series of pavers in the mulch in a particular pattern is an example of rhythm.

Scale

Scale deals with size relationships—between you and your garden, between your garden and your yard, and between one garden element and another. A garden design is most pleasing if plants are in scale with each other and with the landscape as a whole.

▼ Arranging plants from small to large and creating combinations of similar size plants creates calm. An abrupt change, such as the addition of New Zealand flax below, sparks the plan.

Working with scale

An easy way to size up your plants prior to planting is to arrange them from tallest to shortest. Then make planting combinations by pairing plants of similar size.

A gradual transition between sizes of plants has a calming effect. On the other hand one or two abrupt changes can provide a small spark that causes viewers to pause and look again. However, make sure that your changes aren't too abrupt or you'll create unrest in the visitors to your garden.

▲ A plant that is so much larger than its neighbors that it takes over the space is out of scale and does not leave you with a feeling of harmony or balance.

CREATE COMBOS WITH SCALE

Using scale in the garden is all about creating smooth transitions between plants. For the smoothest shifts, pair small plants with medium-size ones or medium-size plants with large ones. If you want to stir up excitement, pair plants of vastly different sizes. Check out the examples in this chart; all the plants listed here thrive in full sun and well-drained soil.

Plant name	Notable characteristic	Zone
SMALL PLANTS—12" TALL OR LESS		
'Blue Clips' bellflower	Blue flowers in summer	3–9
'Bijou' blanket flower	Red-and-yellow flowers in summer; drought tolerant	3–8
'Eenie Weenie' daylily	Dwarf plant with yellow flowers	3–9
'Elijah Blue' blue fescue	Ornamental grass with blue-green foliage	4–8
Geranium	Purple, pink, or white flowers in spring or summer; attractive foliage	Depends on species
Pinks	White, pink, or red flowers in late spring to early summer	3–8
'Sentimental Blue' balloon flower	Purple flowers in midsummer	4–8
'Silver Carpet' lamb's-ears	Fuzzy silver foliage	
Thrift	Pink spring flowers and grasslike foliage	4–8
MEDIUM PLANTS—12" TO 36" TALL		
'Autumn Joy' sedum	Deep rose flowers in fall; bronze seed heads in winter	3–10
Bearded iris	Available in many flower colors; blooms in late spring to early summer	4–9
Clustered bellflower	Blue flowers in early summer	5–7
'Hameln' fountain grass	Almond seedheads in fall	5–8
'May Night' salvia	Purple flowers in summer	4–7
'Moonbeam' coreopsis	Pale yellow flowers all summer	4–9
Purple coneflower	Purple daisylike flowers in summer; long-lasting seedheads	3–9
Rose campion	Burgundy summer flowers and silver foliage	4–9
White gaura	Summer-long, dainty white flowers aging to pink	5–9
LARGE PLANTS—36" TALL OR MORE		
'Adagio' miscanthus	Green and white striped leaves	5–9
Bear's breeches	Tall stalks of purple-and-white flowers in late spring or early summer	5–10
Bee balm	Pink, red, or purple flowers in summer	3–9
Garden phlox	Many flower colors available; blooms in summer	4–8
'Gateway' joe-pye weed	Large, airy pink flower clusters in late summer	3–7
Hollyhock	Bold or pastel flowers on upright sturdy stalks in summer	3–8
Hybrid anemone	Pink and white flowers on thin stalks in fall	5–8
Russian sage	Purple flowers in summer and silver foliage	3–10

Upright iris leaves join low-growing geranium and the taller perennial salvia.

Medium purple coneflower and perennial salvia front tall joe-pye weed, which is just beginning to form flower buds.

Medium-size purple asters pair with tall miscanthus in a fall garden. Accompanying the pair are shorter obedient plant and blue star, a spring bloomer.

Color

▲ Monochromatic gardens are composed of only one color but include shades, tints, and tones of that color to avoid monotony. Iris and lavender here are joined by purple-leaf common sage and red-violet ornamental onions.

▲ Not every yellow—or any other color for that matter—is the same, and not every yellow will go with all other yellows. The yellow of this daylily is a buttery golden orange-yellow. It is in the same color "family" as the daisies on the opposite page, but a darker shade.

Color is the fourth element of design. More than any of the other design elements covered previously—line, form, and texture—color is the chief characteristic people think about when choosing plants. And for good reason. Plants often are added to introduce color or vibrancy to the green and muted earth tones that pervade.

Perennials have the ability to color the landscape almost all season. Gardeners in the North often endure winter months without color except for the color of evergreen trees and shrubs; gardeners in the South and some parts of the West put up with a summer dormant season. With a little planning, though, you can enjoy perennial color in nearly every month of the year.

Color defined

Color is tough to describe because everyone sees colors slightly differently. You might perceive the flowers

of crimson pincushion as deep purplish red, but someone else might describe them as brownish red or clear rich red. The blooms of 'May Night' salvia are commonly described as dark blue, but different people might think they're simply blue, or purple, or perhaps bluish purple.

And it's very difficult to describe color with words. Think about how you learned what the color red was. Someone probably pointed to a red object and said "red."

Of course, not all reds are the same, and each of the many different shades of red will look different in the garden, depending on what other colors they are combined with. Think of crimson and scarlet. At their most basic they are red, but scarlet has a hint of yellow

and crimson includes a hint of blue.

The following terms can help clarify color:
● **Hue** This is the basic color, for example red, orange, yellow, green, blue violet.
● **Tint** This is the basic color lightened with white.
● **Tone** This is the basic color that has been softened by mixing it with gray.
● **Shade** This is the basic color to which black has been added to darken the color.

With flowers, you can't mix colors the way you can with paint. It's not possible to go to the garden center and ask the staff to add white to your red flowers to make them lighter. You can however go to the garden center and look for a plant with a lighter red flower or a slightly different color of purple.

▲ Fern-leaf yarrow blooms in a clear bright yellow. It is a hue, or basic color. Because it blooms for much of the summer, take care that other yellows in your garden will work with it.

▲ These golden-yellow daisies bloom in an analogous color to the clear yellow of yarrow. It is more likely a tone, because it is a darker color.

How will you know if the color of your new plants will go well with the colors of the neighboring plants in the garden? One way is to take cuttings with you as you visit the garden center or nearby public garden.

Cut the flowers, wrap them in wet paper towels, and take them on your next visit. Then hold the cuttings up to the flowers of a plant you're considering and see what you think looks best.

This technique works only for perennials that are in bloom at the same time; you'll need to check the garden center or public garden several times in the season for a full summer of colors. You can use this same technique when buying containers or yard art.

Get started with color

If you're not used to working with color and don't know how to combine different colors, you may find a solution at your local paint, hardware, or home improvement store. Pick up some paint chips;

these swatches are free, highly mobile, and easy to store.

Spread the paint chips out on a table and pick out colors that attract you. Arrange the chips on the table until you find color combinations you like. Take these chips with you as you visit a the garden center or public garden to find plants in those colors. Keep the paint chips handy and go check out plants in bloom every few weeks. You will see what is in bloom and be able to identify different plants in your favorite colors for each season.

Let's say that your favorite color combination is purple, red, and yellow. In late spring to early summer, you might find red-flowered maiden pinks, 'May Night' perennial salvia in deep blue, and 'Bartzella' a yellow peony. For midspring blooms in a partially shaded area you might choose a red columbine, a dark blue pasque flower, and a yellow-

flowered leopard's bane. For summer blooms in full sun, you might select yellow coreopsis, red cardinal flower, and purple stoke's aster.

For each season select plants of your chosen color

scheme and add other plants in complementary colors as you have room. If you don't have time to check out plants each season, flip through the encyclopedia at the back of the book and use the charts

► Take paint chips or strips with you when shopping for certain color combinations of perennials.

THE COLOR WHEEL

Simply the colors of the rainbow arranged in a circle, a color wheel is one of the most valuable tools a perennial garden designer can use. The arrangement of the colors is what makes the color wheel so useful. It comes in handy as a guide to color combinations.

● **Complementary** Colors across from each other on the wheel are called complementary colors. Red and green are complementary as are yellow and violet and orange and blue.

● **Analogous** Colors that are beside each other on the wheel are known as analogous—or harmonious—colors. Violet and red-violet are analogous colors as are red and

red-orange, and blue and blue-violet, and blue and blue-green.

● **Triad** A color triad is made up of colors that are separated by three colors on the wheel, for example red, yellow, and blue or blue-violet, red-orange, and yellow-green.

By selecting complementary, analogous, or triad colors, you are almost guaranteed to get a good color scheme. For example if your favorite color is yellow and you want to use it in the garden throughout the year, pair it with an analogous color, such as green, in spring. Change things up in summer by mixing yellow flowers with purple flowers. End the bloom season with a color triad of yellow, blue, and red in fall. Use the encyclopedia at the back of this book to find plants in the right colors over the seasons.

Yellow yarrow and violet clematis bloom in complementary colors.

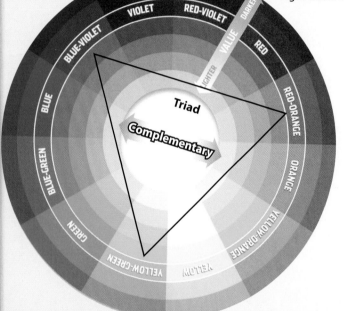

Colors opposite each other are complementary colors. Those beside each other are analogous. Colors three slots away form a triad. Shades are found on the outside edge of the color wheel, tints are the ones next to the center. Tones are in between.

Violet bellflower flowers and a red-violet pinks cultivar make an analogous color combination.

on pages 76 to 79 to learn when plants in your chosen colors are in bloom and which complementary plants you can use to fill the gaps.

If you simply can't decide on a color scheme and all the paint chips are starting to look the same, try using a color wheel instead.

Set the mood with color

Colors are classified as either warm or cool. Warm colors

are red, orange, and yellow; cool colors are green, blue, and purple. Color can have a dramatic psychological impact on people.

For example, schools are generally painted cool colors because they are calming and relaxing. And red is rarely used in prisons because of the unrest it can cause.

You can use colors to either provide excitement in your life or to help convey a sense of peace. If you are a high-

energy, always-on-the-go, excitable person, you might enjoy the excitement of red and orange flowers. They are bold and easily make a statement. On the other hand, you may need cool colors to help you relax when you finally sit down.

If you are a more relaxed, go-with-the-flow person, perhaps the cool colors may appeal to you. They help maintain a sense of serenity. However if your job is

monotonous and your days lacking in excitement, perhaps you would prefer warm colors in your garden.

Warm and cool colors can work together; you don't need to create a garden built on only one or the other. For example, choose a plant with bold red or yellow flowers as a focal point and surround it with more calming cool colors. This helps the focal point to stand out.

Be aware, too, that reds,

▲ Cool blue foliage and flowers calm the garden.

yellows, and blues may be cool or warm depending on how they are mixed. For example crimson, which is tinted with blue, is a cool red. Scarlet, red mixed with yellow, is a warm red. Chartreuse is a warm green because it contains so much yellow, while blue-green is a cool color.

PLEASING PASTELS

Pastels are soothing and calming. A garden of pink, lavender, blue, and light purple is a relaxing and inviting place to sit. Look to all the shades of pink for variety, but select more than just pale tints; pale pinks can get lost in bright sunlight. Surround light pink bloomers with plants bearing deep mauve or dusty rose-colored flowers. Add a splash of blue and gray to round out a pastel garden.

Monochromatic color schemes

Monochromatic color themes are built using only one color. Begin by choosing the main color for your space, purple for example. If you choose flowers that are all the same shade of purple, your garden will have purple flowers all season long, but it will be monotonous. To add variety, you need to use different hues, shades, tints, or tones of purple, as well as dabs of analogous or complementary colors to spark interest. Use paint chips, experiment on paper with crayons or colored pencils, or grab a color wheel to find the one-color shades,

▶ Blanket flower with its red-and-yellow blooms is a perfect example of a hot-colored perennial that brings excitement to a garden.

▲ Pink may be warm or cool, like this pairing, and can be used throughout the garden as part of a combination or in a monochromatic garden.

▲ Thyme demonstrates a few of the many shades, tints, and tones of green available, from blue-green to silver-green, to yellow-green, and clear green.

tones, and tints that will work together.

For example for a purple theme choose plants that bloom in periwinkle, violet, mauve, lilac, and lavender. Add some white and a few light pinks to jazz it up a bit.

By buying plants with these five or six colors, you will have created an entire monochromatic garden. The next step is to select plants that will provide the colors you want throughout the growing season.

Monochromatic themes can be highly effective and relatively simple to design. Just keep in mind that monochromatic gardens must include shades, tints,

and tones of the color and one or two plants that will offset the theme nicely.

If you are more interested in using a complementary, analogous, triad, or any other color theme in your garden, the same steps apply. Choose your main colors, then mix in plants that bloom in shades, tints, and tones of these colors. And if you want some pizzazz, throw in some white, silver, or "black" plants to create a dramatic flair.

Using white, silver, and "black"

Up to this point, there's been little mention of silver, white, or black. Considered neutral,

these colors are excellent for separating colors that might otherwise clash. They can also be used effectively to show off a color theme.

White and silver highlight other colors, especially dark colors. While no plant is actually black, dark foliage and flowers such as deep purple appear to be black from a distance. These dark colors highlight pastels and other light colors.

Versatile pink

Basically, a tint of red (red with white added to it), pink can fit into just about any color theme. There are so many different types of pink:

pastel pink, baby pink, hot pink, red-pink, and purple-pink, and so on. Many species have pink-flowering cultivars.

You can have a monochromatic garden in pinks. Pink goes great with purple, blue, green, and white, but it can also be used effectively with red, orange and yellow. That's because pink can be a cool color (if tinged with blue) or a warm color (if it has a hint of red).

Don't forget green

Although flowers take center stage when it comes to color, foliage also offers great color options. Green is likely the most prevalent color in

gardens. Look closely at all the shades, tints, and tones of green in your garden and you will find an amazing variety in that one color. Green foliage lasts all season long too, so your green combinations are always there when flowers are taking a break.

In addition to green, you'll also find perennials with green, blue, red, yellow, or chartreuse foliage as well as many with variegated leaves.

By using texture, line, and form to work with foliage, you have an almost infinite range of interesting foliage possibilities.

Color in your garden

Now that you've learned about color theory you can learn to apply it in your garden. There are several ways to look at the garden as a whole. You can create small

vignettes of two or three plants and add from there, or you can start with one color theme and work down to the small vignettes. You will learn more about making small vignettes later in this chapter.

For now, keep in mind that color is a powerful design tool. It visually expands or contracts a space. It creates a mood of excitement or calm. And finally foliage as well as flowers have color.

▲ Dark red-purple acts as black in a garden. Dark red and silver are neutrals that help bridge clashing colors. Foliage in these colors can provide the main show during the garden's downtimes.

▶ Foliage provides the main color in this garden, from the chartreuse of sweet flag to the dark red-brown of Japanese maple.

THE SPECTRUM OF COLORS

Use this chart like a color wheel. From left to right the colors go from warm to cool. From top to bottom the colors decrease in intensity, with the top row being the strongest hue and the bottom row the palest tint. The colors across each row are of equal weight.

THE WARM RANGE

 'Paprika' yarrow

Oriental poppy

 Yellow-and-white bearded iris

'Fire and Ice' hosta

 Red asiatic lily

'Enchantment' lily

Yellow chrysanthemum

'Sea Foam' foam flower

 'Anzac' daylily

'Golden Grace' chrysanthemum

Lily

Golden hakone grass

 'Ideal Crimson' pinks

Orange asiatic lily

'Sarah' chrysanthemum

Hosta, similar to 'American Sweetheart'

Autumn sage

'Nicole' chrysanthemum

Evening primrose

'Golden Tiara' hosta

Red-orange daylily

Black-eyed susan

Daylily

Green hosta

'Fires of Fuji' daylily

Yellow torch lily

Cushion spurge

Barrenwort

Crocosmia

Yellow corydalis

Lady's mantle flowers

Hosta, similar to 'Don Stevens'

Butterfly weed

'Baby Sun' coreopsis

Lenten rose hybrid

Lady's mantle foliage

THE COOL RANGE

 'Powis Castle' artemisia

 Delphinium

 Cupid's dart

 'Ville de Lyon' clematis

 'Krossa Regal' hosta

 Globe thistle

 Caryopteris

 Bloody cranesbill

 Lamb's-ears

 Balloon flower

 'Johnson's Blue' geranium

 New England aster

 Blue oat grass

 Delphinium

 'Blackberry Wine' corydalis

 Spiderwort

 Hosta, similar to 'Elvis Lives'

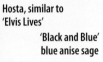 'Black and Blue' blue anise sage

 Jackman clematis

 Stokes aster

 'Blue Panda' corydalis

 Hybrid columbine

 'May Night' perennial salvia

 'Berry Exciting' corydalis

 'Butterfly Blue' delphinium

 'Iso- No-Nami' Japanese iris

 Bearded iris hybrid

 Centranthus

 'Georgia Blue' creeping speedwell

 Siberian iris

 Columbine hybrid

 'Niobe' clematis

 Heart-leaf brunnera

 Clustered bellflower

 Rose verbena

 Lenten rose hybrid

GOOD GARDEN DESIGN | **55**

Know your site

▲ Before starting to design your garden, make a site inventory and analysis to assess the existing features and environmental conditions that you have to work with. The first step is to make a rough sketch of your yard and its features.

▲ Take snapshots of the area to help jog your memory as you work on the plan and to help you find the location that best allows you to view the garden.

▲ Part of the inventory and assessment stage is to measure the size of the area so that you'll know how big the garden can be. This will help you keep the garden in scale with your yard as well guide you to how many plants will fit in it.

Before you begin pairing plants and designing garden beds, study your yard. A couple of simple tools—a site inventory and a site analysis—will teach you about your site quickly and efficiently.

A site inventory is a list of what exists in your yard already so you can work your new garden into the existing features. A site analysis is an evaluation of the environmental conditions so you can make intelligent decisions about what plants might work well in your yard.

Site inventory step 1: Make a sketch

Make a rough drawing of the area in which you're thinking of putting the garden including nearby permanent features. The sketch doesn't have to be to scale, but be as accurate as possible (graph paper will be helpful). Include existing plants, patios and decks, fences, and even places where the dogs always run or the kids routinely cut through the yard.

Step 2: Take pictures

Snap pictures from major viewpoints of the area of the proposed perennial garden. For example, shoot from your deck or patio, kitchen window, or any other spot in which you will spend time viewing the garden.

Also capture images of nearby problem spots or attractive features. These pictures will be handy throughout the design process by reminding you of the specifics of your site.

Step 3: Create a list of must haves

This list should include plants, hardscape elements, garden features—anything you must have in your garden. For example, if you need a spot for a container or a large boulder, include it on your list.

Step 4: Create a list of possibilities

You probably have things you would like to include, for example a birdbath, but that aren't a priority. Maybe you'll add one if you have the money or find one you really like. Keep this list handy so you can incorporate one or more of these features if you find extra space or money.

Site analysis

Once the site inventory is complete, it's time for the site analysis. Up to this point you haven't considered sun or wind exposure, wet or dry soil, or other environmental conditions. While the site inventory lists all the existing and desired features, the site analysis gets down to the nitty-gritty of your particular site. It will reveal the possibilities of your yard.

Six environmental conditions greatly impact plant selection and survival. They are outlined on the site analysis worksheet on page 57 and are discussed in depth in the following sections. After learning about these environmental conditions, fill out the worksheet for your garden space.

Sunlight

Is your site sunny, or partly sunny, or shady? Sunlight or the lack of it has the greatest impact on plant selection. Plants rated for full sun require at least six to eight hours of direct sunlight per day. Shaded areas generally get two to three hours of sun, which might be filtered through trees. Partially sunny areas receive three to four hours of full sun or sun that is filtered through trees. These areas might also receive sun only in the morning or afternoon.

The time of day that an area gets sun makes a difference. Morning sun is not nearly as strong as afternoon sun. Full sun in the morning is equivalent to part shade all day. On the other hand three to four hours of full sun in the afternoon may be enough for full-sun plants because of the intensity of the light. As you are looking at your worksheet, make a note of the hours your garden is sunny.

Soil properties

A soil test will quickly reveal valuable information. Test the soil in your proposed garden plot. For information about having your soil tested, see page 84.

To find out the drainage properties of your soil, try this test: Dig a hole about 1 foot in diameter and a foot deep; then fill it with water and let it drain. This simulates a rainfall that saturates the surrounding soil. Once the hole is empty, fill it again and time how long it takes to drain. Well-drained soil will drain in one to three hours. If it drains in less than an hour, it might drain too quickly. And if water is still standing in the hole three hours after filling, the soil is poorly drained.

Your existing plants can give you a clue about the state of your soil. Are your shrubs struggling even if you are watering adequately and properly? Do the trees drop their leaves earlier in your yard than in your neighbor's? Take an honest look at the existing plants because if they seem to be struggling, the plants in your new garden will struggle too.

Availability of water

Newly planted gardens require regular water during their first few weeks. Even after they're established, most need water during dry spells. How will you water your garden? A watering can, garden hose, and an irrigation system are all options.

Watering deeply and slowly is the trick to adapting plants to drought. Perennials have the ability to form very deep root systems, but shallow watering discourages deep roots. Forcing plants to grow deep roots helps them overcome times of little rain.

If the only way to water is with a watering can, do you have the energy to meet your plant's needs? If you'll use a hose, does your system have enough pressure to run a sprinkler as far as the garden is from the spigot?

Nearby competition

The roots of nearby plants make it tough to prepare soil, and they also compete with new plants for water and nutrients. Some make it impossible to grow other plants. For example, silver and other maples and eucalyptus are so shallow rooted that they leave no room for perennial roots and they are so much more efficient at taking up water that perennials will languish. In addition, seedlings and root suckers from the trees will drive you crazy weeding.

SITE ANALYSIS WORKSHEET

SUNLIGHT
Hours per day of direct light _____
Hours per day of filtered light _____
Sunny Hours: 7 8 9 10 11 12 1 2 3 4 5 6 7 8 9

SOIL
Texture: ☐ Clay ☐ Clay loam ☐ Silt ☐ Silt/loam
☐ Sandy ☐ Sandy/loam
Drainage test:
☐ Less than 1 hour ☐ 1–3 hours ☐ More than 3 hours

HEALTH OF EXISTING PLANTS: _____

WATER
How will you water?
☐ Irrigation system ☐ Hose ☐ Hand watering
Drainage:
☐ Good drainage ☐ Slow drainage ☐ Fast drainage
Typical rainfall in your area _____ inches per year,
which comes during which months _____

ROOT COMPETITION
Types of nearby plants _____
_____

EXPOSURE
☐ Windy ☐ Reflective heat
☐ Permanent structures _____

OTHER
Pets _____
Kids _____
Recreational activities _____
Other _____

Exposure

An area on the south side of a house will be hotter than one on the east or west side, not only because it is sunnier, but because of reflected heat from the house itself. You'll need to choose plants that like the heat. Perennials growing where wind is constant will dry faster and flowers stalks may be knocked over. Knowing this will help you make the right plant choices.

Other landscape challenges

Do you have dogs, cats, or kids to consider? What about recreational activities? How do you use your yard? Understanding these issues, which are different for each garden, will help you plan around them and save you much hassle later.

▲ Try to place the garden far enough away from the children's play area that errant balls and kids don't harm plants.

▲ If your dog has a routine circuit around your yard, it will be hard to change his habits. Think through how you will keep him out of the garden.

▼ The farther away from the spigot your garden, the lower the water pressure exiting the sprinkler as well as the greater the hassle factor in stretching the hose.

Create your design

◄ This new home cries out for a foundation planting. Perennials will bring color to the planting but you must choose ones to complement the house without blocking windows.

Now that you have a basic understanding of the science of garden design, it's time to create the garden. On this and the following few pages you'll find a simple five-step process to take you through the exploration phase to a finished plan that you can use as a shopping list.

As you design your garden—and afterward, once you've installed it—remember to be flexible. There are always unforeseen circumstances that might force you to make changes. Perhaps the garden center doesn't have the cultivars you want. Maybe the plants cost more than you expected.

Even after your garden is planted you might have to make changes to the original planting. For example weather can thwart your most meticulous plans. It might be too hot, too cold, too wet, too dry, or too humid for your plant choices. Or plants that seem to be in their perfect location struggle to survive and must be replaced. Or plants that should survive the winter (or summer) don't. Or a family of deer moved in and took every flower.

Think of your garden as a process and not an end result, and you'll enjoy the adventure.

Step 1: Define your garden

The following nine questions delve into your goals for your garden. By exploring these topics fully you'll be able to move ahead with a solid understanding of your developing garden.

◄ Retaining walls and perennials create a colorful solution to a sloped yard.

Honestly answering the questions is key. Talk to your neighbors, friends, or significant other if you need to. Honest answers will help ensure you have the garden you want, can afford, and can maintain. It's possible to have a perennial garden in any space on any budget, but you need to be aware of your situation before you begin choosing and placing plants. Here are the questions:

1. Why do I want a garden? How will it improve my landscape? Will it have a useful purpose?
2. What is my garden style?
3. Where will I put the garden?
4. Are there colors I want or don't want in the garden?
5. Are there plants I want or don't want in the garden?
6. How much work am I willing to do in the garden?
7. What is my budget?
8. How will my spouse, kids, cats, dogs, neighbors, relatives, or visitors react?
9. Other thoughts and ideas?

● **Why do I want a garden?** Do you need something to look at as you do the dishes, eat breakfast or work on a hobby? Do you want to attract butterflies and hummingbirds, or is your goal to have flowers for arrangements?

Is there a particular season the garden needs to look fantastic? Do you spend a lot of time outside in spring and fall and not as much during the hottest season? Do you live in an area where plants grow year-round, or is your growing season short? If you are always out of the country during May, there is no reason to have your garden looking great that month.

Every garden has a landscape purpose. It might be to dress up a dull corner of the yard. Or you might need to hide an eyesore or deal

▲ Perhaps your style is informal and you want a place to relax and enjoy the colors and scents of the garden.

▲ Maybe you like the rough-and-tumble, overflowing nature of a cottage garden.

with a spot that is wet and muddy all the time.

You will have an easier time creating a garden plan if you know not only why you want the garden, but the landscape purpose the garden will serve. Knowing the function is essential to understanding how the plants will work together.

Put the purpose of the garden in order of priority. For example if one priority is to hide an ugly spot, that is probably at the top of your list. Say attracting butterflies and having a source of cut flowers from May to August are your second and third priorities.

Once you know what you want, then you can use the appropriate design element to achieve the purpose. For example if you're hiding an eyesore, you could use the line of the garden to direct attention away from the problem to another part of the garden. Then you could choose plants to attract butterflies. But because cutting flowers removes the attraction for the butterflies, you'll need to choose a variety of plants and repeat them throughout the garden to ensure there are enough flowers for you and the butterflies.

● **What is my garden style?**
Your garden says a lot about you, just as your home does. Are you a formal person who

likes things neat and tidy or are you the type who likes informality? Perhaps you prefer the organized chaos of a cottage garden or the naturalistic look of the prairie style. Or you might want the garden to match the architecture of your home. For example, if you have a colonial style home, a formal garden would complement the style. Prairie-style and cottage gardens work well with Craftsman-style bungalows.

● **Where will I put the garden?** This choice may be out of your hands. You may be reworking a garden left by the previous owner of your house, or there might be other features in the yard that can't be moved (such as a driveway, garage, shed, or pool) and that force the placement of your garden. The site inventory and analysis will help you find the best place for your garden.

● **Are there colors or plants that I want or don't want?**
Everyone has color likes and dislikes. If you don't care for pink, then selecting a lot of pink flowers doesn't make much sense. If you don't like certain color combinations— red and orange for example— then don't use them. That

doesn't mean you have to stay away from red and orange completely, but select plants that bloom in those colors in different seasons, or place the plants far enough apart in the garden that they don't make a combination. Conversely if you have a favorite plant or color, repeat it throughout the garden.

● **How much work am I willing to do in the garden?**
Perennial gardens are not no-maintenance gardens. You can find ways to reduce the maintenance, but you can't eliminate it entirely. So, do you honestly enjoy spending time in the garden pulling weeds, deadheading, and mulching, or will you hire

▶ For a front yard garden, give your neighbors a view as well as make one that you can enjoy from the house.

Create your design *(continued)*

◀ A garden should reflect whoever you are. Don't be afraid to show your passions, no matter how wild they are.

what role you would like them to play in its establishment and maintenance.

Cats and dogs can be menacing to both young and established plants. You'll need to figure out how to keep them out of the garden or at least to behave appropriately when they are in the garden.

If you are building a garden in the front yard, walk over to your neighbors and take a look at the space from their vantage point. It will give you some new insights into plant placement so that they will have a good view as well. Make sure that visitors can get to the front door through the garden. It is important to consider the garden from many different angles and facets prior to planting to save time, money, and hassle later.

Step 2: Sketch Your Garden

Get a pencil and a piece of paper to make a rough plan. The plan doesn't have to be to scale, though it will be easier to draw if it is. Knowing the exact size of the garden will also help you figure out how many plants to buy to fit. Use graph paper or have 1 inch on your paper equal 2 feet in the garden. This is a good scale for most perennial gardens.

Draw the outline of the garden and indicate which direction is north. Mark any overhanging trees and sketch in fences, driveways, the edge of the house and other rough details to give you an idea of location and scale.

Dividing the garden into thirds may help you place

someone to do the work for you? Even if you enjoy gardening are you capable of doing all of the work? Or do you have enough time to devote to routine maintenance?

● **What is my budget?**
It is possible to create a perennial garden on any budget, but you can't create a $2,000 garden with just $500. Be honest with yourself. And

keep in mind that you'll have to purchase more than just plants. To ensure the garden's success you'll be spending money on bed preparation (amendments, rototiller rental fees and soil amendments). As you get started you'll need standard garden tools, such as spades, trowels, pruners, and stakes if you don't have them already. Over time, you'll be

buying fertilizer and paying a higher water bill in summer. Plus there's always the inevitable replacement plants.

● **How will my spouse, kids, cats, dogs, neighbors, relatives, or visitors react?**
Consulting family members is important, especially if you live with nongardeners or children. Have a talk with them about the garden and

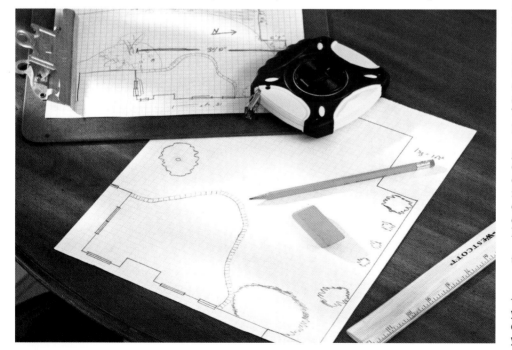

◀ Start by making a rough sketch of your garden. Include nearby features to ensure that you keep them in mind as you make your plans.

Measure out from the center of each plant their full spread to determine the location for their neighbors. Say each plant grows 36 inches wide; they should be 36 inches apart. Each one will spread 18 inches on each side of their center to fill the space.

Spacing plants isn't an exact science. Generally space plants according to their mature spread. A plant that spreads 36 inches across should be 36 inches away from the next plant. If it borders the garden or is next to an object, plant it 18 inches from the object or edge. This spacing is called "on center" in design lingo.

When setting out young plants, this spacing might appear to be too generous. But the plant will grow quickly, and planting it too close to another plant could weaken it and make it more susceptible to pests. In addition, you'll end up dividing and moving plants sooner than you expect.

▲ Lightly write the results of your site analysis and inventory on your plan. You may want to place tracing paper on top of your rough sketch and make notes on it.

the small, medium, and large plants more easily. In most cases the front third of the garden will contain small plants, the middle third medium-size plants, and the back third large plants.

With an island garden, which is viewed from all sides, you'll want to put the largest perennials in the center, small plants at the outer edges, and medium-size plants between the two ranks.

Step 3: Site inventory and analysis

Add your site inventory and analysis notes to your sketch. Use a pencil and write lightly so as not to distract from the outline of your garden. You can also lay a piece of tracing paper over your sketch and note the site inventory and analysis on the tracing paper.

Step 4: Create a bloom chart

On a large sheet of paper, make a list of plants that you already have or that you plan to divide to add to the new garden. Also include plants that you intend to buy. List

them in order by height.

Make columns beside the list for every month of the year, similar to the charts on page 76 to 79. Beside each plant, mark its bloom season and flower and foliage colors.

For example thrift has green foliage all year and pink flowers in spring to early summer. On the chart make a pink line through the months when thrift is in bloom and a green line during the rest of the year.

After completing your chart, you will probably notice flower gaps. Go through the encyclopedia and select a few more plants to fill them. Keep an eye out for plants with eye-catching foliage too—they'll add interest when flowers are hard to come by.

Concentrate the flowering times during the seasons when you're at home and enjoying the outdoors. This step is especially crucial if you live in an area with an extended or even year-round growing season. Aim to have three to five plants of interest each season.

If you live in a cold climate and want color in spring and

fall, select early and late bloomers, add spring bulbs to round out the spring show and perennials that change color in fall to your list.

Be aware that Mother Nature will occasionally decide that late spring bloomers will really flower in midspring or that late-summer bloomers are still going strong well into midfall. However by using this type of chart, you can quickly see if you'll have something interesting to look at for most of your entire growing season.

Step 5: Create your design

Now you are ready to arrange plants. If you are lucky enough to have a very large garden space, you can plant many of each perennial you choose. If your garden is smaller, though, you may not be able to fit in everything you want. Your bloom season chart will come in handy here as well by helping you spread flower color and interest throughout the garden during each season.

Most gardeners use too many different species in

their gardens and too few of each one. Err on the side of using a large numbers of a single perennial rather than on a large number of different plants.

Once you have everything organized by height and flowering season, start looking for pleasing combinations and start filling them in on the plan.

Pick all the plants of one color and scatter them throughout the garden. Then pick their companions that provide the right color combination and place those plants near the first. Keep making combinations and adding plants until you have the area filled.

Ideas to build on

▲ Suppose daylilies are your favorite plant or orange your favorite color. Start with one plant, then look for neighbors that make a good composition.

▲ Catmint blooms at the same time as many daylilies. Its purple-blue flowers complement the orange of daylilies.

▲ Yellow black-eyed susan is a triad color to the blue catmint and is analogous with the orange daylily. All three of these perennials bloom from early to midsummer.

The five-step design process outlined on the previous pages is just one way to design a garden. There are several other techniques you can use to create an appealing perennial garden. Try these ideas for designing your garden around a favorite plant or a favorite color.

Design with your favorite plant

What is your favorite perennial? Perhaps you have more than one. That's even better if those plants bloom during different seasons. Maybe you have a favorite that blooms in spring, another that blooms in summer, and a third that flowers in fall.

Start the process by creating three lists, one for each season. Put your three favorites at the top of each list. Keep your site inventory and analysis handy as you make your list and select companions for them.

Now think about the colors of your favorite plants. To keep things simple, say all three have yellow flowers. Now, do you prefer a complementary, analogous, monochromatic, or a triad color scheme?

If you opt for a complementary scheme, then select a plant with a purple bloom for each season. (Purple—or violet—and yellow are opposite each other on the color wheel.) Now you have six plants for your new garden, three yellow and three purple and three seasons of bloom.

Now add a different color, for example orange. Orange makes a triad with purple and it can be used in an analogous scheme with yellow. (For a discussion of analogous color combinations and triads go to page 50.) Choose one orange plant for each season. Now you have nine plants for the garden.

Next select three or four perennials that flower in a slightly different season. If your spring bloomers all bloom in mid- to late spring,

select one or two that flower in late spring to early summer. If you have many plants that flower in midsummer, select a couple of plants for late summer bloom. Or select complementary foliage plants or summer bulbs to fill this role. Each one of those plants will help set off the plants you have already selected.

At this point your list should be approaching 12 to 15 different perennials, which for many urban lots is enough. It's not an absolute number; you can have many more or fewer plants, depending on the size of your garden. However unless you are trying to create a cottage garden, adding many more species can look busy. Selecting fewer species and purchasing several of each will often generate far more interest than a collection of many individual species.

Finally select a few annuals that go with your color scheme and use those to fill in the gaps. The annuals will ensure that something is in bloom during those inevitable perennial down times. They also allow you to change things a little bit each year, so your garden always looks slightly different.

Nature constantly throws gardeners for a loop. What bloomed in May this year may have flowered in April last year. What made it through the hottest, driest summer on record didn't survive this year's wet summer. You can't plan for all of nature's quirks, but you can hedge your bets by planting a few annuals to keep things going!

Design with your favorite color

Maybe you don't have a favorite plant or perhaps it's whatever one you are standing in front of at the moment. If that is the case, build your garden around a favorite color or color combination.

Flip through books or magazines and check the encyclopedia at the back of this book to find plants in

▲ In fall you won't be able to find plants in the exact shades you use in summer, but you can come close. For example, use goldenrod to provide bright yellow.

▲ A reddish blue aster, such as "Wonder of Staffa', can fill the blue slot.

▲ 'Autumn Joy' showy sedum steps in for orange with russet-red flowers that become deeper russet over time.

your favorite color. Don't worry about what plant it is, or even if it will survive where you live. Once you find all the plants in the garden, sit down to whittle the list to just those that will grow well in your area.

Then start making lists and vignettes as when designing with a favorite plant. Start with a simple color combination such as red and yellow. Find plants that display red and yellow in all three seasons. For example, you could select a red poppy and a yellow iris for late spring bloom, a red lily and a yellow coreopsis or a yellow flowering blackberry lily and red cardinal flower for mid- to late summer color. Yellow and red chrysanthemums can create a stunning effect toward the end of the season. As you choose specific cultivars make sure they bloom at the right times. For example, lilies can bloom from early to late summer.

You may want to tone down these warm colors with white, such as white-flowering phlox or with silver-leaved lamb's-ears.

Once you have a color combination and have identified one or two plants, select one or two more plants in the same colors for each season. When finished you'll have nine to 12 perennials for your garden.

Create a bloom chart like the one on pages 76 to 79 for these plants. Color in the

months when your selections flower or have colorful foliage. Months that have little color will show up readily on the chart. Fill in with two or three perennials that flower during the quiet times. Now you are up to 12 to 15 different species.

Finally select a couple of annuals or foliage plants to provide interest throughout the season. Ornamental grasses, hosta, and yellow waxbells are all excellent foliage plants.

▲ Make combinations of your favorite colors or plants for each season and scatter them throughout the garden. Throw in some silvers, such as lamb's-ears or artemisia to tone down hot colors or soothe clashing color combinations. Add a few annuals and foliage plants or trees and shrubs to carry interest for the entire season.

Create the shape of your bed

▲ The curve of the garden should flow gently. A gently flowing line not only avoids a sense of nervousness or unrest as you view the garden but also eases mowing along the garden's edge.

You might not have the opportunity to design the shape of your garden bed, for example if it's between your walkway and the house or other confined space or it is against a fence. But if you have more flexibility use this chance to sculpt the most pleasing shape possible.

Think about the style of garden you want. Will it be formal or informal? A formal garden will have more straight lines and fewer curves; an informal garden will have more curves and fewer straight lines.

This gets you thinking about the various shapes you could select. A square, rectangle, or triangle has a more formal look than a kidney silhouette.

Don't settle on an exact shape just yet; start thinking about it in terms of style. And remember, a simple shape is usually best. An oval, a kidney-shape outline, or even a triangle will put the spotlight on the plants rather than on the shape of the garden while an octagon or an elaborately curving shape draw the attention.

Next consider the purpose of your plot. If your main goal is to grow flowers for cutting, you might plant in rows in a rectangular bed for easy harvest. A butterfly

◀ Lay hose to outline the garden shape, then check out whether the shape is pleasing. Mow along the hose to test whether the curve really works.

garden on the other hand would probably have a more relaxed appearance.

Consider your viewpoints

After analyzing the style define the views. Will you view the garden from inside the house or from a patio or deck? Are you trying to make a large yard appear smaller or a small yard bigger? Maybe you are simply trying to screen the chain-link fence surrounding a swimming pool. The purpose of your garden will help determine its shape and placement.

Consider the example of screening the fence around a pool. Where will you be when viewing the garden? Inside the fence or outside on the patio? Maybe you split your time and the garden has to look good from both places.

For a garden viewed mainly from the patio, you could build your bed along the fence—curve it for more interest—and place tall plants in back and shorter ones in front. For a more versatile garden, consider an island bed built away from the fence. The tall plants placed in the middle of the bed will be a focal point when

▼ Bricks or concrete edging that is level with the ground provides a convenient mowing strip. The mower's wheels rest on the edging so that you can mow close to the bed without dropping into the garden and scalping the grass.

MAKE A LARGE YARD MORE INTIMATE

If you have a sprawling yard and would like it to appear smaller and more intimate, try these design tips.
● Incorporate plants with large foliage such as hosta or rodgersia.
● Plant in large masses. Massed plants are easier to view from a distance and this will make the garden seem closer.
● Select warm colors. Warm colors are readily visible from a distance. Cool colors become washed out at a distance.

viewed from either the pool or the patio.

Pleasing curves

How do you know if the curves you are creating are too sharp or not curved enough? Curves need to flow; those that are too sharp will cause a feeling of unrest in the garden. Make the curves gentle but noticeable.

Try these two simple tricks using a garden hose and a lawn mower for designing

▲ A stone edging provides a solid front for your plants and prevents you from mowing over them. Stone is heavy and expensive but easy to maintain.

▲ Black plastic edging is relatively inexpensive compared with other edging materials and easy to install on your own. However, if not installed properly, it can be pushed out of the ground as soil freezes and thaws, and it becomes brittle in time.

curves. Outline your bed with the hose; you'll quickly see if the curves are too sharp or not sharp enough.

Then study the outline from your main viewpoints to see whether you have placed the garden in the best location for viewing. Because a hose is generally easy to see from a distance you will know right away if you are placing the garden in the right spot.

Also pay attention to the location of the incurve (the part that curves inward toward the garden). The incurve is good spot for a focal point. (Learn more on page 66.)

Once you think you have the outline of the garden set, take the lawn mower for a run around it. If you can mow the turns smoothly, then the bed is curved just right. You want to avoid

▲ A cut-turf edging looks sharp, especially when the lawn is in excellent shape. It's a simple cost-free edging.

▲ Cut-turf edging requires more routine care to remain sharp and be able to keep grass out of the bed.

having to mow back and forth to get into all the spots around the garden.

Keeping an edge

After defining the shape of your garden, consider how to edge it so that it is easy to maintain. Grass and nearby plants will try to encroach. You can ring your bed with a cut-soil edge or you can use one of the many edging materials available to keep grass and other plants at bay.

Many landscape companies will put a cut edge around your gardens in spring as part of their spring cleanup service. They may use a shovel or a mechanical edger, but the end result should be a nice deep edge. One of the disadvantages of a soil edge is the garden tends to grow a few inches bigger every year, and you may eventually need to put in more plants at the edge of the bed.

Many types of edgings are sold at garden centers and home improvement stores. You'll find plastic, metal, stone, and wood products, each with its advantages and disadvantages. The edgings provide a good way to keep

the garden the same size, and they form an obvious visual separation between the garden and the rest of the yard. However they can look unnatural and be a pain to install. In cold climates, plastic and metal edgings often heave out of the ground during winter, especially if they weren't properly installed.

MAKE A SMALL YARD APPEAR BIGGER

Here's how to make a small suburban lot or urban courtyard feel larger.
● Use cool colors, which give the appearance of distance because they are often a bit harder to see.
● Use fine-textured plants. They are often translucent and allow you to glimpse the plants or objects behind them, increasing the feeling of distance.
● Use fewer plant species or varieties. The garden will appear bigger because of the variety.
● Use strong horizontal lines with fewer curves, which will give the appearance of distance.

Create a focal point

▲ By placing the curve and focal point just beyond an eyesore, you draw attention away from the problem spot. A focal point can also draw you down a path and hide glimpses of what lies beyond so that the journey is even more interesting.

A perennial garden is more than a plot of land on which to grow plants. If positioned thoughtfully it can become the focal point of your landscape—a place to showcase your unique plant combinations and garden art. At the same time the garden has the ability to draw attention away from less than stellar elements such as a utility box or a neighbor's collection of "antique" cars.

Line, the design element discussed on page 35, is a handy tool for creating a focal point. Go to the part of your house where you want to enjoy the best view of your garden. The window will create the frame for your garden in the same way that a frame enhances a picture. Place your garden so it is highly visible from that spot.

If you're more likely to view your garden from the porch or patio, locate the bed where it will naturally draw your eye from those locations.

If you are planning a more informal garden and don't want a straight line between the viewpoint and your garden, put curved lines to work in your favor. When designing the shape of your bed, place a small curve at the spot where you want your eye to be drawn.

The part of the curve that dips in—the incurve—is a natural spot for a focal point, even with a simple shape such as a kidney shape. (On a

◀ A focal point is anything that stands out from the rest of the elements in a garden, such as a bright-yellow container or plant.

▲ Enhance the focal point—the tallest plant or a statue or other piece of artwork—by placing it at the point where a curve dips in. This helps it stand out, making it an even better focal point.

kidney shape, the part where the "bean" dips in is the focal point.) In much the same way as a fireplace or a piano becomes the focal point of a room and all the furniture is placed to highlight that characteristic, an incurve naturally draws the eye to that spot and becomes a great place for a specimen plant or a piece of sculpture.

After determining the focal point's location, select a plant to serve as the center of attraction (if using a plant as a focal point). This plant needs to have a good floral or foliage display and seasonal interest for much of the growing season. In short it needs to be a plant with presence, such as bear's

breeches, black-eyed susan, a large hosta, an ornamental grass, or even a small tree or shrub.

Secondary focal points

A secondary focal point has the important job of supporting and highlighting the main focal point; it also creates rhythm in the garden. In the example using a kidney shape, the lobed areas on either side of the bean's incurve are logical spots for secondary focal points. By placing a different showy plant in either or both lobes, you will maximize the impact of your garden.

Once you have placed those three plants, choose

FOCAL POINT PLANTS

A focal point plant has presence in the garden. It might have beautiful flowers or colorful foliage, or both. It can be a large plant or not so large, but somehow it must stand out in the garden. Here are some surefire focal point candidates.

FOCAL POINTS FOR SHADE GARDENS	
Plant	**Notable characteristic**
Bugbane	Tall plants with slender wands of white to pink in late summer to early fall
'Ghost' lady fern	Low-growing fern with silver fronds
Goatsbeard	Plumes of creamy white flowers on top of tall stems
'Gold Heart' bleeding heart	Bright yellow foliage and pink flowers in spring
Rodgersia	Bold coarse-textured foliage; pink, red, or white flowers in spring, mid-, or late summer
Royal fern	Light green fronds in summer turn bronze in fall
'Sum and Substance' hosta	Large plant with enormous chartreuse leaves that fade to gold
Toad lily	Shiny dark green leaves, unique texture, and orchidlike flowers
Wood fern	Striking texture and upright form from spring to fall; evergreen in some areas
'Variegatum' solomon's seal	Large arching stems and variegated leaves; fragrant white flowers in spring
Yellow waxbells	Dark green maplelike leaves and bell-like yellow flowers
FOCAL POINTS FOR SUNNY GARDENS	
Plant	**Notable characteristic**
Arkansas amsonia	Pale blue flowers in late summer and bright yellow color in fall
Aster	Blanketed with pink, purple, or white flowers in fall
Bear's breeches	Large plant with bold purple and white flower spikes
Butterfly weed	Brilliant orange flowers in summer are followed by seedpods
Black-eyed susan	Bright yellow flowers nearly all summer
Cardinal flower	Brilliant red flowers on tall stems in late summer; colorful foliage all summer
False indigo	Large plant with purple pealike flowers in early spring followed by black seedpods
Fountain grass	Flowing foliage all summer; fluffy plumes in late summer; stands all winter
French lavender	Low-growing, bushy lavender with vibrant purple flowers
'Heavy Metal' switchgrass	Metallic blue foliage and upright growth habit
Helenium	Daisies in shades of red and yellow in mid- to late summer
Mexican bush sage	Evergreen perennial with wands of purple flowers in winter and spring
Miscanthus	Large plant with green or green-and-white striped leaves
New Zealand flax	A rosette of colorful straplike leaves
Purple coneflower	Large purple daisies in summer followed by long-lasting, bold seedheads
Russian sage	Tall plant; silver stems and leaves from spring to fall; blue-purple flower spikes in summer
Yucca	Strong striking form all year

additional plants to complement them. For example, say you used a large bear's breeches as the focal point, several smaller 'Moonbeam' coreopsis planted in the lobes will act as secondary focal points. The foliage of the bear's breeches will set off the fine texture of the coreopsis, and the yellow coreopsis flowers will highlight the dark green bear's breeches leaves. If you don't like yellow, select another bright color, such as pink. Contrast is the key to them working as focal points.

You can also look for complementary, analogous, and triad color schemes (see page 50) when placing your plants. Don't group all the spring-flowering plants together. Sprinkle them throughout the garden and you'll have something to look at all spring.

Direct the eye

How do you make your main focal point work for you? Go back to your yard's unsightly feature that you are trying to hide. If your eyes are naturally drawn to that area of the garden and you would like to draw attention away from it, place the focal point to the right or left of the obtrusion. To do this, move the incurve to the left or right of the object. This will draw your eye to the focal point and away from the eye-sore.

If the feature is particularly ugly or bothersome, you can also use line to draw the eye even more strongly toward your selected focal point. If you make the incurve deeper and extend the sides more, thus naturally creating a frame for your focal point and causing it to stand out even more.

Combine plants

▲ Think of your garden as a series of vignettes so that you're not overwhelmed by trying to fill the entire garden at once. In shade you might start with a foliage combination such as one with lady's mantle and goutweed (*Aegopodium podagraria* 'Variegatum'). A colorful Japanese aucuba in the background and ferns and hosta round out the grouping.

▲ In a sunny site lamb's-ears, perennial salvia, geranium, and rock rose (*Cistus* spp.) can be used in several spots in the garden. The cool colors take the heat out of a hot summer. Daylilies will change the color scheme in a few weeks.

On paper you can create the most appealing plant combinations, but install your garden according to your well-thought-out plan and you're likely to be a bit surprised. Some plants may flower a bit earlier or a bit later than anticipated. Or a perennial might take a liking to the growing conditions and spread, crowding out companions.

Don't look at these challenges as problems. The constantly changing nature of perennials is one of their best characteristics. You have the chance to witness something new and exciting in the garden every year.

▲ Light purple-blue russian sage, dark purple-blue perennial salvia, and rosy pink joe-pye weed and purple coneflower are a calming combination. With the addition of yellow black-eyed susan, the composition becomes vibrant.

Here are a few things you can do to increase your chances of success in the real world and not just on paper.

Make many plant combos

Consider the different features of perennials such as form, texture, and color, which may change from spring through fall. Each of these features generates the opportunity to create a combination.

If you think of your garden as a series of small vignettes, each with its own characteristics, then for each small section of the garden simply choose two or three plants that look good together and move on to the next section. You can pick a foliage combination for the left side, move to a color grouping, then a textural planting, another color combination, and so on.

Instead of worrying about all 1,000 square feet (or whatever size of garden space you have to fill), you only have to worry about 2 to 6 square feet at a time when you think of your garden as a series of vignettes.

Put color to work

Start with either a complementary or an analogous color scheme. Analogous combinations are more harmonious while complementary combinations contrast. Both are pleasing.

When flowers of similar hues are grown together, they blend in nicely. But by adding a perennial that blooms in a complementary color, you can give an analogous scheme needed contrast and create a striking combination.

You can also create different effects by working with tints, tones, and shades within one color range. For example planting light purple and magenta creeping phlox together (different values of purple) with a chartreuse cushion spurge will generate a muted, calm combination.

Contrast that with a rosy-purple common yarrow and golden yellow coreopsis. The yarrow will naturally go through several shades of color as the flowers open then mature, but the addition of a bright coreopsis creates a vibrant combination. This color pairing may not be the most pleasing to you, but you surely will find one you like.

Colors of the seasons

Selecting hues that are associated with the seasons will also help your garden look its best year-round. For example, cool blue and purple are often associated with spring while warmer yellows, oranges, and reds shout summer. And fall offers a cornucopia of deep burgundy, yellow, and orange.

As the seasons change the quality and intensity of the light changes as well. Keep this in mind as you take advantage of seasonal colors. For example, plant pastels in early to midspring when they are readily visible against the backdrop of newly emerging foliage. In summer pinks and other pastels seem to fade during the day in the strong light.

▲ Pink and blue and other pastels are often the color of the spring garden. A splash of orange from an oriental or annual poppy spices it up.

▲ Ornamental grasses, stipa and miscanthus, and silvery lamb's-ears create a striking monochromatic combination accented with white urns.

Add excitement

If you are ready to break away from the expected, try splashes of opposite colors during a growing season. For example, mix some orange poppies into your pastel late-spring garden to add excitement at a time when cooler colors are expected. During the summer months instead of planting all warm-colored flowers, toss in some deep purple (daylily, sea holly, or hardy geranium for example) to tone down red or yellow yarrow, black-eyed susan, and other warm-colored flowers.

If you do decide to go for the pizzazz of unexpected colors, however, don't overdo it. One or two unexpected color combinations will enliven a space. Too much of the unexpected creates chaos.

Beat the heat

Areas with intensely hot, dry summers (southern Florida, Texas, and inland parts of California for example) rely on a bounty of foliage combinations to create interest in hot periods. Great foliage perennials include ornamental oregano, artemisia, sedum, ornamental grasses, and New Zealand flax.

Adding summer-flowering bulbs to the garden is a great way to generate some fantastic flowering combina–

tions. Most are relatively inexpensive and can be added to any garden.

Arum, elephant ears, alstromeria, caladium, crinum, and pineapple lily are a small sampling of what is available. There are summer bulbs that thrive in shade or sun and moist or dry areas. Best of all most are very easy to grow.

Solutions for clashing combos

Occasionally flowers bloom in unexpected colors. The perfect color combination you were planning might end up being an eyesore. Luckily you can remedy color clashes in the garden.

Try placing a bicolored plant in between the two offenders. Many flowers have centers that are a different color. Look for one that is similar to the two colors you are dealing with.

If your two favorite plants are hot pink and yellow but you don't like that color combination, try placing a daylily with a yellow throat and softer pink petals between your two plants. The bicolored plant softens

▶ Their colors and shapes allow birdbaths, sculptures, and other objects to function as focal points. Because most are made from materials that don't deteriorate, they are a permanent focal point, which you can build the entire garden around.

the look. You can also use perennials with white or silver flowers and foliage to calm clashing colors.

Foliage can also generate "neutral" space between two clashing colors. A deep green will set off and highlight almost any bright color. Hosta, bear's breeches, and foam flower are all good foliage selections.

Add art

Plants aren't the only things that can be used to create successful combinations.

Pottery, sculpture, and other artwork can be paired with plants. If you are unsure if your favorite piece of artwork will go well with your chosen color scheme, take it with you when you shop for plants. If the piece is too big to cart around, match a paint chip to it and take that with you.

Your artwork needs a function in the garden or it will look out of place. Let a large piece to serve as a focal point, and nestle smaller objects among the shorter plants at the front of the garden.

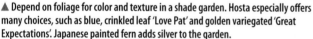

▲ Depend on foliage for color and texture in a shade garden. Hosta especially offers many choices, such as blue, crinkled leaf 'Love Pat' and golden variegated 'Great Expectations'. Japanese painted fern adds silver to the garden.

▲ Golden hakone grass (which also does well in shade), 'Big Ears' lamb's-ears, and thyme make a lovely full-sun foliage composition.

Foliage solutions for shade

Foliage plays a lead role in plant combinations for the shade garden. While color is a key factor in building flowering combinations, texture is the trait of interest in foliage combinations.

Hosta is available in hundreds of cultivars that differ in color, texture, leaf shape, and size. Look to the bold foliage of chartreuse 'Sum and Substance' hosta to catch light and bounce it around the shade garden. Subtle variegations in the leaves of other cultivars provide a similar effect on a smaller scale.

Hostas aren't the only bold foliage plant for shade. Yellow waxbells, rodgersia, and heart-leaf brunnera provide bold texture and a strong presence in any shade garden.

Many ferns have a delicate texture that belies their toughness. A fine-textured fern planted next to a bold-textured hosta or yellow waxbells creates a combination that is pleasing all season long.

Many species of shade plants are available in variegated forms. Toad lily is one of the best fall-flowering shade plants. Its cultivars may have dark green foliage or light green leaves splotched with deep green, or dark green marked with white, or yellow. Use variegation judiciously in your plant combinations. Too many variegated plants together is chaotic.

If you like ornamental grasses but have more shade than grasses will grow in, use sedges in their place. Unlike their weedy relative, yellow nutsedge, most garden sedges are well-behaved garden plants. They are available in a variety of colors including brown, blue, green, and chartreuse, and the foliage may be variegated.

Sedges range in size from 6 to 24 inches tall. Some sedges tolerate moist soils; others thrive in dry sites.

◀ Sedges have texture and form similar to those of ornamental grasses. Use them in a shade garden where few ornamental grasses will grow to create the same effect.

ALL-STAR FOLIAGE PLANTS

Plant	Notable characteristics	Site conditions	Zones
Artemisia	Fine-textured silver foliage; mounding or upright habit	Full sun; well-drained soil; drought tolerant	3–7
Coral bells	Evergreen or semievergreen leaves in shades of green, purple, bronze, silver, or chartreuse	Full sun to part shade; moist, well-drained to dry soil	3–8
English lavender	Fragrant silver-green foliage; purple flower spikes in summer	Full sun; well-drained soil	5–10
Foamy bells	Neat mound of variegated evergreen leaves; showy flower spikes	Full sun to part shade; rich, moist, well-drained soil	4–8
'Ghost' lady fern	Deciduous, upright, spreading fern with brilliant silver fronds	Part shade (morning light will bring out the silver coloring); moist, well-drained soil	3–8
Golden hakone grass	Fountain of variegated green-and-chartreuse foliage; interesting texture	Part sun to shade; moist well-drained, slightly acid soil	5–8
'Karl Forester' feather reed grass	Stiff, upright ornamental grass with dark green foliage and tan flowers	Full sun or part shade; well-drained soil	5–9
Lungwort	Huge white-splattered dark green leaves in summer; pink flowers in spring	Part shade to full shade; moist soil with organic matter	4–8
Miscanthus	Dozens of cultivars; prized for showy seedheads that appear in summer and last through winter	Full sun to part shade; well-drained, average soil	5–9
New Zealand flax	Colorful leaves in solid colors of dark green, yellow green, red, rust, or variegated in these colors plus cream, pink, purple, and burgundy	Full sun; moist, fertile soil	8–11
Variegated fragrant solomon's seal	Upright arching stems of green-and-white foliage	Part to full shade; well-drained moist soil	4–9
Yucca	Spiky gray-green to green to variegated foliage; white flower stalks in early to midsummer	Full sun; well-drained sandy soil	4–11

Artemisia — Coral bells — English lavender — Foamy bells — 'Ghost' lady fern — Golden hakone grass

'Karl Forester' feather reed grass — Lungwort — Miscanthus — New Zealand flax — Variegated fragrant solomon's seal — Yucca

Most prefer moist, shaded areas. If you are growing hosta, astilbe, and ferns, you can readily add sedges to the mix and have the fine texture of a "grass" in the shade.

Sunny foliage combinations

Foliage plants belong in full-sun gardens as much as they do in shade gardens. Ornamental grasses especially ones with variegated or chartreuse foliage are effective in sunny gardens.

Creating color combinations with fall foliage is a great way to add interest to your garden during a time when you may be thinking of putting the garden to bed for winter.

Some perennials such as Siberian iris, Arkansas amsonia, and peony have fantastic fall color.

Extend the season with foliage

Using foliage is the perfect way to create long-lasting combinations, whether your garden is in sun or shade.

Although you can find perennials for a progression of bloom throughout the growing season, not many flower for more than a few weeks at a time. This is a challenge, both good and bad, for the perennial gardener.

Foliage remains on the plant all season long. If you can create effective foliage

Combine plants *(continued)*

THREE TIPS FOR WINNING COMBINATIONS

Perennials in a flowering combination must flower at the same time.
This might seem like an obvious concept, but it is easy to overlook when you are enthralled with a trio of plants you see in a garden, catalog, or the encyclopedia at the back of this book. If you love yellow and purple and decide to pair a yellow yarrow and purple aster, you'll enjoy yellow flowers in summer and purple flowers in fall. Be sure your combinations bloom at the same time for at least a short period. The bloom time charts on pages 76 to 79 will be helpful.

Plants in a combination need to have similar cultural needs.
Lamb's-ear and blue fescue make a fantastic color, texture, and foliage combination, and both plants thrive in full sun and dry soil. But a combination of lamb's-ear and 'Elegans' hosta (a blue-leafed cultivar) doesn't have a chance because of their different needs.

That's an extreme example, but even bee balm and black-eyed susan might suffer during dry years because bee balm prefers moist soil and black-eyed susan needs good drainage.

Add some woody plants.
This advice might seem out of place in a book about perennials, but a small Japanese maple, a crabapple tree, or a flowering shrub such as caryopteris or spirea will add great texture and form to the garden. And many woody plants have colorful foliage (especially in the fall) to provide a backdrop for flowering perennials.

Astilbe, columbine, lady's mantle, and annual sweet william all bloom in late spring to early summer.

Hosta, fern, and astilbe thrive in part shade, however the astilbe needs consistent soil moisture.

Small trees and shrubs provide shade and year-round structure. Some even bring spring flowers or fall color.

combinations, they'll carry your garden when flowers aren't looking their best or there is a lull between blooms.

Foliage also has the ability to outwit nature. Even when flowering occurs earlier or later than usual, foliage fills in the gaps, keeping the garden looking good despite the weather.

Go vertical

Don't forget to add height when putting together plant combinations. Unfortunately lofty plants are relatively rare in the perennial palette. Many perennials top out less than 12 inches tall. More

grow 1 to 3 feet tall. But only a handful of perennials grow as tall as 4 or 5 feet. Adding vines to the mix of tall plants provides you with many more planting options.

A vine can provide that much-needed vertical accent without taking up a lot of soil space. Other tall perennials tend to grow tall and wide; vines grow up, leaving plenty of room for companion plants.

Is there a nearby structure that can support a climbing perennial? Or do you have space to construct a sturdy trellis in the garden? If so take advantage of it.

Vines are especially useful design tools for masking a

◀ Vines and the structure on which they grow add height to a garden, provide color while leaving room for other perennials, and in time fill in to create privacy.

VINES FOR VERTICAL INTEREST

Plant name	Notable characteristics	Size	Site conditions	Zone
Carolina jessamine (*Gelsemium sempervirens*)	Evergreen climber with glossy leaves; clusters of fragrant yellow flowers in spring and summer	10–20' tall and 3–5' wide	Full sun to part shade; moist, well-drained soil	7–9
Jackman clematis (*Clematis jackmanii*)	Large-flowered deciduous vine with velvety purple blooms in mid- to late summer	10' tall and 3' wide	Full sun to part shade; moist, fertile, well-drained soil	4–9
Coral vine (*Antigonon leptopus*)	Fast grower with heart-shape leaves; clusters of pink, white, or red flowers in summer; can quickly invade surrounding plants	25–40' tall and 10' wide	Full sun; moist, well-drained soil	9–11
'Arctic Beauty' kolomitka vine (*Actinidia kolomikta*)	Deciduous climber; purple leaves in spring become variegated green, white, and purple in summer; female plants produce fruit	15' tall and 3–4' wide	Full sun; fertile, well-drained soil	4–8
Passionflower (*Passiflora incarnata*)	Dark green foliage; striking 3-inch-wide purple or white flowers in summer; many species of passionflower available, some of which are extremely rampant in mild areas	6' tall and 2' wide	Full sun to part shade; moist, well-drained soil	6–8
'Variegata' porcelain berry (*Ampelopsis brevipedunculata*)	Marbled, maple-shape leaves decorated with pink, white, and splashes of green; white summer flowers develop into showy blue berries	15' tall and 3–4' wide	Full sun to part shade; moist, well-drained soil.	5–9
Sweet autumn clematis (*Clematis terniflora*)	Deciduous or semievergreen; blanketed with fragrant white flowers in fall; a rampant grower that is relatively easy to control	15–20' tall and 6–10' wide	Full sun to part shade; moist, fertile, well-drained soil	4–9
Trumpet creeper (*Campsis radicans*)	Deciduous; a vigorous grower with woody stems and medium green foliage; tubular orange flowers in summer; a hummingbird favorite; suckers readily	30' tall and 10' wide	Full sun; moist, well-drained soil	5–9

view. For example let a sweet autumn clematis ramble on the trellis. It will create a backdrop of foliage for summer-blooming perennials and sport fragrant white flowers in fall. Think of it as a blooming wall.

There are many great perennial vines. Some have a bad reputation for their aggressive growth habits, but recent breeding has tamed their ways, however you'll need to watch cultivars to ensure you are getting one of these. Other fast-growing vines have not been tamed and become a problem unless you prune frequently to control their growth.

▶ Clematis or another vine climbing the wall of a shed, garage, or other structure effectively draws your eye upward, makes the structure part of the garden, and gives a cottage look to the garden.

Design a year-round garden

▲ In very early summer a white peony is winding down, and blue perennial salvia, ornamental alliums, and purple-pink phlox are at their prime. Yellow yarrow is about to bloom, while lilies are forming buds and miscanthus is emerging from dormancy and putting on growth.

◀ For a short period in midsummer this corner of the garden has few flowers. The lilies have finished blooming and been cut back. 'Lady Elsie May' rose, red and white hardy hibiscus plants, and purple gladiola add some color while the miscanthus, peony, and other perennials add texture and structure.

With some thoughtful planning your perennial garden will have interesting elements every day of the year. The key is to think beyond flowers. If you concentrate only on the blooms, you are missing some of the best ways to generate interest in the garden. You are also missing out on some of the plant world's best combinations.

This doesn't mean you can't come close to having something flowering all the time. In many regions, flowering from March through November isn't unusual and in milder climates most perennial gardens can put on a show year-round.

Flowering times will vary from one area to another. If you are looking in the encyclopedia, you may notice that a given plant is said to bloom in early spring. If you live in a mild winter climate, that plant might actually flower in midwinter for you. If you live in the Midwest or Northeast, you might see flowering in midspring. Keep this in mind as you check flowering times.

A bloom time chart will be handy when designing for seasonal interest. Once you identify your favorite perennials for your garden, make a chart like the ones on pages 76 to 79, coloring in the appropriate flowering months. Then fill in the gaps with foliage plants, bulbs, and plants with colorful fruit or seedheads, as well as plants that striking foliage color, either all year or just in autumn. You will soon discover that you have some interest every day of the year, although some times will be more colorful than others or will have more flowers on display at certain times.

Even if the perennial blooms a few weeks earlier or later than specified in the encyclopedia, by choosing plants that all have the same bloom period, they'll bloom together no matter your location.

If your budget or space is very limited, begin by searching for perennials with longer flowering periods.

Then narrow your choices to plants that also have fall color or interesting foliage or seedheads. Look to plants with variegated foliage, ornamental grasses, and bulbs to round out the seasons and carry your garden through those inevitable downtimes.

Thugs in the garden

Not all perennials are well behaved. You can often spot these plants because their descriptions will generally use words and phrases such as vigorous, spreads but not hard to control, or excellent groundcover. When planning your year-round garden, don't be swayed by the seemingly beneficial characteristics of these aggressive plants.

While some are a bit boisterous, others are downright bullies. If you put them in a garden and let growth go unchecked, they can run rampant. They might crowd out nearby plants and spread beyond the garden border. Nevertheless many of these perennials are great plants and with some work can be made to function in the garden, if you know they are thugs to begin with.

Plants can be aggressive in two basic ways: self-sowing and spreading by roots or rhizomes (horizontal stems).

Prevent excessive self-sowing

The ultimate purpose of a flower is reproduction, which plants accomplish with seeds. The trick with aggressive plants that spread by seed is not to let them go to seed.

Deadheading on a regular basis will stop self sowing. Simply cut the flowering stems off as soon as the flowers fade.

Occasionally you will want some plants such as columbine and hollyhock to reproduce by seed. When you are deadheading you can decide which seedheads to remove and which to leave.

If you are careful you can even place the seeds where you want them and not

where they'd land on their own. Lay the seedhead you cut off on the ground where you want new plants. Soon the seeds will sprout.

Confine spreading plants

For plants that spread aggressively by roots and rhizomes, you need to be territorial with your space. Have a boundary in mind for that plant. Tell yourself, "that plant has x-number of feet to spread and that's all." Once it spreads beyond the allowed area, be ruthless; remove all offending sections. Dig up the parts that are escaping with a shovel.

Generally plants that spread aggressively recover quickly—you don't have to worry about harming the plant. If your spreading plant shows weak growth near the center and vigorous growth around the edges, discard the center and replant the healthy young outer shoots.

A SHORT LIST OF POTENTIAL GARDEN THUGS

Plant name	Notable characteristics
Bear's breeches	Self seeds, especially a problem on the West Coast
Blackberry lily	Self seeds
Common yarrow	The straight species self sows aggressively and spreads
Goutweed (*Aegopodium podagraria* 'Variegatum')	Spreads aggressively
Rose campion	Self sows copiously
Spotted deadnettle (*Lamium* spp.)	Spreads aggressively and self seeds
Spotted bellflower	Spreads aggressively

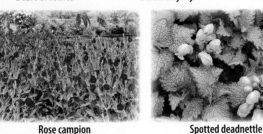  

Bear's breeches   Blackberry lily   Common yarrow   Goutweed

Rose campion   Spotted deadnettle   Spotted bellflower

▲ By September the miscanthus is fully grown and in bloom, joined by a butterfly bush, purple and hot pink asters, daylilies, catmint, and a white hardy hibiscus.

Bloom Times by the Season

Use this chart to help you plan overlapping seasons of bloom for color all year. Because perennials are listed in order of bloom, you can see at a glance which ones bloom together, which ones bloom in succession, and which ones have an extra-long bloom period. Remember that any bloom chart will be only a rough guide, because bloom seasons can differ according to region, weather, microclimate, and cultivar. Blue bars represent bloom seasons.

Plant Name	Spring E	Spring M	Spring L	Summer E	Summer M	Summer L	Fall E	Fall M	Fall L	Winter E	Winter M	Winter L
Christmas rose	■											
Wall rock cress	■	■										
Creeping veronica	■	■	■	■								
Lenten rose	■	■	■									
Lungwort	■	■	■									
Pasque flower	■	■										
Primrose	■	■	■									
Violet	■	■	■									
Barrenwort		■										
Fringecup		■										
Allegheny foam flower		■	■									
Basket-of-gold		■	■									
Bigroot geranium		■	■									
Creeping phlox		■	■									
False solomon's seal		■	■									
Foam flower		■	■									
Avens		■	■									
Gold moss stonecrop		■	■									
Heart-leaf bergenia		■	■									
Heart-leaf brunnera		■	■									
Jacob's ladder		■	■									
Leopard's bane		■	■									
Moss phlox		■	■									
Moss verbena		■	■									
Snowdrop anemone		■	■									
Rock soapwort		■	■									
Variegated fragrant solomon's seal		■	■									
Wherry's foam flower		■	■									
Columbine			■	■								
Goldenstar			■	■								
Lupine			■	■								
Globeflower			■	■								
Bluestar			■									
Firecracker penstemon			■									
Old-fashioned bleeding heart			■									
Rocky Mountain penstemon			■									
Woodland phlox			■									
Arkansas amsonia				■								
Bearded iris				■								
Bear's breeches				■								
Columbine meadow rue				■								
Common foxglove				■								

Plant Name	Spring E	Spring M	Spring L	Summer E	Summer M	Summer L	Fall E	Fall M	Fall L	Winter E	Winter M	Winter L
Coral bells				■								
Dalmatian bellflower				■								
False indigo				■								
Gas plant				■								
Goatsbeard				■								
Hybrid astilbe				■								
Lady's mantle				■								
Masterwort				■								
Nepal cinquefoil				■								
Oriental poppy				■								
Peony				■								
Pinks				■								
Swordleaf inula				■								
Thrift				■								
Thyme				■								
Torch lily				■								
Yellow flag				■								
Bloody cranesbill				■	■							
Common yarrow				■	■							
Foamy bells				■	■							
Fringed bleeding heart				■	■							
Meadow rue				■	■							
Hybrid cranesbill				■	■	■						
Threadleaf coreopsis				■	■	■						
Agapanthus				■	■	■						
Missouri evening primrose				■	■	■						
Spiderwort				■	■	■						
Yellow corydalis				■	■	■						
Common beard-tongue					■							
Lamb's-ears					■							
Maltese cross					■							
Shasta daisy					■							
Astilbe					■							
Bee balm					■							
Bellflower					■							
Butterfly weed					■							
Campion					■							
Catmint					■							
Checkerbloom					■							
Daylily					■							
Delphinium					■							
Dropwort					■							
Fern-leaf yarrow					■							

Left table

Plant Name	Spring E	Spring M	Spring L	Summer E	Summer M	Summer L	Fall E	Fall M	Fall L	Winter E	Winter M	Winter L
Globe thistle				X								
Hollyhock				X								
Japanese iris				X								
Jerusalem sage				X								
Lavender				X								
Lily				X								
Queen-of-the-prairie				X								
Queen-of-the-meadow				X								
Smooth white penstemon				X								
Yellow foxglove				X								
Yucca				X								
Anise hyssop				X	X							
Baby's breath				X	X							
Big blue lobelia				X	X							
Blackberry lily				X	X							
Black-eyed susan				X	X							
Blanketflower				X	X							
Clematis				X	X							
Compact pincushion flower				X	X							
Coreopsis				X	X							
Creeping baby's breath				X	X							
Evening primrose				X	X							
False sunflower				X	X							
Feather reed grass				X	X							
Hybrid garden phlox				X	X							
Hybrid mullein				X	X							
Hybrid speedwell				X	X							
Hybrid verbena				X	X							
Louisiana iris				X	X							
Ornamental allium				X	X							
Ornamental oregano				X	X							
Pincushion flower				X	X							
Rose verbena				X	X							
Spike speedwell				X	X							
Sundrops				X	X							
Tree mallow				X	X							
Yellow meadow rue				X	X							
Crimson pincushion				X	X	X						
Crocosmia				X	X	X						
Stoke's aster				X	X	X						
White gaura				X	X	X						
Gayfeather					X							
Balloonflower					X							
Culver's root					X							
Cupid's dart					X							
Flea bane					X							
Gloriosa daisy					X							

Right table

Plant Name	Spring E	Spring M	Spring L	Summer E	Summer M	Summer L	Fall E	Fall M	Fall L	Winter E	Winter M	Winter L
Hardy hibiscus				X								
Hybrid yarrow				X								
Kamschatka stonecrop				X								
Lavender cotton				X								
Ligularia				X								
Purple coneflower				X								
Rodgersia				X								
Russian sage				X								
Sea holly				X								
Switchgrass				X								
Two-row stonecrop				X								
Caryopteris					X	X						
Golden marguerite					X	X						
Goldenrod					X	X						
Helenium					X	X						
Hosta					X	X						
Hybrid hyssop					X	X						
Hybrid lobelia					X	X						
Joe-pye weed					X	X						
New York ironweed					X	X						
Three veined everlasting				X	X	X						
Wall germander				X	X	X						
Miscanthus					X	X						
Pineleaf penstemon				X	X	X						
Swamp milkweed					X	X	X					
Cardinal flower						X						
Fountaingrass						X						
Mondograss						X						
Muhly grass						X						
Prairie dropseed						X						
Liriope							X					
Aster							X					
Boltonia							X					
Chrysanthemum							X					
Hardy begonia							X					
Obedient plant							X					
Perennial sunflower							X					
Toad lily							X					
Yellow waxbells							X					
Black snakeroot							X	X				
Hybrid anemone							X	X				
Japanese anemone							X	X				
Rose turtlehead							X	X				
Showy sedum							X	X				
Monkshood								X				
White snakeroot								X				
Purple moor grass								X	X			

PERENNIAL BLOOM TIMES

Arranged alphabetically by common name, this chart shows the bloom period of many popular perennials. It also displays peak times for other decorative features such as exceptional foliage, colorful fall leaves, winter structure, or ornamental seedheads. Pink bars show typical bloom times; green bars represent other sources of visual interest. By consulting this chart, you can make beds and borders that look good from spring to fall.

(In the tables below, "P" marks typical bloom times shown as pink bars; "G" marks other sources of visual interest shown as green bars.)

Plant Name	Spring E	Spring M	Spring L	Summer E	Summer M	Summer L	Fall E	Fall M	Fall L	Winter E	Winter M	Winter L
Allegheny foam flower		P	P				G	G				
Anise hyssop					P							
Arkansas amsonia	P	P										
Artemisia		G	G	G	G							
Asiatic hybrid lily				P	P		G					
Aster							P	P				
Astilbe					P	P						
'Autumn Joy' sedum		G	G	G	G	G	G					
Avens		P										
Baby's breath				P	P							
Balloon flower						G	G					
Barrenwort		P	P	G	G			G	G			
Basket-of-gold			P									
Bearded iris				P								
Bear's breeches				P	P	G						
Bear's foot hellebore	P						G	G	G			
Bee balm				P								
Bethlehem sage	P	P		G	G							
Big blue lobelia						P						
Big leaf ligularia		G	G	P								
Bigroot geranium			P	G	G							
Black-eyed susan				P	P		G	G				
Blanket flower				P	P							
Blue oat grass	G	G	G	G	G	G						
Blue star		P										
Bluebeard						P						
Boltonia						P	P					
Bush clematis						P						
Butterfly weed				P								
Cardinal flower						P						
Carpathian bellflower				P								
Catmint			P	G	G	G	G					
Checkerbloom				P								
Cheddar pink				P	P							
Chinese astilbe				P								
Christmas rose	P							G	G	G		P
Chrysanthemum						P						
Clustered bellflower				P								
Columbine		P	P									
Columbine meadow rue				P								
Common beard-tongue				P								
Common sage			P	G	G							
Common yarrow			P	P	P	G						

Plant Name	Spring E	Spring M	Spring L	Summer E	Summer M	Summer L	Fall E	Fall M	Fall L	Winter E	Winter M	Winter L
Compact pincushion flower				P	P							
Coneflower							P	P	G	G		
Coral bells		G	G	G	G	G						
Cowslip	P	P										
Creeping baby's breath				P	P							
Creeping phlox		P										
Creeping veronica				P								
Crested iris		P										
Crimson pincushion				P	P	P						
Crocosmia				P	P							
Daylily				P	P							
Delphinium				P								
English primrose	P											
Evening primrose				P								
False indigo			P									
False solomon's seal	P	P										
Feather reed grass				P	P				G	G	G	
Fern-leaf yarrow		G	G	G	G	G	G					
Fleabane				P								
Foamy bells		G	G	G	G	G	G	G				
Fragrant bugbane							P	P				
Frikart's aster					P	P						
Garden phlox					P	P						
Gas plant			P									
Gayfeather						P			G	G		
Germander					P							
Giant coneflower					P	G	G	G				
Gibraltar bush clover						P	P					
Globe thistle					P							
Gloriosa daisy					P							
Goatsbeard			P									
Goldenrod	P						P	P				
Goldenstar			P									
Ground clematis			P	P								
Hardy begonia						P						
Hardy hibiscus			P	P								
Heart-leaf bergenia	P		G	G	G	G	G	G	G	G		
Heart-leaf brunnera		G	G	G	G	G	G	G				
Helenium			P									
Hollyhock				P								
Horned violet	P	P										
Hosta		G	G	P	P							

Bloom time chart. Columns under each season are E (Early), M (Middle/Mid), L (Late).

Plant Name	Sp E	Sp M	Sp L	Su E	Su M	Su L	Fa E	Fa M	Fa L	Wi E	Wi M	Wi L
Hybrid agastache				■	■							
Hybrid anemone						■	■					
Hybrid astilbe			■									
Hybrid cinquefoil				■	■							
Hybrid foam flower		■	■									
Hybrid lobelia					■	■						
Hybrid mullein				■	■							
Hybrid speedwell				■	■							
Hybrid violet	■	■										
Hybrid yarrow			▭	▭	▭	▭						
Jacob's ladder		■										
Japanese iris				■								
Joe-pye weed							■					
Labrador violet	■	■										
Lady's mantle				■								
Lamb's-ears				▭	▭	▭	▭					
Lavender					■							
Lavender cotton					■	■						
'Lavender Mist' meadow rue					■							
Lenten rose	■	■										
Liriope					▭	▭	▭	▭				
Louisiana iris				■								
Lungwort	▭	▭	▭	▭	▭	▭	▭					
Maiden grass						■	■	■	▭	▭		
Maiden pink				■								
Maltese cross				■								
Marsh marigold		■										
Masterwort				■								
Meadow rue				■								
Meadowsweet				■								
Moss phlox	▭	▭	▭	▭	▭	▭	▭					
Nepal cinquefoil				■	■							
Nettle-leaved mullein				■								
Northern sea oats						■	■	▭	▭	▭		
Obedient plant				■								
Old-fashioned bleeding heart				■								
Olympic mullein				■								
Oriental hybrid lily				■	■		▭					
Oriental poppy				■								
Ornamental onion			▭	▭	▭	▭						
Ornamental oregano				■	■							
Ozark sundrops				■	■	■	■					
Pacific bleeding heart		■	■	■								
Pasque flower	■	■										
Patrinia						■						
Peach-leaf bellflower				■								

Plant Name	Sp E	Sp M	Sp L	Su E	Su M	Su L	Fa E	Fa M	Fa L	Wi E	Wi M	Wi L
Peony			■									
Perennial fountain grass		▭	▭	▭	▭	▭	▭					
Perennial salvia			■	■	■							
Pincushion flower			■	■	■							
Pink coreopsis			■	■	■							
Purple coneflower					■	■	■					
Queen-of-the-prairie			■	■								
Reblooming bearded iris			■	■	■	■						
Reblooming daylily			■	■	■							
Rodgersia		▭	■									
Rose campion			■	■								
Russian sage					■	■						
Sea holly				■	■							
Shasta daisy			■	■								
Showy evening primrose	▭	▭	▭	▭	▭							
Siberian iris			■									
Siebold primrose		■										
Smooth white penstemon	▭			■	■		▭					
Snowdrop anemone		■	■									
Solitary clematis		▭	▭	▭	▭	▭	▭					
Spike speedwell			■	■								
Spotted bellflower				■	■							
Spring cinquefoil		■										
Star astilbe					■	■						
Stokes' aster				■	■							
Sweet violet	■	■										
Switch grass							■	■	▭	▭	▭	
Thinleaf perennial sunflower							■					
Threadleaf coreopsis			■	■	■							
Thrift			■									
Toad lily					■	■	■					
Torch lily			■									
Tree mallow				■	■							
Turk's-cap lily						■						
Variegated solomon's seal		▭	▭	▭								
Wherry's foam flower	■	■	▭	▭	▭	▭						
White gaura				■	■							
Woodland phlox		■										
Woolly speedwell			■	■	■							
Yellow corydalis			▭	▭	▭	▭						
Yellow foxglove				■	■							
Yellow meadow rue				■								
Yellow waxbells								■				
Yucca	▭	▭	▭	■	■							

Planting your perennial garden

▲ Good soil makes for easy planting and healthy perennials.

You may want to jump right in and begin planting your new perennial garden during the first warm weekend in spring—that's when garden centers are overflowing with blooming plants and you're anxious to set healthy, petite perennials in the ground after a long winter.

But planting a garden begins with preparing the soil. Resist the urge to buy plants, and instead focus your energy on building the best soil possible. If you don't take the time to prepare the soil properly, your plants may not reach their full potential. Because perennials grow in the same place for many years, it is important that they have the right soil conditions to begin with.

Trying to fix compaction, drainage, or other soil issues after you plant is nearly impossible, so analyze your soil conditions long before you plant and plan your soil preparation carefully.

Soil preparation is important for perennials because they remain in place for a long time. Simply stated you have one shot to create the foundation for many years of healthy growth.

If you don't want to be limited to growing perennials that tolerate marginal soil conditions and you are not blessed with deep, well-drained soil that is high in organic matter and free of stones, you'll have to do some digging and work in some organic matter.

10 PERENNIALS FOR LEAN SOIL

Many perennials thrive in nutrient-poor soil. Try these 10 species as well as those mentioned in the text on page 80.

Name	Notable Characteristics	Size	Zone
Blanket flower	Long-lasting red and yellow flowers in summer	12–30" tall, 24" wide	4–9
Butterfly weed	Brilliant orange flowers in summer followed by large seedpods	24–36" tall and wide	3–8
Creeping phlox	Shade-loving groundcover with pink, white, or purple flowers in spring	3–6" tall, 12" or more wide	4–8
Perennial flax	Light blue flowers on slender stems in late spring and early summer	18–24" tall and 12" wide	5–8
Pincushion flower	Light blue or pink blooms on wiry stems from summer to fall	18–30" tall and wide	5–8
Sea holly	Unusual flower clusters of steel blue with spiny blue petal-like bracts and stems in summer	24–36" tall, 12–24" wide	5–9
Stokes' aster	Shaggy blue, pink, white, or yellow daisies from summer to fall; evergreen leaves	12–18" tall and wide	5–9
Thrift	Buttons of pink, white, or rosy purple flowers in spring; evergreen tufts of grassy leaves	4–12" tall and wide	4–8
White gaura	Star-shape pink or white blooms on airy stems from midsummer to early fall	12–36" tall and wide	5–9
Yarrow	Red, white, pink, or yellow flowers in late spring and ferny green or silver leaves	12–60" tall, 12–36" wide	3–8

Plants for every soil

Some gardeners are fortunate to have better soil than others and may not need to do extensive soil preparation. Others who want to garden simply cannot do much digging and amending because of arthritis, back problems, or other health issues. You can still enjoy perennials if you are so constrained.

Focus on hardy perennials native to your area or choose old-fashioned perennials like Oriental poppy, daylily, iris, or ladybells. While they may not grow and flower as exuberantly in poor soil (rocky, poorly drained or lean soil that is low in plant nutrients), many of these perennials will provide reliable color in any but the worst of conditions. Perennials grown in lean, unimproved soil are much less likely to fall over or need staking, and frost heaving is also less likely if you live in a cold climate.

Get to know your soil

So many factors influence soil conditions that it is not uncommon for neighbors to have completely different kinds of soil, and the soil in your front yard may even be quite different from the soil in your backyard. You will get to know the areas in your own yard that need more attention to soil preparation and those that have the deepest, most fertile soil.

◄ Before you begin digging up your garden space, check out the soil. Have it tested to learn whether it is sand, clay, or loam, missing nutrients, or needs organic matter. It's much easier to improve soil before the garden is planted than afterwards.

Your soil may be layered with different materials, particularly if you live in an area that is at the boundary between two different soil types. In a similar way the excavation that takes place during home construction often brings large amounts of subsoil to the surface that is higher in clay content than the topsoil, and the soil may be a variable mosaic of subsoil and topsoil.

You may even find construction debris buried in the soil. A layer of sandy soil may sit on top of a clay layer, preventing rapid drainage and causing the sandy layer to remain saturated for long periods.

▲ The soil in a yard may vary from one spot to another. For example near a house foundation, soil is often more alkaline than elsewhere because of the calcium content in the concrete and in the mortar between bricks.

If you live in a stream valley or near a pond or lake, a high water table may impede drainage. A layer of gravel in the soil will slow drainage in the layer of soil above it, causing a perched water table (a water table above the level of the normal water table). To know what to do to prepare your soil properly, you should understand the components that give soil its characteristics.

Components of soil

▲ Earthworms indicate that the soil has enough oxygen and organic matter to support living organisms. As they burrow, earthworms help loosen the soil and work raw organic matter into it. They are essential to a healthy soil.

▲ Sandy soil is comprised of large particles. It is the next stage in the evolution of soil, a step down from rocky soil. Such soil is loose, very well-drained, and relatively low in nutrient content. Perennials adapted to dry, infertile conditions do best in it.

Although soil characteristics vary widely from region to region and possibly even from your front yard to your backyard, all soil is a mixture of three components—clay, silt, and sand. The ratio at which the components are combined gives soil unique properties. Learn the basics about clay, silt, and sand and you'll better understand how to create the best growing conditions for your perennials.

Clay

Clay particles are flat and nearly two dimensional. The particles tend to cling tightly together when the soil gets wet, eliminating air pockets, also called pore spaces. That is why soils high in clay should never be worked when they are wet.

Fortunately in most soils tiny clay particles tend to join together with chemical bonds to form bigger particles. These larger particles may be similar to sand grains in size and do much to open the soil and help it maintain pore spaces.

Compounds excreted by worms and microscopic organisms help to form the glue that keeps the clay particles bonded. Organic matter can be added to heavy soil to help create chemical bonds that encourage the formation of these clay aggregates in a process known as flocculation.

Salt residues can break these aggregates down and create a sticky, pasty soil that is barren, even though it appears to be fertile. Salty irrigation water and deicing agents containing salts can damage soil structure so badly that large amounts of gypsum or lime are needed to restore the soil to a granular consistency. Because lime also raises the pH, use gypsum instead of lime to improve the structure of salt-laden soils that already have a high pH.

▲ pH is measured on a scale of 1 to 10. You can test soil on your own, using solutions and litmus paper from a soil test kit or a meter. The most accurate results come from laboratory tests.

Clay and pH

The pH of a soil is measured on a scale of 1 to 10. One is highly acid; 10 is highly alkaline; and 7 is neutral.

Clay's tiny particles have a large surface-to-mass ratio and lots of binding sites for nutrients, which is what makes it so fertile. But if you need to alter the pH of clay soil, you'll need a lot of lime or elemental sulfur because of these binding sites. (Lime raises pH—makes it more alkaline; sulfur lowers pH—makes it more acidic.)

In high rainfall areas where soils are highly acidic, it is not uncommon to apply 100 pounds of lime per thousand square feet to raise the pH to a neutral level near 7.0. Applied at this rate, the lime will be as much as a quarter inch deep.

On the other hand, high pH clay soils may require up to 75 pounds of elemental sulfur to lower the pH from 8.5 to 6.5. For the best results, have your soil tested and follow the recommendations provided in the results.

Clay's admirable attributes

While clay soils have a bad reputation and are not terribly forgiving if they are mismanaged, they do have some good qualities. The abundance of chemical binding sites means that they hold nutrients very well.

Because clay soil contains lots of little pore spaces and water moves through them slowly, it may retain large amounts of water that plants can use in times of drought.

If the pH is properly adjusted, and the soil is tilled when its moisture content is at the right level, and you supplement the soil with organic matter to keep them porous and open, clay soils can be very productive.

If you are growing bog plants, clay soil is a necessity to hold the nutrients that the plants need. Bog plants grown in sandy soil often look sickly and yellow due to a lack of nutrients.

Silt

Silt particles are a step up in size from clay particles, and their irregular shape prevents them from locking together like clay particles. Most often silt particles move with water or wind, and their presence is an indication that your yard is or once was near a river or stream, or that great dust storms brought much of the soil particles on the wind.

Soils high in silt are apt to erode because the particles are light enough for water to easily move them. They don't form a crust that resists the destructive power of water like clay particles.

Add organic matter to silty soils to help create bonds between the particles and to reduce erosion. Silty soils hold water and nutrients better than sandy soils but not as well as clay soils.

Sand

The largest soil particles are those of sand. Because they don't fit together well at all, they cannot be compacted without a lot of force. If the sand particles are large enough, moving water must be quite powerful to move them and erode the soil.

Sandy soils are common near coastlines and in glacial features called outwash plains. They are often remarkably barren in terms of their nutrient content and they don't hold water well at all. They may be very acidic or quite alkaline as well because they have little organic content to buffer pH change.

Sandy soil can be worked at almost any time without doing any lasting damage to the soil structure. As long as you apply enough organic matter and water regularly during dry periods, sandy soils can be a very good foundation for your perennial garden.

Stonelike soil particles

If you live in or near a mountainous or desert area, you may have other types of soil composed primarily of small bits of stone that are larger than sand.

In these harsh environments most sand, silt, and clay particles may be blown away or washed away to leave behind a thin layer or pockets of soil protected by a covering of stones. In the desert this type of soil is known as desert pavement, and in mountainous areas it is called scree.

These soils can present extreme challenges, and you may want to adopt a strategy to deal with them. Grow perennials that need deep fertile soil in small areas where they will have the most impact in your garden; fill the garden out with native plants that are adapted to the native, unmodified soil. In a mountainous area this might amount to a perennial border with low alpine flowers growing in the natural scree and some larger perennials such as peony punctuating the garden in areas where you have replaced the scree with topsoil or a soil mix.

In the desert your perennial garden might consist of a framework of succulents and cacti with spots of color provided by perennials that you plant in soil generously amended with organic matter and water throughout the growing season.

▲ Rocky soil is composed of very large particles. It is well-drained but not fertile. Only plants requiring excellent drainage do well in it.

▲ Clay soil is sticky and difficult to work, especially when it is moist. Wet clay sticks to tools, becomes compacted where you stand on it as you work, and turns into hard clods when it dries.

Having your soil tested

▲ Home soil testing kits are available. Be aware that they are usually less accurate than laboratory tests and do not provide recommendations for improving your soil. However, they do provide you with a starting point.

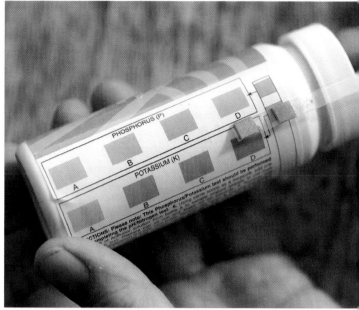

▲ With home kits, you dip a test strip into the soil sample, then compare the color changes against a color key that correlates with soil pH or with the tested nutrient.

If you've never had your soil analyzed to determine its texture and nutrient content, it's best to have it done before you even plan your perennial garden. No matter how well you think you know your soil, you're bound to learn useful gardening information from a soil test.

Contact your local land grant university, state department of agriculture, or county extension service to ask about soil testing services. One of these entities should be able to connect you with a lab that can test your soil.

Some catalogs and garden centers sell equipment for testing soil at home. Home testing equipment often is imprecise, providing only generalized results. A basic soil analysis at a lab is typically quite inexpensive. Considering the nominal cost of a lab soil test and the infrequent need to test your soil, choose a reputable lab.

What is tested?

The lab should test your soil for several parameters. One is the soil texture. This is simply the distribution of the different types of soil particles (sand, silt and clay), and it helps to classify your soil so that fertilization and recommendations for lime or sulfur to adjust pH can be accurate. Soils with well-balanced proportions of sand, silt, and clay are called loam soils. Loam soil is generally the most fertile and easy to manage.

Nutrients are also tested—and which nutrients are tested may depend on where you live. In most regions labs test for nitrogen, potassium, and phosphorus. The nitrogen content may be further analyzed to tell what portion is from a nitrate source and what portion comes from an ammonium source. Where rainfall is abundant and nitrogen leaches out of soils, labs may not analyze the nitrogen content since it is dependent on recent rainfall patterns.

pH readings

Of all the parameters tested, pH is probably the most important. It influences soil chemistry greatly and may restrict the availability of other nutrients. If the pH is too high or too low a soil may not support a good perennial garden even if it has a relatively high nutrient content. At pH extremes (highly acidic or highly alkaline) many nutrients in the soil become less available to plants. If the pH is corrected plants are more likely to be able to absorb the nutrients that they need.

Some labs will test for micronutrients such as copper, sulfur, and zinc. These tests often cost extra, and it is unusual for soils to be deficient in these nutrients. Their availability is strongly controlled by pH; most of them are available in soils that lie between pH 5.5 and 8.0. These tests are not needed in most situations.

Organic matter content

Your soil test results will most likely include the percentage of organic matter in your soil. Maintaining organic matter in the soil is important because it keeps pore spaces open, holds nutrients and water, and slowly releases nutrients as it decays.

It also is the basis on which all soil life depends. A soil without organic matter may be made fertile with granular fertilizer for a short time, but its fertility will be short lived. Organic matter may range from 1 percent to as much as 10 percent in frequently amended garden soils.

Amendment recommendations

The recommendations that you get back from the lab will tell you what you have to add to the soil. They are general recommendations and are not customized for all the different species of perennials you might be planting.

While the lab may ask about broad groups of plants you are growing to give you the right recommendation, it probably won't tell you to manage the soil for your oriental poppies any differently than you manage the soil for your peonies. The crop only comes into play if it has completely different needs. Most labs are concerned with knowing whether you are growing blueberries, turf, flowers, or vegetables and will pay little heed to the different species of perennials that you want to grow.

Most likely the lab will give you some guidance about how much of each type of fertilizer, lime, or acidifying agent you should add. This is usually expressed in pounds per 1,000 square feet. It is best to incorporate these amendments just before you till the ground to prepare it for planting. You don't have to work them deeply into the soil, but for the best results you should evenly mix them into the top four to six inches. Often the lab will

SAMPLE YOUR SOIL

The accuracy of a soil test depends on sending the testing lab a composite soil sample from your garden plot. Follow these simple steps and you can collect a soil sample in less than 10 minutes.

1 Choose 10 random locations in the perennial bed and remove any mulch or organic matter at the top of the soil.

2 Collect a trowelful of soil from each spot, placing it in a bucket. The soil should be from the top 6 inches of the soil.

3 After placing all 10 soil samples in the bucket, mix them thoroughly, breaking up clods and removing any sticks, roots, stones, and other debris.

4 Take the recommended amount of soil, generally 1 to 2 cups, from your sample and send it to the lab.

give you general guidance on adding organic matter, stating that it should be added regularly but not specifying a rate.

Testing for toxic substances

Sometimes gardeners are convinced that toxic elements in their soil are stunting or killing their plants or that someone may have

maliciously applied an herbicide to their plants. While it may seem logical that a soil test can tell you if toxic materials are present, this is often not the case. Testing for toxic substances in soil requires specific, and often costly, tests that are not part of routine soil tests. Regardless of the amount of toxic materials present, they are generally in an insoluble

form that, by the time the sample has arrived at the lab for testing, is inert.

Take heart that most materials are toxic to plants only when soil has an unusually high or low pH. But if you suspect a persistent toxic problem in your soil, contact your local health department, because elevated levels of some materials may be harmful to your health.

Clearing your planting bed

▲ When you are finally ready to work the soil, start by marking the outline of the bed. You can draw it with paint or chalk, then dig out the edge, or simply dig freehand. Get the bed boundaries right, then remove the turf and other vegetation.

◄ To remove turf by hand, push a spade under the grass at the cut edge. With short jabs, slice about 1 inch beneath the turf. Have someone pull back on the sod as you work to ease the job.

Before you prepare your soil for planting, you will have to clear away existing vegetation. Your approach to this depends on the time and effort you want to spend, and on the kind of vegetation growing in the area that will be transformed into your new perennial bed.

It is extremely important to be thorough. If you cut corners you will pay later in time spent removing the vegetation by hand. If you are dealing with tough perennial weeds such as field bindweed, quackgrass, mugwort, or wiregrass, the challenge is even more serious. You will probably not be able to get these persistent weeds under control if you leave any surviving plants or pieces of rhizome (horizontal underground stem) in the prepared soil.

The three basic ways of clearing space for your perennial bed are to physically remove the plants that are growing there, to smother the existing vegetation, kill it with a nonselective herbicide, or to solarize it to kill grass and weed seeds and fungal spores.

Removing vegetation by hand

If you choose to remove the plants by hand, be prepared for some grueling labor. Break the job into manageable sections to avoid muscle fatigue and possible injury. If you have only an hour to spend, plan on clearing an area no larger than 100 square feet.

How difficult this work is depends on the kind of vegetation you are trying to get rid of. If you have bluegrass or fescue turf that is weed free, you can use a flat shovel to cut the sod off the soil. Pare it evenly off the soil surface, and you can use the pieces to repair other spots in your lawn. With a pure stand of groundcover that has horizontally spreading stems, such as English ivy or vinca, you may be able to use your flat shovel to cut away the surface soil containing the spreading stems.

Skimming off sod and groundcover

Whether you are trying to remove turf or groundcover with your flat shovel, your technique is important. You will have to get on your knees for this task, so invest in a good pair of knee pads. And be sure that your shovel is properly sharpened.

Begin by cutting the outline of the area that you want to clear with a flat shovel or a lawn edger. Then get on your knees near the lowest point along the edge of the area to be cleared. Place your tool at a 10-degree angle against the cut that you made to outline the area. Hold the handle with both hands and work it back and forth to slice off the vegetation and the top inch or so of soil. It is the momentum of forward movement that does the work of slicing.

Don't try to force the shovel into the soil with the palm of one hand while holding the shovel with the other. Instead use the power of the rotation of your entire torso and the firm grip you have on the shovel to cut the sod. Textured gloves are a plus to ensure the shovel doesn't slip easily and that you can deliver maximum force to the slicing motion.

If the bed is higher on one side than the other, work from the lower side to the higher so you can more easily keep the shovel roughly parallel to the soil surface as you work. After removing a chunk of sod, look carefully at the soil surface. If you see grass rhizomes or other plant

► Manual sod cutters are available. They keep you off your hands and knees but are not much easier to use for removing sod than a spade. Consider using hand methods only for clearing space for small gardens.

parts that might regrow you are not going deep enough. Don't go any deeper than necessary, since the top few inches of soil contain most of the organic matter and are the most fertile.

Use the skimmed sod for bare spots in your lawn, or compost it. If you are removing a groundcover that has stems running along the soil surface, you may not need to slice through the whole area. Use your shovel to probe for individual crowns where the groundcover has rooted into the soil and concentrate your efforts on these areas to sever the connection between the stems and the soil. You can chop the groundcover into 4-foot segments and roll up the stems as you slice them off the soil surface into a neat 4-foot-long bundle.

Clearing woody plants

Digging up small or shallow rooted shrubs like boxwood or azalea is fairly simple. You can move the shrubs to another location in your yard, or discard them.

Larger shrubs may not be as easy to move. You can cut them as close to the ground as possible and wait for the roots to decay. You may have to paint the cut surface of the shrub with a nonselective herbicide to make sure that it doesn't resprout, and you'll have to work around any major roots that remain in the ground when you prepare the soil and plant your perennials.

Rather than removing and discarding healthy trees and shrubs, consider planting around them. A common problem in new perennial gardens is the lack of depth and focal points. Trees and shrubs can instantly give your garden some character.

▲ Mechanical sod cutters, which you can obtain at rental centers, make slick work of removing grass from the garden area. Use them to clear a large garden space.

Clear your planting bed *(continued)*

◀ Place the cut sod in your compost pile or use it to patch holes in your lawn or share it with friends and neighbors. Rolling makes it easier to carry.

Work with tree stumps

If you choose to remove a tree, you can put plants in handsome containers on the stump and create a perennial bed around it. The damp, dark conditions under the pots will speed decay of the stump, and in the meantime you can use the plants in the container that stand above the surrounding perennial bed as a focal point. Conceal the edge of the stump with a little mulch.

After the stump has rotted, it will provide a small area where the soil is higher in organic matter than the surrounding soil. Ferns, sedges, and other woodland plants thrive in this organic soil mix.

If you have a stump in an awkward location that doesn't really suit your needs for a focal point in the garden, you can have a tree service cut the stump low to the ground and grind or chip up the residual trunk.

Ask your arborist to dig out and chip up the major roots, which extend several feet from the stump. This eases gardening in the area where the tree was located.

Also ask the tree service to leave the stump grindings, if you have space to compost them. After a year of composting, they make a very good mulch.

Replacing lost organic matter

Removing the vegetation by hand saves time. Your soil is ready to cultivate soon after you start work, and you can be on your way to planting in a matter of days.

Unfortunately this method inevitably results in the loss of some soil and organic matter, particularly when you remove sod.

One way to save this resource is to compost the sod. Once it is thoroughly broken down, you can mix into the soil as you plant or use it as mulch. In that way you return the soil and organic matter to your new perennial bed later.

Other methods of clearing the soil, such as smothering, saves a step by leaving the soil and organic matter in place.

◀ Without a grinder, you'll find it difficult to remove tree stumps. You can make the stump an integral and decorative part of your garden. Use it as a support for a container garden or plant moss on it, as in this garden.

Other methods of removing vegetation

▲ Smothering eliminates grass by preventing light and water from reaching it. To smother, cover the area with newspapers along with leaves, grass clippings, or compost to hold it in place. Leave the cover in place for a year to ensure that all roots and rhizomes are killed.

Smothering has become a popular option for busy gardeners who are willing to wait for results and who plan at least a year ahead. The concept is simple: Deprive plants of light and they will soon perish.

Smothering calls for spreading two layers of material over the vegetation—an impervious layer that blocks light and a layer of another material to protect the integrity of the light barrier and hold it in place.

Newspaper, laid at least 10 pages thick and covered with mulch, manure, grass clippings, or chopped leaves, is a popular option. You could use plastic to cover the area, but you'd have to remove it later.

The newspaper eventually decays and you can leave it in place, making it far superior to plastic for this purpose. A smothered planting bed is generally ready for planting in about a year.

Immediate planting option

If you are smothering sod that is growing on well-prepared topsoil, you may be able to plant after you put your smothering layers in place. Simply use a round shovel to cut planting holes through all the layers and the sod. Use extra bits of newspaper to cover the edges of the hole you create, and plant your perennials.

However, if you need to do any soil preparation or if you are dealing with any perennial weeds that spread by underground rhizomes, planting immediately after smothering is not recommended.

Advantages to smothering

The main advantage of smothering is that it takes far less time and energy than removing turf or other vegetation by hand. It can also do a great job of getting rid of tough perennial weeds

▲ Spraying a nonselective herbicide such as Roundup will provide a vegetation-free garden space within one to two months. Spray once, let the grass die, till the soil, water, then wait for weeds to pop up. Repeat until no more weeds sprout.

▲ When using herbicides, adjust the spray to the coarsest pattern possible. This prevents the herbicide from drifting in the wind to nearby plants or to lawn areas you don't want to kill.

▲ Solarization uses the sun's energy to kill vegetation, weed seeds, disease spores, insect eggs, and other soil-borne pests.

such as dandelion, thistle, wiregrass, mugwort, and bindweed. Be aware that these invaders are always waiting to take root in the margins of your prepared bed, so smother a larger area than you need for planting.

Another big plus is that smothering adds organic matter to the soil. It stimulates the earthworm population while feeding all the microorganisms in the soil that need organic matter. The downside is that this method takes longer than most, unless you are killing vegetation on soil that is already suitable for your perennials.

Eradicating vegetation with herbicides

Herbicides can be a good option if you have limited time, are dealing with particularly difficult weeds, and your goal isn't a strictly organic garden.

It's extremely difficult to establish an even outline for a bed when you're spraying herbicide. Take time to create a shield of cardboard, scrap lumber, or plastic before you spray to protect any turf or groundcovers adjacent to the new bed.

Spray the material precisely as directed on the label, and never spray on a windy day. Use a sprayer that can deliver larger droplets and not just a fine mist. Nonselective herbicides such as those containing glyphosate may be applied at almost any time the turf or other vegetation is growing, but they are generally most effective late in the season when carbohydrates are being moved into rhizomes and roots. The material will move with the carbohydrates and kill the underground portion of the weeds as well as aboveground stems.

Because the herbicide enters the plant through the leaves, you don't want to remove any foliage just before treatment, so don't mow the

lawn or prune groundcovers or other broadleaved plants.

You can use a selective herbicide that kills broadleaved plants but not grasses to get rid of groundcover. Materials containing triclopyr work well for this purpose. However, when you use a selective herbicide grassy weeds may remain in the bed to cause problems later.

Monitoring the planting bed

Although the vegetation you treated will die, you'll want to be sure that nothing is lurking in the soil to cause problems after the perennials are planted. Wait several weeks to see if there is any new growth coming from the area, particularly if you are dealing with hard-to-kill weeds like bindweed, thistle, wiregrass, or mugwort.

It's normal for weed seedlings to appear in the prepared bed, and you may want to get rid of them by spraying an herbicide or by tilling the area before you move on to final soil preparation and planting.

Solutions for tough sites

Special measures are needed if you have an extremely weedy area that you want to transform into a perennial garden. You must be sure that all the perennial weeds are dead and that you aren't starting with soil loaded with weed seeds that will create future problems.

Repeated applications of herbicide to kill the seedlings, shallow tilling throughout a fallow season, or soil solarization will ensure that the weed seeds are dead.

Solarization

Solarization relies on the sun's energy coupled with the greenhouse effect to heat your soil above 140°F. At that temperature weed seeds, nematodes, disease spores,

HOW TO SMOTHER VEGETATION

1 Prepare the site by using a mower or string trimmer to cut grass and other vegetation as close to the soil surface as possible. Don't bother to remove the clippings from the ground; they will help to smother the grass.

2 Lay newspapers over the area in a layer at least 10 sheets thick. The inks used in newsprint are not toxic to plants, and you need not worry about any ill effects from them.

3 Thoroughly wet down the newspapers to help hold them in place.

4 Next cover the newspapers with a 4- to 5-inch-thick layer of organic material such as purchased mulch, composted manure, grass clippings, shredded leaves, or compost. If you are smothering a large bed, plan to cover the newspapers with organic material as you go to prevent them from drying and blowing away.

5 Keep the organic topping in place all summer. If it starts to break down, add more to maintain the 4- to 5-inch-thick layer. Keep the area moist to prevent lightweight materials from blowing. Edges tend to dry faster than the interior of the bed. If you live in an area that is humid with ample rainfall during the warmest months, the newspaper should decompose by the end of the growing season. Elsewhere the space will be ready for soil preparation about a year after you lay down the newspaper and mulch. Till the area, working the organic matter into the soil.

and insect eggs present in the soil are killed, but beneficial fungi and bacteria survive.

Solarize soil after you have tilled and prepared it. Start by watering the area thoroughly enough to moisten the top 4 to 6 inches of soil. Position spacers such as bricks or small rocks on the soil surface every 2 to 3 feet, then apply a heavy sheet (6 mil) of clear plastic to the area. Tape any seams or holes with clear tape so the plastic is unbroken and any heat generated stays underneath.

Bury the edge of the plastic in a small trench dug around the perimeter of the bed. In three to four weeks, if sunny, warm weather predominates, the soil will be thoroughly treated and you can proceed with planting.

Solarization is only a viable option if the bed is located in an area that gets at least six hours of direct sun every day, and it may not work as well in cool or cloudy climates.

Amending the soil

▲ Shovel or pour organic matter and other amendments over the soil, rake it evenly over the bed, then till it in. Follow soil test recommendations to learn which amendments and how much of them to use.

After clearing vegetation from your soil it's time to add amendments. Review your soil test results for recommendations. (See more about soil tests on page 84.)

Nearly every soil could use additional organic matter. Considering all the wonderful things it does for soil, you might think that more organic matter is always better. However, too much at one time is not a good thing and may disrupt the natural balance of microorganisms in the soil.

Don't apply more than 2 inches at a time, or a total of 2 inches in a single growing season. If you will be planting right after you work the soil, be absolutely sure that the organic matter is thoroughly decayed. Fresh manure, grass clippings, and compost that has not yet decayed may cause the roots of your perennials to rot when you plant them.

If your site is a low spot that is poorly drained, organic matter may hold on to water and make drainage even worse than it already is. If it is present at a level of the soil that is frequently saturated, it may support anaerobic decay that in turn produces sulfur compounds that give the soil a terrible odor when you dig into it. On such a site consider building a raised bed to correct the drainage problem and prevent poor aeration.

Many organic matter options

Many gardeners have favorite organic amendments. Often these depend on what is locally abundant. Composted dairy manure is popular in Wisconsin, sugar cane waste in South Florida, and seaweed in Maine.

Almost any material will work as long as it is free of weed seeds and is well rotted. Some amendments, such as manures, contain significant amounts of nutrients and will enrich the soil. Some manures—for example, poultry manure—are high in salts and can burn plants unless they are added several months before planting.

Amendments that come from woody plant parts—well-rotted sawdust, wood chips, and leaf mold, for example—generally contain fewer nutrients, but they remain in the soil longer before they are converted into basic mineral elements. But if applied before they are completely decayed, they may rob the soil of available nitrogen, so be sure they are thoroughly decomposed before you incorporate them into your soil.

There has been a trend toward using packaged sources of organic matter, such as Miracle-Gro Garden Soil, which is blended with slow-release fertilizer. Bagged compost, leaf mold, and dehydrated manure are also available at garden centers. These are free of weed seeds and consistent in quality.

A few additives supply little in the way of organic matter, and are used more as fertilizers. Cottonseed meal and blood meal are commonly available sources of nitrogen that may be incorporated into your soil. Bone meal is also a source of phosphorus and calcium.

▲ Common soil amendments include (left to right) sewage sludge, compost, sand, peat, greensand, manure, and gypsum. Not all are suited to every situation.

Amend to adjust pH

Some soil additives—lime, greensand, rock phosphate, and gypsum, for example—come from the ground itself. They can be grouped into two broad categories. Some change the soil pH or the physical properties of the soil while others provide nutrients over the long term.

If you need to raise the pH, lime will do the job. Many forms of lime are available, but by far the most common on garden center shelves is dolomitic lime, which consists primarily of calcium carbonate and magnesium carbonate. Plain ground limestone is simply calcium carbonate. The addition of magnesium may result in greener plants, so dolomitic lime is often preferred.

If you need to drop the pH, sulfur is the answer. Elemental sulfur is unusual in that it must be acted on by microorganisms first before it will produce a drop in pH. It may take several months or more for the sulfur to take effect. Iron sulfate works faster, but more of it is needed to achieve the same results. Aluminum sulfate also works, but can cause aluminum toxicity.

In certain situations gypsum may also drop the pH. However, unless soil drainage is already good, and organic matter content is high, gypsum will have little effect on pH.

Add nutrients

Rock phosphate and greensand are minerals that supply some of the major nutrients that plants need. They are often components of slow-release fertilizers, and if incorporated before planting they can supply a reservoir of nutrients that will meet the needs of your perennials for many years. Use them only if they are recommended by your soil testing lab. Excess nutrients in your soil may contribute to groundwater or surface water contamination.

Synthetic fertilizers are another way to supply nutrients to poor soil. They can be a cost-effective means of applying nutrients, and most are slow release and can give you at least a season's worth of nutrients. Ideally they should be incorporated along with some organic matter that will help to hold the nutrients, particularly if you have sandy soil and live in an area that is prone to heavy rainfall. Apply no more than the amount recommended by the results of the soil test.

Add beneficial bacteria and fungi

The movement toward more organic solutions to garden problems has led to the development of products that contain beneficial bacteria and fungi to inoculate your soil and protect plants from soilborne diseases.

Beneficial microorganisms may be helpful if you are growing perennials that are prone to root rot and crown rot, particularly if you live in an area with humid, rainy summers. Adding well-composted organic matter each year is a good practice and will provide the microorganisms with the food they need.

GROW A COVER CROP

If you are dealing with an area where weeds have long been a problem, and you can plan a year or more ahead, you may want to grow a cover crop or a succession of cover crops in your prepared soil. The cover crop will help reduce the weed seed population and get rid of disease spores in your soil while it builds the soil's organic matter.

In most regions, you can use winter and summer crops to cover the soil throughout the year. You can build nitrogen if you plant a cover crop such as crimson clover or hairy vetch. Annual rye and winter wheat are good for supplying organic matter to the soil. Buckwheat is useful in poor soils and may help to combat weeds. Be sure to turn the cover crop under before it has a chance to set seed.

A buckwheat cover crop helps to build soil fertility.

Preparing soil for planting

▲ Use rototillers with care. Ensure that soil moisture is at the optimum level to prevent compaction. Avoid overworking the soil so that it retains its structure and doesn't become powdery. Small tillers are best suited to small gardens that already have loose easy-to-work soil.

After eliminating existing vegetation and applying any soil amendments, you are ready to till the soil. You can supply the labor or let a rototiller do much of the work. Your choice will depend largely on the size of your perennial bed. It doesn't make much sense to use a rototiller on a very small bed, and hand digging a large bed may take more time than you have to spend.

Soil preparation is by far the most labor intensive of all the chores you will encounter in growing perennials. Do too much too quickly and you'll end up with sore muscles or even a serious injury. The key is to budget the appropriate amount of time for soil preparation and to do it in manageable phases.

If your new perennial border is to measure 30 feet by 5 feet, plan to dig in three phases or to enlist the help of gardening friends or family members. Soil preparation can be invigorating and physically beneficial if you take the time to stretch and warm up, use the right tools and appropriate technique, and pace yourself. If you have more digging to do one day or you're tired, alternate soil preparation with other less strenuous activities.

Improve soil with organic matter

Even if you skip intensive soil preparation, keep in mind that the soil needs organic matter and it shouldn't be compacted if you want to grow something besides dandelions and crabgrass.

Be patient and you can fix a compacted soil that is low in organic matter simply by placing a 1- to 2-inch thick layer of compost, rotted manure, or other decayed organic material on top of the soil. Even if you are not able to work it deep into the soil, earthworms and other creatures will form tunnels and draw the organic matter as deep as 1 foot below the soil surface. This is how nature builds soil, and even if you have the time and energy to do some elaborate soil preparation, you should strive to emulate nature.

Skip double digging

Some books recommend double digging, which

▲ Use a round-point spade (above left), also called a balling shovel, instead of a shovel (below left) to turn soil. Round-point spades have a straight shaft, allowing you to dig efficiently (above right). Shovels have a bent shaft that make them more suited to scooping than to digging.

involves excavating to a depth of 16 inches or more and incorporating organic matter into all layers of the soil. This practice may actually be counterproductive if you have a lot of clay in your soil.

Double digging may bring infertile, sticky clay subsoil to the surface and bury organic matter where it may get waterlogged and hold moisture around plant roots. The best soil may end up at a deep level where lack of oxygen limits root growth. Double digging also creates sharp boundaries between soil types that may impede root growth and the movement of water through

the soil profile. If you decide to double dig the bed, thoroughly mix organic matter throughout the depth of the dug area using one-third organic matter by volume of soil (for example, if digging 18 inches deep in existing soil, work in a 6-inch-thick layer of organic matter) to prevent soil layering and to ensure adequate drainage. Double digging is best reserved for sandy soils that are easy to work.

Mix in amendments

When preparing your soil aim for gradual changes in the soil from layer to layer. You'll want to dig more organic matter into the top layers of soil than into the lower layers, and you may only need to break up the soil at the bottom to improve drainage.

Before you dig make sure that your soil isn't too wet or too dry. You can easily destroy soil structure if you dig when soil conditions are not right. Too wet and the clay particles in your soil may be forced together into large, sticky clods that are impenetrable to roots when they dry. Too-dry soil may turn to powder that forms a crust as soon as it rains.

To create an even gradation in your soil from top to bottom, do all of your soil preparation from the top down. Place no more than an inch or two of decayed organic matter on the soil and use a spading fork to work it into the top 6 to 8 inches. The objective is to turn forkfuls of soil on their side, not to invert them.

Then apply another inch of decayed organic matter along with any other soil amendments you are using and go over the entire area again to a depth of 3 to 4 inches to break up clods and mix in the organic matter and any other amendments. You will end up with soil that is high in organic matter at the top with a gradual decrease in organic matter at progressively deeper levels.

Helpful tools

A plain round point spade is an effective tool for turning over the top several inches of soil. Go over the ground two or three times with the shovel to effectively mix all your soil amendments into the most active and important level of the soil.

A spading fork may be a more efficient tool if your soil is sandy and the clods break apart easily. And if you are preparing the soil anywhere near tree roots, a spading fork is probably the only implement that will work well. Smaller roots can slide between the tines of the fork, and you'll cause less damage to the tree's roots.

CHECK SOIL MOISTURE

Soil should never be worked when it's too wet or too dry. Digging your soil in wet conditions clumps clay aggregates together into larger clods that later bake into hard lumps. Dry conditions can turn clay aggregates into powder that forms a crust on the soil surface when rainfall or irrigation moistens it. Because silt and sand particles are relatively stable, checking soil moisture before you till is not as much of an issue in soils that have little clay in them.

Before you dig or till, check the soil moisture by scooping up a generous handful of soil from the area you want to till. Form the soil into a ball by making a fist. If you are able to squeeze water out of the soil, it is much too wet to till. If it forms a tight ball that doesn't crack when you poke it gently with your finger, it is probably still too wet to till. If the soil won't come together into a loose clump, it is too dry to till. In ideal conditions your soil will form a ball that easily cracks and breaks up into a few large pieces.

When your soil is too dry to till, you can water it for several minutes to bring it to the correct moisture level prior to digging or tilling.

If your soil is too wet and more rain is forecast, tarp the area to prevent further saturation. When the rain has passed remove the tarp so sunlight and air flow can help reduce the soil moisture level.

Soil that is just right forms a ball that easily breaks apart when touched. No water drips from it.

Soil that is too dry to work creates a cloud of dust. You lose your topsoil as it blows away.

Wet soil sticks to your tools, is hard to work, and, if you work it when wet, turns into clods when it dries.

If you are planting in a woodland, you may have to settle for scuffing up the soil in some areas, and mixing in the amendments as well as you can. Be sure to probe for pockets of deeper soil between tree roots and to dig deeper in these areas. You may even want to flag these spots as you go so you'll be able to find them again when you plant.

Use a rototiller with care

A rototiller is a viable option if your soil is relatively free of tree roots and stones. Limit the time spent churning the soil in one area and be sure that your soil isn't too wet or too dry. The action of the rototiller tines striking the soil may create a compacted layer at the base of the tines, and repeated passes with a rototiller will worsen the problem.

▶ A spading fork helps to loosen and break up soil. It is less helpful where you need to turn the soil over and mix amendments into it.

Limit the number of passes, and break up remaining large clods with a rake or hoe. If you have sandy or loamy soil, a rototiller may make fast work of soil preparation.

Fixing drainage problems

Poor drainage is the most common problem that must be addressed before planting a perennial garden. Check drainage by doing a percolation test. Dig a hole that is about one foot deep and fill it with water. After the water has disappeared, fill it again. At least one inch of water should drain out of the soil in an hour's time. If water doesn't drain at least this fast, you may have a drainage problem in your soil.

Improving drainage

Many gardeners are convinced that adding sand to their heavy soil will improve its drainage, but that's not the case if insufficient amounts of sand are added. Until sand makes up half the volume of soil, you may worsen the drainage problem by adding sand. Heavy soils are often high in clay, and when sand is mixed with clay, the clay will simply fill in the pore spaces between the sand particles. Worse yet if a layer of sand is placed under the clay, you get a perched water table. Water held by the small pores in the clay can't drain into the sand until the clay is saturated.

Sand is effective as a soil amendment only if it is combined with large amounts of organic matter and applied over a large area, in a top-down approach, with more sand at the top levels of the soil and a smooth transition to less sand at lower levels.

So how can you fix poorly draining soil? There are several ways. Installing drain pipes and building raised beds are two standard ones.

Drainage pipes

If your yard has a low point where water can drain, then a drainage pipe is an option. Generally the outlet for a drain should be at least 2 feet lower than the surface of the soil in your perennial bed.

For a small garden one trench is usually enough. A large perennial bed may require you to run several parallel trenches through it to ensure that all of the soil drains adequately. Generally drain pipes can be spaced 10 feet apart. Six-inch-diameter pipe is adequate for draining perennial beds.

To install the piping dig a trench at least 18 inches below the grade of the bed. Before you install the pipe, test to see if it drains properly. Place your garden hose at the highest point in the trench and turn on the water. Make sure it runs all the way to the end of the trench where the pipe outlet will be. Adjust the grade of the trench until water flows properly.

Once you're satisfied with the water flow, lay perforated pipe in the trench. It's a good idea to cover the pipe with a layer of gravel to prevent soil particles from clogging the perforations in the pipe. Alternatively you can use perforated pipe wrapped in a geotextile soil barrier.

After placing the pipe, backfill with soil. Because it's easy to forget where the piping is and important that you don't damage it when working in the garden, you may want to place some flat stones a few inches under the soil. Also plant shallow rooted perennials directly over the pipe.

Raised beds

If you don't have a suitable low point near your perennial garden that you can run a perforated drain pipe to, you can build raised beds to give your perennials the drainage they need.

A raised bed simplifies maintenance tasks such as weeding and can allow people with mobility issues caused by an injury or a disease such as arthritis to continue to garden. It also puts small flowers up higher where you can more easily admire them, and it provides the perfect elevated platform for low-growing perennials with fragrant flowers such as pinks that you'd otherwise have to be pick to enjoy them at their full intensity.

Consider your budget and your ability to replace or repair the walls that retain the soil. Treated wood and railroad ties have long been favorites, but in time they may rot and need to be replaced. Stone and interlocking pavers are more permanent but need to be built on a footing in cold areas where frost heaving occurs.

Don't be tempted to build a raised bed directly against

HOW TO DO A PERCOLATION TEST

1 Start by digging a 1-foot-deep hole in the area where you plan to put the garden. You can do this in the prepared bed or strip the sod beforehand.

2 Fill the hole with water, let it drain, then fill it again. Time how long it takes for the water to drain out. Emptying at the rate of 1 inch an hour is ideal.

▲ This cross-section of a drainage trench shows one alternative. The trench slopes from the high point at the rate of 1 inch per 18 feet. You can place gravel or sand in the trench, then lay the pipe on top or set the pipe directly on the bottom of the trench. Use plain perforated pipe or one that is already wrapped in fabric.

your home. Moisture from the soil could rot the building's wall and lead to termite damage.

Your raised bed should contain well-drained soil at least 1 foot deep to grow the full spectrum of perennials, not just the ones that require very good drainage. If you are building a natural stone wall to contain the soil, consider leaving gaps and crevices in it for planting small trailing perennials that will soften the appearance of the wall.

BUILD A RAISED BED

1 For a dry-stack stone wall, start by framing the garden with the stones. Place two or three layers so that the wall is about 6 inches tall, then start adding topsoil.

2 Continue adding layers to the wall and filling with soil until the raised bed is at the desired height. Use only good-quality topsoil.

3 Overfill the raised bed, so that soil will be at the right level when it settles.

4 Raised beds are as pretty as they are functional. They offer many options for your design and let you put your personal stamp on the garden.

Final steps

▲ After the final tilling, smooth the surface of the soil with a rake, removing any high and low spots, which affect drainage. Also remove any rocks or dirt clods. Next, you can spread mulch over the bed and dig through the mulch to plant or put in the garden, then mulch the plants.

When you have done all your soil preparation, you are finally ready to plant—which may take much less time and effort than preparing the soil.

Generally in mild winter climates fall is a better time for planting than spring. Perennials set out in October or November have moist soil conditions all winter to establish healthy, robust roots. If you live in an area with well-defined rainy and dry seasons, plant your perennials at the beginning of the rainy season.

In colder climates winter means frozen soil or the potential for heaving with repeated freeze and thaw cycles. Spring and early summer are the best times for planting perennials because the plants will have an entire growing season to develop strong roots before bitterly cold weather returns.

Spread mulch

Whether you mulch or plant first depends on the size of the plants. If your perennials are in small pots, it will be easier to mulch first and then make small planting holes by plunging your trowel into the ground and pushing soil and mulch aside. But if you are dealing with perennials in quart or gallon pots, plant first so you can make the right-size holes with a shovel; then mulch. If you have a mix of sizes, plant the larger ones first, mulch, and then plant the smaller ones.

About mulches

Various materials are suitable for mulching a perennial bed. The best mulch is well decayed when you apply it. That's because the decay process requires nitrogen—a valuable plant nutrient. Applying mulch that hasn't begun to decay will rob plants of nitrogen. Leaf mold, spent mushroom bedding, finished compost, rotted manure, and decomposed grass clippings are good mulch options. If you use grass clippings, be sure they don't contain herbicides or weed seeds.

Mulches such as sawdust, wood chips, and straw may draw much of the nitrogen out of the soil as they decay, resulting in sickly plants. If you must use a material that is not well decayed, apply a small amount of granular slow-release fertilizer to the soil surface before you mulch.

Mulch quality

The quality of mulches varies greatly. High-quality shredded hardwood bark is comprised nearly entirely of bark. Bark decays very slowly, and while it may take a substantial amount of nitrogen to break it down, the decay takes place over such a long time that it has little impact on soil fertility.

Shredded woody mulch products sometimes contain more wood than is optimal, and often the wood is colored or mixed with soil to give it an appearance that is similar to bark. These dyes may impart an unnatural color, and some may retard decay. Pine bark is a good option if

▲ Different mulches give different effects in the garden. Shredded bark is medium textured and may be dark brown or tan in color.

▲ Pine needle mulch, also called pine straw, is fine-textured. It starts out rich tan-brown, but ages to tan.

▲ Bark chips are coarse textured and, depending on their origins, are generally reddish to dark brown.

▲ The mulch layer should be at least 2 inches deep in order to prevent light from reaching weed seeds to spur their germination and growth. A layer of mulch deeper than 4 inches can cause problems.

▲ Keep the mulch layer 2 to 4 inches away from the plant's crown. Piling it on the crown will lead to rot; keeping it close to the plant provides a haven for voles and other burrowing critters that feed on plants.

you want a natural-looking mulch that doesn't impact soil fertility significantly.

Compost is another option. If your community collects yard debris, composts it, and offers the compost for your use, ask to visit the composting operation— or at least ask how the materials are composted.

Composted yard debris is a good mulch if it is turned frequently and managed so it heats to 160°F or higher. If your community just allows leaves and other yard debris to lie in a stockpile for a year without turning it before it is offered to homeowners, it may contain weed seeds and disease spores that you don't want in your garden.

Regardless of the mulch you choose, examine it carefully before you use it. Most important, give it a sniff. Good mulch has an earthy odor that is not unpleasant. Poor-quality mulch may have a pronounced odor of vinegar, alcohol, sulfur, or ammonia. If you can't stand to smell it for more than 10 seconds, you should not use it around your perennials or other landscape plants. These naturally occurring decomposition products may burn your plants or produce other toxic reactions. If you receive compost with an off odor, spread it out and allow the offending materials to dissipate for several days before you use the mulch.

Spread a thin layer

Never apply mulch more than 2 to 4 inches deep. If the mulch is applied too thick, fungi can grow in it, creating a waterproof mat of fungal threads. Rainfall may run off overly thick mulch. Excess mulch may also cause moisture to sit around the crowns of perennials and rot them.

Some perennials are very sensitive to mulch. Generally any perennials with silvery or fuzzy leaves are likely to be adapted to dry soil conditions and will languish when a blanket of mulch is drawn too close to them. Keep mulch away from the base of their stems.

Lavender, lavender cotton, lamb's-ears, sage, artemisia, and baby's breath are especially sensitive to mulch; if you live in an area where the growing season is humid, it's a good idea to replace the mulch around these plants with a thin layer of pea gravel to provide rapid drainage of surface moisture.

CARING FOR PLANTS BEFORE PLANTING

Try to plant container-grown perennials as soon as possible after buying them. Because weather or a busy schedule sometimes delays planting, here's how to keep your plants in tip-top shape until you can put them in the ground.
● Unpack mail order plants as soon as they arrive. Remove broken or diseased growth and water well.
● If you are holding plants for a week or less before planting in the garden, place them in a shaded spot and water when the soil in the container begins to dry. In hot and windy weather you might need to water plants twice a day.
● Space the containers generously so air can freely circulate around them.
● If you are holding sun-loving plants for more than a week, place them in an area where they will receive at least four hours of sunlight a day.

▲ Mulch gives a tidy look to a garden while it holds in soil moisture and prevents light from reaching weed seeds so that they can't germinate.

Final steps *(continued)*

Transfer the garden plan to the soil

Faced with an array of perennials, a detailed plan, and an empty bed, you may be unsure how to get the plan from paper to soil.

One option is to arrange the plants, still in their pots, on top of the prepared soil according to your design. Remember that the plants will grow significantly over time. Do not space them according to their current size. Using the information in the encyclopedia at the back of this book and on the plant tags, situate the plants according to their expected mature width. Initially the garden will look sparse, but in a few short years the soil will be covered with foliage and flowers.

Another method to assist you in laying out your perennial bed is to purchase colored sand from your local craft store to pinpoint individual plants in the plan

MULCH CHART

Mulch material	Risk of weed seeds	Nitrogen impact	Availability	Cost	Durability	Comments
Straw	Yes	Slight	Widespread	Inexpensive	Single season	Keep bales wet for several weeks to germinate all seeds before applying
Chopped leaves	No	Slight	Widespread	Free or inexpensive	Several months	Best if partially decomposed
Fresh wood chips	No	Severe	Widespread	Free or inexpensive	1–4 years	Use composted chips if possible
Sawdust	No	Severe	Local to regional	Free or inexpensive	1–3 years	Use only after several years of decomposition; do not use sawdust from treated wood
Municipal compost	Yes	None	Local, most often urban and suburban areas	Free or inexpensive	Several months	Quality varies significantly from municipality to municipality
Packaged compost	No	None	Widespread	Expensive	Several weeks	Best used as a soil additive than a mulch
Pine straw	No	Slight	Local to regional	Inexpensive to moderate	1–2 years	May be blown away in windy areas
Spoiled hay	Yes	Slight	Local	Free to inexpensive	Several months to a year	Wear dust mask while using spoiled hay since it may contain mold spores

Straw

Chopped leaves

Wood chips

Sawdust

Municipal compost

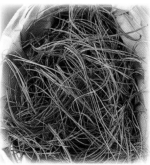
Packaged compost

Pine straw

Spoiled hay

or outline masses of smaller perennials. The sand may help you get the spacing right. And if you are creating a perennial bed that is heavily dependent on color, you can do a final check on color and do any last-minute rearranging to get the color combinations correct by using various colors of sand that match the bloom color of the perennials you intend to plant. The sand will disappear as you plant the plants or you can cover it as you apply mulch to the soil.

▶ Mark the locations for the plants in the garden with landscape paint, sand, or chalk. Set plants in place and leave them for a few days before planting to ensure you are happy with the design.

MULCH CHART *(continued)*

Mulch material	Risk of weed seeds	Nitrogen impact	Availability	Cost	Durability	Comments
Spent mushroom soil	No	None	Very local	Free to inexpensive	Several months to a year	Adds organic matter but not significant amounts of nutrients
Cottonseed hulls	No	None	Very local	Free to inexpensive	Several months to a year	May be blown away in windy areas
Seaweed	No	None	Local to regional	Free to inexpensive	Several months	Adds valuable micronutrients to the soil
Cocoa hulls	No	None	Widespread	Expensive	1–3 years	Deliciously fragrant
Shredded hardwood	No	Limited	Widespread	Moderate	1–3 years	In recent years quality has declined and may vary widely
Shredded pine bark	No	Limited	Widespread	Moderate	1–3 years	Use instead of pine nuggets which can tie up nitrogen
Salt marsh hay	No	Limited	Local to regional	Moderate	1 year	Some concern about environmental impact
Shredded cypress	No	Limited	Widespread	Moderate	Several years	More durable than most mulches

Spent mushroom soil

Cottonseed hulls

Seaweed

Cocoa hulls

Shredded hardwood

Shredded pine bark

Salt marsh hay

Cypress mulch

Planting your perennials

▲ Pressing on the pot as you roll it on the ground will help free a stuck plant from its container. You can also rap the rim of a container against the edge of a flat surface, such as the rim of your wheelbarrow, a tabletop, or a fence post to loosen plants. Hold the plant out of the way as you knock the pot.

Before you plant your perennials, you will want to prepare them. Preparation differs slightly depending on whether you have chosen bare-root or container-grown plants.

Bare root

Bare-root perennials need minimal preparation. If the plants have any broken roots, cut them off. Also trim any roots that are excessively long; they make it hard to dig the hole wide enough to plant them.

If there are remnants of dead leaves or stems near the crown of the plant (where the roots and shoots meet), see if they pull off easily. If so, remove them to reveal buds at the crown.

Roots that look dry often benefit from a good soak in a bucket of water. Soaking the roots is also helpful for perennials if your region is dry or the plants naturally prefer to grow in saturated soil. Never soak perennials that are finicky about drainage. Limit the amount of time the plants soak to an hour or so.

▲ Once the soil is ready, you can finally move on to the fun part—planting—where all your dreams for a garden finally come into being. Dig a wide but shallow hole, loosen the roots a bit, and you're good to go.

▶ One way to free plants from their nursery pots is to step on the pot. The flexing action creates space between roots and pot. Avoid putting your full weight on the pot to prevent damage to the plant.

▶ Match the size of the digging tool to the size of the plant. Use a spade to dig holes for perennials in 1-gallon or larger containers. Using a trowel for such large holes will wear you out and take the fun out of planting.

Prepare container plants

Be sure to water container-grown perennials the day before you take them out of their pots and plant them. They will slide out of the pots much more easily and be less prone to drying out while you are getting them planted.

If you have a hard time removing a plant from a pot, trim any roots growing out of drainage holes and try again. If it still refuses to slide out and the pot is plastic, then place the pot on its side and step on it to flex the plastic. This should create a gap between the pot and the root ball, allowing you to remove the plant. You can also rap the rim of the pot against the edge of a table or edge of a

▲ Potbound roots won't grow out into the surrounding soil. Instead they will continue to follow the circle of the planting hole. Making shallow slices through the roots allows new root tips to branch from the cut ends.

▲ To protect your wrist as you work, grab the trowel handle like you would a glass of water. Pull the trowel toward you to dig the hole. This method keeps your wrist straight and works best when soil is loose and not too wet.

Planting your perennials *(continued)*

wheelbarrow. One or two sharp knocks usually loosens plants. In extreme cases you may have to cut the pot away from the plant.

If you see many roots and little soil on the outside of the soil ball, the plant is root bound. Circling roots are detrimental to growth, so

you'll want to eliminate them before planting. Doing so will help the plant to grow more quickly into the surrounding soil. If you leave them, the

plant may never grow out of its planting hole.

To remove circling roots, you can tease them away from the root ball. Squeeze

HOW TO PLANT CONTAINER-GROWN PERENNIALS

1 Dig a generous hole. For 4-inch or smaller pots, use a trowel for digging. For larger pots use a spade. In old beds where the soil hasn't been worked in a while, make the planting hole one to two times wider than the nursery pot, but no deeper. Dig so that the sides of the hole slope toward the center of the bottom. In well-prepared gardens, dig the hole as wide and as deep as the pot.

2 Check the depth of the hole by setting the pot in it. The plant crown should be level with the surrounding soil. Planting perennials too deep invites stem and crown rot; planting too high so that the perennial's shoulders sit above the surrounding ground is likely to retard plant growth. You can check the level by laying the handle of your spade, a ruler, or other straight object over the hole. The top of the container soil should be even with the bottom of the handle.

3 Take the plant out of the pot by flipping it over, keeping one hand stretched over the soil around the plant. Tap the pot with your other hand until the plant is free of the container. For a stubborn pot roll the pot back and forth on the ground while firmly pressing on it with your hands or your foot.

4 Tease apart any pot-bound roots encircling the root ball. Or make shallow slices around the root ball with a sharp knife, cutting from the bottom to halfway up the root ball.

5 Set the plant in the hole, evenly spreading the loosened roots. Recheck the depth of the crown or top of the potting soil and adjust the depth of the hole as needed.

6 Backfill the hole halfway, firming the soil with your hands. Then fill the hole with water to settle the soil. When the water has been absorbed, finish backfilling the hole; firm the soil and water again. Use a gentle spray, such as from a water breaker or fan-spray sprinkler, to avoid splashing soil out of the hole.

the root ball to loosen the soil and then carefully work the roots free. You can also make shallow slices through the root ball. The roots will branch and grow from the cut ends. This is a little harder on plants than teasing out the roots, but it is less time consuming.

Brush the top of the root ball to see if the crown is covered in soil. The soil should be fairly loose and brush off easily. Remove all of this soil to reveal the crown. You should know where the crown is so that when you plant you position it near the soil surface without burying it.

Some plants are grown in biodegradable pots that you can plant in the ground, pot and all—but only if the roots have begun to grow through the pot and the pot has begun to decay. If the pot is dry and intact and the roots have not penetrated it, it will act as a barrier to establishment of the plant; in this case remove the pot before planting.

Planting perennials

Dig a wide hole no deeper than the height of the root ball. Any deeper and the crown will be buried.

An ordinary hole will do for a container-grown perennial. With a bare-root perennial, forming a small cone of soil in the planting hole helps direct the roots outward from the crown. Plan for some settling of the soil by planting the crown slightly higher than the soil surface; planting a bit high is particularly important if drainage is an issue.

If you are planting masses of perennials with rhizomes that grow in just one direction, dig a trench rather than single planting holes.

HOW TO PLANT BARE-ROOT PERENNIALS

1 Bare-root plants have no soil around their roots. Nurseries often wrap the roots in moist sphagnum peat moss before shipping to prevent drying while the plants are en route. Remove it before planting.

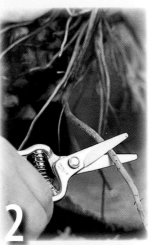

2 Trim any dead or broken roots. Try to keep as many roots intact as possible. The bigger and healthier the root system at planting, the faster a bare-root perennial will take off when growth begins in spring.

3 Fill a bucket with water and soak the roots to rehydrate them. Leave them in the bucket for at least an hour and no more than a couple of hours. Adding a root starter to the water is beneficial.

4 Dig a hole as wide as the spread-out roots and as deep as the roots reach. You can do this while the plants soak or just before planting.

5 At the center of the hole, form a mound of soil to hold the plant at the right depth and help anchor it while you fill the hole. Scrape the dirt in the bottom of the hole into a high enough pile that the crown or eyes (buds on the roots) sit at the soil surface.

6 Leave the plants in the bucket until the moment you are ready to put them in the ground.

7 Set the plant on the mound and evenly spread its roots over the soil. Backfill the soil halfway, and then fill the hole with water.

8 After the water has been absorbed, finish backfilling the hole. Firm the soil and water again. Move the mulch back around plants or add a layer now. Thoroughly water again and keep soil moist until plants become established.

Planting your perennials *(continued)*

A trench makes it easy to set the rhizomes so they all point in the same direction and don't grow into each other or other perennials too quickly. This technique works especially well with Solomon's seal and irises.

Planting among plants

You'll have to navigate around existing perennials when you plant in an established bed. If you have bulbs in the same space, the best time to plant might be spring, when the bulbs and sprouting perennials are easy to see. You can plant in autumn when you are cleaning up the perennial garden if that's a better time to plant in your region and you've marked the bulbs with plant labels or have mapped their location.

Verify that what looks like empty space for a new plant really is and that nearby perennials won't take over that space as they grow. It's a good idea to fortify the soil in these empty areas before you plant by adding a bit of compost or rotted manure and working it into the top several inches of soil.

Be sure you've chosen a plant that fits the spot and that won't overtake neighboring perennials. Then plant your new perennial in the void.

Postplanting care

After you finish planting, touch up the mulch so there's no bare soil exposed to sunlight that will cause the spot to dry out quickly and leave an opportunity for weeds to invade. If you left mulching until after planting, now's the time to put it down. Afterwards water the area thoroughly.

In addition to encouraging root growth, watering settles the soil and helps to eliminate air pockets. Don't rely on a clock to tell you how long to water your perennial bed. Check the progress of the water downward in the soil. Your goal is to moisten the top 8 inches of soil.

If your soil is naturally sandy, you might only have to water the bed for a half hour. You might need to water a dry, heavy soil for several hours to moisten it to the desired depth. If water begins to run off before it has reached 8 inches deep, stop watering for at least a half

▲ When planting within existing gardens, make sure the space is truly empty before digging. Also ensure that adding a new plant doesn't crowd existing plants, taking away space that they need. Neither plant will thrive if crowded. Refresh the soil with organic matter before planting.

▲ Thoroughly water plants right after planting and daily for their first week in the ground. Water every other day during the next week, and every third day during the third week after planting. After plants are rooted and settled in, water weekly.

▲ Using a soaker hose is an efficient way to water. Rather than evaporating in the air, as happens with sprinklers, the water flows directly into the soil surrounding the plant's roots.

▲ If you don't mulch the bed before planting the garden, be sure to mulch afterwards. Leave a 1- to 4-inch mulch-free space around the plants to avoid smothering crowns or providing a home for foliage-feeding critters.

▲ Recutting an edge on the garden once or twice a summer helps keep the garden's good looks tidy and sharp.

hour before turning the water on again.

Edge your garden

Edging neatens your perennial garden's appearance and it helps separate the perennials from adjacent turf or groundcover. Plastic edging, concrete edgers, bricks, or rot-resistant wood are common choices. All should be installed with most of their bulk below the soil surface to give them some stability.

To avoid having to string-trim the boundary between your perennials and nearby turf, you may opt to use a single course of Belgian block cobblestones or concrete pavers to create a vegetation-free track for your mower.

If you lack the budget or time to buy and install one of these edging options, you can use a flat shovel or edger to cut an edge in the sod or groundcover. Be sure to cut several times during the growing season to keep your perennial bed safe from invaders.

You're better off installing edging after you plant the garden so that it doesn't interfere with your work. You can put in the edging or cut an edge in the adjacent sod anytime while the plants are getting established.

Add annual color

In its first year or two, your perennial garden may look a bit sparse. You can give the space color and texture quickly by planting a few annuals around the perennials. Or sow seeds of larkspur or California poppy in early autumn or early spring after planting; they have small leaves that don't cast shade to hamper the growth of your new perennials. These annuals may reseed themselves for many years, politely making way for your perennials as they grow in size.

Use impatiens, caladium, and begonia in a shady perennial garden to provide some color while the perennials are getting established. Avoid large-leaved annuals that cast a lot of shade or grow tall, since they may compete with the perennials and may even cause them to fail due to lack of light.

Caring for perennials

After you've planted your perennials and they start growing, you'll have to give them regular attention to keep them looking their best. Much of the work takes place early in the life of your perennial garden when you are still keeping the weeds out and urging the plants to grow to their full size.

Maintenance is critical early on and you simply can't postpone it. Lack of water or too many weeds can threaten a new perennial bed before it has a chance to become established. It's also much easier to do a little preventive maintenance each week rather than allowing weeds to overgrow the garden, and having to tackle the job of sorting young plants from a jungle of growth. After the plants are fully grown, the big project of dividing your perennials from time to time takes place every few years.

Putting down roots

A perennial garden goes through an establishment phase before it makes the transition to a maintenance phase. While they are establishing plants have not reached their ultimate size or potential, and weeds may attempt to invade the spaces

◄ The first summer after planting your garden will look pretty sparse. You may be tempted to add more perennials to fill the space. That's not a good idea. Instead, concentrate on weeding to eliminate competition and on watering and fertilizing to ensure your plants flourish. If you want, scatter in a few annuals to add more color.

► At last, in year three you'll start seeing the results you hoped for when you planted your perennial garden.

between your perennial plants. You'll have to keep after the weeds to prevent them from gaining a toehold in your garden.

The tender young roots of the perennials that you planted from containers are trying to grow out of the potting soil and into the surrounding soil. Bare-root perennials have to grow an entirely new set of fine roots. Keep the garden soil evenly moist during the establishment phase to encourage the root growth of both types of plants.

When the garden is young you won't reap armloads of flowers. It is a time to be patient and to focus on the ultimate reward that may take several years to realize.

After the first season of growth, your perennials will

begin to come into their own. They will increase in size significantly. Some—for example, yarrow, columbine, chrysanthemum, and iris—reach maturity and full flowering display in their second year. Others, such as peony, hosta, Lenten rose,

and false indigo, may take three or four years to reach their full potential. Unless you're growing a limited number of perennials with similar growth rates, your garden's transition to maintenance will be spread out over several years.

▲ The second summer after planting your garden will still look sparse, although the plants may seem a bit larger than the previous year. No need to worry. Your garden is growing as expected, putting on a good healthy root system.

SLEEP, CREEP, LEAP

Here's a handy saying about the growth pattern of perennials: The first year they sleep, the second year they creep, and the third year they leap. So don't be disappointed by a perennial garden that seems to be stagnant its first year.

Unlike annuals, which send out roots and shoots with fury quickly after planting, perennials take their time establishing vital systems for many years of growing in the garden. Perennials transplanted from quart or gallon containers might flower during their first year in the garden, but don't expect bare-root plants or perennials transplanted from small containers to bloom profusely—these perennials will focus their efforts on establishing a strong root system.

You'll notice some outward and upward growth in the second year after planting. Some perennials such as coneflower are well established by this time and might even be producing offspring by reseeding or forming a spreading clump.

By the third year most perennials are flowering at their full potential and will continue to increase in size if the growing conditions permit it. Exceptionally vigorous perennials are ready to be divided in the third year while other plants will thrive without division for many years.

Controlling weeds

▲ Weeds compete with perennials for resources such as sunlight, water, and nutrients. Remove them before they settle in, and especially before they set seed.

Perhaps the most laborious task of the establishment phase of a perennial garden is weeding. Unlike a vegetable garden or annual flowerbeds, a perennial garden is not tilled every year. Once tough perennial weeds get established, they are difficult to eradicate. Annual weeds may be easier to deal with, but if they are allowed to set seed they may carpet any bare areas in the garden.

You can use various methods to combat weeds: removing them by hand, using preemergence herbicides, and mulching.

Remove weeds by hand

Hand weeding is a viable option if your perennial garden is small and there aren't too many weeds. Some people prefer to bend over and weed, but this may strain your back. Squat or crouch to put your hands in contact with the soil. If you prefer to weed in a kneeling position, use knee pads to ease the wear and tear on your knees.

When you are dealing with taprooted weeds, use a trowel, soil knife, dandelion digger, or hand-hoe to dig the upper part of the root out of the soil. If there seem to be too many weeds to manage with hand weeding, use a hoe. use.

A standard hoe, with a large blade, is useful in the vegetable garden for dealing with weeds between rows and pulling soil up around root crops. But in the perennial garden you may find the large blade ungainly. Choose a standard hoe with a smaller blade, a triangular blade, or a loop blade.

The key to hoeing is to sever the weeds just below the soil surface. Obviously a hoe will mean death to newly sprouted weeds but will only result in a setback for weeds with a deep rhizome or taproot, such as bindweed, dandelion, quackgrass, or thistle.

Repeated hoeing is needed to exhaust the food reserves in weeds with deep roots or rhizomes. If you choose hoeing to combat weeds, carve out time to take care of this task frequently—every two weeks at least. If you allow more time to pass before you hoe, the job will be much harder because the weeds will have developed tougher roots and stems.

Use chemical control

You can use herbicides to control weeds in your perennial bed, but you must be very careful. Always read product labels carefully and be sure to follow the instructions exactly.

In your lawn you can use a wide variety of herbicides that kill broadleaf weeds but don't harm the grass even if the herbicide comes in contact with it. There aren't any products that can selectively kill the established broadleaf weeds but not your perennials. Most perennials are broadleaf plants and will be harmed by lawn weed killers, so take great care if you are treating weeds adjacent to a perennial bed.

If you hire a lawn service to treat the weeds in your lawn, tell them to keep herbicides several feet away from your perennial beds. Also keep any lawn fertilizers that contain an herbicide along with the fertilizer away from your perennials; it could easily kill your plants.

▲ The blade of a diamond hoe is sharp on all sides so it cuts weeds at the roots as you push or pull it through the soil.

▲ Hand weeders slice right under the crown of the plant, severing the roots. Several styles are on the market, and most are available with long handles as well.

▲ A fish tail weeder, also called an asparagus knife, (above right) pries weeds out of the ground. Loosening soil with a garden fork before you pry eases the job.

▲ Hand control methods include hoeing, pulling, and digging.

▲ Apply preemergence herbicide to soil to prevent weeds from germinating. Be sure to apply it *before* seeds germinate.

▲ A selective herbicide such as Brush-B-Gon can kill garden plants. Use a coarse spray and a screen to protect perennials.

▲ Another way to protect perennials while controlling weeds is to paint the herbicide onto the foliage.

Herbicides to prevent weed germination

Nonselective preemergence herbicides are the weed killers most often used in perennial gardens. They target the tiny root that first emerges from a weed seed. Perennials have established roots, and thus are not harmed by preemergence herbicides. If the soil surface has one of these herbicides in it, weeds will not be able to survive the germination process.

Most of these products are granules that you scatter on the soil. It is important not to disturb the soil surface after you apply the herbicide, so they won't work well if you are using them and also hoeing perennial beds.

The granules need to be activated by rainfall or irrigation to diffuse the herbicide throughout the soil surface. Apply the granules just before a rainfall or plan to water the garden after applying them.

Be aware that preemergence herbicides don't selectively work on seeds. If you are planning to sow seeds of annuals in your perennial garden, the herbicide will kill them too. You can get around this by starting your annuals in pots and then planting them into the garden.

Herbicides to eliminate established weeds

You can use nonselective herbicides in the perennial garden during the establishment phase. Limit your use of them to perennial weeds, and be sure to choose one that has no volatile toxic component. Herbicides containing glyphosate fit this description.

Since a nonselective herbicide can kill any vegetation it comes into contact with, you must use it carefully. The simplest method is to purchase ready-to-use product that has its own wand sprayer. With this method you won't have to worry about mixing the correct dilution of the herbicide, and you're less likely to be exposed to any of the herbicide or spill it. Always wear rubber gloves, a long-sleeved shirt and long pants to avoid skin contact when using herbicides.

Be careful not to drip any herbicide on anything other than the perennial weeds that you want to eliminate. Cover nearby flowering perennials plants with large pots for added protection when spraying, or fashion a shield from stiff plastic or metal to prevent spray droplets from inadvertently reaching desirable plants. If you purchase and use the concentrated form of glyphosate, mix only a small amount of herbicide; you will be surprised at how far a small amount of herbicide will go to spot treat persistent perennial weeds.

Apply mulch

Apply mulch to bare soil when weeds have just begun to germinate, and you may be able to smother many of them before they have a chance to make it out of the seedling stage.

If you've already got the weeds under control, mulch will frustrate the attempts of many seeds to germinate and help you to maintain the upper hand. Many different materials can be used as mulch. Some are widely available, and others only locally.

Organic mulches consist of material that will ultimately break down to organic matter. Inorganic mulches are usually crushed stone of some kind. They are rarely used in perennial gardening simply because the soil will be disrupted when you need to dig, divide, and replant individual plants. An important exception is the cultivation of some alpine perennials, where crushed stone may be used as a mulch to keep moisture away from the crowns of sensitive plants. Learn more about mulch on pages 98–101.

Weed barriers such as woven polypropylene and nonwoven synthetic barrier cloth are sometimes used as

▲ A 2- to 3-inch-deep layer of mulch prevents weed seed germination by blocking light. It also holds in moisture and adds organic matter to the soil as it breaks down.

an underlayment for mulch to create a more formidable barrier for weeds. Their use is not really practical in a perennial garden. They may constrict the growth of your perennials as well as restrict the flow of water into the soil. The need to periodically dig and divide perennials also makes weed barriers impractical.

ANNUAL INVADERS

In most regions you'll find two types of annual weeds. Winter annuals typically germinate in the first cool days of fall and may continue to germinate anytime throughout winter if the weather is mild. Chickweed, henbit, and shepherd's purse are winter annuals. They may grow a rosette of small leaves before really cold weather arrives. The weeds begin to grow rapidly in the first warm days of spring, flowering quickly and often setting seed before many perennials begin growing in spring. If you use a preemergence herbicide to combat winter annuals, apply it in early fall.

Summer annuals germinate in response to warming soil in late spring and early summer. Crabgrass, carpetweed, lamb's quarters, and smartweed are summer annuals. An application of preemergence herbicide in spring is helpful in controlling them.

By applying preemergence herbicide in spring and fall you'll be able to eliminate most weeds that try to invade your garden with wind-scattered seeds.

Watering

▲ If you are using a hose and sprinkler, try to keep the sprinkler on a single spot for at least two hours before moving it and be sure to overlap the areas you water.

▲ Snake a soaker hose throughout your garden to water plants. Soaker hoses, like drip systems, apply water directly to the soil so that little is lost to evaporation. When using a soaker hose, leave the water on long enough to ensure the water wets the entire root zone of the plants.

► Covering the soaker hose with mulch hides it and helps hold in moisture.

Watering is perhaps the most important part of maintaining a perennial garden. Although some perennials survive and bloom well on natural rainfall, many regions experience periods of dry weather when plants may need supplemental moisture.

Water is essential to plants. It carries dissolved minerals—the nutrients for plant health and growth—from the soil to the leaves. As water moves through the plant, it gives the plant structure. It exits through tiny pores in the underside of the leaves in a process called transpiration, which helps cool plants on hot days.

Most perennials benefit from about an inch of water a week. Even drought-tolerant plants benefit from regular water until they are established. Afterward they need less frequent moisture. The best way to water perennials is deeply and at length, at least long enough to apply 1 inch of water.

Deep watering encourages a more extensive and stronger root system that is better adapted to drought. The wider and deeper a perennial's root system, the larger the area from which the plant can pull moisture and nutrients. Also water slowly so that the soil can absorb the surface moisture. If you apply water too fast, it runs off and is wasted or it puddles on the ground before it is absorbed. Pooled water can evaporate before it benefits your plants.

How to water

Like many other tasks in landscape maintenance, watering has tended to become automated. Often home irrigation systems are programmed to water for short periods on a frequent basis. Habitual shallow watering is damaging to most perennials, particularly in warm, humid areas where plant diseases are a problem.

It is much better to water plants infrequently but thoroughly. If you are using

▼ Oscillating sprinklers efficiently cover a large area of garden. However, because their water streams shoot high in the air, evaporation is a problem with these types of sprinklers. Use them only when there's little wind.

▲ Automatic irrigation systems take the labor out of watering, but you must pay attention to ensure all parts of your garden receive adequate water and that the sprinkler does not run unnecessarily, for example, when the soil is overly wet.

an automated system, the frequency and length of application for irrigation water depends on several factors. A system that applies a high volume of water quickly should run for less time than a drip system. Program the system so the water is on for 30 to 40 minutes of each hour. The 20- to 30-minute breaks will eliminate much of the water runoff and allow time for the water to soak deeper into the soil. You may need to water more frequently for a shorter period of time if your soil is very sandy. Weather patterns and the types of plants in the garden also affect the frequency and amount of water to apply at each irrigation.

Drip irrigation

If diseases are prevalent where you garden or if water is scarce, you may want to use a drip or soaker system to deliver the water directly to the plant's roots. A soaker hose composed of porous rubber oozes water along its entire length. Drip irrigation is even more efficient because emitters can be placed only by plants that need water. Both types allow you to water even in windy conditions when overhead irrigation may not be practical.

Place soaker hoses under the mulch if possible to

▶ Trees and shrubs in a garden compete with the perennials for water and can dry the soil faster than if only perennials were in the bed. Because water runs off a slope, locate the sprinkler above the garden so that the runoff runs into the garden rather than below it.

ensure that the water goes directly into the soil and does not have to pass through the mulch first. If you place them on top of the mulch, you may have to use a tremendous amount of water to wet the mulch before moisture even reaches the soil surface.

To maintain uniform pressure in drip irrigation lines on slopes, use pressure-compensating emitters. Otherwise high points in the line will be underwatered.

Measure the moisture

Whether you have an automated sprinkler system or a hose-end sprinkler, you may want to set out several empty soup cans to measure how much water is being applied at a time.

Better yet use a long screwdriver or asparagus knife to see how far the water has penetrated into the soil. Plunge the screwdriver into the soil; it should go in easily if the soil is wet. The goal is to moisten the soil to a depth of 8 inches. Check several areas since some sprinklers distribute water very poorly.

Perennials that are growing near trees or large shrubs may have to be given water more often than

perennials in other parts of your garden. Plants in sunny or windy sites also need more water than those in protected, shady sites.

Water with a high salt content isn't good for plants. If your irrigation water has been softened or is naturally high in salt, you may want to follow the example of gardeners who collect water from gutters and downspouts to meet some of their irrigation needs.

Your water source

The vast majority of gardeners use municipal water for their watering needs. Some in rural areas use well water, or water from a stream or pond. Municipal

▲ Whichever type of system you use, you can make sure the root zone is adequately wet by poking the blade of a screwdriver into the soil. The blade should easily slip in 8 inches deep.

water may read as high as pH8 on the scale. Other sources of water are generally better for plants since the pH is usually closer to neutral.

WATER CONSERVATION STRATEGIES

● Water thoroughly and infrequently. Water that gets deep into the soil, where it is available to deep roots, will last much longer than a quick surface irrigation, which is likely to evaporate quickly.

● Arrange plants according to water need. You can limit the size of the area that you have to irrigate frequently if you group perennials that are prone to die in dry periods. Perennials that are drought resistant can fill out other parts of your garden.

● Plant perennials that need reliable moisture near downspouts, on the edge of walkways or drives, and any other place that receives extra moisture in even scanty rain storms.

● Direct water that runs off your roof into a rain barrel and store it for later use. The volume you can collect may surprise you.

● Use soaker hoses or drip irrigation to conserve water and put the water right where it is needed most.

● If you must use a sprinkler to irrigate, do so in the early morning when relative humidity is highest and winds are usually calm.

● Mulch any bare soil in your perennial garden. The mulch will slow down the evaporation of moisture from the soil.

● If your garden has to compete with tree roots, grow moisture-loving perennials in pots and check them daily for water.

Fertilizing

▲ Fertilizer—or plant food—provides the nutrients perennials need to grow and stay healthy. Work fertilizer into the soil before planting and supplement this original feeding every few weeks or months, depending on the type of fertilizer you use.

Feeding your plants is a task that begins when you prepare the soil for planting. The organic matter you mixed in is a good soil conditioner; it is also a nutrient-rich material that is a great slow-release plant food. The soil text most likely recommended that you add specific nutrients to build the soil as you amended it. If you followed the recommend-ations, you won't need to feed your plants again until the next year.

If you did not amend the soil with nutrients, new plants benefit from an application of fertilizer since they have not had time to send their roots into the soil you prepared for them. Use a slow-release material to prevent their tissues from becoming soft and succulent and fair game for pests.

These first fertilizer applications get your plants off to a good start. Regular fertilizing as the plants mature ensures a long, healthy life.

The importance of nutrients

Some people think of applying fertilizer as giving their plants food. Technically, they're not. Plants make their own food by combining the sun's energy with carbon dioxide and water to make carbohydrates in the process known as photosynthesis.

However, fertilizers provide nutrients that the plants use to fuel photosynthesis and so in a way, they are plant food. These nutrients are the catalysts for plant growth and formation of cell structures and enzymes that keep the plant in good shape.

Each nutrient has a special function in the plant. For example nitrogen and magnesium are needed to make chlorophyll molecules— which makes plants green.

Plants must have a base level of nutrients throughout the year, and especially during the most critical stages of plant growth and development.

Use a slow-release plant food to deliver a constant stream of nutrients to perennials. Decaying organic matter in soil and in mulch on the soil surface provides low levels of nutrients as long as weather is warm and moist enough for microbes to break them down.

Depending on which type of slow-release plant food you use, you may need to supplement it during the growing season with fertilizer that feeds plants quickly. Whenever plants show signs that they're not getting enough of a nutrient (see "What nutrient deficiencies look like," below), or right after planting into an older garden or after dividing and replanting perennials.

Types of plant foods

Most fertilizers are dry granules that you place on the soil surface or scratch into the soil around plants,

WHAT NUTRIENT DEFICIENCIES LOOK LIKE

Deficiency	Symptom
Nitrogen	Small leaves, short thin growth; leaves turn uniformly yellow starting at the bottom of the plant; they may take on a reddish hue in severe cases; leaves drop
Phosphorus	Dull green leaves tinged bronze to red to purplish; shoots short and thin
Potassium	Older leaves turn yellow along their margins and eventually die; potassium deficiency is rare
Magnesium	Areas between veins of older leaves turn yellow and die
Boron	Young leaves at end of stems become distorted or thicken (or both) and foliage may develop yellow spots; buds at end of stems cease growth; stems may branch but these new stems are also affected
Sulfur	Uniform yellowing of new and young foliage
Iron	Areas between veins of young leaves turn yellow followed by bleaching of the entire leaf to cream or white
Copper	White mottling on and death of newer foliage; leaves may be small, narrow, and distorted; shoots die back
Manganese	Yellow foliage
Molybdenum	Leaves do not fully expand; color may be bluish green
Zinc	Small narrow leaves in a rosettelike whirl

WHEN TO FERTILIZE AND HOW MUCH TO APPLY

The type of fertilizer you use governs when and how often you need to fertilize as well as how much to apply.

Fertilizer type	Example	Total amount* needed per growing season		When to apply
		100 sq. ft.	10 sq. ft.	
Quick-release powder (the nitrogen dissolves in water and is immediately available)	24-8-16 Miracle-Gro All Purpose or any soluble fertilizer that starts with 20% or more nitrogen (first number)	2⅔ cups or 1⅓ lb	4½ Tbsp	In midspring, when large trumpet daffodils bloom, apply 1½ Tbsp per 10 square feet of garden dissolved in water according to label directions. Apply 1 Tbsp per 10 square feet every 2 weeks until you've supplied the full amount (by midsummer).
	15-30-15 Miracle-Gro Bloom Booster or any high-phosphorus (middle number) soluble fertilizer	2⅔ cups or 1⅓ lbs	2 Tsp	Can be used in place of 24-8-16; apply when flower buds are forming.
	30-10-10 Miracid or any soluble fertilizer with 30% nitrogen	1⅓ cups	5–6 Tbsp	Starting in midspring as large trumpet daffodils bloom, apply ½ Tbsp per 10 square feet of garden every 2 weeks until you've supplied the full amount.
Standard granular (nitrogen dissolves quickly and is available to plants soon after fertilizer is applied)	12-12-12 lawn-and-garden-type fertilizer or other granular fertilizer with 10 to 14% nitrogen	3 cups or 1⅔ lbs	3–8 Tbsp	Scratch half the recommended amount into the soil surface in spring when most of the plants have started to grow. Repeat in late spring when Siberian irises are in full bloom.
Slow-release materials, granular and natural organic products (nitrogen is available only when soil is warm and moist; lasts for 2–3 months.)	14-14-14 Osmocote or other sulfur-coated urea product with 14% nitrogen	2½ cups or 1⅖ lbs	4 Tbsp	Scratch the entire amount into the soil surface in early spring as bulb foliage emerges.
	5-5-5 all-purpose or other fertilizer product with 4 to 6% nitrogen	10⅔ cups or 4 lbs	1 heaping cup	Scratch the entire amount into the soil surface in early spring as bulb foliage emerges. Repeat in autumn when tree leaves begin to fall.

*Use these amounts in the absence of soil test results. They will provide nitrogen at the rate of 2 pounds of nitrogen per 1,000 square feet per year. Some perennials may need more or less than that per year (see the encyclopedia starting on page 156 for species noted as heavy or light feeders). A soil test will tell you which fertilizer formula is best to provide the appropriate amounts of phosphorus and potassium for your garden.

then water in. Others are meant to be dissolved in water before you apply them.

Still others are dry granules coated with a material that governs the release rate of the nutrients; these granules are called prills. Prills are designed to break down in a way that releases nutrients at a constant rate. The coating on prills is slightly soluble in water and as it becomes thinner, the fertilizer is released at an increasing rate. These are known as slow-release fertilizers.

Non-coated plant foods release nutrients rapidly; most are known as fast-release plant foods. Because rain and irrigation water leaches the nitrogen and potassium of these materials from soil and because plants use them quickly, you will need to reapply them more often than prilled plant food. Feeding plants after a long period of rain will give your plants the boost they need.

Prills release nutrients during periods of rainfall, when nutrients are more likely to be leached from the soil, but they don't release all their nutrients at once. They continue to feed plants for several more weeks, depending on the product you use.

Some products contain a mix of prills with varying thicknesses of coatings. In this way the granules release nutrients at different rates. You can find products that feed plants for one to nine months.

Liquid plant foods deliver nutrients in a form that is quickly absorbed by plant roots. Plants can also take in small amounts of nutrients through leaves. Liquid fertilizer is especially helpful for feeding perennials in pots or whenever you need to give your plants a quick boost because they appear to be lacking nutrients.

▶ The label of a plant food specifies how much of each nutrient makes up the product and how much to use. Read the label carefully before feeding your perennial garden.

Fertilizing *(continued)*

▲ A spray of liquid plant food provides a quick boost to plants that are showing signs of needing nutrients. The new feeders use premixed plant foods so there's no guessing about how much to apply and you never have to touch the material.

▲ Plant foods that come in Shake 'n Feed containers make it easy to direct the food exactly where you want it to go. Like the LiquidFeed applicators, you never need to touch the plant food with these containers.

▲ Apply granular materials by hand, sprinkling them in a ring around the plant, 6 inches from the foliage.

Nitrogen, phosphorus, and potassium

All plant foods are labeled with three numbers that denote the percentage of nitrogen, phosphorus, and potassium they contain. Because nitrogen is often the most limiting nutrient, most plant foods contain more of it than other nutrients. Typically phosphorus is not deficient in garden soil to which a complete fertilizer has been added. Unlike nitrogen and potassium, it is not very soluble and does not readily leach from soil. If you mix it in the soil before planting, it most likely will stay there to supply plant needs for many years. Potassium is used in smaller quantities than nitrogen, but it is also readily leached from the soil in areas that get heavy rainfall.

You can send a soil sample to a testing lab for a precise recommendation about the type of fertilizer you should use. Most often the lab will recommend a standard, readily available formulation such as 5-10-5 or 10-10-10.

In addition to nutrients some fertilizer products contain preemergent herbicide. These products are especially helpful in spring and fall when annual weeds are germinating. Avoid using these products if you plan to sow seeds in your garden.

Nitrogen sources
Nitrogen comes in many forms, including nitrate, ammonia, and urea; the labels of all fertilizers specify the sources of the nitrogen and how much of each makes up the product as a percentage. All plants use nitrate for their nitrogen needs. The ammonia and urea in a plant food is converted to nitrate by microbes in the soil, but temperatures must be warm enough for them to work.

Be aware that ammonia-based fertilizers tend to make soil more acidic, while nitrate fertilizers tend to make soil more alkaline. Considering that most tap water tends to be alkaline, ammonia fertilizers are probably the best choice for container perennial gardens, since it is desirable to counteract the high pH of the water.

Many alpine and rock garden plants are sensitive to ammonia and best fertilized with a fertilizer containing potassium nitrate and rock phosphate. Pinks and peony also do best with a nitrate source of nitrogen.

Organic sources Organic plant foods originate from something that was once living and include blood meal, dehydrated manure, cottonseed meal, and fish emulsion. They are often more expensive than conventional plant foods, but have other benefits that may make them worthwhile. For

EXCEPTIONS TO THE RULES

Some perennial species grow best in lean soil, which is low in nitrogen. Others are heavy feeders and require more than average amounts of nitrogen. The following are among the most common perennials with low or high nitrogen needs:

HEAVY FEEDERS
- Astilbe
- Clematis
- Delphinium
- Peony

LIGHT FEEDERS
- Artemisia
- Barrenwort
- Mullein

Leaves that are smaller than normal, older leaves (lower ones) that are pale, and thin stems indicate nitrogen need.

Weak stems, reduced flowering, and rank growth may indicate too much nitrogen.

FERTILIZERS FOR ACID-LOVING PLANTS

Fertilizers for acid-loving plants contain sulfur and certain nutrients, such as iron, that wouldn't normally be available in alkaline soils. The sulfur produces weak sulfuric acid, which helps dissolve nutrients from soils normally too alkaline to release them. Use these products if you want to grow an acid-loving perennial such as gas plant in alkaline soil.

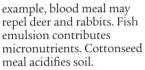

▲ Scratch granular plant foods into the soil after applying them. The different colors and particle sizes of this plant food means that it is not prilled.

▲ Water after applying uncoated quick-release plant foods to ensure they don't burn foliage or plant crowns.

example, blood meal may repel deer and rabbits. Fish emulsion contributes micronutrients. Cottonseed meal acidifies soil.

All organic fertilizers serve as a food source for fungi, bacteria, and other microorganisms in the soil that help to combat soil-borne diseases, and they may encourage the growth of mycorrhizae (beneficial soil fungi) that allow plants to more efficiently absorb water and nutrients. Over time, they help improve soil tilth.

Feeding plants

Your goal when feeding is to ensure the food is evenly distributed to all plants. Use a watering can or a hose-end sprayer to deliver the properly measured proportion of nutrients in liquid plant food. Be sure to mix it thoroughly.

Apply granular plant foods by hand. If using a quick-release materials, wear plastic or rubber gloves, because they will draw water out of your skin and irritate cuts. Use the rate specified on the package, and sprinkle them in a ring around each perennial clump 6 inches from its edge.

Don't let quick-release granules lodge in the foliage or around the crown of the plant. Scratch them into the soil surface. Move mulch aside to apply the fertilizer and then put it back in place.

You can use a rotary hand spreader, but it doesn't let you precisely direct the

fertilizer. And because the plant food will get on leaves and crowns, use it mainly when applying prilled granules. If using quick-release granules, wash leaves off after feeding plants. Or schedule feeding just before a rain or irrigation.

Be safe

Don't be tempted to apply the fertilizer at a higher rate than the label recommends. Granular and liquid plant foods can burn plants if applied too heavily, especially in warm, dry weather. Prilled foods are less likely to burn than the others. However, the rates specified on labels have been tested to supply perennials with optimum amounts of nutrients.

If you spill granular or prilled plant food in the garden, scoop it up and distribute it evenly across the garden. If you spill liquid plant food, water thoroughly to dilute it. Keep plant food away from water features. The nutrients in it can lead to an algae bloom that can kill fish and other aquatic organisms. Also sweep up any plant food you spill on hard surfaces, such as patios and driveways.

Some gardeners think that it is not possible to burn plants with organic fertilizers. This is not true; take care not to apply these fertilizers—particularly fish emulsion, dehydrated manure, and blood meal—too heavily.

▲ Slow-release plant foods feed perennials for several months at a time. Coatings on the granules govern the rate at which nutrients are released to plants.

TIME IT RIGHT

You'll need good timing to ensure that the nutrients are present when the plants really need them. The best time to fertilize is right before periods of active root growth. All nutrients are ultimately water soluble so good soil moisture is essential. If it doesn't rain enough after you fertilize, you'll have to water thoroughly.

In the mildest climates late autumn is the best time to apply slow-release fertilizer. The soil is likely to be moister through winter, and plant root

growth will intercept the nutrients efficiently.

In wintry climates most root growth takes place in spring, beginning when the soil has thawed and warmed sufficiently. Early spring is a good time to apply slow-release fertilizer. If you are growing perennials in containers, use a slow-release fertilizer rated for season-long effectiveness or give them some liquid fertilizer every two weeks or at least every month during the growing season.

Pinching

▲ The trick to growing compact plants with lots of flowers is to pinch them early in the summer. Pinching tames floppy plants and may eliminate the need to stake them.

◀ To pinch, simply grab the tip of a stem and nip it between your fingernails. You can also cut the ends with pruners.

As soon as you have the weeds under control and your perennial garden starts to grow, begin to set aside some time on a regular basis for grooming to keep it looking its best. One of the first tasks to tend to is pinching. This can easily be done as you are checking for new weeds and watching the development of your plants.

If you tend to your perennial garden frequently, you will have fewer dead flowers to mar the display of perennials that are just starting to bloom. This is also valuable time you can use to get an idea of which perennials are doing well in your garden and which are not. One of the routine garden tasks to do is pinching.

Pinch for compact, upright growth

Most perennials don't need to be pinched, but some late summer bloomers—notably asters, bee balm, phlox, and chrysanthemum—tend to grow long floppy stems during spring and early summer. Floppy growth is more likely if your garden has rich soil, ample moisture, and even a small degree of shade.

If you pinch these late bloomers early in the growing

CONTAINER CARE

Perennials growing in containers call for care similar to those that grow in the ground. Here's a rundown of container care basics.

● Watering is the main concern when growing perennials in containers, but you will need to tend to other chores too if you want to get the most out of your container garden. Container plantings dry out more quickly than inground plantings. Plan to water your perennial containers at least every other day during the hottest weeks of summer.

● Fertilizer must be supplied to your container perennials on a regular basis. Choose a liquid fertilizer and apply it at least once a month when the plants are in active growth. As perennials finish their bloom cycle, cut back on fertilizer for the rest of the growing season.

● If your perennial container garden starts to look tired, perk it up with some seasonal annuals. During the dog days of summer, add inexpensive indoor foliage plants to container gardens growing in shade and give new life to the planting. Use pansies and kale to add color during the fall and winter, and in early spring before perennials emerge.

● Check the soil level every fall and spring. Most potting mixes are made primarily of peat, coir, or bark. These decay with time and shrink in volume. Don't be tempted to simply add soil to the top of the pot. If you do so you will bury the crowns of your perennials too deep. Dig the perennials out, remove any hard pockets of soil, and top the pot off with fresh soil before returning healthy divisions to the pot.

● Cleanup in fall can take place after the first hard frost. Carefully remove the dead foliage by pulling it gently away from the plant. If it won't give with a gentle tug, use a garden shears or pruner to cut it away.

● Protect plants in containers from temperature extremes in cold regions. Place them against a wall then insulate with straw or bats of insulation after the first cold snap. Or wrap the plant with bubble wrap to insulate it, then cover it with a tarp or burlap. It's better to keep plants frozen throughout the winter if you live in a cold climate; the objective is to prevent repeated freezing and thawing. You can carry containers over in an unheated garage or in a cold frame, but you must make sure to water them throughout the winter.

Perennials make lovely container gardens. Use them alone or combine them with other perennials or annuals.

Water perennials growing in containers at least every other day, and more often during hot, dry, or windy weather.

If the soil has decomposed, take the plants out of the container, replace the potting soil, and replant.

Insulate containers before winter to prevent the soil from repeatedly freezing and thawing.

season, you won't have to stake them to keep them from flopping over when they start to bloom.

Pinching causes buds on the lower portions of shoots to grow, so that several branches ultimately replace the single shoot that you pinched. Pinch low on the plant, leaving only two to six sets of leaves on the stem.

If you pinch higher, buds all along the stem open in response. The plant's energy then is divided among the many stems, and none of them will be strong enough to produce flowers that reach the plant's full potential.

Start pinching early. When you pinch later in the season (up to a month after growth has started), you will be

removing a larger proportion of the plant than if you pinched earlier. And if you pinch too late, flower buds may be so delayed that the plant may not bloom.

If the growth that comes back after pinching is leggy, pinch again. You can pinch as often as every two weeks, but stop pinching by late spring for summer bloomers such as bee balm and phlox, and by early July for fall-blooming asters and chrysanthemums.

How to pinch

You can use your thumb and forefinger or, if you prefer, hand pruners. Resist the urge

to use grass shears because they don't give you the control you need to pinch each stem at the proper level.

If you want to propagate plants, save the pinched stems. They're cuttings that you can grow into new plants. Dip the cut ends into a rooting hormone to hasten root formation. Then plant the cuttings in pots of moist sand, and cover the pots with ziplock plastic bags. Put the pots on a sunny windowsill and leave one corner of the bag open for ventilation.

Keep the sand moist but not saturated, and mist the cuttings frequently. In a few weeks your cuttings may have enough roots to be moved into small pots, and a few weeks later your potted perennials may be ready to transplant into the garden or share with friends.

◀ Pinching shortens plants and makes them branch more. The result is a stockier plant with more blooms. However, pinching will delay flowering.

Staking

◄ Set stakes in place early in season before plants fully fill out. This will help avoid damaging roots as you insert the stake into the soil.

that spring-flowering bulbs finish blooming and perennials begin their rapid growth. You'll be able to see where your bulbs and perennials are and thus avoid injuring them when you push the stakes into the ground.

Stand tall

There are various ways to support perennials. To emulate nature place tall perennials between shrubs or clumps of ornamental grasses, taking care to give the perennials enough space to develop to their full width.

If grasses and shrubs don't have a place in your perennial garden, you can install structures for tall perennials to grow through. You can save twiggy branches from shrubs and trees you pruned in winter and push them into the soil around perennials that need some extra support. Be sure to anchor them firmly in the soil so they don't topple in windy weather. Twigs work particularly well for short plants with floppy stems like coreopsis, pinks, and low-growing yarrows.

Metal supports are a good solution for herbaceous

S taking is a necessity if you are growing tall perennials or live in a windy area. Many species of perennials naturally grow among shrubs or tall grasses that help to support them; without these sturdy companions to break the wind and help them stand tall, they may fall over, particularly if wind and heavy rain coincide with bloom.

The key to staking is to get the supports in the ground as early as possible before much growth takes place. Aim for the period between the time

▲ Use grow-through supports for multi-stemmed perennials.

▲ Several styles are available. You can find ones with large openings and ones with a grid. Either are effective.

▲ Use two or more grow-through supports for very large plants Set them in place before foliage is more than 6 to 8 inches tall. As plants grow, their foliage will hide the stakes.

▲ To stake plants with one tall flower stalk, place a bamboo stake next to the plant, taking care not to damage roots. Tie the stem to the stake at several places, making sure to keep the stem straight and not pulled back.

▲ Use a figure-eight knot to tie the stem. This allows the stem to sway in breezes, which keeps it from breaking.

▲ Numerous commercial metal stakes are available for single-stemmed flowers. This wavy stake wraps around the stem so that you don't need to tie the plant to it.

▲ Other commercial stakes have hooks or hoops to hold the flower stem. They come in various heights, and you must match the height to the height of the flower stem. The hook or hoop should hold the stem just below the flower.

▲ If flower stems suddenly flop over, you can make an emergency stake with bamboo and twine. However, the plant won't cover up the stake and the flowers won't look natural.

▲ Linked stakes offer flexible support. Each stake hooks onto the next so you can add on as your plants grow. Make sure the height of the stake is below the flowers.

▲ Linked stakes can surround the plant on the outside or can crisscross across the plant.

perennials that die back to the ground each fall. Some gardeners simply leave them in place in the garden throughout winter so they can tell where perennials are planted. Peony, poppy, and delphinium do particularly well when grown with a metal support.

Although tomato cages are often too small for many large tomato vines, they have layers of support at the right levels for most perennials. You can make them even more effective by stringing twine across the horizontal support wires to create a loose mesh through which the stems can grow. Hoops with a horizontal metal grid are available and are a bit sturdier than tomato cages.

STAKING METHODS

Type of stake	Description	Use with these plants
Grid stake	This is a flat, circular grid with three or four legs, which you push into the soil; stems grow up through the grid	Clump-forming perennials such as aster, peony, black-eyed susan, and phlox
Mesh cage	Make a cylinder of chicken wire a bit narrower than the mature width of the plant to be staked; set it over the perennial early in the season; thread a few stakes through the mesh and sink them into the soil for added support	Sprawling perennials such as baby's breath, aster, and yarrow
No-stake staking	Let strong-stemmed perennials, ornamental grasses, and small shrubs hold up floppy neighbors	All perennials
Single stake	Use twine, hook-and-loop plant ties, or padded wire to bind stems to bamboo or wood stakes; many commercial single-stem stakes are also available at garden centers	Tall perennials topped with heavy flower spikes such as foxglove, delphinium, and hollyhock
Tomato cage	Sink a tomato cage in the ground; thread a few stakes through the sides of the cage and sink them into the soil for added support	Clump-forming perennials such as peony, coneflower, and aster
Twig stake	Set sturdy, branched twigs into the soil near a floppy plant for support; prunings from butterfly bush or any other twiggy shrub will do the job	Clump-forming perennials such as shasta daisy and lily

Staking *(continued)*

PLANTS THAT BENEFIT FROM STAKING

Plant	Staking method
Aster	Grid stake, mesh cage, tomato cage
Boltonia	Mesh cage, tomato cage, twig stake
Delphinium	Single stake
Peony	Grid stake, tomato cage
Helenium	Grid stake, mesh cage, tomato cage
Perennial sunflower	Mesh cage, tomato cage

▲ After pruning trees and shrubs, use the trimmings to make a natural stake for your perennials. Insert the cut end in the ground and cut the twigs to about half the height of the mature plant.

If you have a large planting of perennials or are growing a bed of them for cutting, you can use heavy posts and horizontal layers of concrete reinforcing mesh to brace the perennials against wind and storm damage. Although not the most aesthetically pleasing way to support perennials, it will protect them from almost any amount of wind, and it is relatively easy to reach under the mesh from the sides to weed and tend the bed.

Choose a prop tall enough so you can place the supporting layer at a height between one-third and one-half the ultimate height of the plant that you are staking. Tall delphiniums, for example, require a much taller support than peonies.

large perennials like hollyhock. Bamboo stakes work well for most others, including purple coneflower, yarrow, and hyssop.

Unless they are made of metal, stakes deteriorate over time. Take them out of the ground when you clean up the garden in late fall or early winter, or plan to replace them periodically.

Tie up with twine

Stakes and twine provide the best camouflage in supporting perennials. Place stakes in the ground well before the plants are tall enough to need them, and be sure to anchor them well by driving them in as deep as you can.

As the perennial grows tie twine to the stake and loop it around the stems and around the stake again. Don't just wind the twine around the stems and the stake or you will end up with a plant that looks more like a sheaf of grain, and your staking will not be camouflaged at all. Wooden stakes are best for

MAKE YOUR OWN GROW-THROUGH SUPPORT

1 You'll need five or more bamboo stakes, depending on the size of your plant. Insert them so they are equal distance apart around the clump.

2 Tie twine to one stake, string it to the next stake and wrap around it a couple of times. Continue on until you have come to the first stake and completely encircled the clump.

3 Now stretch the twine across the clump to the stake opposite. Wrap the stake, then stretch to the stake opposite it. Continue until you have created a star across the clump.

4 Cut the stakes so they are about half the height of the mature plant.

Deadheading

▲ Deadheading removes faded flowers so that the plant stays neat and doesn't set seed. Because you don't allow seeds to set, the plant will continue to bloom for a longer period.

▲ With daylilies, you can simply break off the spent bloom with your fingers. Check on your plants every day. Spent flowers are very unsightly.

are removed promptly. Removal also prevents seed set and is a must for perennials that tend to seed themselves aggressively, such as black-eyed susan, gayfeather, and garlic chives. Snipping off the developing seeds can also divert the plant's energy into growth and storage of carbohydrates for next year's flowers. Because diseases such as botrytis blight can gain a toehold by infecting fading flowers, deadheading is particularly important in warm, humid weather when the disease organisms are most active.

You may not want to deadhead some plants. Many plants with daisylike flowers, such as perennial sunflower and purple coneflower, attract birds with their ripening seeds. Some plants such as false indigo, woodland peony, and fetid iris have fruits that are as spectacular as the flowers. And the fluffy seeds of butterfly weed delight gardeners and children.

Leave the fading flowers in place if you want any of these lovely and unusual fruits to have a part in the autumn display in your garden. Even if the fruits aren't colorful, they may add some interest to your winter garden. The brown seedheads of sedum, the flat crowns of leftover

Deadheading is the technical term for removing faded flowers from plants. It is not necessary for all perennials but will keep your garden looking its best, particularly if you tend to grow large flowers. Plan to spend a little time removing faded blossoms every few weeks during the growing season.

Getting rid of spent blooms offers several advantages. Some perennials will respond by growing more flowers when faded blossoms

◄ Cut the spent flower at the base of its stem. If you cut just below the flower, they'll turn into dried sticks that detract from the flower show.

Deadheading *(continued)*

▲ Save energy when deadheading plants with numerous tiny blossoms. Use scissors, grass shears, or a hedge trimmer to cut faded flowers all at once.

euphorbia flowers, and the dried spherical orbs of chrysanthemum plants give your garden some winter interest and texture, particularly if you live in an area with long winters and haven't incorporated shrubs into the garden.

How to deadhead

Deadheading can consist of simply snapping off flowers with your fingers as long as the plants have soft, succulent stems that break off easily. Pruners are a better bet, since trying to snap off

▲ Cut the tall single stems of flowers, such as delphinium, so that the cut end is hidden by the plant's foliage (see lines).

spent flowers may injure parts of the plant that still have bloom potential.

How you deadhead really depends on the architecture of the plant. You can let spiky flowers with florets that open progressively, such as gayfeather, bloom themselves out, after which you'll remove the whole flower stalk.

Often you'll want to deadhead as soon as possible after the last flowers fade to force the plant to grow a new rosette of leaves to support next year's flower stalk. Hollyhock, foxglove, lupine, and speedwell may die out if you wait too long and let the plants put their energy into an abundant seed crop.

ENCOURAGE LARGE FLOWERS

Disbudding forces plants to put energy into growing the buds that remain and gives you large showy blooms.

Sometimes you may want to produce exhibition quality flowers in your perennial garden. For the maximum size possible on some flowers, you may have to remove some of the buds that form on the plant long before flowering begins. This will force the plant to put more of its energy into the remaining bud rather than splitting its resources between a lot of much smaller flowers.

Peonies and carnations are often disbudded, and side stalks may be removed from hollyhocks, monkshood, and foxglove. It is important to remove the buds before they get very large to keep the wound caused by the removal as small as possible and to divert the plant's energy into the flower that you want to keep at the earliest stage possible.

This is best done with a very fine garden snipper or your thumb and forefinger. If you use the latter, use a rolling motion to detach the side bud so you don't tear the delicate surface of the succulent stem it is attached to.

▼ Yarrow has branched flower stems, and center buds open first. Cut faded flowers, leaving the buds below to open (first line); remove the entire stem when all flowers have faded (second line). Or cut the entire stem back after the first flowers fade.

◀ On branched stems either the center flower opens first or the side flowers do. Whichever, cut the faded blossoms at the base of their stems, leaving remaining buds to bloom. When no more buds are forming, cut the entire stalk at its base (see lines).

▲ Flower stems of hosta and other perennials come up from the crown of the plant. Cut spent stems all the way back to the ground.

With plants that produce lots of tiny flowers, such as coreopsis, use grass shears or hedge clippers to quickly cut back the forest of stems holding faded flowers. Don't attempt to use your hand pruners to remove individual faded blooms on these plants. This technique takes too long, and you will tire from bending over and making the numerous cuts required to complete the task.

Size up the shearing job first by checking for undeveloped flowers and cutting just above this level. Don't worry if you can't get every faded flower. You can go back and remove any strays that you missed by simply plucking them from the plant.

DEADHEADING TECHNIQUES

KEY

Cut stalk—cut the flower stem just above the ground after flowering has finished to promote growth of a new rosette of foliage
Shear—shear tiny spent flowers near the top of the plant; this may promote growth of latent flower buds lower in the plant
Deadhead—cut the stem just above the first leaf or set of leaves below the spent flower or at the base of the flower stem
Pull—simply pull up the flower stalk when it has died back enough to come out without effort
Don't deadhead—faded flowers are best left on the plant or deadheading isn't needed

Amsonia	Shear or don't deadhead	Hollyhock	Cut stalk
Artemisia	Don't deadhead	Hosta	Pull or deadhead
Aster	Cut stalk	Iris	Pull or deadhead
Astilbe	Cut stalk	Japanese anemone	Don't deadhead
Balloon flower	Deadhead	Lenten rose	Don't deadhead
Bear's breeches	Cut stalk	Lily	Deadhead
Bee balm	Shear	Lupine	Cut stalk
Bellflower	Cut stalk	Lungwort	Cut stalk
Bergenia	Cut stalk	Monkshood	Cut stalk
Black-eyed susan	Deadhead or shear	Old-fashioned bleeding heart	Don't deadhead
Blanket flower	Shear	Peony	Deadhead
Bleeding heart	Don't deadhead	Penstemon	Cut stalk
Butterfly weed	Don't deadhead	Phlox	Deadhead
Centranthus	Shear	Pinks	Shear
Columbine	Cut stalk	Poppy	Deadhead
Coreopsis	Shear	Purple coneflower	Deadhead
Coral bells	Cut stalk	Rose turtlehead	Deadhead
Crocosmia	Cut stalk	Shasta daisy	Deadhead or shear
Chrysanthemum	Deadhead	Speedwell	Cut stalk
Daylily	Pull or deadhead	Thrift	Don't deadhead
Delphinium	Cut stalk	Torch lily	Cut stalk
Foxglove	Cut stalk	Yarrow	Deadhead
Gas plant	Cut stalk	White gaura	Shear
Geranium	Shear		
Goatsbeard	Cut stalk		

Maintaining good looks

▲ Containers can step in to fill a void in the garden when the plants in the garden stop blooming or when a plant such as bleeding heart, which goes dormant early, dies back.

▲ Some perennials such as silver mound artemisia become floppy when grown in rich soil. Cutting back won't help. Rather, move the plant to a less fertile spot.

Keeping your perennial garden attractive is an easy chore if you get into the habit of grooming it frequently. Look at your perennials with a critical eye when you weed, deadhead, and do other routine tasks. Simply removing leaves that have faded or have been heavily damaged by insects or disease goes a long way toward making your perennial garden look stellar.

Some perennials, such as bleeding heart and Oriental poppy, tend to go dormant in the heat of summer; you can remove all the foliage from these plants when it pulls easily out of the ground. Try planting a potted aster or chrysanthemum nearby to cover the void.

If you remove some of the most unattractive leaves and cut back damaged plants, you'll be left with healthy foliage and flowers that make your perennial garden look vibrant and lush.

Cut back or replace

It's important to know when to cut your losses—literally. If your columbine has been attacked by leaf miners or rust has turned your hollyhock leaves into a yellow and brown eyesore, you're better off cutting those plants back to the ground to stimulate new, fresh growth. You may get another flush of flowers on some plants that you cut back in midsummer if your growing season is long enough.

Consider removing an unhealthy plant that you've been nursing. Even if you invested a bit of money in it, simply chalk the loss up to experience and replace the plant with another perennial you want to try or a species that has already performed well for you. Generally if a perennial has not performed well for two or three seasons when you have given it the right conditions, it may be time to give the space to another plant.

▲ When flowers and stems have grown long and leggy, cut the plant back to 3 or 4 inches tall.

▲ The plants will look pretty stark for a few weeks, but they'll soon grow back.

▲ Cutting back often spurs the plant into reblooming, often with a show as full as the first flush of bloom.

Recover from storm damage

When a storm flattens your garden or hail shreds your plants, remember that nature's whims are part of gardening, and take the time to note how plants right themselves and quickly grow new leaves to recover.

You can urge them on by staking some of the stems into a more upright position and by removing some of the worst shredded leaves as new ones appear.

If you live where hail is common, you may want to set up a system that provides some protection during storms. Install posts throughout your perennial garden. Twist an eye screw firmly into the top of each post. Purchase shade cloth from a horticultural supplies dealer, and sew grommets into the cloth through which you can thread clip hooks.

When a storm threatens, you can simply clip the cloth to the posts. Because it is made of mesh, it will withstand wind. The cloth will let rain through but not large hail stones, which may bounce off if the mesh is taut enough and melt into the garden if it's not. It's best to place taller posts near the center of the bed so the cloth will slope to the sides.

You can also use the shade cloth to protect your perennial bed from scorching sun on brutally hot days. Vines planted on the posts will help conceal the structure.

DORMANCY

Perennials go through alternating cycles of growth and dormancy. In late summer and early fall, spring-blooming perennials may begin to look tired. They may lose some of their bright green hue, particularly if they encounter hot weather. As fall progresses the leaves may look even tattier until hard frost finally drains them of all life. While the top of the plant is going dormant, buds near the crown are actively expanding, and the roots are growing in the cool, moist soil. Before winter arrives perennials are ready for cold weather and have formed buds for next spring's growth.

Plants grown in freezing climates remain dormant all winter, even if they encounter a period of warm weather. The large mass of soil keeps them cool through most warm spells. Apply a layer of loose mulch to the perennial garden in late fall after you cut back the dead foliage to help moderate temperatures and prevent frost heaving throughout winter.

Plants are not dead during the dormant period. The buds of many species track the amount of cold they receive and will not resume growth until a certain number of hours below 40°F accumulate. That is why peonies don't succeed in subtropical regions, where the soil is never cold for a long period.

Perennials benefit from watering during dormancy if the soil becomes very dry. In wet-winter climates perennials may be subject to rot during the dormant period and may have to be protected from excess moisture.

In subtropical regions the buds on evergreen perennials perceive the length of night to track the seasons. Most subtropical perennials will not resume growth until nights are shorter and days are longer. Although the plants remain evergreen, they are dormant because they are not actively growing.

Some perennials native to deciduous woodlands grow rapidly in early spring before forest trees leaf out and become dormant as the shade intensifies in late spring and early summer. Perennials native to Mediterranean climates may grow during the cool, rainy winter season and become dormant in summer.

Dormant plants create blank, sometimes awkward spots in the garden. Reduce the impact of these gaps by using annual flowers strategically or by planting perennials that emerge very late in spring—such as butterfly weed, aster, and balloon flower—near those that go dormant early.

Consider using a low evergreen groundcover such as thyme, periwinkle, or dwarf mondo grass near the front of your perennial bed to define it in fall, winter, and early spring. To give the bed some depth and interest during the winter you can strategically incorporate dwarf evergreen shrubs such as hinoki false cypress, dwarf alberta spruce, creeping juniper, and barberry.

Woodland perennials grow and bloom before trees leaf out.

Many Mediterranean plants such as allium go dormant in early summer.

Bleeding hearts go dormant in mid- to late summer.

Dividing & propagating perennials

▲ A plant that has outgrown its space is ready to be divided or moved to a spot that offers more room.

One of the best aspects of perennials is that most can easily be divided and the sections replanted to expand your own garden or given to friends. Most perennials need to be divided every few years to keep them vigorous. After several years of rampant growth, they may exhaust the soil and get so crowded that their growth and bloom are reduced. Some perennials never need to be divided. Peony, torch lily, and ferns may be content to spread slowly and increase in size over many years without any overall loss of vigor or flower production. The only reason to dig them up is to create more plants.

After your perennial garden is established, dividing perennials is the most strenuous job that you will have to do. Fortunately it rarely involves the entire perennial garden. If you want to keep the job to a minimum, grow primarily those perennials that need to be divided less often and stagger the job for other perennials so they are on different cycles. It is much easier to divide a few plants every year than it is to divide a large number in a single year.

Dig up clumps and divide the plants into one or more strong new divisions. Dividing rampant perennials

▲ Dig all around the clump 6 to 12 inches away from the crown. Take care to loosen the plant on all sides before trying to pry it out of the ground.

▲ You may need to cut under the clump to break the plant's hold on the soil. Once you've freed it, lift the plant from the ground.

▲ Another technique to use with clump perennials is to insert two garden forks back to back in the clump. Pull the fork handles away from each other and the clump breaks into pieces.

▲ Some perennials with large rhizomes such as iris can be broken apart to divide them.

▲ Small clumps are easy to cut apart with a knife.

is also a good way to keep them in check. If allowed to expand year after year, they may take up large sections of your garden. Dig up those vigorous growers every few years and bring them back to within their original boundaries.

The best time for dividing perennials depends on where you live and the species you are growing. In most regions

fall is the best time for dividing many perennials. In the coldest climates early spring may be the best time. For some perennials such as iris and daylily, the best time to divide is shortly after the plants flower in summer.

How to divide

You'll need a shovel or a spading fork to divide your

perennials. Dig around the clump at least 6 inches to a foot from the apparent edge of the crown. Excavate an entire circle around the plant before attempting to pry it out of the ground.

Once you have it out of the ground, you can tease away most of the soil clinging to the outer roots. With small perennials, you might be able to grasp sections of the

clump and pull apart the plant from the outer edge of the crown. When the plant is large or has many tangled roots, you may have to use a shovel to slice off divisions. If you have two spading forks, place them back to back and use them to lever perennials into two roughly equal divisions.

When you are dividing to increase the number of

▲ Decide how large you would like each division, then cut through the plant with your shovel. Many perennials such as hosta are essentially a large community of small plants with individual crowns. These are especially easy to separate.

▲ Discard parts of the plant that appear unhealthy or that are old and leafless, such as you'll often see in the center of the clump. When you are finished you will still have numerous starts to put in your garden or to give away to friends.

Dividing and propagating perennials *(continued)*

NEW PLANTS FROM STEM CUTTINGS

▲ Take stem cuttings from the tips of stems, which are flexible and not woody like older stems closer to the ground. Make the cuttings 4 to 6 inches long.

▲ Strip lower leaves from the stem of the cutting.

▲ Poke a hole into the potting soil with a pencil, chopstick, or other slender, pointed object. Then stick the cutting in the hole and press the soil back around it. Put one cutting in each pot.

▲ Thoroughly water the soil and let it drain from the soil.

▲ Place a stake in each pot, then cover the pot with a plastic bag. This creates a humid atmosphere that keeps the soil and plant from drying quickly. Don't let the bag touch the cutting. Moisture on it can cause the cutting to rot.

▲ After a few weeks check whether roots are forming. Tug on the plant; if you feel resistance the cutting is rooting. You can take the plants out of the bag, but keep them watered. When roots fill the pot, it's time to transplant.

plants, don't be tempted to make the largest possible number of divisions. Focus instead on making fewer divisions that will take less time to grow into large plants. If you make a lot of small, weak divisions, many may die when confronted with extremes of soil moisture or temperature. You'll have the chance to make more divisions later.

A soil knife may be helpful in dividing a lot of plants, since you can easily thrust it into a tightly knit mass of roots and use it to pry the roots apart. Very tough plants such as ornamental grasses may require the use of a mattock, a machete, or even an ax to chop them into divisions.

Healthy roots and growing buds

Before you plant the divisions, pull any old or dead sections away from the division and prune off any broken or diseased roots. Good divisions have an abundance of fresh roots and a vigorous growing point or bud. The roots are white or light brown and there is evidence of recent new growth. There are no apparent disease or insect problems on the leaves and

HOW TO MAKE MORE PLANTS

Multiply your favorite plants for use in your garden or to share with friends. Acquire new plants through clump division, seeds, root cuttings, stem cuttings, or division of underground structures such as rhizomes, tubers or tuberous roots.

Plant	Multiplication method	Time of year
Aster	Clump division	Fall or early spring as new growth begins
Bleeding heart	Clump division	After foliage withers in midsummer
Chrysanthemum	Clump division	Early spring as new growth begins
Columbine	Seeds	Early spring to midsummer
Daylily	Clump division	Just after flowering
Hardy begonia	Harvest nodules from stem	Collect and sow in prepared soil before first frost
Hollyhock	Seeds	Early spring to midsummer
Iris	Rhizome division	Just after flowering
Oriental poppy	Root cuttings	Just after plant goes dormant
Peony	Clump division	Fall just after leaves freeze or turn yellow
Yarrow	Clump division	Fall or early spring as new growth begins

GET TO KNOW THE ROOTS BEFORE YOU DIVIDE PERENNIALS

Offset Some perennials form offsets—or daughter plants—that are connected to the mother plant. Snap or slice through these connections to obtain pieces with three to seven eyes.

Eyes Multiple eyes or buds form each year at the base of the previous season's stems or on rhizomes or tubers. Each bud will grow into a new stem and eventually form its own set of roots. Cleanly slice anywhere between the eyes to produce divisions that contain at least one eye and some roots. Even the smallest of such divisions will grow, but the best for replanting have three to seven eyes.

Runners Some perennials have underground stems, called rhizomes, or aboveground stems, called stolons. These runners spread from the original plant. Buds on them grow into new plants at a distance from the original; slice the runner to grow the new plant independently.

Taproot Some perennials form one or more roots that grow straight down from the crown. To obtain divisions from a taproot with a single crown, slice off an eye, catching some of the root with it. You can also cut off pencil-thick side roots. Plant these at an angle just below the soil surface.

Forked taproot If a taproot forks below the soil surface and forms multiple crowns, you can split it lengthwise to get several pieces, each with a crown, a portion of taproot, and branching roots or root buds.

 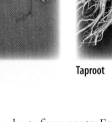  

Offset   Eyes on the root   Runner   Taproot   Forked taproot

roots. If bulbs, corms, rhizomes, tuberous roots or tubers are present on the division, they are healthy and plump.

The best divisions have a very small cut surface where they were once connected to the mother plant. If the cut surface is large, let it dry in a shaded location so the cut no longer presents an opportune place for fungi and bacteria to invade.

Make more plants with root cuttings

Division is only one way to create additional perennial plants from roots. For example oriental poppy grows readily from root cuttings taken in summer or early autumn during the dormant period. The easiest way to propagate oriental poppy is to slice off the upper portion of some of the roots at the edge of the clump.

(Backfill some soil over the part of the clump that you cut when you're done to encourage new growth.)

Look closely at the cuttings; you should find buds at the top of the root pieces. After allowing the cut end to dry, plant the small pieces of root into containers

▲ If rhizomes are too tough to break apart by hand, slice them into pieces with a heavy-duty knife. When dividing iris, pay close attention to the state of the roots. Iris borer enters the plant through rhizomes. If the rhizome is riddled with small holes or it is soft, mushy, and smelly, cut off and discard all affected parts.

▲ Another way to propagate perennials is called layering. Many perennials, including Russian sage, do this naturally. Stems lying on the ground begin to root and grow into new plants. With layering you help the natural process along by holding the stem down with a rock or a peg. When roots form, cut the stem below the roots and move the new plant to another spot in your yard.

Dividing & propagating perennials *(continued)*

◄ If you decide to create a new garden under a tree for your divisions from shade plants, take care when working soil to avoid damaging tree roots. Also be aware that cutting tree roots can lead to suckers growing from them.

of moist potting soil. Let them grow new roots. When new foliage begins, you can plant them into the garden.

With phlox, you can chop up the roots and scatter the pieces on top of damp sand in a flat or container. They will form new plants if you keep the sand evenly moist.

You'll need to grow the tiny plants in pots for several months before they are large enough to plant in your garden.

Plant the divisions

Before you set out the new divisions, prepare the soil for them as you would any new plant. This is particularly true if you want to plant a division in the same location as the tired plant you just divided. Add compost or well-rotted manure to the area or throw

DIVISION INTERVALS

Perennials can be grouped into broad categories based on how long they will continue to grow well without needing division. If a perennial does not appear on this list, take your cue from its growth habits. If it dies out in the center a few years after planting, and the number of flowers decreases, it will need to be divided more often than perennials that consistently flower well and look healthy after many years in the garden.

Divide every 2 to 3 years	Divide every 4 to 5 years	Avoid dividing unless new plants are needed
Aster	Anemone	Astilbe
Bee balm	Bleeding heart	False indigo
Black-eyed susan	Columbine	Lenton rose
Chrysanthemum	Daylily	Oriental poppy
Coreopsis	Pinks	Peony
Iris	Purple coneflower	Torch lily

Aster

Bee balm

Black-eyed susan

Chrysanthemum

Coreopsis

Iris

Anemone

Bleeding heart

Columbine

Daylily

Pinks

Purple coneflower

Astilbe

False indigo

Lenten rose

Oriental poppy

Peony

Torch lily

▲ Peonies form eyes at their crown. Make sure every division has five to seven eyes.

in a handful of slow-release fertilizer to meet the nutrient needs of the plant until the next time you divide. Thoroughly mix these materials into the soil.

Although having organic matter and nutrients in place to support strong, healthy growth is important, pockets of these materials right next to your new division may cause crown rot or root decay in the new plant.

If you are planting groups of divisions, position them so their growing points head in opposite directions rather than toward each other.

MOVING YOUR GARDEN

Thoroughly clean pots before planting divisions to avoid spreading disease to your plants or new garden.

You have put hours of work into your perennial garden, and after several years of planning, careful soil preparation, weeding, and watering, you have achieved the perennial garden you imagined when you started. Then you find out you must move.

It's perfectly normal to not want to leave your garden behind. And because perennials are small, they are easy to take with you and far easier to move than trees or shrubs. For the move to work, though, the climate in your new home must be similar to your current climate. If you are moving from Maine to Florida, few perennials will survive.

Most real estate agents will tell you that landscaping is one of the prime selling points of any property, so it may cost you dearly if you decide to dig up the whole garden. Instead take small divisions from each perennial. Pot the divisions or plant them in a nursery bed in a friend's garden for a few months.

Start preparing for the move several months to a year beforehand. The potted divisions need time to establish a root system before putting them through the stress of moving. Plant them in small containers rather than large ones so their roots will quickly fill the pots. If your move is delayed, you can always bump up the plants to a larger container. Sterilize the pots before planting by soaking them in a mild bleach solution. Use a sterile commercial potting mix to avoid taking any soilborne diseases, insects, or weeds with you. Always pot more divisions than you think you might need. If you don't use them, your new neighbors might appreciate them.

SOME THINGS TO REMEMBER:
- Always check with the state department of agriculture at your destination if you are moving across state lines. Some western states severely restrict the importation of plants. Other states may require that you have plants certified by your current state's agriculture department before the trip.
- Plants that are lovely and well behaved in your current location may be invasive weeds in your new home region. Check with the department of agriculture or a native plant society in your destination location to be sure that you aren't bringing problems with you.
- Inspect all plants before you pack them, and dispose of any sickly specimens.
- Make sure that plants are moist before you pack them. Water plants and let them drain well. After they drain, wrap them in several thicknesses of newspaper and pack them in a sturdy cardboard box. Spritz the newspaper with water to keep the humidity up inside the carton. Do not wrap plants in plastic; it can promote rot if excess moisture remains in the pots.
- Keep plants from heat and sudden changes in temperature during the move. If well watered and kept cool, potted perennials can go three to five days without additional water because they are in the dark and some humidity will be retained by the newspaper.
- Unpack plants immediately upon arrival. Don't wait until you've set up housekeeping to put them in sunlight and give them a drink.

Note your success

It may seem that all the tasks involved in maintaining perennials involve physical labor. However evaluating your garden and planning improvements are just as important as weeding, feeding, and watering.

Set aside time periodically to look critically at your perennial garden. What do you like most about it? What parts appeal to you the least? Are there color combinations

◀ Treat the division as you would any container plant. Dig a wide hole only as deep as the root ball. Set the plant in the hole and backfill halfway. Water to settle the soil, then finish backfilling.

that haven't worked out? Which plants have disappointed you, and which have far surpassed your expectations?

Use the information you gather to plan your next move in the garden. You may decide to completely rework a section of a perennial bed to improve drainage, or you may just want to tweak a bed outline a bit to give it a more pleasing shape.

Make some notes and use a calendar to plan the work. If you continue to make improvements, particularly in the first years of the maintenance phase, you will be generously rewarded with a garden that grows more beautiful every year.

▲ Water thoroughly then mulch the division. If planting near a tree, keep an eye on moisture because the tree's roots will compete for it with the perennial.

Preparing for winter

◄ Fall is a lovely time in a perennial garden. But the changing colors signal that you'll soon need to clean up the garden and ready it for the cold weather to come.

A lthough some perennials are evergreen, most are seasonal plants, and as the season progresses their growth will slow down. Eventually the foliage dries up, leaving only the buds at the crown of the plant. Some perennials develop lovely fall colors, and others simply turn brown.

The first hard frost may turn them black and brown, signaling time to clean up the perennial garden. This task consists mainly of cutting back all the plants and removing the debris. Not all plants need to be cut back at the same time, and you may want to think of your

fall cleanup as a heavier than normal garden grooming.

A few perennials with twiggy growth, such as chrysanthemum, benefit when the top growth is left on the plant until early spring. The mound of branches and dead leaves may help trap snow around the crown, where it can help to insulate tender buds.

Also, cutting back some borderline hardy perennials too early in fall may cause buds at their crowns to begin growing at a time of year when they are susceptible to cold damage. Most of these perennials are native to subtropical or warm temperate climates and may naturally start new growth in fall, even when they are in a colder climate.

Some perennials such as pinks and Lenten rose have evergreen foliage that should be left intact for the winter. In many areas, the cold weather doesn't damage the foliage and you don't need to cut it back even in spring. In very cold regions, though, the leaves become tattered during winter; remove them in spring when new growth appears.

Don't forget to water

Pay close attention to watering in fall and early winter. Perennials tend to make most of their new root growth in autumn, and dry soil will impede root growth.

Without a healthy new set of roots, your perennials will have less chance of making it through a harsh winter. They may also be more prone to frost heaving in areas that have repeated cycles of frost and warmth.

◄ Remove all stakes and drip hoses from the garden. Clean them up before putting them away for the year.

DIVIDE AND ADD BULBS

Fall is a good time to divide spring-blooming perennials that need renewal or restraint. It's also a good time to dig out and discard perennials that have not performed up to expectations. Make plans to replace them with species better suited to the site and your needs next spring.

While you're making design changes, consider adding spring-blooming hardy bulbs around and even beneath late-emerging species such as hardy hibiscus and Japanese anemone. Daffodil, crocus, and grape hyacinth are exceptionally long lived; they will bloom among your perennials for many years. Tulips are lovely but tend to die out in a few years.

Plant bulbs in midfall when the soil has cooled. The bulbs will send out roots in the cool soil in preparation for next spring. A good soaking after planting will encourage healthy growth.

▲ Cover sensitive perennials with 4 to 6 inches of loose mulch such as straw or evergreen boughs to ensure that frost heaving doesn't push them out of the ground. Wait until after frost to apply the mulch.

▲ Cut most perennials to the ground after frost. By removing the dead organic matter, you eliminate the places where disease spores and insects hide out over the winter. In time pests will be reduced in your garden.

Refresh garden mulch in fall, but wait until you've cut back all the other perennials that need to be cut back so the job is easier.

If slugs or snails have been a problem, wait to put down the mulch for a week or two after you clean up the garden so that the soil is exposed to sun. This helps to reduce the pest population. Take care to not pile mulch over crowns of plants and never apply it more than 4 inches thick.

After the soil freezes, put a blanket of straw or loose leaves, or evergreen boughs over the individual plants to insulate the soil and prevent frost heaving. A layer 6 inches or deeper helps protect plants from the worst of winter's cold. If you live where the ground freezes, apply the insulating material after the ground starts to freeze. Snow will do the same job so if your garden is typically snow bound, there's no need for extra mulch.

Place branches from Christmas trees, garland, and other holiday decorations over this mulch to better insulate plants and help to prevent the loose straw and leaves from blowing away.

▶ Preparing your garden for winter ensures that your plants return the next spring, bigger and healthier than ever.

Don't be tempted to pack snow from nearby walks and driveways on top of perennial beds. The extra moisture may keep them too wet in early spring, and the snow from these surfaces most likely contains salt, which can harm the perennials.

Spring wake-up

As days lengthen don't forget to check for signs of new life in your perennial garden. Cut back any perennial foliage that was left behind last fall and gradually pull blanketing materials such as straw and leaves away from plants. Keep them handy so you can quickly cover tender new growth if a late cold snap is forecast. After the new growth is too tall to cover, move the materials out of the garden entirely so the mulch is only 2 to 4 inches deep through the rest of the growing season.

Perennial care calendar

▲ In cold winter areas mulch perennials with straw, evergreen trimmings, or other loose mulch as a protection.

January

In cold winter climates, cover perennial beds with recycled evergreen boughs from garlands, wreaths, and branches from your Christmas tree. Save the trunk of the Christmas tree so you can use it as a stake when spring arrives.

Decide on your goals for the perennial garden this year. Write them down and look at them critically. Make

▼ Set stakes in place as plants begin to grow in spring. This could be February in warm climates or May in cold ones.

sure they will fit with other demands on your free time and adjust them as necessary.

Take a look at perennial catalogs. Circle potential new plants, and do some research in books and on the Internet to find out more about them. Develop a master list of plants you want to purchase by mail order or on the Internet and order them early.

If you have a greenhouse or grow lights, start seeds of perennials now for spring planting.

Check perennials during unusually mild or dry weather and water them if the soil is dry.

February

In mild winter climates, this is the month the perennial garden comes to life. Do your spring cleanup and eliminate any winter annual weeds before they have a chance to set seed. Get stakes and supports in place for tall, floppy perennials.

In cold winter regions, temperatures may begin to fluctuate wildly. Keep the soil in perennial gardens frozen by mulching it with loose straw or dry leaves.

March

In many regions, March marks the transition to spring. Move straw or other winter mulch away from the crowns of your perennials during warm spells, but be prepared to move it back if temperatures are forecast to dip below 20°F.

If spring starts dry and warm, give the perennial garden a good soaking.

Plant some potted spring bulbs in the perennial garden to add spots of color where you need it most. Choose bulbs that live and bloom indefinitely in your region so you can enjoy the spring show every year.

April

Get stakes and supports in place. This is the month of most active growth in the perennial garden—and your last chance to add stakes without damaging plants.

Watch for the arrival of pests such as aphids. Blast them off your plants with a stream of water from the garden hose.

Plant mail order perennials as soon as possible after they arrive. Irrigate if spring rains are sparse.

Eradicate crabgrass and other weeds as they appear. If you allow them to grow, they will be much more difficult to remove later.

May

In many perennial gardens May is the month of peak bloom. Take a photo of your garden every week so you have a record of what bloomed when. You can refer to the photos later when you are considering new plants. Gaps in the flower display will be very apparent in the series of photos, and you can seek plants that bloom during less colorful times in your garden.

Pinch chrysanthemums, bee balm, phlox, and asters now. Cut individual stems back to two sets of leaves.

Don't be tempted to apply fertilizer now. Most perennials won't be able to use the fertilizer during the heat of summer.

Add mulch to bare spots to prevent summer weeds, but be sure you're not accidentally mulching over a late-emerging perennial such as balloon flower or butterfly weed.

June

Keep the garden tidy by deadheading. Trim pinks and yarrow to promote another crop of flowers.

▲ Pinch late-flowering plants from early to midsummer.

Water your perennial garden thoroughly if rain doesn't do the job. If you are using sprinklers, make sure that tall plants aren't blocking the spray.

Divide iris rhizomes late in the month after the last flowers fade.

Pinch chrysanthemums and asters one last time near the end of the month.

Scout the perennial garden for weeds every week.

When hot weather arrives use the beat test (see page 140) to check for mites. Blast them off infested foliage with a jet of water from your garden hose.

▲ Divide iris after they have finished blooming in early summer.

As the leaves mature and the weather warms, container perennial gardens will need more water. Check them at least once a day if it hasn't rained.

July

Divide daylilies after they are done flowering so they have time to establish new roots before winter comes.

Take a critical look at your perennial garden. If there are plants that haven't done well or aren't as colorful as you'd like, plan to get rid of them so you can plant something else in fall or next spring.

Make a trip to your favorite nursery or garden center. Check for perennials that bloom in late summer to add some color during a time of year when color is hard to come by.

If heat has left your perennial garden looking tired, plant inexpensive foliage plants, caladiums, or heat-tolerant annuals among the perennials.

Tend to weeding before that summer vacation, and give your perennial garden a thorough soaking just before you leave.

▶ Prepare a new garden or renew soil in late summer to early fall while the weather is dry and the soil easy to work.

August

Fall-blooming perennials will bloom a lot more if you give them some extra water during hot dry periods.

Tidy up the perennial garden by pulling off dead leaves and trimming back diseased or insect-eaten plants. Most perennials are growing next year's buds near the soil line now, so be careful not to pull too hard on stems that might look dead—you could accidentally damage the buds at the base of the stem.

Pull off old daylily and bearded iris flowering stems as they wither.

If perennials such as lamb's-ear suddenly wilt and die in hot, humid weather, check the soil around the base of the plant. White fungal strands and small round yellow structures that look like mustard seeds indicate Southern blight. Remove all mulch and the soil to a depth of 6 inches. Bury the mulch and soil elsewhere in the garden. The fungus can only survive at the soil surface. Replace with clean, sterile garden soil, and apply a new layer of mulch.

As the nights grow longer and cooler late in the month, you may notice some perennials growing new rosettes of leaves. Encourage this growth by watering regularly if rains fail.

September

Apply a slow-release fertilizer to the perennial garden as the weather gets cooler.

Add some potted asters or chrysanthemums if you need a little extra color.

Add some kale or pansies to container perennial gardens for fall color. In

▲ Keep weeds under control throughout the summer.

mild-winter climates they will provide color all winter and in early spring as well.

October

Divide perennials this month. Add some compost and slow-release fertilizer to the soil if you are planting a division in the same location where the perennial you are dividing originally grew.

Keep the garden watered until the soil freezes.

Plant bulbs among your perennials to provide a spring show. Draw a map so you will know where you planted the bulbs. It will come in handy if you have to dig in the garden when the bulbs are dormant.

November

Autumn leaves make a great mulch for perennial beds. Blow or rake tree leaves onto the beds after cutting back and removing dead foliage from your perennials.

Build your soil by scattering some decayed manure, compost, or leaf mold over the perennial garden after cleanup and before adding mulch.

Protect container gardens from severe winter weather by insulating them with straw or bats of insulation, or move them into an unheated

▲ Clean up frost-nipped plants and other organic debris to prevent diseases from overwintering in the garden.

garage where temperatures fluctuate less.

December

Evaluate your stakes and supports. Rotting ones may need to be replaced. You can build attractive rustic supports from willow branches, grape vines, and wire; they'll add another dimension to your perennial garden.

Consider some of nature's treasures from your perennial garden for holiday decorations. Paint purple coneflower seedheads gold or silver to make bright stars, and stick the fluff from butterfly weed pods onto a gingerbread house or angel wings with spray glue.

Troubleshooting

▲ The size, shape, color, and location of spots on a leaf provide clues to the identity of the fungus or bacteria causing a disease so that you can select the correct treatment.

◀ Yellowing leaves may lead you to suspect that the plant has a disease. However, a nutrient deficiency can be just as likely. Before treating perennials with a pest control, do some sleuthing to find the cause. Otherwise your efforts could be in vain.

E ven the most carefully planned and tended perennial garden encounters a few problems along the way. Insects and diseases may damage the plants enough to blemish the garden that you have worked so hard to grow.

For any insect or disease to reach damaging proportions in your garden, two things must come together:

The right plants must be present. Some insects and diseases attack a wide variety of plants, but they are in the minority. Most pests are associated with only a few plants, often ones in a single genus or plant family. For example, iris borer lays its eggs only on iris roots.

The right environmental conditions must also be present. For the insect or disease to proliferate and cause significant damage, the conditions in which they

thrive must occur. For example powdery mildew occurs when the weather is dry but humid and air cirulation is low.

Perennials and the ecosystem

You may want to keep pests out of your perennial garden entirely. With all the hard work involved in creating a garden, it's easy to understand why. But insects, mites, and the spores of fungi, bacteria are all part of the web of life in the natural world in which your garden grows.

It's impossible to eliminate or intercept every microbe or creature that threatens the garden, so it's best to focus on making your plants as healthy as possible so they can withstand any attack.

Instead of striving for perfection, aim for a balanced perennial garden where insects and diseases may be present but in such low numbers that their damage is not noticeable. If you do this your perennial garden will support a whole ecology of pests and their enemies, and serious problems are few and infrequent.

◀ Caterpillars and other chewing insects eat holes in foliage and flowers. Other insects suck plant sap and transfer disease organisms from plant to plant.

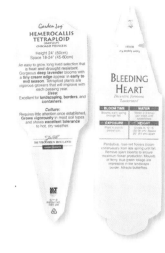

▶ Most plant labels provide information to help you correctly site and care for the perennials.

Choose plants wisely

The root of failure because of insects or diseases often lie in the selection of plants. Colorful images in catalogs or a pristine plant in the garden center may tempt you into buying something that ends up struggling in the conditions you can provide for it. Garden envy is part of every gardener's life. Floridians may long to grow peonies and Minnesotans may wish they could grow the pampas grass, which is an invasive plant in California.

It's great fun to try plants that are reported to be unsuccessful in your area, and you are bound to find some that will grow for you. But the mainstays of your perennial garden should be plants that do particularly well in your climate, soil type, and light conditions.

Be disciplined in plant care

One all-too-common cause of problems is a misunder-standing of what plants really need. Sometimes gardeners assign human qualities to plants and want to, say, give them a daily drink of water or extra fertilizer so the plants grow stronger. Such practices may predispose perennials to rank growth that is attractive to pests and the perfect environment for diseases.

More is not better when it comes to tending your perennial garden. Extra water, extra fertilizer, and extra mulch won't benefit the plants you are trying to grow if you have already supplied them with the optimal amounts. More may instead lead to their demise.

Sometimes even a slight alteration in your gardening practices may bring success where you experienced only failure before. If iris borers have been a problem for you, eliminating mulch may be the key to keeping them out of your garden. If your garden experiences frequent bouts with powdery mildew, thinning out the plants or growing resistant cultivars can help. If chrysanthemums have been a disappointment, perhaps pinching them a bit earlier in the growing season will result in success.

Plant for diversity

The strength of a perennial garden against pests and diseases often lies in its diversity. It's hard to find a perennial bed of any size that contains fewer than 10 kinds of plants. Since many pests are specific about the species

▲ Insects and diseases have greater trouble finding a host when a garden consists of a variety of species. They cannot readily move from plant to plant so populations stay low.

they attack, this diversity means that widespread problems are unlikely. Instead they will be contained to the few plants that are suitable hosts.

Sometimes gardeners are so smitten with one type of perennial that they grow it exclusively. A serious attack by a major insect or disease of this species could wipe out the garden. A one-species garden requires regular, careful attention to avoid problems. One fail-safe is to use annuals and other perennials to weave some diversity into the garden. Often this step also increases the beauty of the garden and shows the plant collection to better advantage.

Limit pest control use

Ironically overuse of some pest controls may also predispose a perennial garden to problems. The reason for this is simple. Harsh pesticides nearly always produce collateral damage by harming beneficial organisms. Good bugs die along with the bad bugs.

Pests and diseases are opportunistic, and if their natural enemies have been removed from the picture, they may have free reign over the garden. In no time at all must spray frequently just to protect your plants because

the pest controls are all that are keeping problems in check.

Think of pest controls as last-resort solutions and apply them strategically, only to the plants that really need to be treated. The remaining plants in your garden will serve as a refuge for all the beneficial insects, mites, and microorganisms. These beneficial creatures can move into the voids created by the spot application of pest control just as soon as the pest control has dissipated.

▲ Plants often tell you when they are in the wrong site. Scorch—dried leaf edges—indicates a plant is getting too much sunlight, wind, or too little water.

▼ A garden consisting of all one type of plant, such as daylilies, is more likely to suffer big losses if a pest moves in than a garden with a variety of plants.

Monitoring for pests

▲ Closely inspect your garden once a week to catch problems early, before they get out of hand.

THE BEAT TEST

Looking for damaged plants is one way to stay on top of pest and disease problems, and you can quickly get a picture of the pests you are dealing with and their numbers if you use this simple monitoring technique. The beat test is a tool you can use to find small insects such as aphids that blend in with the foliage of your perennials and tiny mites that are too small to see.

1 Attach a white sheet of paper to a clipboard. Hold the clipboard under the foliage of a plant you're checking.

2 Gently tap the foliage to dislodge any pests that may be present onto the clipboard.

3 Look at the paper to see if aphids or mites are crawling across it. If dust and debris also drops on the paper making it hard to see the pests, gently blow on the paper. Insects and mites will stay put because they have hooks on their feet to help them grasp the paper fibers while the debris blows off. Watch for tiny moving specks or use a magnifier or a jeweler's loupe to get a closer look at the pests. If your plants are showing signs of damage and you see many specks, you have the evidence you need to know it's time to start treating for the pests.

You need to know what is going on in your perennial garden before you formulate a plan to deal with pests and diseases. The only way to get detailed information is to take a close look at the plants. Do this every week or two through-out the growing season. It's an enjoyable task, and you can proceed at a leisurely pace and get to know and appreciate your perennials on a completely different level of detail.

If you make a minute inspection of your garden, you may be overwhelmed at first. You will find insects at every turn that you have never seen before, and it may seem that each plant is host to some disease or other.

If you realize that your goal should not be about attaining perfection but to instead have a healthy garden, you will quickly realize that most of what you are looking at is no cause for concern. There's no need to identify every insect that you encounter, and it won't pay to agonize over every spot on every leaf. If something is clearly damaging your plants, you do need to be sure that you have correctly identified the insect or disease that you are dealing with so you can select the appropriate control method.

How many pests?

Predicting pest damage is a numbers game. Background

GALLERY OF GOOD GUYS

Every gardener is familiar with a few beneficial insects such as ladybugs. Few are aware of what the different life stages of these insects look like and that mites, true bugs, and wasps are important biological control agents in the garden.

Ladybug

Everyone knows what a ladybug looks like, but few recognize the eggs, larvae, or pupal cases that precede the adult stage of the insect. Several species are found in North America. The imported Asian ladybug has especially become common in recent years.

Adult ladybugs are often sold in garden centers or by mail order. They are collected from locations where they gather to wait out the hottest part of summer, and are then kept under refrigeration until sold. They arrive at the retail outlet or your doorstep ready to fly long distances to get back to their breeding areas from which they were collected, so it is difficult to keep them in the garden in which they are released. It's better to rely on local populations of ladybugs.

Predatory mite

Not all mites are pests. Some, such as the predatory mite, may be present in the garden without you knowing it. When you are doing a beat test to detect mites and small insects on your plants, you might see a few predatory mites moving rapidly across the paper. They are more translucent than pest mites and have longer legs that allow them to move faster than their prey.

Syrphid fly

Also known as flower flies and hover flies, syrphid flies are important predators of aphids and mites. They look like bees or wasps, but their large eyes and single set of wings set them apart from the bees and wasps they mimic. Syrphid flies can usually be found hovering near daisy or carrot family flowers.

Aphidiid wasp

An important parasite of aphids and scale insects, this wasp is a gnat-size insect too small to harm people. It lays eggs inside pest insects; the eggs hatch and develop inside the pest, killing it.

Praying mantid

Often thought to be beneficial, praying mantids actually are not effective predators of common garden pests. They are territorial and never exist in numbers high enough to have much impact on pests. Often their diet consists of bees and butterflies, and so they can be considered pests in a butterfly garden.

Ladybug

Ladybug pupal case

Ladybug eggs

Ladybug larvae

Predatory mite

Syrphid fly eggs

Syrphid fly larvae

Syrphid fly

Aphidiid wasp

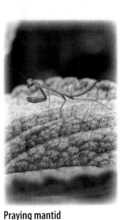

Praying mantid

levels of pest insects and mites are present throughout the growing season, but they won't do much damage if their populations stay low. How do you tell when there are enough pests to cause significant damage? Experience is the best teacher, but numbers are a more objective measure. (See "The Beat Test" sidebar.)

If you count 10 to 20 pest insects or mites per beat test, that's a background amount, which usually does not require treatment. And if the damage is evident on 10 percent of the plant or less, it will not be very noticeable; you can wait a while longer before taking action.

Look for pests frequently so that you can spot them before they do a lot of damage. It's just as important to look for your allies in the garden so you won't be led to take drastic action when nature is at work providing its own pest control.

Beneficial insects and mites can be found in nearly every garden as long as only the least toxic pest controls are used, their use is infrequent, and they are applied to just a few plants.

Common pests

Mites

Spider mites on phlox

Often found on the underside of leaves, mites suck sap out of the leaf surfaces They are actually tiny spiders and not insects at all.

Mites lack wings and spread when blown by the wind. They may hitchhike on plants that you have purchased for your garden.

They favor dry, hot weather and dusty conditions. Because they can multiply quickly in hot weather, it's important to monitor your plants frequently during hot spells.

Damage to perennials: Mites create fine pale yellow stippling on leaves.

Control: Knock mites off plants with a jet of water from your garden hose. Be sure to wash off the underside of the foliage as well. In severe infestations you may have to treat plants with horticultural oil. Predatory mites often keep pest mites under control. The beat test (see page 140) is the best way to determine if mites are present in your garden.

Aphids

Aphids are common pests in almost every garden, and many species exist. All suck sap from plant tissues; they usually

Aphids on hardy hibiscus

prefer to live on the succulent new growth near the tips of stems. You may see white or greenish skins shed by the aphids along with the insects.

Most aphids are female, which have the ability to give live birth to identical females without mating.

Aphids can spread plant viruses. They are active in cool weather and typically disappear in the heat of summer, when predators and parasites tend to reproduce rapidly enough to reduce or eliminate them.

Damage to perennials: Aphids may distort leaves and secrete sugary honeydew, which appears as shiny spots on foliage. The honeydew may support the growth of black sooty mold in areas where there isn't enough rain to wash it off the plants.

Control: A strong jet of water aimed at the growing tips of plants is often sufficient to remove aphids. You can also use insecticidal soap to bring aphids under control. Avoid overfertilizing and overwatering because new, succulent growth promotes higher populations of aphids. Ladybugs, syrphid flies, and aphidiid wasps will usually control aphids if you allow aphid numbers to increase to 10 to 20 per shoot tip; these beneficial insects need to have a threshold amount of aphids present before they lay eggs.

Thrips

Tiny cigar-shape insects that feed inside flowers, thrips arrive in your garden in spring, riding southerly breezes. Or they

Thrips damage to sage

may live in your garden year round, overwintering in the soil under host plants. Because thrips feed on flowers, it doesn't take a high population to do significant damage to your garden. These insects spread some viruses.

Damage to perennials: Thrips have scraping mouthparts, and their damage appears as white streaks in affected flowers. Foliage may also be damaged.

Control: Minute pirate bug is a beneficial insect that appears in the longest days of summer and usually bring thrips under control. Some beetle and mite species also prey on thrips. They are also effectively controlled by pest controls that contain a fungal by-product known as spinosad.

Leafhoppers

As their name implies, these aphid relatives hop away from the plant they are infesting when they are disturbed. Leafhoppers arrive on southerly breezes in spring and are primarily a concern in perennial gardens because they spread the incurable disease known as yellows or aster yellows. They are most damaging in hot microclimates where predators and parasites such as spiders are lacking.

Leafhopper on aster

Damage to perennials: Leafhoppers feed on the underside of leaves and cause a coarse yellow stippling on the leaf surface.

Control: Since they hop away from plants, contact pest controls (ones that must touch the pest) are not very effective. Apply a pest control containing acephate when you notice the damage on the leaves. Select heat- and drought-adapted perennials for gardens in areas with intense reflected heat, such as near driveways, patios, and sidewalks.

True bugs

This broad group of insects includes many beneficial insects and some pests. The species that are most damaging to perennials are the four-lined plant bug and the tarnished plant bug. The four-lined plant bug is yellowish green and has four black lines down its back and wings. The tarnished plant bug is ¼ to ½ inch long and green, brown, or rust colored. It is found in all regions and is unusual in its broad host range.

Tarnished plant bug

Damage to perennials: The four-lined plant bug makes holes in the small leaves near the tips of stems. It is most damaging to plants in the mint and aster families, although it may feed on many other species. The damage usually takes place early in the season, and plants are usually able to outgrow the damage.

The tarnished plant bug distorts new growth by feeding on it. The damage may worsen throughout the season because there are two to four generations each year.

Control: Wash young bugs from the foliage with a strong jet of water, or crush them by squeezing infested growing tips of plants. Horticultural oil and insecticidal soap are effective on the just-hatched insects, which are rather soft-bodied. Pest controls containing pyrethrum or synthetic pyrethroids control the insects for a longer period. A thorough cleanup of the perennial garden may control the bugs because they lay their eggs on the foliage of host plants and the eggs hatch in spring.

Borers

Any pest that feeds within the roots, rhizomes, and stems of a plant is called a borer. The main borer problem in perennial gardens is the iris borer, which is a common pest on bearded iris. It is the caterpillar stage of a drab-looking moth that lays eggs on iris foliage in fall. The eggs hatch in spring after flowering, and the tiny caterpillar bores downward as

Iris borer entrance hole

it feeds, growing much larger when it reaches the rhizome. Even worse, iris borer carries a bacterial disease that rots rhizomes, turning them mushy and smelly.

Damage to perennials: Tall, thick-stemmed perennials may also be attacked by borers. A small hole with a bit of granular material on the outside just below the hole may be the only sign of an infestation. Growth above the borer may wilt and die.

Bacterial rot, which often follows iris borer

Common pests *(continued)*

Control: Keep your garden cleaned up and remove any afflicted plants or plant parts as soon as you notice the problem. Because borers live deep within plants, they're not readily controlled with most pest controls. Keep mulch off iris rhizomes and be sure that the top of the rhizome is planted at the soil surface.

Iris borer damage

Leaf Miners

Leaf miner damage to columbine

These larvae of small flies feed between the upper and lower surfaces of leaves, tunneling through the leaf as they grow. Various species of leaf miners, which often attack only certain plant species, may appear at anytime during the growing season. Chrysanthemum, hollyhock, and columbine are frequently damaged by leaf miners.

Damage to perennials: Leaf miner feeding creates light green or yellow tunnels visible on the surface of leaves.

Control: Since they are sandwiched between the upper and lower leaf surfaces, leaf miners are not easily controlled by pest controls unless they work systemically (the pest control is taken up by plant roots and circulated through all plant tissue). In most cases simply removing infested leaves or shearing the plant back and destroying the clippings effectively eliminates the problem. Leaf miners often are present in weedy areas; mow or clean up these areas frequently to prevent leaf miner problems in your garden.

Caterpillars

Swallow tail butterfly larvae on swamp milkweed

Various caterpillars may chew on the leaves of your perennials. Some, are quite beautiful. For example, the larvae of the monarch butterfly, which feeds on butterfly weed and other milkweeds, is colorfully striped and turns into pupae that appear to be decorated with gold leaf. Other caterpillars, such as cutworms, are less attractive and do more damage.

Damage to perennials: After feeding on foliage some caterpillars leave behind large holes. At times the feeding damage is small and just a few leaves are chewed.

Control: Many gardeners choose to let species of caterpillars that turn into beautiful butterflies live in their gardens. You can pluck caterpillars from plants if they cause unacceptable levels of damage, or you can treat plants with a pest control containing *Bacillus thuringiensis* (Bt). Horticultural oil and

Zebra caterpillar eating iris flower

Arched owlet caterpillar

insecticidal soap usually control young caterpillars. Protect plants from cutworms by placing a collar made from a paper cup with the bottom cut out around newly planted perennials with tender young stems.

Sawflies, which are related to wasps and bees, may look like caterpillars in their larval stage, but aren't controlled by Bt. Hardy hibiscus is the only major species of perennial attacked by sawflies, which you can control with an application of insecticidal soap or horticultural oil.

Grasshoppers

Grasshopper feeding on daylily

Most damaging in the West, grasshoppers often feed on grasses and forage crops. They may become a problem in perennial gardens if farmers working in the fields displace them or if their population becomes high. Hot, dry weather favors them. Adult females lay eggs in the soil.
Damage to perennials: Grasshoppers feed at the margins of leaves, and, if their numbers are high enough, they may quickly strip plants of all leaves.
Control: You may be able to cover a small garden with a floating row cover to protect plants from grasshoppers. You will need to bury the edges in a trench around the garden so that wind doesn't blow it off and the grasshoppers can't get under the cover. The cover should remain in place as long as the grasshopper population is high.

Even after they've been defoliated established perennials usually recover from a grasshopper attack. Keeping adjacent areas mowed during the early part of the season may prevent a large grasshopper population from developing near your perennial garden. A naturally occurring microbe, *Nosema locustae*, provides good control if applied over a broad area while the grasshoppers are small.

Japanese Beetle

Adult Japanese beetles feed on the leaves and flowers of a few perennials and other landscape plants. A small number of them can do a large amount of damage. When the beetles find a suitable food source, they give off a scent that attracts other Japanese beetles. The females periodically lay eggs on the ground; the larvae feed on the roots of grass and are a major lawn pest.

Japanese beetle on tree mallow

Damage to perennials:
Japanese beetle eats the tender tissue between leaf veins, giving it a skeletal appearance. It may eat large holes in the more tender flower petals.
Control: If you and your neighbors control Japanese beetle larvae in your lawns, there will be few adults to cause problems in your perennial garden. A fungus called milky spore is effective in controlling larvae over the long term but may take several years to work after being applied to a lawn. Maintain a healthy, dense lawn and the Japanese beetle will not have a chance to get a toehold in your yard.

Traps that are sold for controlling adult beetles usually attract many more beetles than they ever trap. You can easily knock the beetles off plants into a bucket of soapy water since they instinctively play dead and fall off the plant when threatened.

Japanese beetle damage to hollyhock

Slugs and Snails

Slug and snail damage to hosta

Slugs are similar to snails but lack a hard shell. Both creatures are mollusks, not insects or mites. They prefer damp areas and feed on a wide variety of plants. They glide around on slime that they secrete, and the dried slime trails are often evident near the ragged holes they make in leaves with their rasplike mouthparts.

Damage to perennials: Slugs and snails chew through succulent leaves leaving behind ragged holes. They are common pests in shade gardens and can be particularly troublesome to hosta.

Slug and slime trail on iris bloom

Control: Mulch and plant debris in the garden provide areas that shelter slugs and snails. Clean up debris and consider removing the mulch if snails or slugs are a big problem. Without this protection they are likely to move on. Frequent irrigation creates damp conditions around plants that favor slugs and snails, so water more judiciously. Toads feed on the pests, and installing a garden pond on your property in which toads can breed may help control slugs and snails.

Baits containing iron phosphate are effective and will not harm pets and other animals that ingest them. You can trap slugs or snails in a saucer filled with beer or a yeast solution; renew it every day until the pests are gone. Slugs and snails will not cross a barrier of copper because copper reacts with their slime to form toxic compounds. You can make collars from copper flashing to place around particularly susceptible plants such as hosta.

Voles, Gophers, and Other Rodents

An underground barrier, such as chicken wire stapled to the bottom board of a raised bed prevents burrowing animals from moving in.

Rodents that feed on perennials can do a lot of damage in a short time. Even if they don't feed on your plants, they may damage them with their incessant tunneling. Freshly dug soil is often the first sign of rodents, and wilting plants may be evident where they have been at work.

Rake mulch and debris away from plant crowns to eliminate places where voles and other critters can hide.

Damage to perennials: Wilting plants and plants that easily dislodge from the ground when given a gentle tug signal a possible vole, gopher, or other underground rodent.
Control: Trapping and barriers may offer some control. Knife or scissor traps, which kill the rodent as it tunnels through the yard may be used; check with your local animal control authority or county extension service for advice on the preferred method of trapping in your area.

Barriers of thorny twigs stuck into the soil around perennials or stones placed around plants may discourage these animals. More effective is lining the bottom of a raised bed or planting hole with hardware cloth. Ultrasonic devices sold for repelling rodents do not work in a garden setting.

Clean up debris around the garden to eliminate areas that voles use for protection from birds of prey, snakes, and other predators. Cats may control many of the rodents that can damage the perennial garden, but not every cat is adept at hunting every type of rodent. Blood meal may discourage these animals, but the effect is temporary in most cases.

Rabbits

Rabbits make a clean, straight-across cut.

Although they are fun to watch, rabbits habitually feed on the same plants in your garden and may frustrate your attempts to grow some perennials. They reproduce rapidly, and their population usually cycles with the population of fox, coyotes, and other predators.
Damage to perennials: Rabbits eat succulent new foliage and are often particularly troublesome in early spring when they forage on newly emerged perennials. They often eat from the bottom to the top of the plant and may prefer one side of the plant or garden that is closest to shelter.
Control: Protect your perennial garden from rabbits by constructing a low fence of poultry mesh. The fence needs to extend below the soil surface at least eight inches since rabbits can dig quite well. It doesn't need to be any higher than two or three feet since rabbits cannot climb well. Blood meal may repel rabbits for a short time; it will need to be replenished periodically as its odor dissipates. Repellents such as distasteful sprays or scented items may be temporarily effective. Individual rabbits differ in reaction, so change products often. Dogs and cats may help limit a rabbit population.

Deer

Deer may first be attracted to the lawn but quickly move on to other tasty plants.

By far the most rapidly growing animal pest problem, deer have adapted well to suburban life by feeding on many ornamental plants including annuals, perennials, shrubs, and trees. If you think deer might be browsing in your garden, look for hoof prints in soft soil.
Damage to perennials: Plants may appear as if they were roughly clipped, and deer may pluck succulent blossoms from plants as they appear.
Control: Hunting to thin deer herds in your local area is the best form of control, but may not reduce the population enough to reduce damage to your perennials. An electric fence baited with peanut butter is an effective barrier. Plastic mesh also provides an effective barrier since deer are far sighted and cannot see it. They run into it and it startles them. This type of fence must be firmly anchored to the ground at frequent intervals since deer can easily slink under fences that are not.

Liquid repellents may work for the short term, but if the deer population is high and food is scarce, they will get used to the scent of almost any product that is used. You can also plant a lovely garden of perennials that are not palatable to deer. For a list of deer-resistant plants, see page 25.

A black wire mesh fence is nearly invisible to both you and the deer. It should be at least 8 feet tall.

Common diseases

Many different agents, some of which are not even really considered living organisms cause diseases. As mentioned previously, the right plant and the right environmental conditions must be present for a disease-causing agent or insect to become problematic. With diseases, theses factors need to come together for a critical minimal period of time.

Clematis wilt

Managing diseases in your perennial garden really just entails taking steps to make sure that disease-causing agents are not present and that environmental conditions are not conducive to disease development. If you can avoid overhead irrigation that wets the foliage, you may be able to avoid most fungal diseases. If you are careful to keep mulch away from the crown of the plant (the point where stem meets roots), then the plant will dry more rapidly after rain or irrigation, helping them to escape the fungi that cause crown rot. You can foil some diseases by simply planting disease-resistant plant varieties.

If you choose to use fungicides or other pest controls to combat diseases, be aware that they don't work in the same way as insecticides and mite controls. Most need to be applied as a preventive before disease symptoms appear. Usually an application is timed so the material is on the plant before weather conditions favorable to disease development are forecast. It's much easier to prevent diseases than cure them. The most critical time for applying these protective materials is at the start of the growing season.

Breeders have been actively developing perennials with enhanced disease resistance. Resistance is a relative term, and even the most resistant plant may show some signs of disease under certain circumstances.

Diseases are often opportunistic; they tend to afflict sickly plants that are growing in poor conditions than they do plants that are growing in good conditions. A plant that normally is very resistant to a disease may be made susceptible if it is grown in the wrong soil or is subjected to stressful conditions.

Leaf spots

Bacterial leaf spot on geranium

Fungi, bacteria, and viruses all cause spots on plant leaves, but fungi are the most common cause of leaf spots. Often the spots have a yellow, red, or purple border, and the dead leaf tissue in the middle is tan or brown. The leaf spots may continue to expand if weather conditions are conducive to new infections, and there may be concentric rings of damage. In some instances leaf spots may grow and coalesce to kill entire leaves; they can kill entire stems as well. In this severe form the disease is often called anthracnose. Some leaf spots cause premature leaf loss.

Leaf spots caused by bacteria are generally more irregular than those

Anthracnose leaf spot on toadlily

caused by fungi, which tend to be round or oval.

Spots caused by viruses tend to be bordered in purple, and the plant is stunted. Viruses also cause a kind of mottling or variegation on the leaves.

Control: You can control some leaf spots by thoroughly cleaning up plant debris in the garden before plants begin growing

Leaf spot on black-eyed susan

in the spring. The clean up eliminates overwintering spores that survived on the dead growth from the previous year.

A fungicide labeled for both leaf spots and the plant you want to treat may be useful if you apply it as the new growth begins to emerge. Copper is an effective preventive fungicide, and it is one of the few materials that effectively controls bacterial diseases.

Leaf spots caused by viruses are not curable; remove and destroy afflicted plants if they are stunted and do not look normal. Avoid overhead watering, especially if plants in your garden have suffered from leaf spots in the past; the splashing water may spread spores. Most diseases also need a water film on the leaf surface for several hours for the spores to germinate.

Botrytis blight

Leaf spot on peony caused by botrytis blight

Always an indicator of poor air circulation and high humidity, botrytis blight (also known as gray mold) is a common disease, particularly on faded blooms. The gray fuzz you see on afflicted plant parts are the prolific spore of the fungus that causes botrytis blight. Peony is a frequent target of the disease, but many other perennials may come under attack. Long periods of rainy, cloudy weather

encourage the growth of the fungus. In favorable conditions the disease may also affect leaf and stem tissues.

Control: You can usually control botrytis by thinning out the garden so your perennials have more space around them. When plants are crowded together, dew and rainfall dry slowly, creating favorable conditions for

Botrytis blight on peony blossom

the fungus. Prune nearby shrubs and trees to encourage better air circulation in the perennial garden.

Deadhead perennials frequently because botrytis often gets a toehold in the garden on dead flowers. You can also use a fungicide labeled for the control of botrytis and the plant you wish to treat. Apply it just as the blossoms are starting to open.

Vascular wilt

Sudden wilting, even when the soil is wet and plant roots are intact, is a sure sign of vascular wilt. Often the disease is caused by fungi such as *Fusarium* and *Verticillium,* but bacteria and other agents can cause the disease. The spores are present in soil and plant debris, waiting to attack plants stressed by drought, saturated soil or other environmental factors.

The fungi grow in the water-

Streaking of vascular system from fusarium wilt

conducting vessels in the stem tissue, causing them to become clogged. The leaves begin to turn yellow then wilt because the clogged vessels cannot meet their demand for water. In the final stages roots and stems are killed and the whole plant dies. If you were to cut through the stems, you would see black or brown streaks running through it.

Control: Start with disease-free plants. Avoid planting your garden in soil where plants have died from vascular wilts in the past. If you have spot for a garden, solarize the soil before planting to reduce the number of disease spores (page 90). Make sure that the soil in which the perennials are growing is well drained. Fungicides are not effective in combating vascular wilts after the disease has made it inside the stem tissue.

Powdery Mildew

A white coating on leaves and flowers is the hallmark of this fungal disease. Unlike most diseases that invade the plant tissue and grow among the cells, powdery mildew grows on outside surfaces; it grows "pegs" of tissue into the plants cells and absorb nutrients from the plant sap.

Leaves may be distorted and smaller than normal if the infection is severe. Powdery mildew is unlike most other fungal diseases because its spores are killed by prolonged exposure to water. It thrives in dry but cloudy weather conditions and high humidity. **Control:** Simply washing the foliage with water may kill many of the spores on the leaf surface but doing so may aggravate other fungal disease problems. Pest controls containing potassium bicarbonate, horticultural oil, or neem oil provide good control.

Since most of the disease-causing fungus is on the outside of the plant, powdery mildew is one of the few diseases that can be cured by spraying after it has appeared.

If possible select mildew-resistant varieties. Many good mildew-resistant varieties are available for some of the most commonly afflicted perennials, such as phlox and bee balm. Among them are 'David' phlox and 'Marshall's Delight' bee balm.

Powdery mildew on phlox

Powdery mildew on columbine

Rust

Orange or mahogany spots that rupture the leaf surface are distinct signs of rust. Different species of plants host different species of rust, and most rust fungi have an alternate host that is an entirely different plant species. Rust seldom kills plants. **Control:** Avoid wetting leaves; also clean up all remnants of last year's foliage before new growth begins in spring; rust fungi don't always need to go to their alternate host before causing new infections on your perennials.

Rust on chrysanthemum foliage

Plant a rust-resistant variety when possible. Hollyhock and daylily are common hosts of rust. Daylily rust, a recent import from Asia, is a relatively new disease in North America, catching many daylily growers off guard. There are varying degrees of rust resistance among the hundreds of daylilies available from specialty nurseries, and efforts are being made to identify the most resistant varieties.

Rust on aster from underneath the leaf

Yellows

As its name indicates, this disease manifests itself in a general yellowing of foliage. It is caused by a type of parasitic microorganism known as phytoplasma and is spread from plant to plant by aster leafhoppers. All plants in the aster family are potential hosts, as are many other perennials, including aster, delphinium, black-eyed susan, chrysanthemum, and purple coneflower. Yellows also distorts flowers, causing a proliferation of small blooms that are green and leafy-looking.

Control: Once a plant has yellows, it cannot be cured. Remove the plant from the garden and destroy it. Control leafhoppers (see page 142) to prevent the spread of the disease. Because yellows is often present in weeds it is important to control dandelion, plantain, and other weeds in your lawn and elsewhere in your landscape.

Yellows on purple coneflower

Root rots

Many fungi attack roots, but the water molds that cause *Pythium*, *Phytophthora*, and *Rhizoctonia* root rots are the most common. Poor drainage and saturated soil conditions favor water molds. Even though the soil is moist and the stems are intact, plants may wilt because of the sudden death of much of the root system. The dead roots are brown and shriveled, and the outer portion of the root easily pulls off.
Control: Make sure the soil in your perennial bed drains well and avoid frequent irrigation that makes the soil soggy. Extremes of drought and saturated soil may predispose plants to root rot. High salt content, due to salty irrigation water or overfertilization, may also make roots more susceptible.

Rhizoctonia root rot on baby's breath

Fungicides are available for use as a soil drench, but they are not a cure; they merely prevent new infections. If your soil is poorly drained, stick to perennials that like wet conditions such as cardinal flower, joe-pye weed, and Siberian iris.

Southern blight

This fungal blight is a common problem wherever hot and humid weather is common during the growing season. Plants die quickly, and rot is evident in the crown of the plant. White strands of fungus are often visible on the dead stems near the soil surface. Yellow spores that look like mustard seeds are often seen near the crown of a dead perennial. Southern blight is favored by frequent watering, acidic pH, and mulch that touches or covers the crown of plants. Some plants, such as lamb's-ear, may recover to some extent, but most perennials are killed by this disease.
Control: Keep mulch away from the crowns of your perennials and water infrequently but thoroughly. Deep tilling before planting to bury the spores is helpful, since they may persist for many years in the soil and burial deprives them contact with the crown of any plant.

You can place a thin mulch of pea gravel around the crown of susceptible perennials to create an environment that is less hospitable for the fungus. Solarizing your soil (see page 90) kills spores near the soil surface where they can cause damage. Any fungicides you apply must be done preventively as a drench, which usually is not practical to do in perennial gardens.

Petiole blight on hosta caused by southern blight

Crown rot on hosta caused by southern blight

Viruses

Almost all plants carry one kind of virus or another. Some viruses cause few noticeable symptoms, but others stunt plants and produce yellow or mottled spots on the leaves. Impatiens necrotic spot virus causes tan spots bordered in purple. In some cases, viruses drastically reduce flowering. Viruses spread when infected plants are propagated by cuttings or division. Aphids, thrips, and leafhoppers also spread the disease organisms from plant to plant.

Control: Viruses don't always cause significant damage to perennial plants. If any of your plants are severely stunted by a virus, remove them from the garden and destroy or discard them. Control aphids, thrips, and leafhoppers to limit the spread of viruses.

Hosta displaying streaking and variegation typical of a Hosta X virus disease

Nematodes

Nematodes are tiny roundworms that make up a significant portion of soil life. Many species of nematodes play a vital role in soil ecology, and a few cause plant disease.

Plants suffering from root-feeding nematodes become severely stunted and turn yellow because of the decreased ability of the roots to take up nutrients. Infected roots have many round or spindle-shape galls on them. Foliar nematodes feed on leaf tissue and infect tender new foliage as it emerges in spring. They cause the areas between the major veins in the leaves to turn brown and die. Hostas and Japanese anemones are commonly afflicted by foliar nematodes.

Control: Because nematodes cannot withstand much heat, soil solarization is effective. You can also control foliar nematodes by cleaning up all leafy debris in the garden by early winter. Dig and divide affected perennials and dip the divisions in hot water to kill the nematodes. The dip should

Nematode damage on butterfly bush *(Buddleia)*

be between 120° and 140°F; leave the divisions in the dip for 10 minutes. After dipping plunge the divisions into cool water and plant them immediately in a location away from where the original plant grew.

Mutations and Reversions

Sometimes an otherwise healthy plant may have a branch or other part with flowers of a different color or leaves that are variegated. These are caused by chance mutations that do not affect the overall health of the plant. If the mutation is attractive, you can propagate it by divisions or cuttings. Similarly cultivars of perennials that originated as a chance mutation of another cultivar may spontaneously revert to the original form.

Control: No control is needed, but if you want to maintain the original form of the plant remove the mutated portion.

The mottling on a few leaves of this peony results from a mutation. Several clues help you tell whether it's a virus or mutation. Virus-free mottling is random, affects just one plant, does not "bleed" from the veins, and fades in dim light.

PEST DETECTIVE

The following chart will help you figure out which pest, or pests, are attacking your perennials. Often multiple pests are at work on a single plant, and the plant may show several symptoms. This chart covers some of the most prominent garden pests.

1. IS THE PLANT WILTING?
   Yes. Go to number 8.
   No. Continue to number 2.

2. DOES THE FOLIAGE APPEAR TO HAVE BEEN EATEN OR CHEWED?
   Yes. Go to number 10.
   No. Continue to number 3.

3. DO THE LEAVES HAVE A STIPPLED APPEARANCE OR DO THEY APPEAR TO HAVE TUNNELS?
   Yes. Go to number 11.
   No. Continue to number 4.

4. ARE THE FLOWERS DAMAGED?
   Yes. See thrips (page 142), Japanese beetle (page 145), and botrytis blight (page 149).
   No. Continue to number 5.

5. ARE THE ROOTS DAMAGED?
   Yes. Go to number 9.
   No. Continue to number 6.

6. ARE LEAVES MARRED WITH COLORED SPOTS OR A FUZZY OR RUSTY COVERING?
   Yes. Go to number 12.
   No. Continue to number 7.

7. DOES THE PLANT HAVE UNUSUAL LEAVES, STEMS, OR FLOWERS?
   Yes. Go to number 13.
   No. Continue to number 8.

8. CAREFULLY EXAMINE A PORTION OF THE ROOTS OF THE WILTING PLANT. DO THEY APPEAR TO BE HEALTHY?
   Yes. See vascular blight (page 149).
   No. Go to number 9.

9. EXAMINE THE DAMAGED ROOTS. WHICH DESCRIPTION BELOW BEST CLOSELY DESCRIBES THE DAMAGE?
   Roots are severed a few inches below the crown of the plant. See voles, gophers, and rodents (page 146).

   The roots have pronounced round galls or growths. See nematodes (page 152).

   The roots are mushy and decaying. Or the growth near the crown of the plant is decaying. See borers (page 143), root rot (page 151), and Southern blight (page 151).

10. EXAMINE THE LEAF DAMAGE. WHICH DESCRIPTION BELOW BEST DESCRIBES THE DAMAGE?
   Large sections of leaves are missing, primarily on the uppermost part of the plant. See deer (page 147).

   Large sections of leaves are missing, primarily on the bottom part of the plant. See rabbits (page 147).

   Ragged roundish holes mar several leaves. See slugs and snails (page 146) and caterpillars (page 144).

   Many leaves are damaged and large portions of the plant may be defoliated. See Japanese beetle (page 144) and grasshoppers (page 145).

   Small holes can be seen on young, succulent new leave and stems. See true bugs (page 143).

11. EXAMINE THE LEAVES CLOSELY. WHICH DESCRIPTION BELOW BEST DESCRIBES THE DAMAGE?
   The stippling or raised surface is pale yellow. See mites (page 142) and leafhoppers (page 142).

   The surface of the leaf is smooth, but light green or yellow tunnels are visible. See leaf miners (page 144).

12. EXAMINE THE SPOTS CLOSELY. WHICH DESCRIPTION BELOW BEST DESCRIBES THE SPOTS?
   The discoloration is rust colored. See rust (page 150).

   The leaves appear to be covered with a powdery white substance. See powdery mildew (page 150).

   The spots are shiny or appear to be a black sooty substance. See aphids (page 142).

   The spot is bordered with a purple, brown, red, or yellow ring. The interior of the spot may be tan or brown, dead tissue. See leaf spots (page 148).

13. EXAMINE THE UNUSUAL GROWTH. WHICH OF THE FOLLOWING BEST DESCRIBES THE GROWTH?
   There's general yellowing of the foliage along with a possible proliferation of flowers that are green and leafy. See yellows (page 151).

   Leaves are mottled or variegated and may be distorted (twisted). Plant growth is stunted and flowering is reduced. See viruses (page 152).

   The plant sports an unusual branch or flower exhibiting a different color or growth pattern. See mutations and reversions (page 152).

Control methods

◀ A strong blast of water controls aphids because as it knocks them off the plant, their mouthparts rip off. This is a type of physical control.

▲ Mechanical controls, such as deer fences, prevent the pest from reaching the plants or the garden.

Chemical pest controls were once the standard treatment for many pest and disease problems. With mounting concerns about the environment, more gardeners are now trying to avoid the use of these materials in their gardens.

Various nonchemical control methods— with no potential for harm to the environment—are effective against many pests and diseases. These measures won't control every problem, and there is no reason why they cannot be used in tandem with pest control treatments, particularly if the pest control you choose isn't very toxic and targets only the pest.

Physical control

Physical control uses physical means to limit pest damage. While you are tending your perennial garden, you can squash pests or their eggs to prevent further damage. If this approach is a bit too hands on for you, you can drop them in a bucket half-filled with soapy water.

Many insects are beneficial, so be sure the insects you are killing are actually troublemakers. You can prevent the spread of disease by removing infected leaves as soon as you see damage and also by cleaning up the garden, especially in fall to prevent harmful organisms from surviving winter in your garden.

Mechanical control

Mechanical control is the use of some type of barrier to keep pests from reaching plants. Controls used for deer and rodents are usually mechanical controls, as are copper barriers used to keep slugs and snails away from plants they like to eat.

Cultural control

Cultural control is the manipulation of the growing conditions to favor plants and thwart pests and diseases. Limiting nitrogen fertilizer to plants that are susceptible to aphids is an example of cultural control.

Because many fungi require a protracted period of moisture before spores can germinate, cultural control is perhaps the most powerful tool in disease control. By avoiding overhead irrigation or limiting it to the early morning hours, you avoid having the foliage wet long enough for disease spores to germinate.

Biological control

Biological control is the use of beneficial organisms to combat an insect or disease problem. You could purchase

▲ Cultural controls involve manipulating the growing environment. For example, scratch fertilizer into the soil near heavy feeders rather than applying it to the entire garden to prevent problems in perennials that prefer infertile conditions.

▲ When the pest population is so large and active that other controls don't work, it's time to apply chemical pest controls.

beneficial insects for biological control in your garden, but often they do not stay in your garden. However, if you limit pest control applications and grow a diversity of plants that produce pollen and nectar, you will probably have an abundance of insects, mites, and other organisms working with you to control pests.

Quarantine

Quarantine is the stockpiling of plants that you have recently purchased or received in a remote part of your yard so you can determine if pests or diseases are present on them before planting them in the garden. Even plants from a reputable nursery may have low levels of pests or diseases on them that were suppressed by frequent pest control application at the nursery. In your garden, these problems may multiply once the effects of the pest controls wear off. Delay planting new perennials in your garden until you are sure they are not harboring pests and diseases that are new to your garden.

Chemical control

Chemical control is the use of traditional pest controls to keep pests in check. If you have concerns about health and environmental hazards when using these materials, be aware that not all pest controls are equal in toxicity, and many have little impact on the environment.

Start with reduced-risk pest controls, such as horticultural oil. Many of these materials kill through physical methods, preventing pests from becoming resistant to them. For example, horticultural oil smothers insects, and insecticidal soap burns the skin of soft-bodied insects. Soaps and oils will not control all problems that you encounter in your garden, and from time to time you may want to use a more conventional pest control on a tough pest or disease.

Systemic pest controls are taken up by the plant and move within the plant to provide protection from pests for a certain period of time ranging from a few days to a full season or longer in the

case of some new controls. Limit the use of the most toxic pesticides because they may harm beneficial organisms and result in the pest rebounding because of the loss of these controls.

Some gardeners want to tend a completely organic perennial garden—meaning they use no chemical fertilizers or pesticides in the garden. Organic options may not provide the same level of control as more conventional pest controls, and some organic controls may actually be more toxic to the environment and disrupt beneficial organisms more than conventional non-

organic controls available for the same problem. Organic gardening is primarily concerned with the source of materials used in the garden and does not necessarily concern itself with the cost or impact of the materials.

Resistant plants

Resistant plants are not damaged as often or as seriously as more susceptible varieties. If you have a choice, always choose insect- and disease-resistant cultivars. Resistance is not immunity, and in the right conditions plants may still be attacked by insects and diseases.

▲ Planting pest-resistant perennials prevents many diseases from ever moving into a garden. 'David' is a mildew-tolerant phlox.

Encyclopedia of perennials

▲ Surround yourself with beauty by selecting the best plants for your garden. In this encyclopedia you will find a diverse array of plants for all regions. You'll find ones that speak to your heart as well as thrive in your yard. You'll learn about the conditions they need for growing.

Perennials can make your garden a delightful place to work, play, and entertain. In previous chapters, you've seen how planning ahead helps make your dream garden a reality, saving you time and money in the process. Finding healthy plants and planting them right moves you further down the garden path. Maintaining your garden keeps it vigorous and protects it against the pests and diseases that sometimes visit your yard.

Now it's time to look at specific plants and select the ones that are best for your garden. This encyclopedia features more than 400 perennials. It explains the plant's preferred growing conditions, any special needs, day-to-day growing tips, and advice for using the plant.

In the encyclopedia you'll find a few bulbs, such as lilies, and woody plants, such as clematis, common sage, and caryopteris. These plants are particularly well-suited to combining with perennials. In some regions, a few such as caryopteris have a similar life cycle to that of perennials, dying to the ground in winter and reappearing from the roots the next spring.

Key to the entries

The encyclopedia is organized by common names. However because of the inconsistencies in common names, botanical names are given as well. When shopping for plants, the botanical name will ensure you're getting the plant you expect. You'll also find cross-references within the encyclopedia to help guide you to the entry for any perennial you want to learn more about.

Next you'll find a pronunciation guide to the botanical name. Many new gardeners are fearful of looking foolish when trying to pronounce botanical names. The truth is, Latin is a dead language and most people, including the experts, mangle it. Although the guide is simply one way of pronouncing the words, it will give you the courage to speak with confidence and fool even the haughtiest botanical snob.

Following the pronunciation, you'll find a quick guide to the plant. Here you'll learn the main reason for growing it (its features), its hardiness, bloom time, size and shape, as well as its preferred site preferences.

Hardiness tells you whether a plant will survive winter in your region. The range of hardiness zones listed is only a rough gauge of a plant's ability to withstand summer stresses in a region, such as heat, humidity, drought, wind, and pests.

Bloom time uses generalized terms because spring, summer, and fall arrive at different times around North America. For example, early spring occurs when the earliest bulbs and trees begin to bloom in your region, which may be February in warm climates and late April in cold ones.

▲ 'Paprika' yarrow is a relatively new cultivar with bright red flowers all summer long. It does best in warm, dry climates with low humidity. When not in bloom, the foliage makes a lovely gray-green groundcover.

▲ 'Star Gazer' lilies are nearly everyone's favorite, with their sweet scent, moderate size, and pastel pink blooms.

Fall is when trees, shrubs, and other plants prepare for a dormant period, changing foliage colors and begin dropping their leaves. This may occur in late November or in December in warm climates and in early September in cold ones.

Light required provides an approximation of how much sunlight the plant needs during the growing season to be healthy, develop to its full potential, and bloom well. Where high heat and humidity are the rule, a plant may do better with less light than normal. In cool climates it may thrive in much more light.

The description goes into more detail about the plant's attributes and about using it in your garden. Care provides more in-depth information about the plants' site needs and explains whether it has any specialized care needs that deviate from standard perennial care. It tells you when and how to plant the perennial as well as how often to divide it and when or if you need to deadhead, stake, or pinch. You'll also find information on pests that

may be troublesome.

Species and cultivars tells you about outstanding cultivars available for each species and about their cousins or related species. If no other cultivar or species is listed, the main entry is the only ornamental choice or the only one on the market. As much as possible, the species and cultivars listed provide choices for all parts of North America.

Most of the perennials in the encyclopedia are easy to locate at nurseries and garden centers throughout North America. Unusual selections are available by mail order.

▲ Shasta daisies are great in a cottage garden or anywhere you'd like an informal planting.

▶ Peonies, such as 'Coral Supreme', are plants for cool climates rather than the South. They're a traditional flower for Memorial Day decorations.

Agapanthus (*Agapanthus* hybrids)

ag-uh-PAN-thuhs hybrids
Features: Large blue flowers
Hardiness: Zones 7 to 11
Bloom time: Late spring to early fall
Size: 1 to 5 feet tall, depending on cultivar
Shape: Low mound of foliage with tall upright flowers
Light: Full sun to part shade
Site: Well-drained soil

Agapanthus

Description: This South African native produces dense round umbels of bell-shape blossoms at the tops of long stems. Plants range from 1 to 5 feet tall when they are in bloom and are half that size around. They eventually grow into large clumps of glossy, strappy evergreen leaves that are attractive even when plants are out of bloom. Flower colors vary from pale to deep blue and white.

Let the tall flower stalks weave among the other perennials in your garden to provide large dots of blue throughout the space. Or grow agapanthus en masse for a swath of vivid blue. Plants do well in large containers, a boon to gardeners in cold climates. Agapanthus makes dramatic cut flowers, and flowers last five to seven days in a vase. The dried seedheads also add interest to arrangements.

Care: Agapanthus does best in full sun or light shade. Provide afternoon shade in very hot climates. They'll grow in heavy shade, but blooming is greatly reduced.

Agapanthus is available as ready plants in containers or as bare rhizomes. If using rhizomes plant the roots 1 inch deep, spacing them 1½ to 2 feet apart. When planting in containers use one rhizome in a 12-inch pot or three in a 20-inch pot.

Water regularly during the first year to encourage plants to grow a healthy root system. After they are settled in, water when the top 3 inches of soil are dry. Deadhead spent flower stems.

Divide plants every two or three years in early spring. If growing plants in containers, let them become rootbound before dividing. This usually takes four or five years. In cold regions bring containers indoors over winter.

Species and cultivars: 'Back in Black' has dark purple-blue flowers

White agapanthus

on top of dark black-green stems. Flowers of 'Blue Heaven' are a dark sky blue. The plants grow 1½ to 2 feet tall. 'Danube' has violet-blue flowers marked with purple. 'Peter Pan' grows just 8 to 12 inches tall and blooms in blue. 'Snow Storm' offers snow white blooms on 2- to 2½-foot-tall and wide plants. The foliage of 'Tinkerbell' bears creamy white stripes along the edges, and the flowers are pale blue.

Amsonia (*Amsonia* spp.)

am-SONE-ee-uh species
Features: Pale blue flowers, brilliant fall color, lacy texture
Hardiness: Zones 3 to 9
Bloom time: Late spring
Size: 1 to 3 feet tall and wide, depending on species
Shape: Mounded to round
Light: Full sun to part shade
Site: Moist, well-drained soil of average fertility

Arkansas amsonia in autumn

Description: Amsonias are shrubby perennials noted for their fine texture and two or three seasons of garden interest. Two species make up the group, Arkansas amsonia and blue star amsonia. Both grow in tidy mounds and bloom with clusters of starry light blue flowers on the tips of their stems in mid- to late spring. The blooms of Arkansas amsonia are a little steelier blue and darker than those of blue star. The plants also have narrower leaves and foliage that turns brilliant yellow in fall. Both amsonias remain attractive in the winter landscape until beaten down by heavy snows.

Care: Amsonia requires little care. Grow it in full sun or under trees that cast light shade, such as honeylocust or young birch trees. If shade is too deep, plants will become floppy. Stake them or cut them back to 6 inches after blooming has finished to encourage more compact growth. Amsonia does best in moist, well-drained soil of average fertility, but it will tolerate wetter and drier soils. However plants become floppy in soil that is too rich or fertile; again cut them back. Cut stems exude a milky sap.

The flowers are followed quickly by abundant seedpods and, in the right conditions, amsonia self-seeds aggressively. Deadhead after blooming to keep the number of volunteer seedlings under control.

Species and cultivars: Arkansas amsonia (*A. hubrechtii*) grows 2 to 3 feet tall and has steel blue flowers and bright yellow fall color. Zones 5 to 9.

Blue star (*A. tabernaemontana*) is a carefree native plant that resembles Arkansas amsonia except for its wider, darker green leaves, slightly coarser landscape texture, and lack of fall color. It grows a little more upright than Arkansas amsonia and is a little shorter (1 to 3 feet tall). Zones 3 to 9.

Jones bluestar (*A. jonesii*) has blue-tinged ivory flowers in late spring to early summer. Foliage changes to yellow in fall. It tolerates as little as 10 inches of water a year and as much as 30 inches. Plants are slow to establish; but once settled in they are long lived. Zones 4 to 8.

Anemone *(Anemone ×hybrida)*

uh-NEM-own-ee HI-brid-uh
Features: Pink, white, or dark rose flowers
Hardiness: Zones 5 to 8
Bloom time: Late summer to fall
Size: 1 to 3 feet tall, 2 to 3 feet wide
Shape: Spreading irregular mound
Light: Partial shade to full sun
Site: Moist, fertile, well-drained soil high in organic matter

Description: From late July until frost and sometimes even for a few weeks after frost, pastel, 2-inch-wide cupped flowers dance on slender stems above the foliage of hybrid anemones. The graceful blooms may be single or semidouble and come in white or shades of pink. Each has a ring of golden stamens at the center. The long, sparse flower stems give the plant a see-through quality. Flowers are excellent cut, and you can use the seedheads in flower arrangements.

Plants have large leaves that are lobed like a maple. The foliage hugs the ground, standing no more than 2 or 3 feet above the ground until plants bloom. Flowers rise above the plant on 3-foot or longer stalks. Because of the plant's ultimate height and slowness to send up shoots in spring, it's best to grow it in the middle of the border. Some cultivars vigorously spread by rhizomes and, once established, quickly grow into large masses that crowd their neighbors.

Hybrid anemone

Care: Grow hybrid anemones in moist, fertile, well-drained soil with plenty of organic matter. Partial shade is best, especially in the South where they can suffer from high heat and humidity. In cooler northern regions they'll do fine in full sun.

Plant anemones in spring. Some cultivars can be slow to become established and bloom; just give them time. Cut the plants back in late fall after frost has stopped growth. In Zone 4 mulching heavily after frost often enables you to grow anemones, which are not hardy in your area.

To control the spread of the anemones, dig up and discard the rhizomes that grow beyond the space designated for the plants. Often the rhizomes have few roots; if you want to propagate your plants, pot up the rhizomes and let their roots develop before repotting them in the garden or passing them on.

Snowdrop anemone

Species and cultivars: In bloom 'Honorine Jobert' is 3 to 4 feet tall and covered with abundant 2-inch-wide pure white single blooms. Plants spread but do so less rapidly than other cultivars. 'Queen Charlotte' grows 3 to 5 feet tall and displays 3-inch-wide pink semidouble flowers with bright golden stamens. 'Party Dress' is 3 to 4 feet tall and 3 feet wide with large pink double blooms. 'Bressingham Glow' has rose-red flowers on 2- to 3-foot-tall stems.

Japanese anemone *(A. hupehensis)* is similar to hybrid anemones, but plants are shorter (2 to 2½ feet tall) and bloom a little earlier than hybrid anemones. Flowers vary from rosy mauve to bright pink. 'September Charm' is a 24-inch-tall cultivar. Its single flowers are rich pink on the inside and darker pink on the outside. 'Prince Henry' has semidouble deep rose blooms. Zones 5 to 8.

Snowdrop anemone *(A. sylvestris)* is a spring blooming, spreading perennial with fragrant white flowers and yellow stamens. Plants grow 6 inches tall by 12 inches wide, forming tidy clumps. The attractive leaves are deeply lobed. Zones 4 to 8.

Artemisias *(Artemisia spp.)*

ar-tem-ISS-ee-uh species
Features: Silvery fine textured foliage. Drought tolerant and deer resistant.
Hardiness: Zones 3 to 7, depending on species and climate
Bloom time: Not grown for flowers
Size: 1 to 3 feet tall depending on species
Shape: Mounded to upright to spreading
Light: Full sun
Site: Poor to average soil, excellent drainage

Description: Grow artemisias for their magnificent fuzzy silver foliage that complements nearly all other perennials and helps pull together the diverse colors within a garden. The plants make good backdrops for blue and purple flowers, such as those of speedwell and perennial salvia. The silver foliage also harmonizes with ornamental grasses such as 'Sapphire' blue oat grass and burgundy-leaved 'Rubrum' fountain grass, a tender perennial. Flowers are tiny and rarely noticeable. Most artemisias are well behaved but some, such as white sage artemisia, spread rapidly.

Care: Grow artemisias in full sun in infertile to average sandy soil. Plants are drought tolerant and need excellent drainage and good air circulation around them. Roots rot in wet soil; plants growing in soil that is poorly drained are unlikely to survive winter, even where hardy. Artemisias also have a problem with humidity. Shear plants that become floppy or open in the center by one-third to one-half. Most artemisias are woody. Prune to control size and shape in spring after plants leaf out. Cut herbaceous species to the ground in fall.

'Powis Castle' artemisia

Silver mound artemisia

Species and cultivars: Beach wormwood *(A. stelleriana)* with its broadly lobed furry leaves and tiny yellow flowers may be confused with dusty miller. It's an excellent species that tolerates salt spray. Plants grow 1 to 2 feet tall and 2 to 3 feet wide. 'Silver Brocade' is a shorter cultivar, only 6 to 8 inches tall by 12 inches wide. Its woolly white leaves are ideal for softening the edge of containers and low stone retaining walls. Zones 3 to 8.

Fringed sage *(A. frigida)* grows 8 to 18 inches tall and about 12 inches wide. The silver-gray leaves are finely cut, soft, and evergreen. Small yellow flowers are borne in profusion on slightly nodding stems in spring. Plants grow well in full sun or part shade in most soils. They prefer a pH of 6 to 8.5. Watering promotes rapid growth but may cause crown rot; 8 to 12 inches of water a year is adequate. Remove spent flower stems to keep plants neat. Zones 3 to 8.

Silver mound artemisia *(A. schmidtiana)* forms 1- to 2-foot-tall mounds of soft, fine textured silvery foliage. It grows best in cool climates and infertile soil. Where the climate is too hot and humid or the soil too fertile, plants languish, becoming floppy and open in the center and eventually failing. Silver mound looks stunning with 'Blue Clips' Carpathian bellflower, 'Purple Rain' salvia, 'Walker's Low' catmint, and 'Royal Candles' speedwell. It is not a spreader. Zones 3 to 9.

White sage *(A. ludoviciana)* grows rampantly, forming upright spreading masses of 2- to 3-feet-tall stems with aromatic silver leaves. Give plants plenty of room to expand. White sage is not a low maintenance choice for a garden, but it is especially useful for holding the soil on a hillside in hot, dry areas. It does well throughout the West. Zones 4 to 9. 'Silver King' and 'Silver Queen' are aggressive silver-leaved spreaders. 'Valerie Finnis' is a hardier, more moderate spreader with silvery white leaves. It is 18 inches tall by 18 to 24 inches wide and a better choice for gardens. Zones 3 to 8.

Hybrids: 'Huntington', with its aromatic, filigreed silvery leaves, grows 18 inches to 5 feet tall, depending on its location. It is tallest in frost-free climates. Zones 5 to 7. 'Powis Castle' grows 2 to 3 feet tall and wide or larger on the West Coast, and forms an upright mound of lacy silver leaves. It does especially well in warm climates. Zones 6 to 8.

Asters *(Aster spp.)*

ASS-tur species

Features: Late season blooms in pink, rose, white, purple, or lavender
Hardiness: Zones 4 to 9
Bloom time: Mainly late summer to fall
Size: 1½ to 5 feet, depending on species
Shape: Upright to rounded, depending on species
Light: Full sun
Site: Well-drained soil

Description: Asters are staples of the perennial garden. Treasured for their bright-hued fall flowers, a few asters actually bloom from June to October. The aster family is one of the largest in the plant world, and dozens are available for use in gardens. Most are easy-care perennials. All have daisy flowers in rosy reds, hot pink to light pink, all shades of purple, and almost blue. In some species the daisies are 1 to 2 inches across; others are only ½ inch or so wide. Asters are naturals for meadow and prairie gardens, but they're just as appropriate for perennial gardens and for containers with ornamental grasses.

Care: Most asters require full sun; white wood aster thrives in sun and partial shade. In the South asters may be short lived. Growing them in a shady area, especially one that

'Hella Lacy' New England aster

receives afternoon shade, will help plants survive the high heat and humidity. Plants growing in shade often become floppy, and tall plants can become lanky. Stake to keep plants upright, using grow-through supports, or pinch stem ends once a month from spring to early summer.

Deadhead routinely to prolong bloom and control self-sowing. Cut plants back after they bloom in late fall. Divide plants every two to three years in spring to control spread and renew plant vigor. Discard the oldest central section.

Powdery mildew, rust, wilt, and a viral disease known as aster yellows is a common problem. Select disease-resistant cultivars and plant asters in well-drained soil where they will have good air circulation. Water early in the day so that foliage dries quickly. If your asters develop wilt or aster yellows, it's best to dig them up and discard the plants. Do not plant new asters in these spots. Aster yellows are spread by insects with piercing-sucking mouthparts, such as thrips and aphids. Controlling the insects will help prevent the disease.

Species and cultivars: Calico aster *(A. lateriflorus)* is a 2- to 3-foot mounded, shrubby plant with white daisies in late summer to fall. 'Lady in Black' is distinguished by its handsome blackish purple foliage. It has small white flowers in September and October. Zones 5 to 7.

Frikart's aster *(A. ×frikartii)* is a 2- to 3-feet-tall and -wide summer bloomer. Plants form tidy mounds and are disease resistant. Straight species have lavender-blue daisies that last eight weeks or longer. 'Monch' is 2 feet tall and has lavender-blue semidouble blooms from June to September. 'Wonder of Staffa' is similar but slightly taller with paler blue flowers. Zones 5 to 8.

New England aster *(A. novae-angliae)* is one of the best known garden asters; however the

Calico aster

New York aster

straight species is rarely grown. Upright plants are 4 to 6 feet tall and have large, 2-inch-wide, many-petalled daisies in autumn. 'Purple Dome' is only 18 inches tall and has bright purple flowers in September and October. 'Alma Potschke' blooms from August to frost with bright, red-violet daisies; it grows to 4 feet tall. Zones 4 to 8.

New York aster *(A. novii-belgii)* is even better known and more widely grown, with more than 100 cultivars available. Also called michaelmas daisy, it grows 1 to 6 feet tall and 3 feet wide and has violet daisies in late summer to fall. 'Alert' grows 12 to 15 inches tall and wide and has large red-purple daisies. 'Mt. Everest' has white flowers and grows 3 feet tall and wide. Zones 3 to 8.

Smooth aster *(A. laevis)* has yellow-centered blue daisies and grows 3 to 4 feet tall. 'Blue Bird' is 3 to 5 feet tall with yellow-centered violet-blue flowers in cone-shape clusters in September and October. It is mildew resistant. Zones 3 to 8.
Hybrids: 'Woods Pink' grows 18 inches tall and has pink single flowers from August through October. Plants are mildew resistant. Zones 4 to 8.

Astilbe *(Astilbe spp.)*

uh-STILL-bee species
Features: Feathery plumes in pink, red, white, or lavender
Hardiness: Zones 4 to 8
Bloom time: Early, mid-, or late summer
Size: 6 to 40 inches tall, 18 to 36 inches wide
Shape: Airy, upright clump while in bloom; mounded when not
Light: Partial to full shade
Site: Moist, well-drained soil

Chinese astilbe

Description: Astilbe brings a graceful note to shady landscapes and brightens a shade garden. The flower cluster may be a tight upright spire, a compact steeple, or a loose drooping plume. Foliage forms a bronze to green ferny 6-inch to 3-foot-tall mound; the flowers rise above the plants another 1 to 2 feet. Mass astilbes as a groundcover or group them in perennial beds and borders—along with blue-leaved hosta and Japanese painted fern—or next to a pond or stream. The arching plumes rise above the foliage and look good in fresh or dried arrangements. Astilbes bloom in early, middle, or late summer, depending on the type.
Care: Astilbe requires consistently moist, well-drained soil

in partial to full shade. If plants do not receive enough moisture, their leaves dry out and turn brown. Deadhead early blooming species to encourage rebloom. Cut plants back in late fall or early in spring before new growth begins. Astilbes rarely require dividing but if you want to propagate plants, divide them in fall. Plants also spread by seed; if using astilbe as a groundcover, avoid deadheading to encourage self-sowing. Few pests bother astilbe; its main problem is intolerance to drought.
Species and cultivars: Chinese astilbe *(A. chinensis)* and its cultivars tend to be more drought tolerant than other astilbes. They bloom in late summer. 'Pumila' is a compact plant, 10 inches tall and 12 inches wide in bloom and only 6 inches tall when not in bloom. It has lavender-pink plumes and dark bronzy green leaves. It makes an excellent groundcover or edging plant. 'Superba' grows nearly 4 feet tall with magenta flowers and shiny dark green leaves.

Pink hybrid astilbe

'Fanal' astilbe

'Visions in Pink' offers fluffy pale pink blooms on a 1½- to 2-foot-tall plant. Its foliage is bluish green. Zones 4 to 8.
Hybrids: Most other astilbes are lumped into the general category of hybrids. Among the best is 'Sprite', which grows 12 to 18 inches tall. It has shell pink plumes in mid- to late summer, followed by reddish brown seedheads. 'Deutschland' is another good choice. It grows 24 to 30 inches tall with ivory plumes in late spring and early summer and dark green leaves. 'Rheinland' grows up to 30 inches tall and wide, has clear pink flowers, and blooms in early summer. 'Fanal' blooms in midsummer with dark red blooms. It grows 24 inches tall and 18 to 24 inches wide and has red-bronze leaves.

Autumn fern *(See Ferns)*

Avens *(Geum species)*

GEE-um species
Features: Dazzling hot-hued blooms and handsome foliage
Hardiness: Zones 5 to 7
Bloom time: Late spring through summer
Size: 10 to 12 inches tall to 2 feet in bloom, 1 to 2 feet wide
Shape: Mounded
Light: Full sun, afternoon shade in warm climates
Site: Fertile, well-drained, moist soil

Description: Grown for roselike flowers in electric hues of red, orange, and yellow, avens is a hit at the front of the

Avens with lady's mantle

perennial border, especially when massed for impact. The long blooming flowers grow on wiry stems that are good for cutting and for bringing life to the garden as they blow in the wind. The flowers rise above a compact basal rosette of hairy leaves that have zigzag or scalloped edges.

Avens attracts butterflies and looks good in and out of bloom. Good partners include violet-blue 'May Night' salvia and yellow 'Goldquelle' cut-leaf coneflower.

Care: Avens can be short lived. But if you provide the necessary growing conditions to keep plants vigorous, you should be able to keep your plants for many years. These conditions include cool temperatures and consistent moisture.

Avens does best in cool climates. In warm climates try to cool plants by making sure they have shade from harsh afternoon sun. Water abundantly. Provide continuously moist but well-drained soil during the growing season. In winter soggy soils will kill plants. Fertilize in spring and deadhead to extend blooming. Plants rarely need division.

Species and cultivars: Chilean avens (*G. chiloense*) grows 2 feet tall and 1½ feet wide and have single or double scarlet flowers. Plants bloom in spring. 'Mrs. Bradshaw' has semidouble scarlet flowers on 1- to 2-foot-tall and 2-foot-wide plants. Blooms of 'Dolly North' are tangerine-gold and semidouble; plants grow 2 feet tall and 1 foot wide. 'Lady Stratheden' bears buttery yellow semidouble blooms in loose clusters. It grows 15 to 24 inches tall by 24 inches wide. Zones 4 to 7.

'Mrs. Bradshaw' avens

Avens (*G. coccineum*) is a later bloomer than Chilean avens. The brick red flowers start in late spring and last through June. Plants grow 1 to 1½ feet tall and 1 foot wide. 'Borisii' has orangy-red single blooms all summer; it grows 10 to 18 inches tall. 'Werner Arends' offers long-lasting clear orangy-red semidouble flowers. Zones 3 to 7.

Water avens (*G. rivale*) thrives in cool, wet situations. Plants grow 8 to 12 inches tall and bloom in late spring to midsummer. 'Leonard's Variety' has coppery-pink blooms in mid- to late summer. Zones 3 to 8.

Hybrids: 'Fireball' has large, 1½-inch-wide semidouble orange-yellow blooms. Plants grow 2 feet tall and wide. Zones 5 to 7.

Baby's breath *(Gypsophilia paniculata)*

jip-SO-feel-yuh puh-NICK-yew-law-tuh
Features: Clouds of tiny white flowers
Hardiness: Zones 3 to 8
Bloom time: Summer
Size: 18 to 36 inches tall, 36 inches wide
Shape: Low mounds of foliage from which tall flower stems emerge
In- and out-of-bloom size: 18- to 36-inch by 36-inch open mound
Light: Full sun
Site: Well-drained alkaline soil

Baby's breath with annuals

Description: Baby's breath makes the perfect backdrop for showy garden flowers. You may know it as the filler florists add to their packages of cut flowers. In bouquets—fresh or dried—its dainty flowers are the perfect foil for red roses. In a garden baby's breath plays the same role; use it as a filler or as a background in perennial borders and containers.

The flower stems create the plant's presence in the garden. These tall, stiff, many-branched stems are an airy mass highlighted by a cloud of tiny white blooms. Out of bloom or after cutting all the flower stems for bouquets, a low mound of foliage hugs the ground. Baby's breath belongs in the middle of the garden where the nonblooming plant doesn't detract from the scene and the blooming plant weaves among its neighbors to create living bouquets.

Care: Baby's breath is easy to grow in full sun and light, well-drained alkaline soil. Plants do poorly in acid soil; add lime if your soil is acidic. Baby's breath needs average moisture and fertility. Deadhead plants to promote reblooming. Taking off spent bloom stems to the base may stimulate another flush of flowers in fall. Do not divide plants. You may need to stake plants; use grow-through supports.

Species and cultivars: 'Bristol Fairy' grows 2 to 3 feet tall and has white double flowers. 'Flamingo' is a 3- to 4-foot tall plant with double pink blooms. 'Pink Fairy' grows only 18 inches tall and has double pink flowers that last into fall.

Creeping baby's breath (*G. repens*) grows just 8 inches tall and 12 to 20 inches wide. White, pink, or purplish flowers arise from its bluish-green foliage. Plants are charming at the front of the border, in rock gardens, or at the edge of a path. 'Rosea' is shorter at 8 inches tall and has pale pink blooms. Zones 3 to 7.

Baby's breath blooms

Balloon flower *(Platycodon grandiflorus)*

Platte-ih-COH-done grand-ih-FLOR-us
Features: Lovely blue-violet, white, or pink flowers
Hardiness: Zones 3 to 8
Bloom time: Summer to fall
Size: 24 inches tall, 12 inches wide
Shape: Upright
Light: Full sun to partial shade
Site: Well-drained, slightly acid soil

Balloon flower with astilbe

Description: Balloon flower takes its name from its puffy colorful buds that open into large, cupped, pointed stars that are long lasting in the garden and in a vase. Blooming begins in early summer and with deadheading can last through much of the summer. The flowers develop at the tip of the strong, upright stems. Plant form varies from upright-columnar to vase-shape. The dark green foliage has an interesting coarse texture that complements the other perennials in your garden.

Balloon flower looks enchanting near the front of the garden and pairs well with finer textured and mounded plants, such as fleabane, blanket flower, butterfly weed, artemisia, yarrow, and catmint. Low mounded varieties are good for rock gardens and edging.

Care: The only condition necessary for healthy balloon flowers is good drainage. Some will need staking, especially tall plants in hot climates or those planted in shade. Use a grow-through support or brace each stem. Short varieties form dense mounds and need no support. Deadhead flowers individually; plants exude a sticky milky sap that is not harmful to you or the plant. Because balloon flowers emerge later in spring than most other perennials, mark their location in fall to ensure you don't damage their crowns or roots when working in the garden the next spring. Plants rarely need to be divided and moving them is difficult. Balloon flowers are pest and disease free. If you leave the seedheads, they often self-sow. That's a problem only in small gardens or when growing both tall and dwarf varieties. Seedlings can outcompete the smaller varieties and replace them.

Balloon flower with phlox and coreopsis

Species and cultivars: 'Albus' grows 24 to 30 inches tall and has large white flowers. 'Astra Pink' grows 10 inches tall; its pink blooms are marked with darker pink veining. 'Fairy Snow' is a 12-inch-tall plant with white blooms decorated with blue veining. 'Hakone Blue' has double blue flowers; plants grow 20 inches tall. 'Hakone White' is similar but with double white flowers. 'Hime Murasaki' is an 18-incher with big blue-violet blooms. 'Mariessii' blooms in mid- to late summer with blue-violet flowers on 24- to 30-inch-tall stems. 'Sentimental Blue' grows just 6 to 8 inches tall and has long lasting 3-inch-wide blue flowers.

Barrenwort *(Epimedium spp.)*

epp-ih-MEAD-ee-um species
Features: Petite blooms, heart-shape leaflets, and red to copper fall foliage.
Hardiness: Zones 4 to 8
Bloom time: Spring
Size: 4 to 12 inches tall, 12 to 18 inches wide
Shape: Mound
Light: Partial to full shade
Site: Moist, well-drained to dry soils

Description:
Barrenwort spreads at a moderate pace, forming a graceful, dense groundcover. It thrives in dry shade, growing well in shady rock gardens and under shrubs and dense-canopied trees. Most plants have an upright, mounded shape when not in bloom. The flowers add another 2 inches or so to the plant's height. The flowers dangle on wiry stems above the foliage; they're dainty and not showy from a distance but are a welcome sight nonetheless. Plants bloom in early to midspring. The flowers, which have spurs that spread out from the center of the bloom, appear in spring and look like a bishop's miter, hence another common name for the plants: bishop's hat. Flower colors among the different species vary and may be white, pink, purple, red, or two-toned.

Red barrenwort

Foliage is evergreen but can become tattered during winter in cold climates. New leaves open bronze, then turn green.

Care: Barrenwort requires little care. It flourishes in fertile, well-drained soil high in organic matter and also does well in dry shade. Barrenwort thrives in all but the darkest corners. Plant it under deciduous trees or where it will receive some shade. Maintain consistent moisture for the first season in the garden. Remove tattered foliage early in the growing season to tidy up the plant and to make its delicate spring flowers easier to see.

Species and cultivars: Featherleaf barrenwort *(E. pinnatum colchicum)* produces yellow

'Rose Queen' long-spur barrenwort

flowers on 12-inch stems that top an 8-inch clump of dark evergreen foliage. Zones 5 to 8.

'Fröhnleiten' *(E. ×perralchicum)* is an attractive, vigorous 4- to 18-inch-tall evergreen groundcover with nodding yellow blooms on straight stems above the leaves. Zones 5 to 8.

Longspur barrenwort *(E. grandiflorum)* grows into 12-inch-tall spreading clumps. Its light pink 1¾-inch-wide blooms are the largest of the group. Look for 'Rose Queen', which has crimson flowers, or 'White Queen', whose blooms are silvery white. Zones 5 to 8.

'Niveum' young's barrenwort *(E. ×youngianum)* grows 6 to 8 inches tall with red-flushed leaves in spring and fall and tiny bright white flowers in late spring. Zones 5 to 8.

Red barrenwort *(E. rubrum)* has ¾-inch red-and-yellow flowers. Its foliage is red along the edges and has rosy undertones. For the reddest foliage plant this barrenwort under deciduous trees where it will receive lots of light before the trees leaf out in spring. Zones 5 to 8.

'Sulphureum' bicolor barrenwort *(E. ×versicolor)* has yellow flowers with coppery new leaves. It is a spreading evergreen that grows 8 to 12 inches tall and up to 36 inches wide. 'Versicolor' has small pale purplish-pink blooms with a yellow center. Zones 5 to 8.

Basket-of-gold *(Aurinia saxatilis)*

oh-RIN-yuh sax-uh-TILL-iss
Features: Abundant tiny gold blooms
Hardiness: Zones 3 to 7
Bloom time: Spring
Size: 6 to 12 inches tall, 12 to 18 inches wide
Shape: A rounded mound
Light: Full sun
Site: Very well-drained soil

Description: Basket-of-gold is a short-lived perennial, but while you have it, it is dazzling. The neon yellow flowers create a carpet of color. The flowers are low, just above the foliage, and provide the main show.

After flowering basket-of-gold's grayish-green leaves take over, forming a low mat that makes a fine counterpoint to the blooms of the other perennials in the garden. Tuck plants into odd corners of a rock garden or into the crevices of a dry laid stone wall. Put them along a path to soften the edges or let plants trail over a wall.

Basket of gold with New Zealand flax

Basket-of-gold complements spring bulbs and other colorful, low-spreading plants such as moss phlox, blue corydalis, and verbena.

Care: Basket-of-gold thrives in poor, dry soil. Plant it in masses about 8 to 12 inches apart in full sun and very well-drained soil. Overly wet soil leads to root rot and plant death. It needs no fertilizer and requires watering only during drought. Divide in fall if necessary.

Heat and humidity contribute to the short life of basket-of-gold, which is often grown as an annual in the South. It also succumbs to the same types of pests that affect cabbages and other cruciferous plants, which are related.

Species and cultivars: Several fine cultivars are available. 'Compacta' grows 8 to 10 inches tall and has bright yellow flowers. 'Sulphurea' grows 6 to 8 inches tall with lemon yellow blooms and gray-green foliage. 'Citrina' is 6 to 8 inches tall with lemon yellow blooms. Flowers of 'Sunnyborder Apricot' have an apricot tint. Those of 'Golden Queen' are pale yellow.

Basket-of-gold

Beach wormwood *(See Artemisias)*

Bear's breeches *(Acanthus spp.)*

uh-CAN-thuh-us species
Features: Dramatic texture and height; long lasting hooded flowers on stiff, erect spikes
Hardiness: Zones 5 to 10
Bloom time: Late spring or early summer depending on climate
Size: 2 to 5 feet tall, 3 to 4 feet wide
Shape: A large, coarse mound with tall upright spires
Light: Full sun to partial shade in cool regions, shade in hot areas
Site: Well-drained, loose, average to fertile soil

Bear's breeches

Description: This plant is like a living sculpture. In fact its sturdy 4-foot spires of white flowers and huge, dark glossy leaves served as models for the carving adorning classical Corinthian columns.

Leaves are spined and thistlelike but not dangerous. In warm climates they are evergreen. Because its greatest height is achieved only when plants are in bloom, place it in the middle of your garden or in the front if the other plants blend with it. Avoid putting it in the back of the border where you'll miss its fine architectural form, which is apparent whether the plant is in or out of bloom.

Plants grow slowly at first, then pick up speed. They have the potential to grow into a large colony. Native to the Mediterranean region, bear's breeches combines well with silver mound artemisia, porcupine grass, golden-edge creeping thyme, cushion spurge, and pearly everlasting. It blooms at the same time as daylilies, meadowsweet, and balloon flower. The spikes are interesting additions to fresh and dried flower arrangements.

Care: Bear's breeches prefers average to fertile soil and regular moisture, but it will tolerate poor, dry soil once it is established. Soil must be well drained; wet feet can kill the plants. In loose soil spiny bear's breeches forms large colonies. Plants spread by roots; even small root pieces left in the ground after moving the plant can grow into new plants.

Deadhead when the spent flower spikes deteriorate, usually some weeks after blooming. Fresh basal leaves will emerge, although the plant will not bloom again. If most of the foliage looks good, remove individual scraggly leaves. In the North mulch to protect roots in winter. Let the foliage, which is evergreen in warm climates, remain on the plant through the winter. Cut off tattered leaves in spring. Powdery mildew, snails, and slugs may affect this plant.

Bear's breeches

Species and cultivars: Balkan bear's breeches (*A. hungaricus*) grows 2 to 4 feet tall by 2 to 3 feet wide. Reddish-purple hoods top its pale pink flowers, which rise on 3-foot spikes. Zones 6 to 9.

Common bear's breeches (*A. mollis*) grows 5 feet tall by 3 feet wide. It produces large, glossy leaves and purplish flower stems with mauve-hooded white flowers. Zones 6 to 10. Golden bear's breeches (the cultivar 'Hollard's Gold') has gleaming chartreuse leaves.

Spiny bear's breeches (*A. spinosus*) has white flowers with showy purple hoods. It grows 3 to 4 feet tall by 3 feet wide. Zones 5 to 9.

Bee balm *(Monarda didyma)*

mow-NAR-duh DID-ih-muh
Features: Shaggy flowers in scarlet, pink, purple, or white
Hardiness: Zones 3 to 9
Bloom time: Early summer
Size: 24 to 30 inches tall, 36 to 48 inches wide
Shape: Spreading, bushy clump
Light: Full sun to partial shade
Site: Moist, well-drained, somewhat fertile soil with abundant organic matter

Description: This mint relative is a must for butterfly and hummingbird gardens. Plants bloom in early to midsummer with 1- to 2-inch-diameter whorls of red, pink, purple, or white flowers.

In bloom bee balm has a lively appearance that is just right for prairie gardens and naturalized areas. Flowering plants can rise 3 to 6 feet tall, depending on the cultivar. Out of bloom bee balm forms a low, 1- to 2-foot-tall spreading mat. You can use bee balm in the middle of a more formal border, but you'll have to keep its aggressive spread in check.
Care: Bee balm tolerates most soils and grows well in sun

Bee balm

to partial shade. It does not tolerate drought or high humidity and may need staking when growing in rich garden soils. Deadheading or shearing after flowering helps prolong bloom; however the first flush is always the showiest. Powdery mildew seriously disfigures bee balm foliage and eventually leads to the plant's decline. To avoid problems grow mildew-resistant cultivars, keep space around plants to ensure good air circulation, and water enough to keep soil moist (not dry or waterlogged). If mildew affects the leaves, cut down old stems, leaving the fresh growth, and discard the mildewed parts.

'Petite Delight' bee balm

Bee balm spreads freely by rhizomes (it is a mint relative). Parts that have moved out of their designated spaces are easy to dig up and discard or share with friends. Divide bee balm every two to three years when the plant's center dies out.
Species and cultivars: The following are mildew-resistant cultivars: 'Blue Stocking', which is 2 to 4 feet tall and has whorled violet-blue flowers. 'Colrai Red' is 36 inches tall with red flowers. 'Gardenview Scarlet' grows 3 feet tall and has rosy red blooms; 'Jacob Cline' can reach 5 feet tall; it has large red flowers. 'Marshall's Delight' grows 3 to 4 feet tall. Its rose-pink flowers bloom longer than most other bee balms, from July to September. 'On Parade' grows 30 inches tall and has rich purple-red flowers set in nearly symmetrical rows. It blooms in July. 'Petite Delight' is 15 to 18 inches tall with bright lavender-pink flowers.

Bellflower *(Campanula spp.)*

cam-PAN-yew-luh species
Features: Bell-shape blue, pink, or red blooms
Hardiness: Zones 3 to 8
Bloom time: Late spring to midsummer
Size: 9 to 36 inches tall and wide, depending on species
Shape: Upright in bloom, mounded when not in bloom
Flowers: Violet, blue, or white; form depends on the species
Light: Full sun to partial shade
Site: Neutral to slightly alkaline well-drained soil of average fertility

Description:
Bellflowers are among the finest of perennials. Although they are classic cottage garden plants, their variety in size, shape, and texture makes them appropriate for use throughout a landscape. Some are diminutive ground-huggers with airy flowers; others are tall and upright with stately spires of

Spotted bellflower

bloom. Some form tidy clumps; others spread widely in the garden. All have bell-shape flowers that face either up or down. Colors range from white to pink to violet to red.

Clustered bellflower

Grow the tallest bellflowers in masses in the middle of the garden, along with foxglove, garden phlox, and red valerian. Plant shorter varieties at the front of the border. Bellflower's tendency to self-sow or to spread suits cottage and informal gardens. The blooms make lovely, long-lasting cut flowers.

Care: Bellflowers are easy to grow in full sun to partial shade and neutral to slightly alkaline well-drained soil of average fertility. They do not tolerate drought, full shade, hot summer nights, or wet soil. Deadhead to extend flowering. Some bellflowers, especially taller ones, require staking.

Divide plants every three to five years or when clumps start to deteriorate. Transplants readily reestablish. Self-sown seedlings often come true to the "mother" plant. Harvest stems for cut flowers just before flower buds open.

Species and cultivars: Carpathian bellflower (*C. carpatica*) is a good choice for rock gardens and for edging. It forms a dense, spreading clump dotted with 1-inch flowers. Zones 3 to 9. The cultivars 'Blue Clips' and 'White Clips' have blue and white flowers, respectively. Flowers of 'Pearl Deep Blue' are vivid blue-violet.

Clustered bellflower (*C. glomerata*) sports tight clusters of upward-facing violet blooms on 24- to 36-tall stems in early summer; flower stems need staking. Zones 3 to 8. 'Superba' has deep purple flowers and is more heat resistant than other cultivars.

Dalmatian bellflower (*C. portenschlagiana*) is a groundcover that grows 4 to 8 inches tall and 2 feet wide. Blue-violet flowers appear in late spring to early summer. Zones 3 to 8.

Peach-leaf bellflower (*C. persicifolia*) is among the daintiest campanulas. It grows 12 inches tall and wide with very fine foliage. In June and July, short spires of violet, blue-violet, white, or pink flowers on wiry stems rise from above the plant, giving an airy effect. The stems often need to be propped up, but you can allow them to weave through neighboring plants. Zones 3 to 7. Cultivars include 'Chettle Charm', which has creamy white blooms edged in lavender-blue on 2½- to 3-foot stems. 'La Belle' offers double sky-blue blooms on 2-foot-tall stems. 'Telham Beauty' has large lavender-blue bells that rise 30 inches above the plants.

Spotted bellflower (*C. punctata*) sends up 1- to 2-foot-tall spires of tubular white blooms, marked inside with pink or purple, from mid- to late summer. This bellflower spreads rapidly, and the flower stems often need staking. Zones 5 to 9. 'Cherry Bells' has long, downward-facing bright pink blossoms in early summer; a mound of light green leaves grows up to 20 inches tall when the plant is not in bloom. 'Bowl of Cherries' has dark purple-red blooms; those of 'Hot Lips' are pale pink, speckled with burgundy on the inside.

Big Betony (Stachys grandiflora)

STAY-kiss grand-IH-floor-uh
Features: Pinkish purple spiky flowers
Hardiness: Zones 2 to 8
Bloom time: Late spring to early summer
Size: 9 to 18 inches tall, 12 inches wide
Shape: Flattened clump of foliage with upright flower spikes
Light: Full sun to light shade
Site: Rich, moist, well-drained soil

Description:
If you are familiar with lamb's-ears, you may be surprised to learn that big betony is a close relative of that plant. Unlike its cousin big betony has deep green, arrow-shape leaves with a pebbly surface that form a clump. Eight-

Big betony

to 10-inch-tall, upright flower stems of pinkish purple appear from late spring to early summer and last for several weeks. Plants are especially effective grown in groups of three or more. They also are spectacular near water gardens, although they will not stand up to continuously wet soil.

Care: Plant big betony in a sunny spot in rich soil. Water regularly and mulch to keep soil moist but not soggy. Deadhead spent flower stems; plants do not rebloom. Big betony suffers in high heat and humidity. Providing part shade and watering consistently helps ease some of their pain but don't expect them to be long-lived in the humid South.

Species and cultivars: 'Superba' is more floriferous with rosy pink flowers.

Betony (*S. monieri*) is almost a twin of big betony. It grows 18 to 20 inches tall and 18 inches wide and has dense rosy pink spiky flowers. 'Hummelo' has lavender-rose flowers in midsummer. Zones 4 to 8.

Blackberry lily (Belamcanda chinensis)

bell-am-CAN-duh chi-eye-NEN-sis
Features: Orange or yellow-orange flowers
Hardiness: Zones 5 to 10
Bloom time: Midsummer
Size: 1½ to 2 feet tall, 40 inches in bloom, 1½ feet wide
Shape: Upright
Light: Full to part sun
Site: Well-drained light soil

Description: This undemanding Asian native is valued for its imposing flat fans of foliage and crimson-speckled blossoms. The flower buds open in succession, each bloom lasting a day. When the fruit pods slit open in fall, they reveal clusters of shiny black berries.

Swordlike foliage and tall flower stalks set off this fast-growing plant. Good companions include ornamental grasses, cushion spurge, blanket flower, and globe thistle.

Blackberry lily in fall

Care: This plant is not a good candidate for areas with cool, moist summers or wet soil in winter. Deadhead by removing individual blossoms as they fade. Plants are short-lived, but they self-sow. Divide plants every two to three years to renew the planting.

Blackberry lily is susceptible to iris borers and iris soft rot. Check for leaf damage in spring; remove and destroy all foliage and stems in fall.

Species and cultivars: 'Freckle Face' is a short version with pale orange blooms. 'Hello Yellow' is pure yellow without spots.

Black-eyed susan *(Rudbeckia fulgida)*

Rude-BECK-ee-uh FULL-geh-duh
Features: Large yellow daisies
Hardiness: Zones 3 to 8
Bloom time: Summer
Size: 2 to 2½ feet tall, 2 to 3 feet wide
Shape: Mounded clumps
Light: Full sun
Site: Average to moist, well-drained soil

Description:
Black-eyed susan with its handsome foliage and dark-centered brassy gold daisies is a sure sign of summer. Having a few plants in your garden assures colorful blooms for nearly the entire season. Plants have dark green, coarse-textured foliage. Flowers rise just a few inches above the mounds of

Black-eyed susan

foliage on stiff, strong stems; they maintain the clumpy shape of the plants. The coarse texture and mounded shape of the plants complement finer-textured and upright plants.
Care: Black-eyed susan thrives in garden soil of average fertility and moisture. Water regularly until the plants become established (well rooted). After they settle into the garden, they live up to their wildflower origins and require few extra resources. Deadhead regularly to keep plants in bloom and avoid reseeding. Divide plants every four to five years; they are easy to move. Cut back plants in fall unless you would like to let birds feed on the seeds; leftover seeds will sprout the next spring. Plants are pest free.
Species and cultivars: 'Goldsturm' is bushy and vigorous with long-blooming, black-centered golden-yellow daisies. It grows 24 inches tall and wide. 'Pot of Gold' grows 12 inches tall. Its golden-yellow blooms last from midsummer to fall. The variety fulgida is similar to the straight species,

but it sheds its petals, leaving brown cones to decorate the plant.

Cutleaf coneflower *(R. nitida)* forms 3-foot-tall mounds of deeply lobed foliage from which droopy, bright yellow daisies with green centers rise on tall stems. Depending on climate, wind exposure, and soil fertility, the plant may need to be supported with stakes and string or let nearby shrubs and ornamental grasses hold up the flower stems. Zones 6 to 8. 'Autumn Sun' coneflower stands out for its handsome

'Goldsturm' black-eyed susan

flowers, vigorous green foliage, and towering height. Flowering begins in mid- to late summer and extends to fall. 'Autumn Sun' produces blooms with droopy yellow rays around a green center. Butterflies visit this outstanding plant when it's in bloom, and songbirds enjoy the seedheads later in the year. 'Autumn Sun' coneflower belongs in wildflower gardens, at the back of informal borders, and in prairie plantings; it makes a handsome cut flower. This cultivar is also sold as 'Herbstsonne'.

Giant coneflower *(R. maxima)* is a stunning plant that forms a mound of huge, silvery blue leaves from which droopy yellow daisies arise on tall stems. The brown seed-bearing centers of the daisies can grow 7 inches long; they attract goldfinches. The flower stems reach 6 to 8 feet tall and need no staking. Zones 5 to 9.

Gloriosa daisy *(R. hirta)* is a drought-tolerant short-lived perennial or biennial. It grows 12 to 36 inches tall, depending on the cultivar. 'Becky' grows 12 to 15 inches tall and wide. Flower colors may be yellow, gold, orange, reddish bronze, or a combination of colors, all with a black central cone. Plants are heat and drought tolerant and do well in containers. 'Prairie Sun' grows 30 inches tall and 12 to 18 inches wide with a loose upright shape. It has orange and lemon-yellow daisies with a pale green cone. 'Toto' hybrids grow to 10 inches tall and 12 inches wide. The 4- to 5-inch-wide daisies in gold, lemon, or mahogany with gold tips bloom from June to September. The double daisies of 'Cherokee Sun'

'Prairie Sun' black-eyed susan

are a mix of golden-yellow, orange, bronze, and mahogany with a dark reddish brown center. Zones 5 to 7.

Black snakeroot *(See Bugbane)*

Blanket flower (*Gaillardia* hybrids)

guh-LARD-ee-uh hybrids
Features: Colorful daisies
Hardiness: Zones 3 to 8
Bloom time: Early summer to fall
Size: 12 to 30 inches tall, 24 inches wide
Shape: Loosely upright to sprawling
Light: Full sun
Site: Sandy, well-drained soil high in organic matter

Description: This cheery perennial brings warmth and bright color to perennial gardens. Blanket flower's 3- to 5-inch-wide red, orange, yellow, and multicolor daisies attract butterflies. The flowers are good for cutting, adding vivid hues to arrangements. Plants are fast-growing and form an expanding clump, thanks to their

Red blanket flower and yellow coreopsis

horizontal spreading roots. With their large flowers on long stems, they can also look like a tangle of stems and flowers. Some cultivars are tidier. Good companions for blanket flower include yarrow, crocosmia, coreopsis, blackberry lily, daylily, white gaura, and ornamental grasses.
Care: Blanket flower tolerates heat, drought, and poor soils. It tends to be short-lived. Plants grow best in well-drained soil of average fertility but tolerate poor soil. They are healthy and vigorous except in soggy conditions where crown rot may develop.

Stake plants with grow-through supports to control their sprawl. Seedheads give plants a ragged appearance and detract from the fresh flowers. Deadheading keeps plants tidy. It can also keep them from becoming too tangled and prevent self-sowing. Most cultivars do not come true from seed.

Divide blanket flower every two or three years in spring. They are easy to move. Cut back plants in fall to clean up the garden. In areas with heavy snow, mulch plants to protect their crowns.
Species and cultivars: 'Baby Cole' grows 6 to 8 inches tall and 15 to 18 inches wide. It has 3-inch-wide, yellow-tipped red daisies with a wine-red central disk. 'Bijou' at 8 to

'Arizona Sun' blanket flower

10 inches tall is a dwarf version of the cultivar 'Goblin'. It has yellow-edged red flowers. 'Fanfare' is a 12- to 15-inch-tall and 15- to 18-inch-wide plant. It's a relatively new cultivar with tubular orange daisies tipped in yellow with a yellow-burgundy center. It has a dense, mounding form. 'Goblin', which is also sold as 'Kobold',

is one of the easiest to find gaillardias. It grows 12 inches tall and has deep red blooms edged in yellow from July to frost. 'Maxima Aurea' has golden-yellow daisies and grows 24 to 30 inches tall; 'The Sun' is similar but grows only 15 inches tall. 'Oranges & Lemons' has an stronger upright habit to 26 inches tall. Its pale orange flowers are tipped in yellow. 'Torchlight' grows 30 inches tall and has yellow-edged orange-red flowers.

Slender blanket flower (*G. pinnatifida*) has yellow daisies with large red centers all summer. Plants grow 1½ feet tall and wide. It is particularly well adapted to arid sites in the warm and cold deserts and the Great Plains. Zones 5 to 8.

Bleeding heart (*Dicentra* species)

die-SEN-truh species
Features: Heart-shape flowers
Hardiness: Zones 3 to 8
Bloom time: Spring or summer, depending on species
Size: Depends on species
Shape: Rounded or flattened mounds, depending on species
Light: Partial to full shade
Site: Rich, moist, well-drained, humusy soil

Description: Bleeding heart encompasses two groups of plants. Old-fashioned bleeding heart makes up one group; Pacific and fringed bleeding hearts fall in the second. All have delightful heart-shaped flowers in white or pink.

Old-fashioned bleeding heart (*D. spectabilis*) is a large, 2 to 3 feet tall and wide, slow-growing, irregularly rounded plant. Long, arching branches bearing dangling hearts reach out from the plant in early spring. This gives the effect of horizontal branching, a sort of oriental look. Foliage is light yellowish green and deeply lobed. Plants

Old-fashioned bleeding heart

often go dormant in mid- to late summer, leaving a large hole in the garden. Locate old-fashioned bleeding heart in the center or back of the garden and pair it with neighbors that will hide the empty space.

Pacific bleeding heart (*D. formosa*) and fringed bleeding heart (*D. eximia*) are like twin sons of different mothers. Their appearance is nearly the same: short (9 to 12 inches tall and wide), flattened mounds of dark blue-green, fernlike lobed foliage. Pacific bleeding heart is native to the West and is slightly more drought tolerant, while fringed bleeding heart originated in the East. Flowers of both species appear above the foliage on 12 to 18 inch tall stalks in late spring; plants rebloom sporadically throughout summer. Plants spreads quickly by roots and seeds to form a lovely groundcover in shady areas and woodland gardens.
Care: Old-fashioned bleeding heart does not tolerate wet soil. Full sun, dry soil, and high heat send it into dormancy. There's no need to deadhead spent flowers; the flowers are self-cleaning and plants will not rebloom. Division is also rarely necessary. Moving plants can damage the roots, which are brittle, and plants reestablish slowly. Old-fashioned bleeding heart is pest free.

Caring for Pacific and fringed bleeding heart is similar to

Fringed bleeding heart

old-fashioned bleeding heart. Plants can take a little more sun and do not go dormant in summer. Deadheading encourages rebloom of these bleeding hearts. Pacific bleeding heart self-sows. Deadheading before seeds form prevents self-sowing and keeps the garden looking neat. If necessary, cut back tattered foliage as the season progresses. Fungal diseases may affect leaves.

Species and cultivars: Old-fashioned bleeding heart: 'Alba' has pure white flowers and long-lasting bluish green leaves. 'Gold Heart' blooms in pink. It has brilliant chartreuse leaves that scorch if they receive too much sun. Zones 2 to 8.

Fringed bleeding heart: 'Snowdrift' has pure white flowers. 'Stuart Boothman' has pink flowers above deeply cut, silvery blue-green foliage. Zones 3 to 9.

Pacific bleeding heart: 'Adrian Bloom' produces ruby-red flowers and has blue-green foliage. 'Aurora' has small soft-white blooms and ferny blue-green leaves. 'Bacchanal' offers dark brick-red flowers above pale green leaves. 'Luxuriant' has rosy pink blooms and blue-green foliage. Zones 3 to 9.

Hybrids: 'King of Hearts' has abundant wide, deep pink flowers above compact grayish green foliage; it is disease free. Blooming begins in early summer. In cool climates, it can continue through summer; in warmer areas, blooming stops in summer but often resumes in early fall. 'Ivory Hearts' has pure white flowers above compact, but vigorous, 12-inch-tall and -wide clumps of blue-green foliage. Flowering begins in midspring.

Blue fescue *(Festuca glauca)*

fess-TOO-kuh glaw-cuh
Features: Silvery blue foliage
Hardiness: Zones 4 to 8
Bloom time: Not grown for flowers
Size: 6 to 10 inches tall and wide
Shape: Rounded tufts
Light: Full sun to light shade
Site: Well-drained soil

Description: This fine-textured compact grass creates dots of blue in a garden. Blue fescue is semi-evergreen except in its northernmost range. However it looks best in spring and summer, when the foliage is fresh. In most areas, cold weather damages foliage, which then browns out. Blue fescue makes a fine groundcover and is a

Blue fescue

good complement to other low-growing perennials. The linear blue foliage adds elegance in flower borders. Plants bloom and the flowers mature to tan seedheads, which you may or may not find attractive.

Care: Grow blue fescue in average to dry, lean to somewhat fertile, well-drained soil in full sun. Plants will grow in light shade, but foliage color is best in sun. Deadhead seed heads if you don't find them attractive. Trim dead or damaged foliage in spring. The clumps die out in their centers. Divide plants every few years to freshen the clump, removing older and dead parts.

Species and cultivars: 'Blue Fox', which may be sold as 'Blaufuchs', grows to 12 inches tall and has silvery blue leaves. 'Blue Glow', also known as 'Blauglut', offers icy-blue foliage on 8 to 10-inch-tall plants. 'Blue Sea' grows just 6 inches tall and has grayish-blue tufts. 'Boulder Blue' has intense blue foliage. 'Elijah Blue' forms an 8- to 10-inch-tall compact, rounded tuft of fine blue leaves. 'Sea Urchin' (or 'Seeigel') forms a dense, 10-inch-tall blue tuft. 'Superba' has very fine blue foliage and grows to 10 inches tall.

Tufted fescue *(F. amethystina)* grows 9 to 18 inches tall with blue-green foliage. 'Klose' has attractive olive-green foliage and grows just 8 inches tall.

Blue fescue seedheads

Blue oat grass *(Helictotrichon sempervirens)*

hel-lick-toe-TRY-con sem-per-VIE-renz
Features: Blue foliage
Hardiness: Zones 4 to 7 (8 on West Coast)
Bloom time: Not grown for flowers
Size: 1½ to 2½ feet tall and wide
Shape: Rounded clumps
Light: Full sun
Site: Well-drained, moderately fertile, neutral to slightly alkaline soil

Description: With its gray-blue foliage, blue oat grass looks a little like blue fescue, but it grows into much larger clumps. The fine-textured 2-foot-tall and -round tuft of silvery blue evergreen foliage is perfect for dry areas. Tan oatlike flowers sway above the foliage in summer and turn a golden wheat color in fall. This grass looks beautiful with the powdery blue-green foliage of giant coneflower and 'Chocolate' white snakeroot.

Care: Blue oat grass grows best in sites with dry soil and excellent drainage. Cut plants back in late winter. Divide

Blue oat grass

'Sterling Silver' blue oat grass

Pink and white boltonias

them every three years. In humid climates plants are prone to fungal diseases such as rust, which limits their use in the South. Mulch plants over winter in Zone 4.

Species and cultivars: 'Sapphire' is bluer than the species. Although it is more tolerant of its growing conditions, the best color develops in cool climates. Plants grow 2½ feet tall. 'Sapphire' is rust resistant.

Blue avena grass *(H. sempervirens)* grows 4 feet tall and 2 feet wide and has stiff blue-gray foliage. Plants bloom in midsummer and are suitable for dry climate gardens.

Blue star *(See Amsonia)*

Boltonia *(Boltonia asteroides)*

Bowl-tone-ee-uh ass-ter-OID-eez
Features: White daisies; late-season color
Hardiness: Zones 4 to 8
Bloom time: Late summer to early fall
Size: 1 to 2 feet tall; 5 feet tall when blooming
Shape: Mounded, upright while in bloom
Light: Full sun to partial shade
Site: Moist, well-drained soil of average fertility

Boltonia

Description: Boltonia looks like a giant bushy aster. It produces abundant 1-inch-diameter yellow-centered white daisies. These grow in open clusters on sturdy branched stems and offer late-season interest in a garden. The flowers attract butterflies and are good for cutting. When not in bloom the mounds of narrow grayish green leaves are not showy. Boltonia pairs well with blue star, joe-pye weed, 'Silver Feather' maiden grass, and 'Cloud Nine' switch grass. Let it naturalize in informal or wildflower gardens.

Care: Boltonia is a low-maintenance, mildew-resistant perennial that grows best in full sun to partial shade in moist, well-drained soils of average fertility. It needs no staking unless grown in exposed windy sites, partial shade, or extremely fertile soils. Cut plants back to 1 foot in late spring to encourage branching and sturdier form. In favorable conditions boltonia's root system expands fast, and the plant can become enormous. Control its spread by

dividing plants every three to four years. Provide shade in hot climates.

Species and cultivars: 'Pink Beauty' has pink flowers on 5-foot stems, silvery blue leaves, and a more relaxed habit than the species. 'Snowbank' is a smaller choice, to 3 to 4 feet tall, with white flowers.

Bugbane *(Actaea simplex)*

ACK-tee-uh SIM-plex)
Features: Wands of white blooms; interesting foliage
Hardiness: Zones 3 to 7
Bloom time: Midsummer to fall, depending on species
Size: 2 to 3 feet tall and wide, 3- to 6-foot flower stems
Shape: Large mound from which upright spiky flowers arise
Light: Part sun to full shade
Site: Well-drained, fertile soil

Description: Bugbane forms neat 3-foot-tall clumps of coarsely lobed foliage. The foliage is striking; even when not in bloom, the plant is a handsome counterpoint to other perennials in the garden. Elegant upright to arching spikes of white flowers rise above the foliage on tall sturdy stalks and last for several weeks. The blooms of some have a pleasant smell; others . . . you want to avoid getting too close to them when they are in bloom. Bugbane is a slow-growing plant. Try it with hosta, rodgersia, heartleaf brunnera, toad lily, and monkshood.

Care: Bugbane performs best in moist, well-drained, loamy soils high in organic matter. It prefers shade or partial shade in warm climates; heat and drought can be detrimental. It can tolerate full sun in the North as long as the soil stays consistently moist. You may need to stake plants where light is strongly one-directional; use grow-through supports. Deadheading is not necessary. Cut plants back in fall or early spring. Bugbane rarely needs division but if you want to share plants, divide them in spring. Plants are pest free.

Bugbane with larkspur and poppy

Species and cultivars: 'White Pearl' is a loose, shrubby perennial with abundant, dense white spikes held high above the pale green leaves. Bugbane's purple-leaved cultivars look handsome throughout the entire growing season because of their striking foliage, which ranges from greenish purple to dark bronzy purple. Twelve-inch creamy white flower spikes on branched stems rise high above the mass of dark leaves. 'Atropurpurea' is a splendid accent for the shade garden, whether grown alone or in groups.

It looks elegant massed at the back of the border and in woodland gardens with ferns and hardy begonias. 'Brunette' fragrant bugbane has pinkish white blooms on 3- to 4-foot stems and dark bronzy-purple leaves. 'Hillside Black Beauty' offers 12-inch-long creamy white fragrant flower spikes on 5-foot stems and deep coppery purple leaves.

Black snakeroot (*A. racemosa*), a bushy perennial native to Eastern North America, has fragrant white bottlebrush flowers in mid- to late summer. Zones 3 to 7.

'Hillside Black Beauty' bugbane

Butterfly weed *(Asclepias tuberosa)*

ES-clep-ee-us two-burr-OH-suh
Features: Brilliant orange flowers
Hardiness: Zones 4 to 9
Bloom time: Early to midsummer
Size: 2 to 3 feet tall and wide
Shape: Shrubby
Light: Full sun
Site: Light, lean, well-drained soil

Butterfly weed with false sunflower

Description: Valued for its fiery orange blooms, this butterfly magnet belongs in wildlife gardens, mixed borders, and meadow and prairie gardens, where it harmonizes with red, yellow, and other hot hues. Many kinds of butterflies sip its nectar, and monarch caterpillars devour its lance-shape leaves, although the damage doesn't harm the plant.

Butterfly weed, a type of milkweed, is generally healthy and easy to grow. It is a coarse-textured, vase-shape perennial that is sturdy, clump forming, long lived, and slow growing. Plants emerge late in spring so label their location lest you forget where you planted them. The flowers appear in large clusters; the seedheads look good in dried arrangements. Combine butterfly weed with finer-textured, mounded perennials; good companions include blue oat grass, catmint, coreopsis, and fountain grass.
Care: Grow butterfly weed in full sun and light, lean, well-drained soil. It needs heat to prosper and bloom well; it is not suited to cool summer climates or sites with poor drainage, especially over winter. Plants self-sow; deadhead before seeds form if you don't want butterfly weed to spread. Deadheading also produces a second flush of bloom. (Milkweeds exude a white sap when stems are cut.) Butterfly weed's long taproot makes it difficult to transplant

and divide. To ensure success cut through the top of the root to obtain several eyes and a large slice of root. Plants are generally pest free, but they do attract aphids.

Swamp milkweed

Monitor plants and use insecticidal soap if aphid populations become damaging.
Species and cultivars: 'Gay Butterflies' grows 2 to 3 feet tall. Because it is obtained by seed, plants may have yellow, orange, or red flowers. 'High Yellow' has bright yellow flowers.

Swamp milkweed (*A. incarnata*) is a native species that does well in moist sites. It produces fragrant pink flower clusters on top of its 4- to 5-foot-tall stems from summer through fall. Deadhead to ensure rebloom. 'Ice Ballet' grows 40 inches tall and has long-lasting white flowers. 'Cinderella' has lovely rose-pink blooms and grows 3 to 5 feet tall and 1 to 3 feet wide. Zones 3 to 7.

California fuchsia *(Zauschneria californica)*

zosh-NAIR-ee-uh cal-if-FOR-nih-cuh
Features: Bright red flowers
Hardiness: Zones 7 to 10
Bloom time: Summer
Size: 1½ to 2 feet tall, 3 feet wide
Shape: Rounded, arching mound
Light: Full sun
Site: Well-drained, sandy to loamy soil

Description: California fuchsia dazzles the garden with its long red tubular flowers that attract hummingbirds. Plants grow as upright-to-arching mounds with rigid, brittle stems. They bloom all summer. The gray-green leaves are covered with soft hairs.

This handsome perennial is a good choice for informal plantings, wildflower gardens, and container gardens. Its short, spreading underground stems are effective on slopes. Good companions include artemisia, hyssop, penstemon, evening primrose, and yucca. California fuchsia is also sold as *Epilobium canum canum*.
Care: California fuchsia grows in deserts and dry slopes from sea level to 10,000 feet in elevation. It does best in well-drained, sandy to loamy soil and full sun. Plants are very drought tolerant. They can become invasive. Trim plants in winter or early spring to control plant size and shape.
Species and cultivars: Arizona fuchsia (*Z. c. latifolia*) is a shrubby perennial

California fuchsia

that grows 3 feet tall and 2 feet wide. Flowers are scarlet red. Water regularly during the first year to help plants settle in. After becoming established plants are drought tolerant. Hot weather is necessary to grow strong roots; plant Arizona fuchsia in spring. Zones 5 to 10.

'Orange Carpet' hummingbird flower *(Z. garrettii)* forms a 4- to 6-inch-tall mat of foliage topped with long scarlet-orange flowers. Plant it in well-drained, compost-enriched soil and water regularly. Zones 5 to 10.

Campion *(Lychnis* spp.*)*

LICK-niss species
Features: Large clusters of vibrant flowers
Hardiness: Depends on species
Bloom time: Early to midsummer
Size: Depends on species
Shape: Irregular upright clump
Light: Full sun
Site: Moist, well-drained soil

Rose campion

Description: Two important garden plants fall into this group: arkwright's campion *(L. ×arkwrightii)* and rose campion *(L. coronaria).* Several traits bind them together: their short lives, the swollen nodes on their stems, and their large, brilliantly colored flower clusters that with deadheading can last all summer.

Rose campion stands out for its silver woolly foliage and loud magenta flowers. The large gray-green leaves form a low basal rosette from which gray, branched, 2- to 3-foot-tall flower stems emerge. Plants bloom little the first year, heavily the second, and deteriorate the third, but they self-sow. Rose campion is charming in cottage gardens, where its short life and abundant seedlings add spontaneity to the garden. Grow it with lamb's-ears and prostrate rosemary. Zones 4 to 10.

Arkwright's campion offers brilliant orange-red flowers in early summer and bronzy foliage. Plants grow 18 to 24 inches tall and 12 inches wide. It is hardy in Zones 6 to 10.
Care: Provide moist, well-drained soil in full sun or light. Keep foliage of rose campion dry to avoid problems. Do not place mulch over the crown of the plant and do not overwater or overfertilize; both actions will weaken the plant. Cut back dead stems in late fall.
Species and cultivars: Rose campion: 'Alba' grows 2 feet tall and has white flowers. 'Gardener's World' is 2 feet tall with 1- to 2-inch-wide, deep purple-red double flowers from late June to early August. Plants do not self-sow. 'Oculata' grows to 32 inches and has white flowers with a cherry pink eye.

Arkwright's campion: 'Vesuvius' grows 18 inches tall and has orange-red blooms in late spring to early summer and red-tinged leaves. 'Orange Dwarf' looks like 'Vesuvius' but grows 8 to 15 inches tall. 'Orange Gnome' is just 8 inches tall with dark purple-red foliage.

Maltese cross *(L. chalcedonica)* has four-petaled, brilliant scarlet flowers in dense clusters at the tips of 1½- to 2-foot-tall plants. It blooms briefly in early summer. 'Carnea' has pink flowers on 4-foot-tall plants. It blooms repeatedly from early summer on if deadheaded. Zones 3 to 8.

Ragged robin *(L. floscuculi)* is a multistemmed upright perennial with gray-green foliage and rose to red flowers with deeply cut petals. Plants grow 1 to 2 feet tall and 1 foot wide. 'Nana' is a 4-inch-tall dwarf with red flowers in spring and grassy gray-green leaves. 'Jenny' grows 16 to 18 inches tall and 15 inches wide. It offers a mass of soft lavender-pink blooms in early summer. Zones 3 to 8.

Rose campion with trumpet lily

Cardinal flower *(Lobelia cardinalis)*

LOW-bee-lee-yuh car-DIN-al-iss
Features: Red flower spikes
Hardiness: Zones 3 to 9
Bloom time: Late summer
Size: 20 inches tall, 3- to 4-foot flowers, 12 inches wide
Shape: Clump, upright in bloom
Light: Full sun to partial shade
Site: Moist to continuously moist, fertile, well-drained soil

Description: Cardinal flower looks attractive massed at the edge of lakes, streams, and ponds. Its tubular scarlet flowers attract bees, butterflies, and hummingbirds and occur in tall spikes from summer to early fall. Foliage is vivid green, sometimes tinged with bronze. Good companions for cardinal flower include gooseneck loosestrife and hybrid astilbe.
Care: Give fast-growing cardinal flower full sun in cool climates and afternoon shade in warm ones. The sunnier the location the more water cardinal flower will need. It thrives in moist to wet, fertile, acid soil with abundant organic matter. Deadheading extends blooming. Prune back dead stems in late fall or early spring and divide every few years. This trouble-free perennial is often short lived, but because it self-sows it's not always lost from the garden.
Species and cultivars: Big blue lobelia *(L. siphilitica)* produces 24- to

'Hummingbird Pink' cardinal flower

36-inch-tall blue flower spikes all summer. Like cardinal flower it prefers a site with abundant moisture and partial shade, but it can get by in drier soil. 'Alba' grows 3 feet tall and has white flowers. It needs less moisture than the species. Zones 4 to 8.
Hybrids: 'Cranberry Crush' grows 20 to 24 inches tall and has cranberry red spikes and a tight form. 'Flamingo' is 20 inches tall with pale pink spikes from July to September. 'Grape Knee-hi' grows to

Cardinal flower

25 inches and has deep purple blooms from midsummer to midfall. 'Gladys Lindley' is 4 feet tall with creamy white flowers. 'Queen Victoria' grows 24 to 36 inches tall and 18 to 24 inches wide. It has mahogany leaves and scarlet spikes from July to September. It is hardy in Zones 6 to 8. 'Ruby Slippers' has beet red blooms.

Caryopteris (Caryopteris ×clandonensis)

carry-OP-ter-iss clan-DOHN-en-siss
Features: Fluffy blue flower clusters; gray-green leaves
Hardiness: Zones 5 to 9
Bloom time: Late summer to early fall
Size: 3 feet tall and wide
Shape: Rounded mound
Light: Sun
Site: Dry, well-drained soil of average fertility

Caryopteris

Description: This deciduous flowering shrub belongs in sunny perennial borders. In some regions it acts more like a perennial than a shrub. Its frothy blue flower clusters and low mounded shape pair well with ornamental grasses and late-blooming perennials such as 'Low Down' perennial sunflower, sneezeweed, and daylily. Caryopteris has fine-textured, aromatic, lance-shape leaves ranging from gray-green to variegated and chartreuse, depending on the cultivar. It's an airy shrub that works well in midborder as a backdrop for other plants. You can also mass it for more impact.
Care: Caryopteris is a woody shrub that is treated like a perennial in some regions because only its roots are hardy in Zone 5. It flowers on new wood, so winter dieback is not a problem. Cut away the dead stems in early spring; consider waiting until new growth appears because lower stems may be alive. Grow caryopteris in full sun and dry, well-drained soil of average fertility. Thin out some shoots on dense plants to improve air circulation.
Species and cultivars: 'Arthur Simmonds' is particularly cold hardy but is otherwise like the species. 'Blue Mist' grows 2½ feet tall and wide and has powder blue flowers. Flowers of 'Dark Knight' are dark blue. It does best in average to dry soils. 'First Choice' has dark

Caryopteris flower detail

purple blooms that develop earlier than those of other cultivars. 'Petite Bleu' grows just 2 feet tall and 3 to 4 feet wide. 'Pink Chablis' grows only 1 to 2 feet tall and 3 to 4 feet wide. It blooms in pink. 'Summer Sorbet' has variegated dark grayish green leaves edged in chartreuse. Both 'Sunshine Blue' and 'Worcester Gold' have yellow foliage. Blooms of 'Worcester Gold' are lavender-blue.

Catmint (Nepeta racemosa)

NEP-ih-tuh ray-see-MOH-suh
Features: Billows of blue flowers, fragrant gray-green leaves
Hardiness: Zones 4 to 7
Bloom time: Early summer
Size: 18 to 24 inches tall and wide
Shape: Mounded to upright, depending on species
Light: Full sun, afternoon shade in warm climates
Site: Well-drained soil

Description: When not in bloom, catmint forms an attractive shrubby mound of branching stems covered in small scented gray-green leaves. Long clusters of small blue flowers cover plants in early summer. In full bloom, catmint creates swells of cool blue in the summer landscape. Used as edging, its long-blooming flowers and aromatic leaves soften paths and bring cool hues to the garden. Catmint looks wonderful massed as a low-maintenance, drought-tolerant groundcover. Place it in several spots repeated along the front of the garden to pull together the many hues of all the perennials. Catmint is a great companion for coarser-textured, taller plants such as bearded iris, yarrow, blackberry lily, and

'Walker's Low' catmint

Catmint flower detail

purple coneflower. Or try it with 'Creme Brulee' coreopsis, roses, 'Happy Returns' daylily, and 'Biokovo' cranesbill. Although related to catnip, catmint has little attraction for cats.

Care: Catmint thrives in full sun and well-drained soil. It does very well in heat, wind, drought, and even tolerates being walked on. Plants however do not tolerate hot humid weather. Deadhead by shearing the plants. Cutting stems back by one-third to one-half after the first flush of bloom makes plants more compact and encourages rebloom later in the season. Some species can be floppy; stake them with grow-through supports or pea brush. Divide in spring or fall every three to six years; plants are easy to move. Clean up the plants in late fall or early spring, cutting stems to the ground.

Species and cultivars: 'Blue Wonder' is a 12- to 15-inch-tall groundcover with 6-inch flower spikes. It has more flowers and bigger leaves than the species. 'Dropmore' forms 12- to 18-inch-tall mounds and has large (bigger than the species) deep lavender flowers in June and July. 'Kit Kat' is a compact plant with dark purple-blue blooms. 'Six Hills Giant' is one of the largest selections; it grows 30 inches tall and has large leaves and flowers. The violet-blue blooms are carried on 1-foot-long stems. 'Snowflake' is a 12- to 15-inch-tall plant with summerlong white flowers. Despite its name 'Walker's Low' is not a low-growing catmint. It grows 18 to 24 inches tall with lavender-blue blooms. Plants will sprawl unless propped up.

Giant catmint *(N. grandiflora)* grows to 3 feet tall and has long-lasting, lavender-blue flowers. Blooms of 'Dawn to Dusk' are light pink. Zones 5 to 7.

Siberian catmint *(N. sibirica)* grows 2 to 3 feet tall. It is more cold hardy than other catmints but can be invasive. 'Souvenir d'Andre Chaudron' has abundant spikes of large brilliant blue flowers. Zones 3 to 7.

Celandine poppy *(Stylophorum diphyllum)*

sty-LOFF-or-um die-FILL-um
Features: Golden orange flowers
Hardiness: Zones 4 to 8
Bloom time: Mid- to late spring
Size: 18 inches tall, 12 inches wide
Shape: Irregular clump
Light: Part shade to shade
Site: Well-drained organic soil

Description: The golden flowers of celandine poppy help light up a shade garden. Foliage is dark gray-green with deep lobes.

Celandine poppy

Plants form clumps and grow at a moderate to fast pace. Good companions include yellow corydalis, gold-leafed hostas, coral bells, jacob's ladder, and bellflowers.

Care: Grow celandine poppy in a shady spot with rich, well-drained soil. Celandine poppy does not tolerate heat or sun. Deadhead to prevent self-sowing; plants will not rebloom. They do not need to be divided, nor do you need to cut them back in fall. Their foliage decomposes over winter. Plants are pest free.

Celandine poppy buds

Centranthus *(Centranthus ruber)*

sen-TRAN-thus ROO-ber
Features: Iridescent reddish pink flowers
Hardiness: Zones 5 to 11
Bloom time: Summer
Size: 2 feet tall and wide
Light: Full sun
Site: Well-drained alkaline to neutral soil

Centranthus

Description: Easy-to-grow centranthus is one of the longest-blooming perennials in the garden. Pale green to silvery green foliage sets off its dense clusters of reddish pink flowers. The plants start blooming in late spring to early summer and continue through late summer as long as you deadhead. The flowers are especially beautiful combined with silver-leaf plants such as artemisia and lamb's-ears; dark-foliaged perennials and shrubs make a fine backdrop, setting off centranthus plants.

Care: Grow centranthus in full sun and well-drained, neutral to alkaline soil. Plants do not tolerate the heat and humidity of the South. Water regularly, especially during centranthus' first year in the garden to establish a deep root system. Deadhead to encourage rebloom and prevent self-sowing. Because plants are short lived, letting a few volunteers pop up will ensure that centranthus remains in your garden. Cut back plants in fall or early spring before growth begins. Divide centranthus every two to three years.

Species and cultivars: 'Albus' blooms in white; 'Coccineus' flowers are dark rosy red.

'Coccineus' centranthus

Checkerbloom *(Sidalcea malviflora)*

sigh-DAHL-sea mal-VEH-floor-uh
Features: Spikes of pink, white, or purplish flowers
Hardiness: Zones 4 to 8
Bloom time: Early to midsummer
Size: Depends on cultivars
Shape: Mounded, upright in bloom
Light: Full sun to partial shade
Site: Moist, well-drained soil

Checkerbloom with black-eyed susan

Description: Like its big cousin, the hollyhock, this short-lived perennial creates a vertical accent in gardens. Checkerbloom looks like a thick, multistemmed hollyhock, however it is half the size, making it ideal for both small and large beds and borders. It blooms with dense spikes of long-lasting flowers that have five silky smooth petals, some fringed at the tips. The flowers top thin but rigid stems that are good for cut flower arrangements. Most checkerblooms in garden centers are hybrids, rather than the straight species. Depending on the cultivars they grow 15 to 48 inches tall and bloom in July and August. Good companions include 'Hameln' dwarf fountain grass and 'Goldrush' goldenrod.

Care: Checkerbloom prefers climates with cool summers and does poorly in heat and humidity. It is easy to grow in moist, well-drained, average garden soil. Deadheading extends flowering and reduces self-sowing. After blooming cut checkerbloom to the ground, particularly if it wanes in summer's heat. Cutting after the first flush of bloom stimulates fresh basal growth and the prospect of more flowering. Pick off Japanese beetles by hand and discard. Divide plants every three to four years. Cut plants to the ground in late fall or early spring.

Species and cultivars:
'Bianca' grows to 3 feet and has white flowers. 'Brilliant' is 28 inches tall. It has vivid red blooms on erect stems and shiny leaves with shallow lobes. 'Elsie Heugh' is 36 inches tall with fringed pink blooms. 'Little Princess' has lavish light rose-pink blooms and grows 2 feet tall. 'Party Girl' is a 2- to 4-footer with spikes of 2-inch-wide rose-pink flowers from midsummer to fall. 'Rosanna' with its rose-red flowers grows 3½ feet tall.

'Party Girl' checkerbloom

Christmas fern *(See Ferns)*

Chrysanthemum *(Chrysanthemum* hybrids*)*

kris-ANTH-eh-mum hybrids
Features: Lavish, brightly colored flowers
Hardiness: Zones 5 to 9
Bloom time: Late summer to early fall
Size: 12 to 36 inches tall and wide
Shape: Mounded
Light: Full sun, partial shade in the South
Site: Average to fertile, well-drained soil

'Marilyn' chrysanthemum

Description: Mums liven up the garden when most plants have finished blooming. Their long-lasting handsome flowers come in red, pink, yellow, orange, violet, green, white and all shades in between. Plant size and shape varies among the cultivars, but most mums are rounded to upright mounds 1 to 2 feet tall. Flowers also vary. Some cultivars have round flowers like globes; others have daisy blooms. Petals can be flat, hooked, fringed, or rolled like quills.

Mums enhance fall beds and borders and pair well with 'Autumn Joy' sedum, boltonia, fall-flowering asters, and ornamental grasses. They look striking in containers, whether grown alone or with ornamental grasses and trailing greens. The flowers attract butterflies.

Because shorter days trigger flowering, select the right mum for your climate. Early bloomers suit areas with early frosts; mid- to late-season bloomers are better for the South. In mild climates planting early, mid-, and late-season bloomers prolongs flower interest. Many cultivars are little more than throwaway plants, bred for the florist trade and meant to provide just one season of bloom. Others thrive in gardens for many years. The greatest selection is available in late summer and early fall; some of these will be short lived. If you're looking for garden plants rather than porch decorations, ask the nursery staff which ones they offer are hardiest.

Care: Plant mums four to six weeks before the last frost. If you can find them in spring, planting then allows maximum root development so the mums have a better chance of surviving the winter.

Avoid sites with poor drainage, especially ones that stay wet over winter. Mums do not tolerate wet soil but require regular watering. Pinch plants several times between late spring and early summer (Memorial Day to July 4 in the North, early August in southern areas) to create tighter, bushier plants

'Sheffield' chrysanthemum

with more blooms. Pinching delays flowering by a few weeks. If you prefer looser, bigger, earlier-blooming plants, avoid pinching and stake the plants in late spring so they don't fall over.

Fertilize plants for lush flowering until you see budded blooms. Once they are in bloom, deadhead old flowers to make way for the new. Divide plants every two years or so in spring, removing any dead material. After plants have finished blooming, trim them back to 6 inches and mulch for winter protection. You also can cut back plants the next spring.

Chrysanthemums are susceptible to a host of pests including aphids, Japanese beetles, spider mites, slugs, leaf spots, mildew, and rust.

Species and cultivars: 'Cambodian Queen' has dark pink single blooms with yellow centers in the fall. Zones 3 to 7. 'Clara Curtis' forms a 2-foot mound of 3-inch fragrant yellow-centered pink daisies in August and September. Zones 5 to 9. 'Gypsy Wine' is an early-blooming dwarf cultivar with scented wine red pompoms. 'Hillside Pink Sheffield' has light salmon pink daisies in September and October. Zones 4 to 9. 'Marilyn' offers abundant white double flowers from September to frost.

Cinnamon fern *(See Ferns)*
Cinquefoil *(See Nepal cinquefoil)*

Clematis *(Clematis spp.)*

CLEM-at-iss or clem-IT-iss species
Features: Blue, violet, red, or white blooms
Hardiness: Zones 3 to 7
Bloom time: Late spring to late summer
Size: Depends on species
Shape: Vining or mounded
Light: Full sun to partial shade
Site: Moist, fertile, well-drained soil

Description: Although woody plants clematis belong in perennial gardens. Vining types weave among the plants, adding dots of blue, white, purple, or red, or form a colorful backdrop on walls and fences behind the garden. Shrubby types form bushy upright or sprawling mounds of blue or white flowers. Among the shrubby types are solitary clematis *(C. integrifolia),* tube clematis *(C. heracleifolia),* ground clematis *(C. recta),* and durand clematis *(C. ×durandii).*

Solitary clematis makes a bushy, sprawling little mound that looks charming when its woody but flexible stems lace among those of nearby plants. Starting in late spring small blue-violet bells nod among green leaves for much of the growing season. The main show occurs early in the season but continues sporadically throughout summer. Airy seedheads persist into fall and resemble puffs of curling silken threads. Plants grow 1½ to 3 feet tall and wide; they tend to sprawl and need some support. Combine it with spring-blooming shrubs. The shrubs will support the scrambling clematis, and the clematis will bring

'Rosea' solitary clematis

spring-to-fall visual interest to the shrubs. Or grow it among early-blooming, strong-stemmed perennials such as blue star or false indigo. Massed on its own it creates a bushy deciduous groundcover.

Solitary clematis

Tube clematis is considerably larger, 2 to 3 feet tall and wide, with clusters of tiny blue flowers in late summer. The branching stems are stiffer, or woodier, than solitary clematis, but plants still sprawl. Foliage is much different from other clematis; leaves are composed of three lobed leaflets. Like other clematis fluffy seedheads replace the flowers. Tube clematis tends to readily self-sow.

Ground clematis is a summerlong bloomer covered with large clusters of fringed white flowers. Plants sprawl on the ground; staked they can reach 4 feet tall and 3 feet wide. Grow this sprawler staked and upright or let it run through shrubs and other perennials.

Durand clematis is a large-flowered, nonclimbing clematis. Its yellow-centered deep blue blooms open bell-shape, then flatten out like other large-flowered clematis. Plants form 3- to 6-foot-tall sprawling clumps.

Tube clematis with red Asiatic lily

Solitary clematis is one of the parents of durand clematis.

Flowers of vining clematis vary greatly. Some plants have large circular blooms with colorful centers; others offer dainty nodding bells. Flowers may be single, double, or multipetalled. Colors generally are in shades of blue, purple, white, or red, but a few species have yellow flowers.

Care: Clematis are low-maintenance plants. They grow best in full sun and moist, fertile, well-drained soil. To help nonclimbing types appear taller, use pea stakes or grow-through supports for a natural look. Mulch the root area to shade and cool the soil. Cut plants back to a pair of buds about 6 inches from the ground before they leaf out in spring.

Vining clematis grow best with cool roots and foliage exposed to sun. Plant them so their roots are in shade. A thick mulch of bark chips also helps keep roots cool. Good drainage and moderate moisture are essential. Support stems on netting, fencing, or a light trellis, or let them weave through the other plants.

To aid survival plant vining clematis deep enough to bury 2 to 3 inches of stem. The stem will send out roots; if the plant wilts after planting, this buried stem ensures the plant will sprout from the base.

Prune to control growth, encourage flowering, and remove dead stems. The key to pruning is first determining whether your clematis blooms on stems that were formed the previous year, the ones that form during the current year, or both. Prune vines that bloom on last year's stems after their flowers fade. These clematis include spring- and midseason-flowering varieties.

Prune clematis that blooms on the current year's growth in late winter or early spring. These are usually late-flowering clematis. Cut young plants to 1 foot above the ground for the

'Duchess of Albany' scarlet clematis

first two or three years, then to 2 feet above the ground for older plants. Clematis that bloom on new wood can quickly become overgrown.

Prune clematis that blooms on both the previous year's stems and then have a later flush of bloom on the current year's growth in late winter or early spring. Pinch occasionally to stimulate branching.

Clematis are generally pest free, but they are susceptible to wilt disease. Plants will seem healthy, then suddenly wilt. New growth may sprout from the base of the plants.

Species and cultivars: 'China Purple' tube clematis grows 30 inches by 36 inches and has flaring deep blue-violet bells in summer, followed by silky seedheads. Its large dark green leaves and upright stems make this plant look shrubby and coarse textured. Some people call this fragrant tube clematis. 'Alblo' (sold as Alan Bloom) has large, vivid blue flowers rising above deep green leaves. These plants stand up better than most tube clematis; however they will sprawl in shade. Zones 3 to 7.

Purple-leaved ground clematis, the cultivar 'Purpurea', has small but lavish clusters of fragrant, starry white flowers complemented by foliage that opens purple and turns green as it matures. Zones 3 to 7.

'Caerula' solitary clematis has porcelain blue flowers on 1- to 2-foot-tall plants. Zones 3 to 7.

Vining clematis: Alpine clematis (C. alpina) has bluish violet bell-shape flowers. Zones 6 to 8

Anemone clematis (C. montana) is a dainty, fast-growing climber with white flowers. The variety rubra has pink flowers. Zones 5 to 8.

Armand clematis (C. armandii) is an evergreen species with showy white fragrant flowers and shiny dark green leaves. It blooms on old wood. Zones 7 to 9.

Scarlet clematis (C. texensis) has small nodding, pink, bell-shape flowers. Zones 4 to 8.

Viticella clematis (C. viticella) has delightful nodding flowers in colors ranging from blue to purple to rose-purple, as well as small tidy foliage. Zones 5 to 7.

Hybrid clematis: Most of the showy large-flowered vines are hybrids. 'Nelly Moser' has pinkish flowers with dark pink stripes; those of 'Miss Bateman' are creamy white with red centers. 'Candida' is white with yellow centers; 'Ville de Lyon' blooms are red; 'Madame le Coultre' is white. Jackman clematis (C. ×jackmanii) has large violet-purple flowers in early summer and sporadically throughout the summer. 'Comtesse de Bouchaud' has silvery rose blooms all summer. Blooms of 'Niobe' are deep ruby red with yellow centers. This cultivar blooms from late spring to summer.

Columbine *(Aquilegia spp.)*

ack-will-EE-gee-uh species
Features: Pink, blue, white, red, and yellow flowers attract hummingbirds
Hardiness: Zones 3 to 9
Bloom time: Mid- to late spring
Size: 1 foot tall, 2 to 3 feet in bloom, 1 to 1½ feet wide
Shape: Rounded clump
Light: Partial shade to full sun
Site: Rich, moist, well-drained soil

Description: Perfect for perennial, cottage, and woodland gardens, these old-fashioned columbine come in many new colors and forms. The nodding blooms rise above the foliage on short, sturdy upright stalks. Flowers have curved spurs at the back that resemble frilly caps. Cut flowers look charming in spring arrangements. Good companions include foam flower, woodland phlox, toad lily, and fleece flower.

Columbine

Care: Columbine prospers in sun to partial shade in moist, well-drained soil high in organic matter. It has a short life span but self-sows readily. Break off dried seedpods and shake the seeds where you would like new plants to grow. To avoid unwanted self-sowing and to lengthen the season of bloom, deadhead the plant before it goes to seed. Remove any leaves with narrow tan leaf miner tracks and discard them in the trash. Renew the plant by cutting it to the ground after flowering.

Species and cultivars: Canadian columbine (A. canadensis), a tall North American native reaching 36 inches by 12 inches, has ferny foliage. The droopy flowers with upright spurs are red on the outside and light yellow on the inside. 'Little Lanterns' grows 8 to 10 inches tall and wide. It has red-and-yellow flowers. Zones 3 to 8.

Rocky Mountain columbine (A. caerulea) is a short, 1- to 2-foot-tall columbine with long-spurred blue-and-white blooms. Zones 3 to 8.

Hybrid columbines: These generally have large upright

Hybrid columbine

flowers in a wide range of colors on tall stems. Zones 3 to 9. McKana Hybrids are 2 to 3 feet tall with flowers in white, yellow, red, pink, blue, and lavender. 'Nora Barlow' grows 3 feet tall and has shaggy double flowers in dark rosy pink and white. 'Lime Frost' grows 14 to 18 inches tall with variegated yellow-and-green-splotched leaves.

Coral bells (*Heuchera* spp.)

HEW-ker-uh species
Features: Colorful foliage, dainty flowers
Hardiness: Zones 3 to 8
Bloom time: Late spring to early summer
Size: 6 to 10 inches tall and wide, 12- to 24-inch flower stems
Shape: Low mound with airy flowers
Light: Full sun to partial shade
Site: Moist, well-drained soil rich in organic matter

Coral bells

Description: Grow coral bells for spectacular foliage that provides months of interesting color and texture long after the flowers fade. The semievergreen to evergreen leaves are mostly rounded and lobed; some are ruffled and frilled. They vary in hue from green, chartreuse, lime, silver, and pinky beige to wine red, blackish maroon, and chocolate brown. Colorful veins often etch contrasting patterns on coral bells' upper surface. Silvery veils cover the leaf surface of some varieties; others have contrasting edges or undersides. Every year new cultivars that extend the color range even further arrive on the market.

The foliage is the show, but plants have tiny red, pink, or white flowers on long slender stalks that rise high above the plants. Red flowers stand out, but the other colors need to be appreciated up close. The loose flower spikes attract bees, hummingbirds, and butterflies and make long-lasting cut flowers.

Coral bells suit cottage and woodland gardens. Use them to edge beds and paths or mass-plant them under trees as a groundcover, in containers, and at the front of perennial and mixed borders. Good partners include hosta, Japanese painted fern, and astilbe.

Care: These low-maintenance perennials like moist, well-drained, somewhat acidic soils high in organic matter. Give them full sun in cool climates, part shade in warm ones. Deadhead to extend blooming and remove flower spikes at the base when they finish blooming. If you don't

Coral bells

find the flowers attractive, cut the stalks to the ground before they bloom. Cut back dead leaves in spring. If any leaves are damaged during the growing season, remove them at any time and new foliage will emerge from the base. Coral bells can compete with tree roots if topdressed with

1 to 2 inches of compost every fall. Prevent frost heaving and winter damage by mulching with evergreen boughs. Root weevils sometimes cause problems. Divide plants every few years to stimulate more flowering.

Species and cultivars: Coral bells (*H. sanguinea*) have green leaves and colorful pink, red, or white flowers. Plants grow 12 to 18 inches tall by 12 inches wide. 'Chatterbox' is a long bloomer with salmon-rose buds that open to pink. It grows 10 inches tall, with flowers rising to 22 inches above the foliage. 'Ruby Bells' has brilliant red flowers on 16-inch-long stems. Foliage is 8 to 10 inches tall. Zones 3 to 8.

Small-flowered coral bells (*H. micrantha*) grow 12 to 24 inches tall and have sparse, yellowish white flowers. 'Palace Purple' is one of the oldest cultivars in this group. It has large bronzy purple leaves and creamy flowers on 18-inch stems. Plants will reseed. Zones 4 to 7.

Hybrids: 'Amber Waves' has 12-inch flower stems bearing light rosy blooms above an 8-inch mound of ruffled amber gold leaves. 'Amethyst Myst' forms a 9-inch mound of plum-purple leaves fogged with silver. 'Bressingham Bronze' forms 8- to 12-inch mounds of coppery brown leaves with pointed lobes. 'Chocolate Ruffles' offers purplish flowers on 30-inch stems over a 10-inch mound of ruffled leaves that are chocolate on top and burgundy on the bottom. 'Ebony & Ivory' has ivory flowers on 22-inch stems above a 10-inch mound of ruffled, very dark purple leaves. 'Harmonic Convergence' has silver-mottled bronze foliage and showy fringed pink flowers. 'Lime Rickey' blooms in white on 17-inch stems. It forms 8-inch mound of ruffled chartreuse leaves in spring that mature to lime green for the rest of the summer. 'Petite Pearl Fairy' blooms in pink on 8-inch stems. Foliage is a 3- to 4-inch mound of bronzy purple leaves. 'Raspberry Ice' has dark purple foliage touched with frosty silver and showy two-toned pink blooms. Flowers rise 24 inches over the 12-inch mound of foliage. 'Saturn' grows 15 to 18 inches tall with dark veins over pewter leaves with reddish edges.

Coreopsis (*Coreopsis* spp.)

core-EE-op-siss species
Features: Long-blooming yellow daisies
Hardiness: Zones 4 to 9
Bloom time: Summer
Size: 6 to 36 inches tall, 12 to 36 inches wide
Shape: Mounded to loosely columnar
Light: Full sun
Site: Moist, well-drained soil

Description:
Valued for their long-blooming yellow daisies that attract butterflies, coreopsis bears golden yellow, pale lemon, pink, or bicolor flowers from early summer to midsummer and longer

Coreopsis

with deadheading. A distinctive feature of the flowers is the notching at the tips of the petals. Some types are short and mounded with fine texture; others are more upright,

Coreopsis

especially when in bloom, with a coarser medium texture. In the larger species flowers rise above the plants on long slender stems. On short species the blooms hover just above the foliage. Grow coreopsis in containers, sunny borders, or wildflower gardens with companions such as Arkansas amsonia, perennial salvias, ornamental mullein, speedwell, or ornamental grasses.

Care: Coreopsis needs full sun and moist, well-drained soil; it tolerates heat and drought but does not do well in wet soil in winter. Deadheading faded flowers prolongs blooming and prevents self-sowing. You may be tempted to simply pop off faded blooms from the long-stemmed flowers, but doing so detracts from the plant's looks. Cut plants back after the first flush of flowers to encourage rebloom. In late fall or early spring, cut plants to the ground. Coreopsis sprawls in rich, wet soil and needs support. Tall cultivars may require staking. Use crutches, such as pea brush or grow-through supports. Divide plants in spring every three years.

Plants are generally pest free. Four-lined plant bugs can feed on foliage. Powdery mildew or rust may develop in shaded sites.

Species and cultivars: Lanceleaf coreopsis (*C. lanceolata*) grows into a large 2- to 2½-foot-tall plant with 2-inch-wide golden yellow daisies. 'Goldfink' is a 10-inch dwarf with golden blooms. 'Sterntaler' has 2½-inch golden daisies with a burgundy-brown eye. Zones 3 to 8.

Pink coreopsis (*C. rosea*) grows into 1- to 2-foot-tall and wide mounds with fine-textured threadlike leaves and tiny rose pink daisies. Zones 7 to 9. 'Sweet Dreams' has 1-inch-wide raspberry-centered white daisies. Zones 6 to 8.

Tickseed coreopsis (*C. grandiflora*) grows with a 12-inch-tall whirl of foliage near the ground from which the yellow daisies arise on stems up to 24 inches long. Plants are short lived but wonderful while you have them. 'Baby Sun' is a finer-textured tickseed coreopsis with 2-inch golden yellow daisies on 20-inch-tall stems. 'Early Sunrise' offers showy 2-inch-wide orangy-gold, semidouble to double daisies on 18-inch-long stems. Flowers of 'Rising Sun' have mahogany-red centers; blooms are held on 3-foot stems. 'Sunray' blooms with frilly, brilliant gold double daisy flowers on 16- to 18-inch-long stems. Zones 4 to 9.

Threadleaf coreopsis (*C. verticillata*) is similar in appearance to pink coreopsis but has yellow daisies. It is fast growing and long flowering with a mounded, spreading form and fine-textured leaves. It grows 2 to 3 feet tall. This coreopsis is often self-cleaning; however cutting plants back after the first round of blooms ensures a good show later on. 'Moonbeam' is one of the earliest and best-known cultivars. It has small pale yellow daisies. 'Creme Brulee' grows into 1-foot-tall and 3-foot-wide clumps. Its butter yellow daisies are held on sturdier stems than those of 'Moonbeam'. Plants have good powdery mildew resistance. 'Zagreb' is an 8- to 10-inch-tall cultivar with yellow flowers. Zones 4 to 9.

Hybrids: 'Tequila Sunrise' offers red-centered, yellow-orange flowers and olive green leaves with creamy yellow edges. (Zones 6 to 9) 'Jethro Tull' has dense golden yellow daisies with unusual quilled (rolled) petals. Zones 4 to 9. The Limerock series incorporates a number of fine-textured plants similar to pink coreopsis. They are tender perennials that may be hardy to Zones 7. In colder regions they are well worth growing in containers or as annuals. 'Limerock Ruby' has rose red flowers. 'Limerock Dream' blooms with apricot pink daisies. Flowers of 'Limerock Passion' are lavender-pink.

Cranesbill (*See Geranium*)

Crimson pincushion (*Knautia macedonica*)

KNOT-ee-uh mass-ih-DON-ih-kuh

Features: Crimson red blooms on wiry stems
Hardiness: Zones 5 to 9
Bloom time: Summer
Size: 12 to 15 inches tall, 10 to 12 inches wide
Shape: Weaver
Light: Full sun
Site: Well-drained, somewhat fertile, alkaline soil

Description: Crimson pincushion is a long-blooming perennial with lovely pincushion-shape wine red flower heads on long, wiry stems. When plants first start blooming, the flowers rise above a low mound of slender leaves, but the long stems soon flop over. Instead of staking the stems, plant crimson pincushion with open perennials that can support it, such as coreopsis, baby's breath, or 'Purple Rain' salvia. This short-lived perennial attracts bees and butterflies. It has an informal, untidy look that is well suited to cottage gardens. Cut flowers are excellent in fresh or dry arrangements.

'Egyptian Rose' crimson pincushion

Care: This low-maintenance perennial prefers full sun and well-drained average garden soil. Deadhead to prevent self-sowing and divide crowded clumps. Plants grown 18 inches apart may look sparse in spring. By midsummer though, the plant has filled in.

Species and cultivars: 'Mars Midget' is 15 to 18 inches tall with ruby blooms from summer to fall. 'Melton Pastels' hybrids grow 24 to 30 inches tall. The arching stems carry pink, crimson, salmon, or light blue pincushions from early to late summer.

Crimson pincushion

Crocosmia *(Crocosmia hybrids)*

crow-CAUSE-me-uh hybrids
Features: Yellow, orange, or fiery red blooms
Hardiness: Zones 5 to 11
Bloom time: Mid- to late summer
Size: 2 to 3 feet tall, 1½ to 2 feet wide
Shape: Vase-shape clump
Light: Full sun
Site: Rich, moist, well-drained soil

Crocosmia

Description: Brilliant flower color, unique texture, and outstanding plant form make crocosmia an exceptional choice for perennial gardens. The bright green sword-shape leaves spread out from a central clump like a vase. Along the top of sturdy, arched stems, rows of knobby buds open to 2-inch-wide bright yellow, orange, or red flowers that flare like a trumpet. Planted in groups or masses, crocosmia is a perfect midsize choice for tropical gardens and hot borders. Good partners include ornamental grasses and orange-, yellow-, and white-flowered perennials. Cut flowers are stunning in arrangements.

Care: Crocosmia grows from corms, which are hard, scaly, enlarged underground stems. It tolerates heat and humidity but prefers full sun and rich, moist, well-drained soils. It does poorly in wet soil, poor drainage, and drought.

Plants are sometimes listed as hardy only to Zone 6, but winter losses are usually caused by poor drainage rather than cold temperatures. Older plants with large root systems are usually hardier. Cover new plants with a thick mulch for the first year or two after planting.

Clip off the entire flower stalk once the last bud on the stem has finished blooming. Divide plants in spring every three years or so.

Species and cultivars: 'Babylon' has deep reddish orange blooms on 30-inch-tall stems. Foliage is 18 inches tall. Flowers of 'Emberglow' are orange-red with a hint of blue. 'Emily McKenzie' has bright orange flowers with a deep red throat; its flower stems reach 2 to 2½ feet tall. Blooms of 'George Davison' are a soft yellow-orange. 'Irish Sunset' blooms are vivid yellow tinged with orange. 'Jenny Bloom' has vivid yellow flowers on 30-inch stems. 'Lucifer' has fiery red blooms on 36- to 42-inch-tall stems.

Crocosmia

Culver's root *(Veronicastrum virginicum)*

vur-ON-ih-kay-strum ver-GIN-ih-come
Features: Bluish white spires
Hardiness: Zones 4 to 8
Bloom time: Mid- to late summer
Size: 4 to 6 feet tall, 2 to 4 feet wide
Shape: Upright clump
Light: Part to full sun
Site: Moist organic soil

Culver's root   Culver's root flowers

Description: Culver's root is a giant architectural perennial for the back of a garden. A midwestern native, it grows in tall clumps at a moderate pace. The dense, branched flower spikes, which look similar to those of speedwell, open from the top down. Foliage grows in whorls around the flower stems. Use culver's root to provide a vertical accent for large mounded plants such as hardy hibiscus.

Care: Culver's root tolerates heat and humidity. Deadhead to prolong blooming. Cut plants back in late fall or early spring. If your plants are floppy, stake them with grow-through supports.

Cupid's dart *(Catananche caerulea)*

cat-uh-NAN-key see-RULE-ee-uh
Features: Pale blue flowers
Hardiness: Zones 4 to 7
Bloom time: Mid- to late summer
Size: 2 feet tall, 1 foot wide
Shape: Rosette of foliage from which wiry flower stems arise
Light: Full sun
Site: Well-drained sandy soil

Description: Cupid's dart is a, delicate see-through plant with leafless flower stems bearing papery blue flowers with a dark eye. Its rosette of gray-green foliage hugs the ground; in bloom the wiry flower stems rise to 24 inches. Plants grow quickly into clumps. Plant cupid's dart in front of perennials that help the

Cupid's dart

Cut spent cupid's dart flowers to prolong bloom.

flowers stand out, such as sedum, butterfly weed, gas plant, or artemisia.
Care: Cupid's dart grows best in well-drained soil; avoid sites that stay wet in winter. Plants are heat and drought tolerant but do not thrive in high heat and humidity. Deadhead to prolong bloom. Cupid's dart does not need to be cut down in fall because stems and foliage decompose rapidly over winter. Divide plants every two or three years. Plants are short lived.

Cushion spurge (Euphorbia polychroma)
yew-FOR-bee-uh poly-CHROME-uh
Features: Chartreuse flower bracts
Hardiness: Zones 3 to 10
Bloom time: Early to midspring
Size: 12 to 20 inches tall, 24 inches wide
Shape: Rounded mound
Light: Full sun to part sun
Site: Well-drained soil

Description:
Cushion spurge has clusters of tiny flowers backed by showy long-lasting yellow bracts on top of each stem in early to midspring. It is a strongly mounded, clump-forming plant. Good companions include midseason tulips in pinks, red-violets, and purples, creeping phlox, dwarf bearded iris, and penstemon. The form and texture of cushion spurge complement

Cushion spurge

peonies. Their stems hide the foliage of fading spring bulbs.
Care: Cushion spurge tolerates heat, wind, and alkaline soil but does not do well in high humidity or in wet or poorly drained soil. The best site has full sun to light shade and well-drained soil. Where summers are hot plant cushion spurge in light to part shade.
Deadhead to prevent self-sowing; plants will pop up everywhere if you leave the spent flowers. Plants can also open in the center after they bloom. Cut them back by half or more to refresh the foliage. Cut stems leak a milky sap; this doesn't harm the plants, but it can irritate skin and cause a rash.
Divide plants every five to six years to reduce crowding.

Plants are easy to move, but they wilt for several days afterwards. Keep them well watered until they settle in.
Few pests bother cushion spurge.
Species and cultivars: 'Bonfire' is spectacularly colorful with a combination of purple, red, orange, and chartreuse leaves at the tips of the

'Lacey' variegated cushion spurge

stems and sulfur yellow bracts. Zones 5 to 9. 'First Blush' produces light green leaves variegated with cream along the edge and, in spring to early summer, flushed with rose pink. Yellow bracts surround rose red flower buds. Zones 4 to 7.

Cutleaf coneflower (See Black-eyed susan)

Daylily (Hemerocallis spp.)
hem-er-oh-KAL-iss species
Features: More than 30,000 varieties in every color but pure white and blue
Hardiness: Zones 3 to 10
Bloom time: Late spring to frost, depending on cultivar
Size: Depends on cultivar
Shape: Arching fountain with upright flower stems
Light: Full sun to partial shade
Site: Moist, fertile, well-drained soil

Description: Valued for their striking appearance and adaptability, daylilies are perpetual garden favorites. Each flower lives for a day, giving the plant its name. Colors range from hot red, orange, and yellow to cool pink, purple, and combinations of colors. Blooms are shaped like trumpets and may be long, short, or flattened. The edges of the trumpets may be plain or ruffled. Most daylilies have single flowers, but there are extra frilly double-flowered cultivars.
Peak bloom is midsummer, but this varies according to the cultivars. Some cultivars bloom in late spring; others bloom in early, mid-, or late summer. Repeat bloomers have several flushes throughout the summer. And a few superstars bloom from late spring until frost. For summerlong bloom combine cultivars from each bloom group.
Flowers may skim the top of the foliage or rise several feet above it. Most daylilies are clump forming and spread at a

Daylily

moderate rate. Some spread quickly and make good groundcovers. There are a few evergreen daylilies. These do best in the South.

Daylilies and daffodils combine well; daylily's grassy leaves emerge in time to mask the dying spring bulb foliage. Daylilies look wonderful with ornamental grasses, salvia, and nettle-leaved mullein. Showy but easy, they blend beautifully with most other perennials.

Care: Daylilies prefer well-drained, humus-rich soil of average moisture and fertility, but they will grow just about anywhere. These garden heroes adapt to heat, drought, shade, salt, wind, flooding, and foot traffic. They also survive competition from tree roots. Daylilies are so tough you can plant them or divide them at any time during the growing season.

Feed your plants moderately but regularly. Break off individual faded blooms at the base; remove the entire flowering stalk once it has finished flowering. Divide plants every three to five years when you start seeing fewer flowers.

Snails, slugs, deer, rabbits, and woodchucks eat daylilies. Daylily rust and leaf streak may infect these plants. Planting them where all their cultural preferences are met helps control diseases.

Species and cultivars: With more than 30,000 cultivars, this is only a small selection.

'El Desperado' is 28 inches tall with large mustard yellow flowers that have a burgundy-purple eye, frilly red edge, and green throat. Reblooming 'Happy Returns' is just 18 inches tall and has lemon yellow flowers from May to September. The large lemon yellow flowers of 'Hyperion' are fragrant. They bloom in June and July. Plants grow 36 inches tall. 'Stella de Oro' is a sturdy 12-inch-tall repeat bloomer with gold flowers from June to September.

The following are All-American Daylily Selection award winners: 'Bitsy' has lemon yellow flowers from spring to fall. It grows vigorously, 17 to 28 inches tall. 'Black-Eyed Stella' has large, showy gold flowers with a dark mahogany eye from late spring to fall. It is 17 to 28 inches tall. Late-blooming 'Lady Lucille' has huge, 5- to 6-inch red-orange flowers and shiny leaves. The 22- to 30-inch-tall plants are pest and disease resistant and readily visible from afar, especially when massed. 'Lullaby Baby' grows 24 inches tall and has ruffled, fragrant creamy pink flowers with a green throat. It is an early to midseason rebloomer. 'Persian Market' has salmon pink blooms with a rose halo for at least 90 days in summer. 'Plum Perfect' has purple blooms with a darker purple eye, gold throat, deep purple veins, white midribs, and ruffled edges. It is a vigorous, long-blooming, semievergreen plant that thrives in light shade. 'Red Volunteer' offers gigantic velvety red blooms for six to eight weeks starting in midseason. Plants grow 29 to 33 inches tall and are daylily rust resistant.

Daylily

Delphinium *(Delphinium elatum)*

dell-FIN-ee-um ee-LATE-um
Features: Luxurious spikes of blue, white, pink, or purple
Hardiness: Zones 3 to 7
Bloom time: Early to midsummer
Size: 2- to 3-foot foliage, 1- to 7-foot spire, 3 feet wide
Shape: Mound to spire
Light: Full sun to light shade
Site: Rich, moist, well-drained, slightly alkaline soil high in organic matter

Description:
Delphinium's lush flower spires of blue, pink, white, and purple will wow you. The spikes are comprised of single or double spurred flowers. Some cultivars have white centers, called bees, for a pretty bicolor effect. Out-of-bloom plants form 18-inch-tall mounds of coarse-textured leaves. In bloom the flowers rise 3 to 6 feet over the foliage.

Delphinium

Plant tall cultivars at the back of sunny cottage borders where they tower over other plants. Shorter varieties belong in midborder; dwarf plants are charming at the front of the border and in rock gardens. Combine delphiniums with tall, later-blooming perennials, such as joe-pye weed, hyssop, and bugbane.

Care: Delphiniums do best in cool summer climates. They do not tolerate wind, heat, drought, or poorly drained soil. Plant them in a spot that receives afternoon shade. If soil is acidic, apply lime to raise pH. Deadhead delphinium to a fresh shoot when flowers fade. After all flowering finishes cut spikes back to the basal leaf mounds; new flower spikes may appear later in the season. Cut bloom stalks to the ground after all flowering ceases.

Thin the shoots on established plants in early spring, allowing five to seven shoots per clump. As they develop stake individual flower stems, tying them at 12-inch intervals.

Divide plants in fall every three years. Cut plants down in late fall and remove and discard all foliage to reduce pest problems.

Delphinium

Delphiniums are susceptible to leaf spot disease, powdery mildew, and stem and crown rot, as well as insects such as slugs, snails, and stem borers. Remove and discard all discolored foliage and flowers. Avoid crowding plants. Grow new plants in beds that have not held delphiniums for several years.

Species and cultivars: Chinese delphinium (*D. grandiflorum*) grows 1 to 2 feet tall and has a loose habit of branching racemes in shades of blue. Also known as larkspur, plants are short lived. 'Blue Dwarf' is a small plant with 10-inch spikes of gentian blue blooms all summer. 'Blue Butterfly' grows 14 inches tall and has deep blue flowers with a hint of purple. Flowers of 'Summer Blues' are sky blue. Those of 'Blue Mirror' are bright blue. Zones 3 to 7.

Hybrids: Belladonna-type: These hybrids have loose, branched flower stalks and perform better in warm climates than other delphiniums. Plants grow 1 to 2 feet tall and bloom in shades of blue on 3- to 4-foot-tall stems. 'Bellamosum' has dark blue flowers. Plants in the Connecticut Yankee series have white, blue, lavender, or purple flowers. Zones 3 to 7.

Pacific-type: This group boasts showy spikes of clear, brightly colored double flowers. Magic Fountain Series delphiniums are 2½- to 3-foot-tall bushy plants with dark eyed blue, pink, and white flowers. New Millennium Hybrids include 'Blushing Brides', which have rosy lavender flowers on 6-foot stems, and 'Pagan Purple', with reddish purple blooms on 4-foot stems. 'Round Table Hybrids' bloom in light blue, deep blue, lavender, violet, white, purple, or bicolors on 5- to 6-foot-tall stems. 'Summer Skies' have sky-blue flowers on 5-to 6-foot stems in early summer. Zones 2 to 7.

Dropwort *(See Queen-of-the-meadow)*

Evening primrose *(Oenothera spp.)*

EE-noth-er-uh species
Features: Showy yellow or pink flowers
Hardiness: Zones 4 to 9
Bloom time: Summer
Size: Depends on species
Shape: Upright to spreading, depending on species
Light: Full sun
Site: Well-drained soil

Showy evening primrose

Description: This group of fast-growing native plants brings color to gardens growing in even the harshest conditions. From early to midsummer—or longer—large, rich yellow, pink, or white cupped flowers bloom at the ends of robust stems. Some species creep along the ground; others form a low mound of leaves from which the flowers arise on sturdy 1- to 2-foot-tall stems.

The name evening primrose comes from the fact that flowers open at night. Some *Oenotheras* bloom during the daytime; these are known as sundrops. Each flower lasts only a couple of days, but new flowers are constantly opening.

Grow evening primrose with other vigorous spreaders in wildflower gardens, meadows, or in perennial borders. They

look striking with catmint, bigroot cranesbill, blanket flower, and 'Karl Foerster' feather reed grass.

Care: Evening primrose and sundrops grow and spread quickly through a garden, some from seedlings, others from rhizomes. They can take over if you are not diligent about pulling seedlings or ripping up spreading rootstocks. Deadhead to extend flowering and prevent excessive self-sowing.

Ozark sundrop

After flowering finishes cut back upright growers by one-third to stimulate fresh vegetative growth or cut them all the way back to the evergreen basal rosette of foliage.

To control spreading lift surplus plants each year and give them to friends. Divide plants every four or five years in spring or early fall; discard the old central portion of the clump. Evening primrose is pest free but may have occasional problems with mildew and may develop root rot when soils are too moist.

Species and cultivars: Missouri evening primrose (*O. macrocarpa*) is a Midwest native. Its gray-green foliage grows 6 to 12 inches tall with ruddy, creeping, spreading stems. From late spring to early fall, 5-inch-wide golden cupped blooms cover plants. Flowers open in late afternoon and close the following morning; they last just one day. Zones 4 to 10.

Showy evening primrose (*O. speciosa*) is an upright plant with flower stems reaching 18 inches tall. Its white flowers open at dusk and close the next morning; in cloudy weather they remain open all day. As blooms age they change from white to rose pink. 'Siskiyou' grows 10 to 12 inches tall and has fragrant 2-inch light pink blooms from late spring through summer. It spreads fast and needs excellent drainage. Zones 5 to 11.

Sundrops (*O. fruticosa*) are fast-growing upright spreaders that reach their maximum size in one to two years. Their large yellow flowers sit atop sturdy stems that arise from basal rosettes of evergreen foliage. The rosettes turn mahogany red in cold weather and form an appealing groundcover when plants are not in bloom. Sundrops are native to eastern North America and thrive in moist, well-drained soil. The pink-and-white spring foliage of 'Fruhlingsgold' changes to variegated green with creamy white edges as the season progresses. Its 1½-inch fragrant, gleaming yellow flowers are borne on 15-inch stems in early summer. 'Highlight' is also 15 inches tall when in bloom. Its lightly fragrant 2-inch-wide yellow flowers form clusters of blooms from June to August. 'Fireworks' has red 18-inch-tall flower stems topped with yellow flowers that open from red buds in June and July. Zones 4 to 9.

White-tufted evening primrose (*O. caespitosa*) forms dense rosettes 6 to 12 inches tall and 1 to 2 feet across. The cupped flowers are 2 to 4 inches wide, white aging to pink. They lie above the tufted foliage, open in the afternoon, and close the following morning. Plant them in well-drained, gritty soil with no organic matter mixed in. Avoid wet sites especially during winter. This species requires less than 8 inches of water per year, but additional watering will increase flowering. Zones 4 to 9.

False indigo (Baptisia australis)

bap-TISS-ee-uh ah-STRAL-iss
Features: Long spikes of violet-blue blooms; drought tolerant and deer resistant
Hardiness: Zones 3 to 8
Bloom time: Late spring
Size: 3 to 4 feet tall; 3 feet wide
Shape: Broad oval
Light: Full sun to part sun
Site: Lean, well-drained to dry soil

Description: This perennial's lupine blue spires appear from late spring to early summer, followed by handsome, nodding black seedpods. The pods, used as rattles by pioneer children, make a clattering noise when shaken. Attractive blue-green leaves resemble those of clover. Blooms and seedpods are valued for flower arrangements. Use false indigo for screening, at the back of perennial borders as a backdrop for showy shorter flowers, in containers, and in prairie and meadow gardens.

False indigo

Care: Although false indigo takes a while to establish, it's worth the wait. This easy-care, long-lived perennial resists pests and diseases and is drought tolerant. It grows best in lean soil in a sunny, well-drained spot. After flowering false indigo may need staking, especially if you let the seedpods remain on the plant. Set grow-through supports over the plants in spring before foliage grows too tall or cut back the plant by one-third after it blooms to promote sturdier, more compact growth. A deep taproot makes false indigo difficult to transplant and divide so choose its location carefully. Cut plants back to the ground in late fall or early spring.

Species and cultivars: Lesser wild indigo (*B. a. minor*) looks similar to the species but is smaller, growing just 2 feet tall and wide. Its violet-blue flowers appear in early to midsummer. Zones 3 to 8.

False indigo

White wild indigo (*B. alba*) has purplish new growth and long-lasting white flowers on a 2- to 3-foot plant. Zones 5 to 8.
Hybrids: 'Purple Smoke' has open spikes of smoky purple-blue flowers on charcoal stems in late spring and early summer. Plants grow 48 to 52 inches tall and have gray-green foliage. Zones 4 to 9. 'Carolina Moonlight' provides delightful spires of pale yellow flowers over blue-green leaves. Plants grow 40 to 50 inches tall. Zones 4 to 9.

False solomon's seal (Smilacena racemosa)

smy-lass-SIGH-nuh ray-see-MOH-suh
Features: Gracefully arching stems; showy white flower plumes
Hardiness: Zones 3 to 8
Bloom time: Spring
Size: 3 feet tall, 2 feet wide
Shape: Upright to arching
Light: Partial to full shade
Site: Moist, well-drained, moderately fertile soil with abundant organic matter

Description: In nature false solomon's seal grows densely clustered in rich woods. Its broad pointed green foliage has smooth edges and parallel veins running lengthwise down the

False solomon's seal

blades. From April through May or June, showy pyramidal plumes of tiny, fragrant white flowers bloom at the stem tips. After flowering dense clusters of small berries appear at the stem tips, ripening from mottled green to bright red. In fall the foliage turns yellow.

Grown in masses, false solomon's seal beautifies wild gardens, woodland edges, the banks of shady ponds and streams, and shady borders. Combine it with ferns, hostas, or snowy woodrush, a shade-tolerant ornamental grass. Both solomon's seal and false solomon's seal produce leaves along curving stems. You can tell the plants apart by the way they bloom.

Care: Grow false solomon's seal in somewhat fertile, acid soil rich in organic matter. It prefers a cool location, uniform moisture, good drainage, and partial to full shade. To propagate plants divide in spring.

Species and cultivars: Starry false solomon's seal (S. stellata) produces small clusters of starry, greenish white flowers at the tips of leafy stems. It grows 1 to 2 feet tall and wide and does best in partial shade and dry, sandy soils. Zones 3 to 7.

False sunflower (Heliopsis helianthoides)

he-lee-OP-siss hee-lee-AN-thoy-deez
Features: Yellow daisies
Hardiness: Zones 3 to 8
Bloom time: Early to late summer
Size: 3 to 6 feet tall, 2 to 4 feet wide
Shape: Bushy, upright clump
Light: Full sun
Site: Well-drained, organic soil

Description: Large, 3-inch-wide colorful blooms and a long bloom time make false sunflower indispensable to informal gardens. Plants are clump forming and fast growing. The plants and flowers look similar to true sunflowers; one difference between the two is that false sunflower blooms earlier. Use as a backdrop to the garden or partner with shorter, finer-textured perennials, such as lavender, catmint, peony, or salvia. Cultivars have better form and showier flowers than the straight species.

Care: False sunflower tolerates drought, part shade, a wide soil pH range, and heavy clay soil. It does not do well in wet or poorly drained soil. In hot regions midday shade helps cool the plants.

'Loraine Sunshine' heliopsis

Deadhead to prolong bloom and prevent self-sowing. Seedlings do not come true to the parent and are usually inferior to the original plant.

Floppy stems on false sunflower mean one of several things. The plant needs a sunnier location, soil drainage is too slow, or plants need more water and fertilizer. Increase watering and fertilizing early in the season; improve drainage around the plant and prune overhanging branches to let in more light; or move the plant to a sunnier, better-drained site.

Species and cultivars: 'Summer Sun' has soft yellow double flowers. It grows 3 feet tall. It is more heat tolerant than the species and does better in the South than other cultivars. 'Prairie Sunset' blooms for eight weeks at a time. Its lovely yellow daisies have a red eye; foliage is tinged purple. Plants grow 4 feet tall and 2 to 3 feet wide. 'Loraine Sunshine' has unusual white foliage with dark green veins and yellow daisy flowers. Plants reach 30 inches tall.

False sunflower

Feather reed grass *(Calamagrostis acutiflora)*

cal-uh-muh-GRAWS-tiss uh-cute-ih-FLOOR-uh
Features: Ornamental grass with upright flowers
Hardiness: Zones 5 to 9
Bloom time: Early summer
Size: 2- to 3-feet tall, 5 feet with flowers, 18 to 24 inches wide
Shape: Cascading, upright in bloom
Light: Full sun to light shade
Site: Well-drained soil

Description: Feather reed grass changes alluringly through the seasons. Spring brings a fountain of light green leaves, which by early summer are topped with tall, feathery pink inflorescences. These change to light purple by early summer, then ripen into golden wheatlike sheaves by midsummer. The seedheads remain attractive into fall, and

plants maintain their erect architectural form through winter. Use feather reed grass singly or in groups in prairie gardens, perennial beds, mixed borders, and containers. It makes a fine vertical accent. Cut seedheads for fresh or dried arrangements.

Feather reed grass, white coneflower, fountain grass

Care: Plants prosper in sun to partial shade and moist, well-drained soil rich in organic matter. They tolerate a variety of soils and conditions, including wet clay and salty seasides. Divide plants in spring after new growth begins but before flowering begins. Leave the foliage and seedheads for winter interest. Cut plants to the ground in late winter or early spring. If growing in part shade, plants bloom later.

Species and cultivars: 'Karl Foerster' forms a stiff 5-foot by 1½- to 2-foot column when in flower. It has lustrous dark green deciduous leaves. Foliage of 'Avalanche' is variegated with a white streak down the center. 'Avalanche' grows 4 to 5 feet tall. 'Overdam' has variegated leaves, this time with white stripes around a green center. It grows 3 feet tall.

Ferns

Features: Unique texture and handsome foliage colors
Hardiness: Zones 3 to 8, depending on species
Size: Less than 1 foot to 6 feet, depending on species
Light: Partial to full shade
Site: Rich, well-drained soil

Description: Ferns are a natural for woodland gardens and shady beds and borders. Dozens of species are available for use in shady backyards. Combine ferns with other shade-loving perennials such as hosta, astilbe, solomon's seal, and Bethlehem sage. Individually they are graceful in form. Massed as a groundcover under high-canopied trees, they add drama and refinement to the landscape.

Care: Most ferns grow easily in partial to full shade and moist, well-drained, slightly acid soil rich in organic matter; a few prefer wetter sites. Divide ferns in spring or fall and keep divisions well watered.

Species and cultivars:
Christmas ferns *(Polystichum* spp.) are

Christmas fern

Hay-scented fern

upright, evergreen ferns with medium to bold texture and lustrous green fronds. Give them moist, well-drained soil in light to full shade. They tolerate slightly alkaline soils. Provide continually moist soil. Remove brown foliage as new growth emerges. **Christmas fern** (*P. acrostichoides*) produces fronds up to 3 feet long. Although new fronds are erect, they sprawl on older growth to form a striking, slightly glossy mound. Because of its compact, mounded shape and evergreen foliage, this fern looks good in woodland settings and shines in partly shaded borders. Zones 4 to 10. **Western sword fern** (*P. munitum*) has glossy dark evergreen fronds that make an erect, arching clump of medium texture about 3 to 4 feet tall and wide. This fern looks outstanding planted in moist, shady woodland gardens in soil rich in organic matter. Plants do best in coastal environments. Zones 5 to 10. **Soft shield fern** (*P. setiferum*) produces feathery, dark evergreen fronds that grow in a whirl, giving plants a shuttlecock shape. It grows 3 to 4 feet tall and 3 feet wide. This erect fern adds an exotic touch to woodland gardens and shady borders. Plant it in beds with hosta under ornamental trees. Soft shield fern dies back in cold-winter climates. 'Congestum' is 8 inches tall with crowded, overlapping segments that give the grayish green fronds an intricate texture. 'Herrenhausen' grows 10 to 12 inches tall with lacy fronds. It is a good choice for growing in containers. Zones 5 to 7. **Tassel fern** (*P. polyblepharum*) has dark glossy evergreen fronds. It grows 18 to 24 inches tall and just 10 inches wide. Zones 6 to 10.

Hay-scented fern (*Dennstaedtia punctilobata*), gets its name for the scent of its fronds when they're bruised. It is an upright native fern with lovely yellow-green arching lacy fronds. Plants grow 3 feet tall and wide. They tolerate a wide range of conditions but do best in partial to deep shade and rich, moist, well-drained, slightly acid soil. Once established hay-scented fern tolerates dry shade. Plants grow and spread quickly, naturalizing into a beautiful woodland groundcover. Zones 3 to 8.

Lady ferns (*Athyrium* spp.) comprise a large group of variable, deciduous, upright to spreading ferns. Plants grow best in soil with a neutral pH and in part to full shade. **Japanese painted fern** (*A. nipponicum* 'Pictum') is one of the best known to gardeners. Its silver fronds licked with red and blue rise from

'Cruciatum' criss-cross lady fern

burgundy-red stems. Plants grow 12 to 18 inches tall and up to 24 inches wide, and make elegant and colorful garden or container accents. Japanese painted fern grows in dark garden corners but is at its most colorful if it receives at least a few hours of morning light. Zones 4 to 9. 'Pewter Lace' is a 12-inch-tall fern with dark-centered silvery gray leaves. Zones 5 to 8. 'Red Beauty' is similar to 'Pictum' with silver, red, and green fronds on 12- to 18-inch-long red stems. But the stems and veins are much redder.

Although somewhat variable, fronds of **lady fern** (*A. filix-femina*) are denser and more finely divided than Japanese painted fern. These plants have a delicate lacy appearance and grow 2 to 3 feet tall. They can be evergreen in mild climates. Lady ferns are easy to grow and tolerate dry soil. They will grow in full sun if given plenty of moisture. Zones 4 to 9. The cultivar 'Frizelliae', called the tatting fern, looks like strings of green pearls. This odd plant grows about 1 foot tall. Zones 3 to 10.

Hybrids: 'Branford Beauty' has silvery fronds with red stems, similar to those of Japanese painted fern. It grows 2 feet tall and wide. 'Ghost' offers erect all-silver fronds 2 to 3 feet tall.

Maidenhair ferns (*Adiantum* spp.) are airy, delicate-looking ferns with broad leaflets on slender stalks that originate from the tip of stem like an umbrella. They are lovely when grouped in a shady border, rock garden, or woodland garden, creating a fine-textured mass. Plants prefer neutral to alkaline soil well enriched with organic matter. Provide continuous moisture. Grow them in full shade to part sun. **Northern maidenhair ferns** (*A. pedatum*) have upright blackish purple stems topped by arching branchlets arranged like fingers on a hand. This tough but dainty deciduous fern grows about 2 feet tall and wide and prefers dappled shade. New growth of 'Miss Sharples' emerges light yellow-green; leaflets are larger than the species on this cultivar. Fronds of 'Japonicum' emerge pinkish bronze. Zones 3 to 9. **Himalayan maidenhair fern** (*A. venustum*) is a semievergreen fern growing 8 to 12 inches tall. New fronds emerge bronzy pink in spring and age to light bluish green in summer, and yellowish brown in fall. Stems are purplish black. Heat and humidity are detrimental to these ferns. Zones 5 to 8.

Japanese painted fern

Northern maidenhair fern

Osmundas (*Osmunda* spp.) are among the largest ferns suited to home gardens. They require very moist soil to survive. Grow them in light to full shade. **Cinnamon fern** (*O. cinnamomea*), a deciduous fern, grows wild in moist to wet soils in sun or shade. Its sterile light green fronds on the outside of the clump can reach 5 feet tall and 2 feet wide. In the center of the plant are erect, reddish brown spore-bearing fronds from which the plant gets its name. These grow 3 feet tall. This fern looks striking at the edge of ponds and woodlands. Zones 4 to 9. **Interrupted fern** (*O. claytoniana*) grows into a clump up to 3 feet tall and twice as wide. Its upright fronds bow at the top. In the center of each green frond, leaflets bearing spore cases develop, hence the fern's name. Interrupted fern looks particularly striking in spring when these fertile leaflets turn rich blackish brown. Zones 3 to 6. **Royal fern** (*O. regalis*) forms a 2- to 6-foot-tall well-shaped clump in wet, boggy, or lakeside soils. The deciduous foliage is leathery light green, turning an attractive gold tone in fall. Zones 4 to 9.

Ostrich fern (*Matteuccia struthiopteris*) grows in a vase-shape clump 3 feet tall and wide. In the right conditions plants may reach 6 feet tall. If you want the classic fern look in your garden, this is the one for you. Plants spread rapidly by thick braided rhizomes and are too aggressive to combine into tidy combinations with other shade perennials. Let it spread into a tall, vigorous groundcover that will make your shady area look like a primeval jungle. Plants do best in shade and in average to moist soil. They'll tolerate some sun as long as the soil never dries. Even in shade fronds become scorched and die back when soil is too dry. Zones 3 to 8.

Cinnamon fern

Sensitive fern (*Onoclea sensibilis*) is a wide-spreading, 2-foot-tall fern with light green fronds. It makes an excellent groundcover for moist shade and is frequently found growing at the edge of moist woods. Zones 3 to 8.

Wood ferns (*Dryopteris* spp.) are medium-size woodland ferns. They are tough and adaptable, with strong forms and bold texture. Some species are evergreen; others are deciduous. Grow them in neutral to acid, well-drained, fertile, organic soil, and light to full shade. Divide plants every three years or so to maintain their symmetrical form. However if never divided the ferns can grow into large attractive clumps. **Male wood fern** (*D. filix-mas*) forms a 3-foot by 3-foot clump of fronds. In protected places it may remain evergreen through the winter. Zones 3 to 8. **Autumn fern** (*D. erythrosora*), an evergreen, produces coppery new growth that turns green with age; it has ruddy fall color. Plants grow about 18 inches tall and wide. **Goldie's fern** (*D. goldiana*) forms 4-foot by 2-foot clumps of light green fronds. Zones 6 to 8. **Marginal shield fern** (*D. marginalis*) has evergreen fronds. It grows about 18 inches tall and 24 inches wide. Zones 3 to 8.

Fleabane *(Erigeron speciosus)*

ee-RIJ-er-on spee-cee-OH-suss
Features: Showy pink, white, yellow, or purple daisies
Hardiness: Zones 4 to 9
Bloom time: Midsummer to fall
Size: 2 to 12 inches tall, 18 to 30 inches in bloom, 24 inches wide
Shape: Low rosette from which upright flower stems rise
Light: Full sun
Site: Sandy, well-drained soil

Description: This dainty yet bushy North American native looks like aster but is even easier to grow. Its 1- to 2-inch-wide yellow-centered pastel daisies appear earlier than those of aster; plants start blooming in midsummer and often remain in bloom until fall. Colors range from pink and purple to yellow and white. The native species is rarely grown; cultivars have better form and color. Short fleabanes look charming massed in rock gardens. They also

White fleabane with purple lantana

work at the front of borders and on the edges of beds. Taller varieties look good grouped in the middle of a border. Good companions include dwarf blue fescue, northern sea oats, and 'Moonbeam' coreopsis. Grow fleabane in groups of three or more for seasonlong color.

Care: This low-maintenance perennial is free from pests and diseases. It likes moist, well-drained soil of average fertility but adapts well to leaner sites. Short alpine fleabanes need quick-draining soil. Stake tall varieties. Pruning fleabane to 6 inches after blooming renews the leaves and makes the plant more compact. Divide plants every three years in spring to maintain vigor.

Species and cultivars: Beach fleabane (*E. glaucus*) has pale mauve flowers with yellow centers from late spring to midsummer. A California native, the 12-inch-tall by 18-inch-wide plants can be found growing on sand dunes. 'Albus' is a white-flowered cultivar that grows 8 inches tall. 'Sea Breeze' has large pink daisies with a fat yellow center. They grow 24 to 36 inches tall. Zones 5 to 10.

Hybrids: 'Azure Fairy' is lavender-blue with semidouble blooms. 'Darkest of All' shows its rich blue-violet flowers on 24-inch-tall stems. 'Prosperity' has lavender-blue blooms and grows 18 inches tall. 'Rose Jewel' blooms in lilac-rose and grows 15 to 18 inches tall.

Fleabane

Fleeceflower *(Persicaria* spp.*)*

per-sick-AIR-ee-uh species
Features: Colorful flower spikes or foliage
Hardiness: Zones 3 to 7, depending on species
Bloom time: Mid- to late summer
Size: Depends on species
Shape: Upright or creeping, depending on species
Light: Full sun to light shade
Site: Well-drained moist soil of average fertility

Description:

Fleeceflowers are lovely garden perennials with showy flowers and/or foliage. Unfortunately they are related to some nasty weeds, a trait that scares many gardeners away. Some species are sturdy upright plants; others creep along the ground. All have upright flower spikes and fat swollen joints on their stems. Blooms may be white, red, or pink. Plants are coarse textured.

'Painter's Palette' Virginia fleeceflower

Care: Provide well-drained moist to wet soil in full sun or part shade. Sun and moisture requirements vary among the species. Deadhead by removing the entire flower stalk to prevent self-sowing and keep plants tidy. Plants are sturdy and do not need staking. Divide plants every 3 to 5 years in spring or as often as necessary to restrict spread. Fleeceflowers are pest free.

Species and cultivars: Himalayan fleeceflower *(P. affine)* is a creeper with dense, 12-inch-tall rose red flower spikes from summer to fall. Plants require moist, well-drained sites in full sun. They prefer cool climates and are not invasive. Foliage turns bronze in fall. 'Darjeeling Red' has long rose red flowers above deep green leaves in late summer to fall. 'Superba' has pink flowers from early summer to fall. It grows just 6 inches tall and 12 inches wide. You may find it also sold as 'Dimity'. Zones 4 to 9.

Mountain fleeceflower *(P. amplexicaulis)* is a stout, upright plant 2 to 4 feet tall and 3 feet wide. Plants are not invasive, but they can group into large clumps. Cool, moist sites are best. In warm climates ensure a plentiful water supply. 'Firetail' has crimson flower spikes from early summer to fall. Plants grow 4 feet tall and wide. 'Taurus' has brilliant scarlet spikes from early summer to midfall. Plants are 2½ feet tall and 4 feet wide. Zones 4 to 7.

Detail of mountain fleeceflower

Virginia fleeceflower *(P. virginianum)* has gone by several names in the past few years, including tovara. Because the cultivars are better than the species, look for this perennial by its cultivar name. Virginia fleeceflowers are sturdy upright plants that grow 2 feet tall and wide. Like other fleeceflowers they need moist, well-drained soil, although they can tolerate drought. Plants grow slower in dry soils and do not do well in drying winds. Flowers are not showy; they're tiny on whiskerlike stalks. Plants readily reseed, so deadhead to prevent self-sowing. 'Painters Palette' has beautiful variegated foliage, bright green marked with yellow, white, and rusty pink. 'Variegatum' is variegated white; stems are red. Zones 4 to 8.

Foam flower *(Tiarella* spp.*)*

tea-uh-REL-uh species
Features: White or pink blooms, ruddy bronze fall color
Hardiness: Zones 3 to 8
Bloom time: Midspring
Size: Depends on species
Shape: Creeping or mounded
Light: Partial to full shade
Site: Moist, well-drained, humus-rich soil

Description: Foam flowers are aptly named for their foamy clusters of creamy white flower spires. They have coarsely lobed hairy leaves. Two species comprise this group: Allegheny foam flower *(T. cordifolia)* and wherry's foam flower *(T. wherryi)*. Both thrive in shade and woodland conditions.

Allegheny foam flower spreads vigorously by stolons, forming a handsome groundcover with good red to yellow fall color. Its foliage may be evergreen in temperate areas. In spring the petite star-shape white flowers appear in fluffy spikes above the leaves. Plants

Foam flower

grow about 6 inches tall and spread indefinitely. They are not invasive but weave around their neighbors.

Wherry's foam flower is a lovely small, clump-forming plant. Clumps grow 6 to 9 inches tall and enlarge to 12 inches wide or more by stolons. Like Allegheny foam flowers they have tiny white flowers on upright flower stems in spring.

Grow foam flowers with ferns, bleeding heart, and yellow waxbells. They are especially pretty with bleeding heart, lenten rose, barrenwort, bellflower, and dropwort.

Care: Plants tolerate light foot traffic but not drought. Space them about 12 to 15 inches apart. Deadhead wherry's foam flower and clump-forming cultivars to prolong bloom. Removing spent flowers from Allegheny foam flower may stimulate more blooming, but the appealing foliage looks good even if you don't deadhead. Divide plants every three or four years to contain their spread. You can also keep foam flower in check by pulling out runners, which you can pot up and give to your friends. Do not cut plants back in fall. Foam flowers are basically pest free, but root weevils may be a problem.

Detail of foam flower

Species and cultivars: Allegheny foam flower: The pink flower buds of 'Oakleaf' open to pink flowers that fade to white.

Wherry's foam flower: 'Heronswood Mist' has white blooms on pink stems and mottled cream-and-green foliage with pinkish new growth. Plants grow into 12-inch-tall clumps.

Hybrids: 'Black Snowflake' has dramatic semievergreen leaves with dark purple veins and nearly black new growth; coloring is stronger in cool weather. Flowers are creamy white. Plants grow 12 inches tall. 'Elizabeth Oliver' makes a dense 12-inch-tall groundcover covered with pale pink spikes in spring. Its deeply lobed foliage is marked with maroon. 'Jeepers Creepers' is another groundcover type growing 12 inches all. The large creamy white flower spikes are set off by deeply lobed leaves with black markings through their centers. 'Pink Skyrocket' offers large, long-lasting pink flower spikes. Plants grow 12 inches tall. 'Pirate's Patch' blooms profusely with white flower spikes on 10-inch-tall stems that rise above the 5-inch mound of leaves marked in the center with reddish black.

Foamy bells (×Heucherella spp.)

hew-ker-ELL-uh species
Features: Abundant white, pink, or cream flower spikes
Hardiness: Zones 4 to 8
Bloom time: Spring
Size: 5 to 9 inches tall and wide, 10 to 18 inches tall in bloom
Shape: Mounded
Light: Full sun to partial shade
Site: Rich, moist, well-drained soil

Foamy bells

Description: Grown for abundant foamy flower spikes and handsome tight mounds of leaves, this hybrid perennial results from a cross between coral bells and foam flower. Plants show the best of traits from both parents. They do not reproduce; instead the energy that would have gone to making seeds is put into forming lavish wands of delicate pink, white, or tawny flowers.

The evergreen leaves grow in neat mounds that sometimes change color as the season progresses. Foliage varies from marbled greens to purple, bronze, chartreuse, and yellow. Some cultivars have silver overlays or colorful decorative veining on the leaves.

Foamy bells looks terrific at the front of the perennial border. Use it for edging or as a leafy accent between shrubs. Grow it on its own in containers alone or with other plants. Cut the flowers for long-lasting bouquets. Foamy bells harmonize with catmint, cranesbill, and hosta.

Care: Pest- and disease-resistant foamy bells is easy to cultivate in rich, moist, well-drained soil high in organic matter. Partial shade is ideal, but foamy bells can adapt to full shade. Green-and-purple-leaved cultivars also do well in full sun, but yellow or pale-leaved plants may burn. To preserve soil moisture mulch around plants but don't cover the growing point. Deadheading promotes more flowers. Divide foamy bells in spring or fall every few years, discarding the center and replanting the vigorous edges.

Species and cultivars: White foamy bells (H. alba) have white blooms similar to coral bells on 15- to 20-inch stems from early to midspring. 'Bridget Bloom' has light pink blooms on 14-inch-long spikes in late spring to midsummer.

Hybrids: 'Quicksilver' offers 18-inch-tall white spikes on dark stems that open from pinkish buds. The dark bronzy foliage has a silver overlay between the veins. Leaves change from red to green to dark bronze over the season. 'Kimono' blooms with 18-inch tawny spikes rising from a 9-inch leafy mound. Spring leaves are variegated green, silver, and purple. Foliage changes to a metallic rose over winter. 'Kimono' requires part shade. 'Sunspot' offers electric yellow leaves splotched with scarlet and 16-inch pink spikes. Foliage of 'Stoplight' is larger, with a larger scarlet splotch in the center. It blooms in white on 12-inch stems.

Fountain grass (Pennisetum alopecuroides)

pen-iss-SEE-tum al-oh-pek-yer-OI-deez
Features: Graceful form
Hardiness: Zones 5 to 9
Bloom time: Late summer
Size: 3 feet tall, 4 feet in bloom, 2 feet wide
Shape: Cascading fountain
Light: Full sun
Site: Well-drained fertile soil

Description: One of the most useful grasses for perennial gardens, fountain grass is a graceful ornamental grass with arching, glossy green foliage that sways in the wind. The fine-textured leaves remain green into fall, and then change to gold before bleaching to almond for winter. In late summer, August to October, long foxtail plumes open green and mature to silvery pink or white. The seedheads ripen to tan and remain upright on the plant until walloped by winter ice and snow. Grow large fountain grass cultivars

Fountain grass

Seedheads of fountain grass

with tall asters at the back of the border or in the middle of the garden for an attractive late-season display. Small cultivars look charming in containers and around mailboxes or lampposts mass-planted with 'Happy Returns' or 'Black-Eyed Stella' daylilies. They add an airy, fine texture to the front of beds and along borders and can be grouped for maximum effect. The bottlebrush blooms are excellent for cutting. **Care:** Fountain grass prefers full sun and moist, well-drained, somewhat fertile soil. In warm climates it may self-sow to the point of invasiveness. Before buying this grass check with your local cooperative extension service to see which cultivars grow best in your area. Division is easy. Cut plants to the ground in early spring.

Species and cultivars: 'Hameln' grows 24 inches tall and wide. Its leaf blades are thinner than the species. Plumes are creamy white blooms and form in midsummer. 'Little Bunny' grows just 8 to 12 inches tall. It's a profusely flowering green-leaved miniature. 'Little Honey' is a variegated version of 'Little Bunny'. 'Moudry' grows 2 to 3 feet tall and has dark brown to black bottlebrush flowers in late fall. 'National Arboretum' is also a 2- to 3-foot grass. It has dark green leaves and dark brown flower spikes. Zones 5 to 8.

Foxglove *(See Yellow foxglove)*

Fringe cup *(Tellima grandiflora)*

TEA-lih-muh grand-IH-floor-uh
Features: Dense evergreen foliage
Hardiness: Zones 5 to 8
Bloom time: Midspring
Size: 8 inches tall, 24 inches wide
Shape: Low, spreading mound
Light: Part to full shade
Site: Well-drained organic soil

Fringe cup

Description: This dense-mounded evergreen perennial makes a fine edging for a shade garden, and a gray-green point of contrast among forest greens, bronzes, and blue-greens. Its tiny fringed flower cups bloom on wiry naked stems. The green blooms age to pinkish green by midspring. Good companions for fringe cups include blue-leaved hostas, columbine, meadow rue, fringed bleeding heart, dwarf goatsbeard, dropwort, purple-leaf coral bells, and astilbe.
Care: Fringe cup tolerates drought and competition from tree roots, making it an excellent choice for growing under trees. It does not do well in wet soil, high humidity, and heat, especially when soil is poorly drained. Deadhead to keep plants neat. If you want the plants to naturalize, leave the seedheads in place. Mulch with 1 to 2 inches of compost in fall or early spring. Divide plants every four to five years to maintain vigor and to renew the soil.
Species and cultivars: 'Purpurea' is more floriferous and has pink flowers.

Gas plant *(Dictamnus albus)*

dick-TAM-nus AL-bus
Features: Huge spikes of white flowers; attractive mound of foliage
Hardiness: Zones 3 to 8
Bloom time: Midspring
Size: 1½ to 2 feet tall, 3 feet in bloom, 2 to 3 feet wide
Shape: Mounded, upright spire in bloom
Light: Full sun to partial shade
Site: Moist, somewhat rich, well-drained soil with a neutral to slightly alkaline pH

Description: Gas plant is an impressive sight when it is in bloom and later when its wand of ripened seedpods opens into a host of nut-brown stars in the fall. Its starry, white or rose-pink flowers open on tall spikes over shining dark foliage. Plants are worth growing for the tough, handsome, glossy feathery foliage alone. Flowers and leaves have a lemony scent.

Each flower has five petals unevenly spaced around a group of long, prominent stamens. The flowers give off a gas. Light a match beside a flower in the evening and you'll see a flash of flame.

Gas plant's flower spikes and seedpods add a welcome vertical note to the perennial border. It looks attractive silhouetted against dark shrubs and planted with peony, coral bells, lady's mantle, or daylily. The foliage color and texture contrast nicely with Siberian and Japanese irises and with threadleaf coreopsis.
Care: Slow-growing gas plant takes its name from the combustible oil produced by the seeds

'Alba' gas plant

'Purpureus' gas plant

and flowers. The oil may irritate skin, so wear gloves when working with this plant, which is mostly healthy and free from pests and diseases.

Gas plant does not tolerate poor drainage or hot nights (over 80°F). It's a heavier feeder than most perennials, so fertilize regularly. Floppy stems mean the plants need water. Because stems are strong and woody at the base, plants usually do not need staking. Leave flower stems to provide fall and winter interest, cutting plants back in spring. Deadhead as flowers fade if you do not desire seedpods.

Plants rarely require dividing. They have a taproot and can be difficult but not impossible to move. Move or divide gas plant in spring or early fall. Gas plant is host to larvae of black and giant swallowtail butterflies.

Species and cultivars: 'Purpureus' has purplish pink flowers with dark stems and veins.

Gayfeather *(Liatris* spp.*)*

LIE-ay-triss species
Features: Tall purple flower spikes, fine texture
Hardiness: Zones 3 to 9
Bloom time: Early to midsummer
Size: 12 inches tall and wide, 2- to 5-foot flower spike
Shape: Upright in bloom, grassy clump out of bloom
Light: Full sun
Site: Fertile, well-drained soil

Spike gayfeather

Description: This native prairie plant stands tall in a garden. Slender but sturdy upright flower stems arise from a short clump of fine-textured grassy foliage. The stems have grassy leaves as well, so the overall effect is of handsome bottlebrushes planted in your garden. The fuzzy rosy purple flowers are densely packed along the top foot of the stem and open from the tip down, providing several weeks of color.

Gayfeather adds a useful vertical accent in perennial borders, in containers, and in cut flower arrangements. It is a good choice for wildflower and wildlife gardens, attracting bees and butterflies.

The fine-textured foliage offers an attractive contrast to larger, coarser foliage, and the flower spikes partner well with mounded plants, ornamental grasses, and perennials with daisy flowers. Good partners include tree mallow, daylily, rudbeckia, purple coneflower, golden marguerite, geranium, false sunflower, hardy hibiscus, or iris.

Care: Drought tolerant once established, easy-to-grow gayfeather thrives in average garden soil and is pH adaptable. Plants tolerate heat and wind. Tall species may need staking, especially if they grow in average to dry soil. Use individual stakes or grow-through supports set up in early spring.

Deadhead to extend blooming, tidy plants, and prevent self-sowing. After flowering finishes remove the spent stems at their base. Cut back plants in late fall or early spring.

Divide gayfeather in spring every three to five years, as necessary, to maintain the vigor of the plant. They grow

from cormlike roots and are easy to move. Few pests and diseases trouble spike gayfeather, though slugs and snails can cause problems.

Species and cultivars:
Kansas gayfeather *(L. pycnostachya)* grows to 5 feet tall, topped with 1½-foot flower spikes in mauve-purple. The flower stems are less sturdy than those of spike gayfeather and should be staked. Plants require a moist, well-drained site, and they must have excellent drainage over winter.

The flowers of **rough gayfeather** *(L. aspera)* grow in widely spaced, 1-inch-wide tufts along the flower stem. Plants are 3 to 4 feet tall.

Kansas gayfeather

Spike gayfeather *(Liatris spicata)* grows 3 to 4 feet tall and 2 feet wide. The blooms make up 6 to 15 inches of the flower stem. It has mauve-purple flowers in early to midsummer. 'Alba' grows 40 inches tall and has white flowers. 'Floristan Violett' is 3 feet tall with violet spikes on strong stems. It's a good choice for cut flowers. 'Floristan White' is similar, but it blooms in white. 'Kobold' grows just 2 feet tall and has rosy-purple spikes. 'Kobold Original' is shorter at 14 inches tall.

Geranium *(Geranium* spp.*)*

Ger-AIN-ee-um species
Features: Mounds of pink, rose, red, purple, violet, or magenta flowers
Hardiness: Depends on species
Bloom time: Spring or summer, depending on species
Size: Depends on species
Shape: Mounded or spreading clump
Light: Full sun to shade
Site: Moist, moderately fertile, well-drained soil

Description: Dozens of species comprise this group of perennials. All have coarsely lobed hairy leaves that grow into spreading clumps or rounded mounds. All have five-petaled, saucer-shape flowers from which the stamens and pistil poke out. When the petals drop the ripening fruit left at the end of the stem looks like a bird's beak, hence another common name for this group: cranesbill. This beaky fruit is the only trait that ties perennial geraniums to annual geraniums, which are not geraniums at all but pelargoniums.

All geraniums are good for carefree color. Most make fine front-of-the-border plants and blooming groundcovers. Others belong in the

Geranium with scabiosa

Detail of geranium blossom

middle of the garden because of their size. The majority are refined plants, but some have a rangy habit and are best suited to wildflower gardens. Some geraniums bloom in mid- to late spring and then sporadically throughout the summer. Others bloom all summer. A few geraniums develop reddish fall color. In warm climates the foliage can persist into winter. Geraniums are good facer plants for hiding the base of leggy shrubs.

Care: Geraniums do best in full sun to light shade. In hot, humid climates, they'll do better in a site with all-day dappled shade or morning sun and afternoon shade. Deadheading is not necessary for rebloom. After the first flush of flowering has finished, shear the plants near the base. This stimulates growth of fresh foliage that will look much tidier, and it prevents self-sowing. New leaves fill in quickly, creating a solid light green mass. In late fall or early spring, trim back frost-killed foliage. Divide plants every five to six years to renew vigor. Plants are easy to move.

Species and cultivars: **Armenian geranium** (*G. psilostemon*) is the tallest geranium. It grows to 4 feet tall and 3 feet wide. Blooms are an incredible hot magenta color with a dark eye. Plants require light shade and moist soil. Zones 5 to 7.

Bigroot geranium (*G. macrorrhizum*) blooms in spring with bright magenta flowers. It forms a dense, adaptable weed-smothering 18-inch-tall groundcover. Although full sun and well-drained moist soil are best, bigroot geranium does well in dry shade. Try it on a sunny dry-laid stone retaining wall or under a tree. The medicinal-scented light green leaves develop attractive red and yellow fall color. Although many cranesbill species need cutting back after bloom to keep leaves fresh and growth compact, bigroot cranesbill looks good all season. 'Bevan's Variety' has summerlong deep magenta flowers on compact mounds of aromatic foliage 1 foot tall and 1½ feet wide. 'Lohenfelden'

Bloody cranesbill

offers long-lasting pale pink flowers on 8-inch-tall by 20-inch-wide plants. It has red fall color. 'Minor' has long-blooming magenta flowers and red to yellow fall color. It grows 9 inches tall and 36 inches wide. Zones 3 to 8. 'Ingwersen's Variety' has 1-inch-wide pale pink blooms and red to orange fall color. It grows 14 inches tall and nearly 4 feet wide. Zones 5 to 8.

Bloody cranesbill (*G. sanguineum*) is a free-flowering plant that tolerates heat and cold better than other geranium species. Brilliant magenta flowers cover the plants from spring into summer. Plants typically grow 1½ feet tall and 3 feet wide. The variety strianum is only 6 inches tall and has red-veined pale pink flowers. 'John Elsley' has carmine-pink flowers and small tidy leaves. It blooms in late spring to early summer. Plants grow 16 inches tall and wide. The vivid carmine-rose blooms of 'Max Frei' are striking. Plants are more compact, growing 1 foot tall and 1½ feet wide. 'Album' has white flowers. Zones 3 to 8.

Cambridge geranium (*G. ×cantabrigiense*) is a short, 6- to 8-inch-tall groundcover geranium with purple-violet flowers. The flowers produce little seed so plants bloom for long periods, starting in spring and extending into summer. 'Biokovo' has pinkish white blooms in early summer and orange to red fall color. It grows 9 inches tall and 24 inches wide. The flower color of 'Karmina' is a deep rich raspberry. 'St. Ola' has white flowers from May to July. Zones 5 to 7.

Grayleaf cranesbill (*G. cinereum*) is a diminutive spreading plant growing 6 to 12 inches tall and wide with pale purple blooms in spring. Plants do best in mild climates, such as that of the Pacific Northwest. 'Ballerina' has pale pink flowers with purple-red eyes. It grows 5 inches tall and 10 inches wide and is a good selection for rock gardens. 'Rothbury Gem' offers bright pink blooms with a magenta eye on compact 5-inch-tall plants. Zones 5 to 7.

Meadow cranesbill (*G. pratense*) is one of the largest geraniums, reaching 3 feet tall and 2 feet wide. Plants bloom in late spring with purple flowers. Plants tend to be lanky; cut plants to the ground after flowering to prevent self-sowing. New foliage will be more compact. 'Midnight Reiter' has dark purple foliage and violet flowers. 'Summer Skies' has double violet-blue flowers above 2-foot-tall and wide mounds of gray-green foliage. The foliage of 'Victor Reiter Jr.' starts out dark purple and then fades to purple-tinged green. The pink flowers bloom throughout the summer. Zones 5 to 7.

Geranium

Hybrids: Some of the best geraniums for gardens are the hybrids. Many offer compact tidy form and summerlong color. 'Ann Folkard' has rich magenta-purple blooms with a dark eye and yellowish foliage, 1 foot tall and wide. Zones 5 to 8. 'Brookside' flowers are blue with a white eye; foliage turns red in fall. Plants grow 2 feet tall and 3 feet wide. Zones 4 to 7. 'Jolly Bee' has 3-inch-wide blue blooms with a white eye and grows 2 feet tall and 3 feet wide. Zones 5 to 8. 'Pink Penny' is a sport of 'Jolly Bee' with bright pink blooms. Zones 5 to 8. The 2½-inch violet-blue saucers of 'Rozanne' last from early summer to fall. Plants have marbled dark green leaves that change to mahogany in the fall. They grow 20 inches tall and 24 inches wide. Zones 5 to 8. 'Sweet Heidi' blooms are brilliant purple-blue with a white eye. Zones 5 to 8.

Geum (*See Avens*)
Giant coneflower (*See Black-eyed susan*)

Gibraltar bush clover *(Lespedeza thunbergii)*

less-ped-EASE-uh thun-ber-GEE-eye
Features: Purplish pink blooms on arching stems, blue-green leaves
Hardiness: Zones 5 to 8
Bloom time: Late summer to early fall
Size: 3 to 6 feet tall, 3 to 10 feet wide
Shape: Fountain
Light: Full sun
Site: Light, well-drained soil

Gibraltar bush clover

Description: Small purplish pink flowers coat the stems of gibraltar bush clovers. For most of the summer the strong columnar shape forms an upright accent in a garden. In bloom the plant becomes a fountain of color when its long stems arch under the weight of the lavish pink-purple blooms. The flowers, which attract bees, occur in droopy spikes along the stems and in massive hanging clusters up to 24 inches long at the branch tips.

Gibraltar bush clover is actually a woody shrub. The fast-growing plants can grow 6 feet in a season. New cultivars on the market are more compact and are ideal for use in perennial gardens.

Bush clover adds brilliant color to late-season borders. It pairs well with ornamental grasses and shorter, coarser, mounded plants. Good companions

'Pink Fountains' gibraltar bush clover

include tall yellow 'Herbstsonne' black-eyed susan and 'Giraffe' maiden grass. Or let its long curving stems and vibrant blooms soften the harshness of a ledge or high wall.

Care: Bush clover is a woody perennial or deciduous flowering shrub that grows easily in well-drained soil of average fertility. It tolerates heat, drought, wind, and a wide pH range, but too much moisture can cause rot.

Deadhead to prolong bloom. Cut stems to the ground in late fall or to live wood in early spring. Luckily bush clover rarely requires division. Dividing it is a difficult task. Plants are generally pest free, but leafhoppers may disfigure foliage in early summer.

Species and cultivars: 'Albiflora' has white flowers. Those of 'Edo Shibori' are bicolor white and mauve-pink. It grows 2 to 3 feet tall. 'Pink Fountains' has rich pink blooms in mid- to late fall on 4- to 5-foot plants. 'Spilt Milk' has variegated green-and-cream foliage and dark purple-tinged

stems. Lavender flowers appear in midsummer and again in fall on 4-foot plants. 'Yakushima' grows just 1 to 1½ feet tall and has violet-blue flowers.

Globe thistle *(Echinops bannaticus)*

ECK-in-ops bun-NAT-ih-cus
Features: Attention-grabbing deep blue globes
Hardiness: Zones 4 to 9
Bloom time: Midsummer
Size: 3 feet tall, 2 feet wide
Shape: Coarse mound, columnar in bloom
Light: Full sun
Site: Somewhat fertile, well-drained soil that is neutral to slightly alkaline in pH

Description: Intense blue spheres cap this tough perennial that produces coarse grayish green leaves with hairy white undersides. Erect branched flower stems emerge from the basal foliage. The 1- to 2-inch-diameter flowers start out dark blue but take on a lighter tint as summer progresses. They attract bees and butterflies. The deeply cut thistly foliage has sharp spines. Use it in fresh and dried flower

Globe thistle with gayfeather and bee balm

arrangements. In the garden globe thistle looks stunning with purple coneflower, coreopsis, and Russian sage. It suits well-drained cottage gardens, roadside beds, seaside plantings, and sunny borders.

Care: Globe thistle is easy to grow. It tolerates heat, drought, and infertile soils. Stake when growing in fertile soil, where it becomes floppy. Without grooming plants can look rangy

Globe thistle flower

by summer's end. Keep them tidy by deadheading, which also prevents self-sowing. Plants may flower again if pruned to basal leaves after blooming. Pests and diseases rarely trouble globe thistle. If necessary divide in spring by separating offsets.

Species and cultivars: 'Taplow Blue' blooms with silvery blue globes. 'Blue Globe' has deep blue flowerheads up to 2½ inches wide. Zones 3 to 8.

'Arctic Glow' globe thistle *(E. sphaerocephalus)* forms 2-inch white balls on reddish stems. Zones 5 to 8.

Globeflower (*Trollius* hybrids)

TROLL-ee-us hybrids
Features: Lemon yellow flowers
Hardiness: Zones 4 to 7
Bloom time: Midspring
Size: 1 to 1½ feet tall, 2 to 3 feet in bloom, 3 feet wide
Shape: A low mound of foliage, airy upright flower stems
Light: Part sun to full shade
Site: Rich soil with plentiful organic matter and moisture

Globeflower with iris

Globeflower flower detail

Description: Globeflower offers beautiful accents to the spring garden. Its lemon yellow to orange flowers, layered like buttercups, rise high above the mound of shiny foliage on strong, nearly leafless stems. Good companions for globeflower include celandine poppy, bugbane, corydalis, golden hakone grass, and lungwort.

Care: Plants tolerate a wide range of soil pH as well as full sun and wind if the soil is well drained and constantly moist. They do not do well in drought or in hot areas. Feed globeflower heavier than average perennials. Deadhead spent flowers.

Plants rarely require division. They are generally pest free but may suffer from powdery mildew in dry sites.

Species and cultivars: 'Cheddar' has soft yellow flowers. Those of 'Orange Princess' are large, double, and orange. **Orange globeflower** (*T. chinensis*) is a tall, 3 to 4 feet, late-blooming species, typically blooming in midsummer. 'Golden Queen' is the most available cultivar. It has single golden orange flowers with long stamens. Zones 3 to 7.

Gloriosa daisy (*See Black-eyed susan*)

Goatsbeard (*Aruncus dioicus*)

uh-RUNK-us die-oh-IK-us
Features: Open plumes of white flowers
Hardiness: Zones 3 to 7
Bloom time: Early summer
Size: 2 to 3 feet tall, 4 to 6 feet in bloom, 4 feet wide
Shape: Irregular mound, upright airy column of flowers
Light: Light to part shade
Site: Moist, well-drained soil

Description: This grand shade dweller has ferny deep green leaves and long creamy white flower plumes that bloom in early summer. It is a huge plant, especially in bloom, with coarse-textured foliage. Grown by a shady brook or in a moist woodland garden, goatsbeard is an attractive specimen as well as a fine companion for ferns and big-leaved hostas. The seedheads provide winter interest;

Goatsbeard

however they're not that attractive in your summer garden.

Care: Goatsbeard thrives in partial shade with plentiful moisture. It is not a good choice for the hot, humid South but does well almost everywhere else. In cool-summer climates plants will grow in full sun; in warm climates it must receive shade during the heat of the day. If grown where the roots are moist and where temperatures are relatively cool, goatsbeard will be trouble free. Where plants are too hot, leaf spot and rust diseases can develop. If allowed to be too dry, leaf scorch singes the edges of the leaves.

Deadhead if you don't want to keep the seedheads for winter interest. Cut the flower stems back to the top of the foliage, where the leaves can hide the cuts. Plants sometimes self-sow; pull unwanted seedlings. Established plants have sturdy roots that are hard, if not impossible, to dig.

Species and cultivars: 'Kneiffii' grows 3 feet tall in bloom; half of the height is the flower stalk. It has finely cut lacy foliage and creamy plumes. **Dwarf goatsbeard** (*A. aethusifolius*) grows just 8 to 12 inches tall and up to 18 inches wide. It has small, tight ivory blooms. The lacy foliage and mounded form are perfect for edging a path and in the front of a shade border.

Goatsbeard flowers

Golden hakone grass (*Hakonechloa macra* 'Aureola')

ha-cone-ee-KLO-uh MAC-ruh or-ee-OL-uh
Features: Golden foliage
Hardiness: Zones 5 to 8
Bloom time: Not grown for blooms
Size: 1 to 1½ feet tall, 1½ feet wide
Shape: Cascading fountain
Light: Part sun to shade
Site: Rich, well-drained, slightly acid soil

Description: Golden hakone grass produces an elegant mound of narrow, arching, vivid yellow leaves marked with skinny green stripes. It is especially useful for bringing bright color into a shade garden. Use it singly in a container or massed for bold effect at the front of shady borders. Its graceful habit softens the hard edges of architectural features and brings bright color and

Golden hakone grass

contrast to rock and woodland gardens. The golden color of the foliage looks smashing with hostas, especially ones with yellow-variegated leaves.

Care: Plants grow best in partial shade and moist, well-drained soil rich in organic matter. Remove faded foliage in spring before new leaves begin to grow.

'Aureola' hakone grass

Species and cultivars: The straight species has medium green foliage and looks somewhat like a bamboo, without the rampant spread. 'Albostriata' has darker green leaves with slim white stripes along the margins. 'All Gold' is just like it sounds; foliage is completely yellow. Plants grow 8 to 12 inches tall. 'Beni-kaze' has consistent red fall color; foliage is green during the summer. Plants grow 2 to 3 feet tall.

Golden marguerite (*Anthemis tinctoria*)

ANN-them-us tink-TOR-ee-uh
Features: Yellow daisies
Hardiness: Zones 3 to 7
Bloom time: Early to midsummer
Size: 2 to 3 feet tall, 2 feet wide
Shape: Low clump of foliage with flowers rising above
Light: Full sun to part shade
Site: Well-drained soil

Description: These masses of bright yellow daisies are fast growing and spread by offsets and seed. The fragrant, finely

Golden marguerite   Golden marguerite with snapdragon

divided deep green foliage and upright habit combine well with daylily and fountain grass.

Care: Provide full sun to light shade and regular watering. Plants tolerate drought and heat. Deadhead to prolong blooming and prevent self-sowing. Stake with grow-through supports or cut plants back after blooms fade to promote fresh foliage growth. Fertilize lightly to prevent plants from becoming floppy. Divide plants every two to three years, before the oldest central portion of the clump dies out. Plants are basically pest free but may develop powdery mildew.

Species and cultivars: 'Moonlight' has pale yellow flowers and grows 2 feet tall. 'Kelwayi' has more finely cut foliage and brighter yellow flowers. Plants are 3 feet tall. 'E.C. Buxton' has lemon yellow flowers and finely cut foliage.

Dwarf marguerite (*A. biebersteiniana*) offers silver filigreed foliage and yellow daisies for much of the summer. Plants grow 10 inches tall and 15 inches wide. Zones 4 to 9.

Goldenrod (*Solidago* spp.)

saul-ih-DAY-go species
Features: Plumes of golden yellow flowers
Hardiness: 4–9
Bloom time: Late summer to fall
Size: Depends on species
Shape: Upright, spreading clump
Light: Full sun to light shade
Site: Sandy, lean to somewhat fertile, well-drained soil

Description: These fast-spreading perennials bring brilliant yellow flowers, not hay fever, to late summer and fall gardens. They are native North American plants, well known as roadside plants. Cultivated varieties have tamed the ragged appearance of the native plants but kept their ability to adapt to many situations.

Plants grow 1 to 3 feet tall, depending on the species, and have an upright habit until blooms form. The flowers of some radiate from a central point on long stems; those of others form an upright plume.

Stunning at the front or in the middle of late-season perennial borders and able to

Goldenrod

Goldenrod

grow in just about any soil, goldenrod is also appropriate for butterfly, meadow, and wildflower gardens. Grow with other fall bloomers, such as Russian sage, aster, and ornamental grasses.

Care: Goldenrods are deer resistant and tolerate drought. They do best in well-drained soil and full sun, although they can take some light shade. Fungal diseases bother some goldenrods, but most species are sturdy, healthy, and easy to grow. Division is seldom necessary to manage spread. You will want to deadhead to prevent self-sowing.

Species and cultivars: 'Fireworks' rough-stemmed goldenrod (*S. rugosa*) has 18-inch-long tapering clusters of bright yellow flowers that arch over 3- to 4-foot-tall and wide plants. Zones 4 to 9.

'Golden Fleece' goldenrod (*S. sphacelata*) is a compact plant growing 1 to 1½ feet tall and wide. Ten-inch-long sprays of yellow flowers emerge in late summer, arching at the tips and creating a mass of color. Zones 2 to 9.

'Goldrush' goldenrod (*S. cutleri*) grows 12 to 14 inches tall with masses of bright yellow flowers from early August to September. It is suitable for the front of the garden, and the flower stems are good weavers. Zones 4 to 9.

Hybrids: 'Golden Baby' has large, broad, bright yellow flower plumes from late summer into fall that look fabulous in the garden and make excellent cut flowers. Plants grow as a 20-inch-tall mound. Zones 4 to 8.

Goldenstar (Chrysogonum virginianum)

kriss-OH-go-num ver-gin-ee-AIN-us
Features: Yellow flowers
Hardiness: Zones 5 to 9
Bloom time: Late spring and summer
Size: 3 to 4 inches tall, 12 inches wide
Shape: Creeping mat
Light: Sun to partial shade
Site: Well-drained soil of average fertility

Goldenstar with columbine

Description: Long-blooming goldenstar has five-petaled, vivid yellow blooms. The hairy-stalked flowers face upward in contrast to the fuzzy bright green leaves. Stems form a thick mat and spread quickly but not aggressively. The foliage of this eastern United States native is herbaceous in cool climates and evergreen in warm climates.

Care: Low-maintenance goldenstar performs best in moist soils of average fertility but high in organic matter. It thrives in sun to partial shade and needs good drainage.

Species and cultivars: 'Allen Bush' is a 10- to 12-inch-tall groundcover with small yellow flowers. 'Pierre' forms a 6-inch-tall clump and has larger flowers than the species. 'Australe' is an 8-inch-tall groundcover. Its golden blooms appear from April to June and in September and October. Plants have dark glossy green leaves.

Goldenstar

Goldies fern *(See Ferns)*
Hardy ageratum *(See Joe-pye weed)*

Hardy begonia (Begonia grandis)

beg-OWN-yuh GRAND-iss
Features: Striking heart-shape leaves; sprays of pink flowers
Hardiness: Zones 6 to 9
Bloom time: Summer to fall
Size: 1½ to 2 feet tall, 1½ feet wide
Shape: Spreading mound
Light: Partial to full shade
Site: Moist, fertile, well-drained soil

Hardy begonia

Description: Hardy begonia adds elegance and color to shady garden areas. Its big leaves are heart shape at the base, olive green on top, and red flushed on the bottom with red veins and stems. The pink flowers cap red stems and fall in loose, droopy sprays. Plants naturalize by means of tiny bulbs that form where leaf stems attach to the main stems. The little bulbs fall to the earth in autumn and sow themselves in the soil. Grow hardy begonia in woodland gardens and shady borders or as a groundcover in partial shade. It blends well with low ferns, hosta, and Siberian bugloss.

Care: Hardy begonia comes up late in spring. It prefers moist, fertile, well-drained soils high in organic matter. Avoid wet soils. Deadhead faded blooms to extend flowering. Cut plants to the ground in late fall and apply a generous layer of mulch for winter protection.

Species and cultivars: 'Alba' has nodding clusters of pink-tinged white flowers. Its stems and leaves are greener than the species. 'Heron's Pirouette' is just 15 inches tall with deep pink flower clusters that are larger than the species and extra large leaves. 'Wildwood Premier' has drooping pinkish white blooms in late summer and early fall. Its leaves are red flushed all over.

Hardy hibiscus (Hibiscus moscheutos)

high-BISK-us moss-KEW-tohs
Features: Bright, bold, tropical-looking pink, red, and white blooms
Hardiness: Zones 5 to 10
Bloom time: Mid- to late summer
Size: 3 to 6 feet tall, 3 to 4 feet wide
Shape: Upright oval
Light: Full sun
Site: Rich, consistently moist soil with abundant organic matter

Description:
Perfect for borders with a tropical look, hardy hibiscus produces dark-eyed, dinner plate-size brightly colored flowers that attract butterflies and the admiration of garden

Pink hardy hibiscus

visitors. The species can grow 6 feet or more tall, but breeding has resulted in cultivars that never rise more than 2 to 3 feet. You will undoubtedly find a selection to fit your garden, no matter what its size.

Hardy hibiscus starts flowering when many perennials are winding down. It makes a stunning garden specimen or a striking late-summer informal hedge. For outdoor drama grow it with plume poppy and ostrich or royal fern. Hardy hibiscus contrasts well with vertical perennials and fine-textured perennials such as iris, gayfeather, joe-pye weed, obedient plant, and culver's root.

Care: Plant hardy hibiscus in moist to soggy soils with plentiful organic matter. It is native to marshlands and does not tolerate drought. Water regularly, especially during dry spells. The plants also require warm temperatures to bloom well.

Fertilize regularly during the growing season. The best flowering and plant health are achieved with full sun and adequate air circulation, but hardy hibiscus also grows in partial shade. The strong stems need no staking. They even stand up in windy locations, although the flowers may be shredded.

Cut plants back to about 6 inches in late fall. Flag their locations in your garden because they emerge late in spring. Divide hibiscus every 7 to 10 years; you may need to use a saw to cut through the woody roots. Japanese beetles and caterpillars are the main pests of hardy hibiscus. Pick these off by hand.

Species and cultivars: Plants in the Disco Belle

'Lord Baltimore' hardy hibiscus

Series are short, 20 to 30 inches tall, with 9-inch-wide pink, rose red, and white blooms. 'Lady Baltimore' is 4 to 6 feet tall with 6- to 8-inch-wide, dark-eyed ruffled pink flowers and deeply cut leaves. 'Lord Baltimore' is a little shorter, 4 feet tall, but it has larger, 10-inch-wide bright red flowers.
Hybrids: 'Kopper King' grow 3 to 4 feet tall with 12-inch-wide red-eyed white flowers in August and September. Its foliage is a ruddy copper with a rusty underside. Hybrids in the Cordials Series have large flowers, maple leaf-shape foliage, and grow about 4 feet tall. 'Brandy Punch' blooms in pink, 'Cinnamon Grappa' in scarlet red, and 'Cherry Brandy' in rose-red.

Red hardy hibiscus

Hay-scented fern (See Ferns)

Heart-leaf bergenia (Bergenia cordifolia)

burr-JEAN-ee-uh cord-if-FOH-lee-uh
Features: Leathery evergreen leaves, pink flowers
Hardiness: Zones 4 to 10
Bloom time: Spring
Size: 12 inches tall, to 18 inches in bloom, 12 inches wide
Shape: Mound of cabbage-shape leaves
Light: Sun to partial shade
Site: Moist soil of average fertility high in organic matter

Description: Admired more for its bold-textured clumps of cabbage-shape leaves than for its pink flowers, heart-leaf bergenia brings architectural beauty to gardens. Its thick shiny evergreen leaves are deer resistant and gleam like polished wood. The foliage is so leathery that it squeaks when you rub it between your fingers, giving it the nickname pigsqueak.

In spring this low-maintenance mounded perennial produces clusters of pink cupped flowers held above the leaves on fat reddish stalks. Unless temperatures are harsh, the foliage takes on magnificent reddish to bronze hues in fall. Some cultivars are especially colorful when compared with others. Plants are evergreen in mild climates and semievergreen in all but the coldest climates.

Bergenia spreads slowly and makes an outstanding impenetrable groundcover when mass planted in partial shade. It looks good in rock gardens and at the front of the perennial border growing with ferns, cranesbill, Bethlehem sage, and lady's mantle. Bergenia holds its shape

Heart-leaf bergenia

Heart-leaf bergenia blossoms

even under a blanket of snow.

Care: Bergenia is easy to grow in partial shade and moist soil of average fertility but high in organic matter. Provide part shade or afternoon shade in southern areas. Plants don't do well in areas with excessive heat or drought. In cold areas protect plants from bitter winds, which will scorch and shred the leaves.

Because it's an evergreen wait till early spring to cut plants back. Then cut off only the leaves showing winter damage. Remove flower stalks once flowers fade. Divide plants if they become crowded. Slugs can feed on the foliage.

Species and cultivars: Leather bergenia (*B. crassifolia*) is similar to heart-leaf bergenia. It differs mainly by the fact that its flower stalk rises higher above the foliage and is more branched. This species is especially recommended for dry shade in California and other areas. 'Red Star' has large rose red flowers; its foliage stays green all year. Zones 4 to 8.

Hybrids: 'Bressingham Ruby' has dark rose pink flowers and burgundy fall color. The flowers of 'Bressingham White' open pink and change to white. 'Magic Giant' has rosy blooms on red stems and huge purplish leaves that turn bronzy purple in winter. 'Ruby Elf' is short, to 6 inches tall, with reddish lavender blooms in spring and ruby red winter color. 'Winterglut' has red flowers in spring and dark green leaves that turn rich mottled red and orange in fall.

Heart-leaf brunnera *(Brunnera macrophylla)*

BREW-ner-uh MAC-roh-phi-luh

Features: Large heart-shape leaves; airy clusters of tiny blue flowers
Hardiness: Zones 3 to 7
Bloom time: Midspring
Size: 1 foot tall, 1½ feet in bloom, 2 feet wide
Shape: Coarse, rounded mound
Light: Partial shade
Site: Consistently moist soil high in organic matter

'Jack Frost' heart-leaf brunnera

Description: In spring a cloud of tiny blue flowers resembling forget-me-nots hovers above brunnera's low mound of dark green leaves. The fuzzy dark green heart-shape leaves look spectacular planted along a woodland path or massed in dappled shade under a grove of birches. Ferns, primroses, jack-in-the-pulpit, and pink bleeding heart make fine

companions. Variegated cultivars lighten dark corners of a shade garden, particularly when planted in a mass.

Care: Heart-leaf brunnera prefers partial shade but can grow in full sun or in cool-summer climates in consistently moist soil high in organic matter. In hot climates brunnera's foliage may scorch. Variegated varieties are especially prone to scorch. Remove the damaged leaves. The foliage has prickly hairs, so you'll want to wear gloves when working with the plants.

Variegated heart-leaf brunnera

After blooming cut off flower stems at the base to tidy up the plant and prevent self-sowing. Or leave the seeds if you plan to use the plant as a groundcover. Deadhead variegated cultivars before seeds form. The seedlings do not resemble the parent plant; they tend to have the dark green foliage of the species and be more vigorous than the cultivar. Divide plants as needed every 5 to 10 years.

Species and cultivars: 'Hadspen Cream' has dark green leaves with creamy white edges. It is a little smaller than the species, 10 to 12 inches tall and 15 to 18 inches wide. 'Jack Frost' offers 3- to 5-inch-wide silver leaves with narrow green edges and darker decorative veins. It is dramatic whether you see it close up or from a distance. It is somewhat more heat tolerant than other heart-leaf brunneras. 'Langtrees' has splashes of silver around the edges of its dark green leaves. 'Looking Glass' is silver all over with leaves that cup under. The silver foliage helps the blue flowers stand out. 'Silver Wings' has gray-green leaves with large silvery splotches between the veins; it is a sport of 'Langtrees'.

Helenium *(Helenium autumnale)*

hell-EEN-ee-um aw-tum-NAL-ee

Features: Daisies in autumnal colors
Hardiness: Zones 3 to 8
Bloom time: Midsummer to fall
Size: 3 to 5 feet tall, 2 to 3 feet wide
Shape: Upright clump
Light: Full sun
Site: Moist to wet average soil

Description: Gardeners value this plant for its long-lasting daisies that bloom in autumnal shades of yellow, orange, and red starting in midsummer. Each flower has a brown or yellow central dome surrounded by drooping wedge-shape petals of red, orange, yellow, copper, or bronze. Helenium is a sturdy, adaptable plant native to wet meadows of eastern North America. It grows 3 to 5 feet tall, depending on cultivar and moisture availability. Flowering lasts 8 to 10 weeks or longer.

Helenium suits the middle to back of the perennial border, where it glows when grouped with maiden grass, tall asters, and other late-blooming perennials. Its informal character and love of moisture make it good for moist meadow gardens and wildflower gardens. Its 2-inch blooms attract butterflies, and the seedheads are interesting over the winter.

Care: Grow helenium in moist to wet soils in full sun. Don't let the soil dry out. Stake tall varieties in early spring while they are still small or cut back plants in late spring or early summer to make plants more compact. Deadhead to encourage rebloom. Feed lightly in spring and after flowering with a balanced fertilizer.

'Mardi Gras' helenium

Divide plants in spring or fall when they become crowded. Ensure that plants have plenty of room to provide them air circulation to help prevent powdery mildew and leaf spot disease. If these are present, cut down the plant after flowering and discard the stems in the trash.

Detail of helenium bloom

Species and cultivars: Hybrid 'Butterpat' is a 4-foot-tall cultivar with golden flowers that have yellow centers. 'Bruno' blooms in late summer with large-centered, crimson-orange daisies. 'Chelsey' has nondrooping crimson flowers marked with yellow and a dark brown center. 'Double Trouble' offers double yellow, nondrooping flowers around a large round yellow center. 'Indian Summer' has coppery red flowers with a yellow center. It grows 40 inches tall. 'Mardi Gras' is a summer bloomer with nondrooping orange-red flowers splashed with yellow around a dark brown cone. It grows 3 feet tall. 'Moerheim Beauty' is short at 2 to 3 feet. Its rust-red blooms age to orange and gold. 'Wyndley' grows 2½ feet tall and has coppery brown flowers.

Hollyhock *(Alcea rosea)*

al-SEE-uh rose-EE-uh

Features: Old-fashioned spires of bright pink, red, maroon, purple, yellow, or white
Hardiness: Zones 3 to 8
Bloom time: Early to midsummer
Size: 3 feet tall, 4 to 8 feet in bloom, 2 to 3 feet wide
Shape: Mounded, upright in bloom
Light: Full sun
Site: Fertile, well-drained soil

Description: Valued for its size and color, this short-lived perennial has lofty floral wands that look stunning at the back of a border, growing against a brick, adobe, or clapboard wall, or silhouetted against a dark yew hedge.

Hollyhock blooms open from the bottom to the top of the spike throughout the summer, attracting butterflies and hummingbirds. Plants are fast growing with large, coarsely lobed leaves at ground level. Short varieties make good container plants. Grow hollyhocks in cottage gardens with roses, white daisies, and clematis.

Care: Hollyhocks thrive in rich, well-drained soil with plenty of moisture. Stake tall varieties. Deadhead after flowering for a tidier look, unless you want seeds to ripen and self-sow. When plants begin to look tacky, cut tall flowering stems back to fresh leaves. Plants are easy to start indoors from seed, and they readily self-sow and spread across a garden. The volunteer seedlings often bloom in different colors than the original plant.

Dark red hollyhock

Japanese beetles, leaf miners, and hollyhock rust are serious problems. Select rust-resistant cultivars when buying plants. Pick off and destroy leaves with telltale leaf miner trails.

Detail of pink hollyhock bloom

Species and cultivars: 'Chater's Double Hybrids' have double blooms in pink, red, maroon, salmon, violet, white, and yellow. 'Crème de Cassis' grows 5 to 6 feet tall with large, heavily veined, white-rimmed dark raspberry flowers. Plants may have double, semidouble, and single flowers all on the same stalk. The blooms are more brightly colored in warm regions. Plants are reliably perennial. 'Nigra' shows off deep maroon single flowers on 5- to 6-foot-tall spikes. 'Queeny Purple' is just 2 to 3 feet tall and 1 to 1½ feet wide. It easily stands erect without staking. The 3- to 4-inch-wide double purple blooms last over a long season. 'Old Barnyard Mix' has 3- to 5-inch-wide yellow-centered single flowers in bright pastels, deep jewel colors, and bicolors, including yellows, oranges, and rosy and brick reds. Plants grow 5 to 6 feet tall and 2 feet wide and are rust resistant.

Fig-leaf hollyhock *(A. ficoides)* blooms in yellow and has irregularly lobed leaves that look like those of a fig. In bloom plants reach 5 to 7 feet tall. They are reliably rust free and cold tolerant. 'Happy Lights' blooms in yellow, white, red, pink, and shades of the colors. All have a yellow eye. Zones 3 to 8.

'Peaches 'n' Dreams' hollyhock

Hosta *(Hosta* spp.)

HOSS-tuh species
Features: Colorful mounds of foliage
Hardiness: Zones 3 to 8
Bloom time: Summer
Size: Depends on species or cultivars
Shape: Mounded
Light: Partial shade
Site: Moist, rich, well-drained soil

Description: Grown more for its bold leaves than for flowers, hosta is a star of the shade garden. The leaves come in a wide array of colors, including brilliant gold, gray-blue, light to dark green, and variegated with cream, yellow, or white. They may be medium to coarse in texture with surfaces that are puckered, wavy, or smooth.

'Golden Tiara' hosta

In summer one-sided stalks of white to lavender, occasionally fragrant flowers open above the foliage. In some species the flowers rise well above the plants on lanky stems that detract from the plant, especially once the flowers fade. In others they stay close to the foliage and open on short stalks. Flowering is one of the traits breeders have been working on, and cultivars may display large bell-shape blooms on short, tidy stalks, or they may not bloom at all.

Use hosta as an accent, massed as a groundcover, in rock gardens, woodland gardens, shady perennial borders, and Japanese gardens. Combine it with mat-forming perennials or ones that have strong vertical lines or fine-textured foliage. Good companions include lungwort, goatsbeard, woodland phlox, heart-leaf brunnera, Japanese anemone, bugbane, corydalis, bleeding heart, solomon's seal, and toad lily. Hosta stands out in containers, whether used alone or in mixed plantings. The long, stiff flower stalks make excellent cut flowers.

Care: Hostas require full shade and plentiful moisture in hot climates. In cool climates they do better with some morning sun and can even tolerate full sun. Yellow-leaf

Detail of blue hosta

cultivars are more likely to do well in sun than blue-leaf cultivars.

Alkaline soil is acceptable, but hostas will not tolerate drought. Before planting improve the soil with compost or well-rotted manure to ensure a fertile, well-drained bed.

Because hosta's leaves are its main attraction, some gardeners cut off the flower stems before they bloom. You may want to wait until the flowers form before deciding whether to let your plants bloom. Weak floppy flower stems always detract from the plant, but cultivars with large flowers on sturdy stems are attractive. Large blue-leaf hostas produce more flowers when deadheaded.

Use a continuous-release product at spring planting or apply soluble fertilizer starting three weeks after setting hostas in the ground. Stop fertilizing hosta about six to eight weeks before the first fall frost.

Prune back the plant after foliage dies in fall. The first frost usually turns hosta into a watery mass.

Most hostas are long lived. Divide crowded plants in spring or fall when necessary. Lift root clumps and divide them with a sharp spade. Replant sections with healthy roots and top shoots and then apply water and mulch. Discard divisions lacking vigorous roots and shoots.

Snails and slugs are frequent hosta pests, as are rabbits and deer. Voles and root weevils feed on the roots. Hail storms can leave gaping holes in hosta leaves. Before treating plants for suspected insect damage, make sure your plants are infested with snails and slugs. Thick-leaved hostas with quilted leaves are more slug resistant.

Species and cultivars: There are thousands of hosta species. This is just a small sample of choices you may find. If you cannot find an exact cultivar in your area, chances are a

'Frances Williams' hosta

similar plant will be available.

Blue: 'Blue Mammoth' has puckered light blue leaves. It grows 45 inches tall and 70 inches wide, making it a good screen or focal point. Foliage is slug resistant. 'Camelot' has powder blue foliage on 14-inch-tall, 40-inch-wide plants. 'Hadspen Blue' has heart-shape, thick gray-blue leaves. Plants grow 18 inches tall and 48 inches wide; they are slug resistant. 'Halcyon' is a midsize classic blue hosta with spear-shape leaves. 'Love Pat' forms compact, 3-foot-tall and -wide mounds of silvery blue. It has lovely, large white flowers on short stalks.

Variegated white: 'Christmas Candy' has white leaves with a slender streak of green along the edges. It grows 16 inches tall and 20 inches wide. 'Fire and Ice' offers bright white leaves with green edges and compact size, 8 to 10 inches tall and 12 to 15 inches wide. The puckered leaves of 'Golden Meadows' are variegated green, white, and chartreuse. In sunny sites the chartreuse bleaches to white. 'Minute Man' has pure white margins around dark green centers on cupped and slightly wavy foliage. It is 1½ tall and 2½ feet wide. 'Orphan Annie' is tiny at 2 inches tall and 4 to 6 inches wide. It has wide creamy leaf margins around a green center.

Variegated yellow: 'Frances Williams' has rounded corrugated blue-green leaves with gold borders. It grows 32 to 36 inches tall and 36 to 42 inches wide. 'Golden Tiara' has small heart-shape leaves edged in gold. It forms dense, heavy-blooming clumps 8 to 12 inches tall and wide. The purple flowers barely rise above the foliage. 'Golden Tiara' is a good edger. 'Gold Standard' is a medium-size hosta with gold-green leaves highlighted with blue-green variegation, especially along the margins. The big leaves of 'Guacamole' have a bright golden center and green edge. Intensely

Hosta

fragrant, white to light lavender blooms appear in August. Plants grow 28 to 32 inches tall and 42 to 48 inches wide.

Yellow: 'August Moon' has heart-shape gold or chartreuse leaves, depending on the amount of sun plants receive. It grows 1½ feet tall and 4 feet wide. 'Sun Power' has oval-pointed chartreuse leaves, a vase-shape habit, and grows 2 feet tall and 3 feet wide. 'Sum and Substance' has huge, round, puckered chartreuse leaves that can reach 20 inches across. Plants grow 2 feet tall and 3 to 6 feet wide. It is sun tolerant. 'Zounds' is a heavily textured gold cultivar with cupped leaves; it grows 2½ feet tall and 4 feet wide.

Green: 'Baby Bunting' is tiny, forming 4- to 6-inch-tall and -wide clumps of gray-green. 'Elegans' siebold hosta (*H. sieboldiana*) has large, heart-shape, bluish green leaves with corrugated texture. 'Krossa Regal' is an older cultivar with oval frosty blue leaves growing in a vase-shape habit, 30 inches tall and 48 inches wide. Blue hosta (*H. ventricosa*) has large heavily textured dark bluish green leaves. It grows about 18 inches tall and spreads rapidly. Fragrant hosta (*H. plantaginea*) is an unassuming yellow-green hosta, 2 feet tall and 4 feet wide, with fragrant white flowers on 5-foot stems. 'Aphrodite' offers pure white, fragrant double flowers.

Hyssop *(Agastache* spp.)

ag-us-TAY-key species
Features: Fragrant foliage and spiky flowers
Hardiness: Zones 5 to 10, depending on species
Bloom time: Midsummer to fall
Size: 2 to 4 feet tall, 2 to 3 feet wide, depending on species
Shape: Upright to mounded
Light: Full sun to partial shade
Site: Well-drained average garden soil

Anise hyssop

Description: This group of long-blooming perennials offers delicious colors in nectar-rich flowers that appeal to insects, butterflies, and hummingbirds. Several species make up the group, each with grayish green leaves that have an anise scent and taste like licorice. The hybrids have the most colorful flowers.

Hyssop suits the middle or back of the border, giving excellent support to showier perennials. Plants tend to have sparse foliage at their base, and shorter perennials in front will help to hide the bare feet, as does growing anise hyssop in a mass. Use anise hyssop in containers and fresh flower arrangements or dry the blooms for later use.

Care: These easy-care perennials thrive in well-drained soil and full sun. In rich, wet soils or when given too much fertilizer, plants will grow lanky, flop over, and have problems with winter hardiness. Plants prefer average amounts of water but will tolerate drought, heat, and humidity once they are established.

Cut plants back to the ground in fall. Hyssop has no serious pests or diseases and is rabbit and deer resistant. Giant hyssop and the hybrids may need winter protection in cold parts of Zone 5.

Species and cultivars: Anise hyssop (*A. foeniculum*) grows in upright columns 1½ to 2½ feet tall and wide. Short dense flower spikes bloom at the tops of the plants. Plants will self-sow; unless you plan to grow a field of anise hyssop, deadhead and keep an eye out for seedlings. Foliage is flavorful and is often harvested for use in tea and cooking. Plants may suffer from powdery mildew in hot, dry years. Zones 5 to 10.

Korean hyssop (*A. rugosa*) grows 2 feet tall and 1 foot wide. The dark violet-blue flowers are bottlebrushy like those of anise hyssop but somewhat fatter. 'Alabaster' has white flower spikes and coarse-textured leaves. Plants tolerate temperate sites with average rainfall and watering. Zones 5 to 8.

Threadleaf giant hyssop (*A. rupestris*) is native to mountain ranges in the southwestern United States. In their native habitat, plants can grow 4 feet tall. In gardens they usually stay around 2 to 3 feet tall. Flowers are a brilliant mix of red-purple-orange, hence another name for the plant is sunset hyssop. Flowers last eight weeks or longer, starting in midsummer, and plants often rebloom after deadheading. Plants require excellent drainage for survival. Zones 4 to 8.

Texas hyssop (*A. cana*) has dense spikes of raspberry red flowers. Like Korean hyssop it can tolerate regular garden sites in full sun as well as dry soil. Plants grow 1 to 3 feet tall. Zones 6 to 9.

Hybrids: Flowers, shape, size, and growing requirements of these hybrids are similar to threadleaf giant hyssop. 'Apricot Sunrise' has spikes of light orange flowers. 'Ava' has rich, dark raspberry pink flowers on 4- to 5-foot-tall plants. 'Big Bazooka' has large bubble-gum pink blooms. 'Desert Sunset' offers multicolored blooms of orange, lavender, and pink. Plants are a fine choice for dry gardens but also adapt to regular garden conditions. 'Firebird' has raspberry red flowers and is 3 feet tall and 2 feet wide. It is hardy only to Zone 6.

'Tutti-Frutti' hyssop

These hybrids are more like anise hyssop in flower shape and color. 'Black Adder' has dark violet-blue blooms. It grows 1 to 3 feet tall, does well in part shade, and prefers average moisture conditions. 'Blue Fortune' grows 3 to 4 feet tall and 2 feet wide. It has dense, bright blue-purple flowers from July to September. Zones 6 to 9. 'Tutti Frutti' grows 4 to 6 feet tall and 2 feet wide and has lavender-pink flower spikes with sweet fruit-scented leaves. Zones 6 to 10.

Interrupted fern *(See Ferns)*

Iris (*Iris* spp.)

Features: Purple, blue, white, pink, burgundy, yellow, and bicolor flowers
Hardiness: Depends on species
Bloom time: Spring to early summer, depending on species
Size: 6 to 48 inches tall, depending on species
Shape: Upright clump
Light: Full sun to partial shade
Site: Moist, moderately fertile, well-drained soil

'Electric Days' Japanese iris

Description: Irises are among the most spectacular and popular garden perennials. The flowers of all irises have a distinctive three-part symmetry consisting of three falls (the petals that hang down) and three standards (the petals that stand up). But in other respects the flowers and foliage vary.

There are two major groups of irises: rhizomatous and bulbous. The majority of cultivated species and hybrids, and the ones people most commonly think of when referring to iris in a perennial garden, grow from rhizomes. These also fall into categories: bearded, beardless, and crested.

Bearded iris are the late spring and early summer-blooming iris that make up the vast majority of garden irises. They are called bearded because of the dab of fuzzy hairs in the center of the falls. Flower colors range over the entire spectrum (indeed iris means rainbow). The colors include striking bicolors and even browns and near black. Only true red is missing. Among this group are German iris (*I. germanica*) and sweet iris (*I. pallida*).

Beardless iris have smooth falls with neither a beard nor a crest. This group of spring and early summer blooming irises includes Siberian (*I. siberica*), Japanese (*I. ensata*), Louisiana irises (*I. fulva*), and yellow flag (*I. pseudoacorus*).

Crested iris have a central ridge—or crest—down the center of the falls. Dwarf crested iris (*I. cristata*) and roof iris (*I. tectorum*) are two of the best known in this group.

Combine irises with mounded and finer-textured plants

Bearded iris

such as aster, yarrow, golden marguerite, coreopsis, and catmint. Other good companions include ornamental grasses with cranesbill, coral bells, and lady's mantle. Siberian iris is perfect for perennial borders and pondside plantings. This fast-growing, trouble-free perennial produces blooms above the leaves in early summer. All irises are excellent for cutting.

Care: Irises grow in most types of soil as long as drainage is good. They should be planted so that their rhizome is just at the surface of the soil. Fertilize and water moderately and provide full sun.

Species and cultivars: The great majority of irises on the market are hybrids. Hundreds of them, especially bearded iris, are available. Like hostas you may not be able to find every cultivar in your area, but you will find one that speaks to you.

Bearded iris (*Iris* hybrids, germanica-type) grows 8 to 36 inches by 12 to 24 inches. It produces upright fans of broad, sword-shape leaves from

'Rare Treat' bearded iris

rhizomes on the soil surface. Flowers may be fragrant and range in size from 1 to 8 inches. Plant rhizomes an inch deep so the tops are above ground. Add bone meal to the soil when planting. Remove bloom stalks and any brown leaves after flowering. Divide plants every three to four years, keeping only healthy rhizomes with roots and top shoots. Bearded iris is susceptible to iris borer, iris weevil, slugs, snails, rhizome rot, and crown rot. Discard affected parts in the trash. Zones 3 to 10.

'Beverly Sills' blooms in pink. 'Chasing Rainbows' has

'Yodo No Kawase' Japanese iris

apricot-caramel standards and orchid-violet falls with orange beards. 'Harvest of Memories' is a deep yellow rebloomer; plants bloom in spring and fall. Flowers of 'Hello Darkness' are nearly black. 'Strike It Rich' is bright yellow. 'World Premier' offers white standards and rich blue falls. 'Warrior King' blooms in a deep reddish brown.

Crested iris bears fragrant, yellow crested lilac-blue flowers on 2- to 3-inch stems. Leaves grow 4 to 6 inches tall. This southeastern United States native makes a dense groundcover in dry shade and pairs nicely with barrenwort and bleeding heart. 'Alba' has yellow crested white flowers and is less vigorous than the species. Zones 3 to 8.

Japanese iris has showy horizontal blue, purple, pink, or white blooms in late spring or summer. It grows 5 feet by 3 feet with tall, sword-shape leaves. It thrives in full sun to partial shade and rich, moist to boggy, acid soil. 'Caprician Butterfly' has 8-inch white double flowers with violet veins. 'Variegata' blooms in purple and has variegated green-and-white leaves. Zones 4 to 9.

Louisiana iris grows 18 to 60 inches tall and spreads fast in boggy soils. Its beardless flowers attract hummingbirds and butterflies and come in copper, blue, purple, yellow, pink, and white. This iris tolerates heat and thrives in the South. Zones 4 to 9.

Roof irises have interesting flattened foliage that

provides a unique texture to the plants. The late spring to early summer blooms come in blue or white. Plants grow 12 to 18 inches tall and 3 feet wide. Zones 5 to 8.

Siberian iris is elegant, tough, and blooms in colors ranging from blue to lavender to pink, white, yellow, and all shades in between. Although the flowers are not long lasting, the narrow, grassy foliage forms lush green clumps that stay attractive all season. Plants grow 2 to 3 feet tall and 2 feet wide.

Siberian iris prefers moist, fertile, well-drained, slightly acid soils, but it adapts to many other conditions. Plant it in early spring or late summer, spaced about 2 feet apart. Keep the roots just below the soil surface. Water regularly until established, after which the plant will tolerate drought. Divide plants every three to four years in spring or late summer to keep them blooming and vigorous. Divide more frequently in fertile soils to manage the plant's spread. The first year after division, flowering may be reduced, especially if you replant small segments. Zones 3 to 9.

'Butter and Sugar' has white standards and yellow falls. 'Caesar's Brother' is deep violet. 'Coronation Anthem' has dark blue falls with a white splotch and lighter blue standard. 'Lavender Bounty' has pale lavender standards and darker lavender falls.

Sweet flag, also known as orris root, has upright sword-shape leaves like bearded iris. Each flower stem carries two to three fragrant bluish purple flowers. Sweet flag is easy to grow and durable and is less likely to succumb to iris borer than germanica-type bearded irises. 'Argentea Variegata' has a wide white stripe on each leaf. It grows 12 inches tall with lilac flowers. 'Aurea Variegata' has a wide creamy yellow stripe up each leaf. Zones 4 to 8.

Yellow flag has long, supple upright leaves 3 to 5 feet long. The light yellow flowers have slender falls and standards. Plants bloom from late spring to early summer. They require moist to wet soil. Grow them in part shade in areas with hot summers. Zones 3 to 9.

and lady's mantle.

Care: Jacob's ladder needs moisture and good drainage. It may decline in extreme heat, drought, and high humidity but tolerates shade and alkaline soils. It may need staking. Remove flower stems after blooming. Doing this promptly keeps the plant attractive, prevents excessive self-sowing, and may promote later flowers.

Detail of Jacob's ladder flowers

Species and cultivars: 'Apricot Delight' has pink blooms and green foliage. 'Brise D'Anjou' has violet-blue flowers in early summer and ferny variegated leaves edged in cream. 'Bressingham Purple' starts as an 8-inch mound of purple leaves in spring, matures to green, and then turns purple again in fall. The lavender-blue flowers are carried on 15-inch-tall stems. 'Snow and Sapphires' is also variegated white and green. Foliage is evenly ranked along a central stem, and flowers bloom on 30-inch-tall stems. Zones 3 to 7. 'Stairway to Heaven' has lavender-blue spring flowers and pink-tinged white-variegated green leaves that are broader than those of 'Snow and Sapphires' and 'Brise D'Anjou'.

'Purple Rain' Jacob's ladder (*P. yezoense*) produces a 24-inch mound of ferny purple leaves with clustered blue flowers in late spring and early summer. Zones 6 to 9.

Japanese anemone *(See Anemone)*
Japanese iris *(See Iris)*
Japanese painted fern *(See Ferns)*

Jacob's ladder *(Polemonium caeruleum)*

pole-MOAN-ee-um see-RULE-ee-um
Features: Blue-violet or white flowers; foliage gives the effect of a ladder
Hardiness: Zones 3 to 8
Bloom time: Mid- to late spring
Size: 8 to 12 inches tall, to 24 inches in bloom, 18 to 24 inches wide
Shape: Clump to upright in bloom
Light: Full sun to partial shade
Site: Moist, well-drained soil rich in organic matter

Description: The leaves of this handsome, fine-textured plant resemble rungs on a ladder. Clustered blue-violet or white blooms top narrow flowering stems that rise above the dense mound of basal foliage in mid- to late spring. Jacob's ladder looks lovely in lightly shaded beds, borders, and woodland gardens, planted in groups with hosta, Bethlehem sage,

Variegated Jacob's ladder

Jerusalem sage *(Phlomis russelliana)*

FLOW-miss russ-EE-lee-ay-nuh
Features: Tiers of glossy yellow flowers, gray-green foliage
Hardiness: Zones 4 to 8
Bloom time: Late spring to early summer
Size: 2 to 3 feet tall and wide
Shape: Upright
Light: Full sun to light shade
Site: Light, well-drained soil

Description: Jerusalem sage blooms with the first hot days of summer, undaunted by the heat. Its distinctive spires of glossy yellow flowers and its carpet of wavy gray-green leaves make it a handsome addition to any sunny border. The hooded flowers form in widely spaced tiers, whorled around a stem and underpinned with rough-looking foliage. Good companions

Jerusalem sage

include penstemon, catmint, artemisia, torch lily, and evening primrose.

Care: Good drainage and plenty of sun are the keys to success with Jerusalem sage. It is unfazed by heat and thrives with little water. Deadhead to prolong bloom. In cold climates mulch in late fall to ensure winter hardiness.

Jerusalem sage flowers

Joe-pye weed

(Eupatorium maculatum)

yew-pat-OR-ee-um mack-yew-LAY-tum

Features: Jumbo mauve flowers on tall burgundy-streaked stems
Hardiness: Zones 3 to 7
Bloom time: Late summer
Size: 4 to 6 feet tall, 4 feet wide
Shape: Upright clump
Light: Full sun to partial shade
Site: Moist, well-drained, fertile soil

Joe-pye weed with feather reed grass

Description: This striking plant is ideal for cutting, for wildflower gardens and moist meadow gardens, and for the back of large late-summer borders. It has 10- to 12-inch rosy flower clusters atop 5- to 6-foot burgundy-mottled stems covered with leaves up to 1 foot long. The plant forms a coarse-textured informal clump that holds its own in the largest perennial garden, especially when massed. Good companions include 'Silberfeder' maiden grass, 'Cloud Nine' switch grass, and 'Herbstsonne' and great rudbeckia to bring nonstop goldfinches and butterflies to the garden in late summer and fall.

Care: Joe-pye weed prefers moist soils. Its stems are sturdy and usually need no staking. Limit its height by pinching stems in early summer. Dig up and remove excess plants and seedlings to keep plants under control. Deadhead to prevent self-sowing and to tidy plants. Powdery mildew can be a problem. To deter it

Bee on blossom of joe-pye weed

thin stems for improved air circulation. Divide in spring.

Species and cultivars: 'Atropurpureum' has burgundy blooms and red-tinged leaves. 'Bartered Bride' has white flowers. 'Gateway' is a more compact form that grows to 5 feet tall.

Hardy ageratum *(E. coelestinum)* has fuzzy purple-blue flowers from late summer to fall. Plants grow in mounds and may be much wider than tall. They spread quickly by shallow stolons below the soil surface. 'Alba' blooms in white but is otherwise similar. Zones 4 to 10.

White snakeroot *(E. rugosum)* has white, fuzzy, ageratum-like flowers on 5-foot plants. 'Chocolate' has erect dark purple stems and deep bronzy purple leaves that turn greener as the season progresses. In autumn creamy white flower clusters cover this gorgeous cultivar. Plants grow 3 to 5 feet tall by 2 to 3 feet wide. They readily reseed, and seedlings resemble the parents. Zones 3 to 7.

Lady fern *(See Ferns)*

Lady's mantle *(Alchemilla mollis)*

al-chem-ILL-uh mall-is

Features: Unique pleated leaves; tiny chartreuse flowers
Hardiness: Zones 4 to 7
Bloom time: Late spring to midsummer
Size: 1½ to 2 feet tall and wide
Shape: Ground-hugging mat
Light: Partial shade
Site: Moist, well-drained soil

Lady's mantle

Description: This plant's mounded foliage is ideal for softening the edge of a path or creating a lush groundcover in a lightly shaded spot under a tree. The velvety leaves are pleated when they open and then fan into a scalloped to rounded shape. Slightly cupped, the foliage often holds early morning dewdrops. Clusters of greenish yellow flowers appear on arching stems in early summer. The bright chartreuse hue combines well with both pastel and primary colors in borders and bouquets. The blooms are charming dried and are long lasting in fresh bouquets.

Care: This easy-to-grow perennial flourishes in moist, well-drained soils and partial shade. In cool climates lady's mantle also thrives in full sun. If you grow lady's mantle as a groundcover, let some of the plants go to seed so they will spread. If your design calls for a single clump or a small group, remove the faded flowers to prevent self-sowing. In spring before new growth emerges, remove last year's dead leaves. Spring is also the time to divide lady's mantle, though it rarely requires it. As summer progresses you can renew any shabby plants by cutting back the leaves. Space lady's mantle plants 12 to 18 inches apart for a lush mass. A tough plant, lady's mantle is basically pest and disease free, except for

Detail of lady's mantle foliage

occasional attacks by spider mites. **Species and cultivars:** 'Thriller' is more erect than the species and has larger leaves. It grows 18 inches tall.

Alpine lady's mantle (*Alchemilla alpina*) grows just 5 to 6 inches tall. It has small white-edged gray-green leaves, deeply divided into six lobes. The chartreuse flowers are in 6-inch-wide clusters. Plants self-sow and are good in rock gardens. Zones 3 to 7.

Lamb's-ears (*Stachys byzantina*)

STAY-kiss biz-an-TEEN-uh
Features: Woolly gray foliage
Hardiness: Zones 3 to 10
Bloom time: Early summer
Size: 8 inches tall, up to 18 inches in bloom, 24 inches wide
Shape: Low irregular mound
Light: Full sun
Site: Dry, sandy to loamy, well-drained soil

Lamb's-ears foliage

Description: Most folks remember the first time they touched lamb's-ears—their feelings of surprise that something so soft, furry, and almost white is a common garden plant. Everything about lamb's-ears but its flowers wears a thick, furry whitish coat. Pink-purple bloom spikes cap thick, rigid whitish stems. Some people like the flower spikes for their vertical interest. Others remove the stalks before they have time to grow for the sake of the wonderful leaves. Grow this drought-tolerant plant in dry, sunny borders and on top of terraces and retaining walls. Lamb's-ears make a good groundcover that many weeds find hard to penetrate. Good companions include 'Biokovo' cranesbill and 'Crème Brulee' coreopsis.
Care: Lamb's-ears grows best when you meet its needs, which include full sun and very well-drained soil. Divide plants every five years or so to control vigor and keep it in check. In moist soils, the 4-inch leaves of lamb's-ears may start to rot and need some deadleafing by midseason.
Species and cultivars: 'Big Ears' (also sold as 'Helene Von Stein') has few to no flowers. It makes a superb 8- to 10-inch-tall groundcover with leaves twice as big as the species. This heat-tolerant cultivar is very desirable. 'Primrose Heron' forms a dense 6- to 8-inch-tall clump of cream-yellow

cupped leaves. 'Silver Carpet' does not bloom; it forms a dense 8-inch-tall carpet of silvery leaves.

Shrubby lamb's ears (*S. inflata*) offers white-stemmed spikes of pink flowers in early summer. Plants grow 12 inches tall and 10 inches wide. They have dark gray leaves. Native to mountains in the Middle East, shrubby lamb's-ear is especially tolerant of well-drained, infertile soil, making it a good choice for xeric gardens. Zones 5 to 9.

Flowers of lamb's-ears

Lavender (*Lavandula angustifolia*)

lav-an-DEW-luh an-gus-ti-FOL-ee-us
Features: Fragrant purple flower spikes; aromatic silver-green leaves.
Hardiness: Zones 5 to 10
Bloom time: Summer
Size: 2 feet tall, 3 feet in bloom, 3 feet wide
Shape: Fine-textured upright clump
Light: Full sun
Site: Well-drained, somewhat fertile, somewhat alkaline soil

Description: This evergreen woody shrub is a staple of herb gardens, Mediterranean gardens, and sunny perennial borders. Bees and butterflies like the fragrant two-lipped, tubular purple flowers growing on long, delicate spikes above the slender gray-green leaves. Both flowers and foliage produce a sweet, clean, lingering aroma. Lavender is a frequent ingredient in potpourri and fresh and dried flower arrangements. It appreciates the sharp drainage of rock gardens and makes a handsome short hedge or mass landscape planting. For an attractive combination grow lavender with Knock Out roses and wall germander.
Care: Lavender is heat-, drought-, and wind-tolerant and needs full sun and excellent drainage to survive. It does not tolerate high humidity, wet soil, or poor drainage. Shear faded blooms after flowering for a denser shape and to promote reblooming.

In spring wait until new growth has broken before cutting plants back. Don't cut them down completely, but prune them as you would a shrub. Remove dead or damaged stems and then shape plants as desired.

Because plants are woody, you cannot divide them. You can propagate lavender by stem cuttings.

Root rot may occur when grown in wet conditions.

To dry lavender, cut flower spikes when they are partly open. Bundle stems in groups up to 1 inch in diameter and hang them upside down in a dark, dry

Lavender

Detail of 'Hidcote' lavender flowers

area that has good air circulation. Store in an airtight container.

Species and cultivars: 'Blue Cushion' forms a pillow of silvery leaves 16 inches tall and has blue flowers. 'Hidcote' is 2 feet tall with deep purple flowers on a compact silver plant. 'Loddon Pink' is just 18 inches tall and has light pink flowers. 'Munstead' is also 18 inches tall with blue-purple blooms. Both 'Munstead' and 'Hidcote' do especially well in cold regions. 'Nana Alba' is a 12-inch-tall lavender with white flowers.

'Grosso' (*L. ×intermedia*) grows to 2 feet tall with long spikes of dark violet flowers. This cultivar is grown for its intensely fragrant essential oil. Zones 6 to 9.

Spanish lavender (*L. stoechas*) grows into a 2- to 3-foot-tall rounded silver bush sporting lilac-purple "rabbit ears" underscored with wands of dark purple bracts. 'Kew Red' offers magenta pink flowers in spring and early summer and can reach 4 feet tall. 'Otto Quast' blooms in royal purple from late winter to early summer. 'Hazel' blooms heavily in spring on 2½-foot-tall and 3-foot-wide plants and often reblooms in fall. 'Lemon Leigh' has chartreuse flowers on 2-foot-tall plants. 'Willow Vale' is more upright, 3 feet tall and 2 feet wide, and blooms in lavender-purple. Zones 7 to 10.

Hybrids: 'Dilly Dilly' is 12 inches tall with purple-blue flower spikes.

Lavender cotton *(Santolina chamaecyparissus)*

san-TUH-lean-uh cam-uh-sip-uh-RISS-us
Features: Shrubby mound of evergreen aromatic silvery foliage; tight round yellow blooms
Hardiness: Zones 6 to 10
Bloom time: Summer
Size: 1 foot tall, 1½ feet in bloom, 2 to 3 feet wide
Shape: Round mound
Light: Full sun
Site: Average garden soil

Lavender cotton with a purple sedum

Description:
Grown for its silvery evergreen leaves, lavender cotton resists deer and rabbits and looks good year-round. The foliage is fuzzy, fragrant, and fine textured with tiny, toothed edges. Use this woody perennial as an edging in rock gardens or perennial borders. Mass it as a groundcover. Or shear it to make a low, dense formal hedge in herb and knot gardens. Lavender cotton

does especially well in dry, low-maintenance gardens. Its round, brilliant yellow flower buttons bloom in summer on the tips of stems. Good companions include yucca, heart-leaf bergenia, and Japanese blood grass.

Care: Lavender cotton tolerates heat, drought, and salt spray but dislikes high humidity. Well-drained soil year-round is a must. To keep them dense and compact, prune plants to 6 to 8 inches tall before growth starts in spring. For hedges forego the flowers and clip the foliage as often as necessary to maintain

Detail of lavender cotton leaf

a clean shape. If you like the button flowers, trim plants right after they bloom.

Species and cultivars: 'Nana' grows 10 inches tall. Its foliage is strongly scented.

Lenten rose *(Helleborus orientalis)*

hell-eh-BOR-us ore-ee-ent-AL-is
Features: Early flowers in white, green, red, purple, or yellow; leathery evergreen leaves
Hardiness: Zones 4 to 9
Bloom time: Early spring, late winter in mild climates
Size: 1½ to 2 feet tall, 2 to 2½ feet wide
Shape: Loose, coarse-textured mounds
Light: Partial to full shade
Site: Rich, humusy, well-drained soil

White Lenten rose

Description:
This sturdy, deer-resistant shade lover stands out for its long-lasting 2½-inch flowers, unusual seedpods, and bold umbrella-shape dark green leaves that complement more delicate plants. The single or double flowers are cupped and nodding. They bloom in late winter or early spring and last for months. Colors range from green, white, and yellow to pink, purple, maroon, and red. Some may be spotted or washed with another hue. The clustered seedpods look sculptural. Grow lenten rose in woodlands or shady borders. Mass it for a groundcover under the canopy of trees. In the North lenten rose tolerates more sunlight.

Care: Provide a shady site with moist, well-drained soil. Plants do not grow well in wet or poorly drained soil or in windy areas. They will tolerate dry and alkaline soil. Lenten rose can tolerate and even thrive in full sun if the climate is cool and plants have ample water.

Fertilize as new growth emerges in spring. Lenten rose requires slightly more fertilizer than other perennials. Plants do not require deadheading but they may self-sow. The resulting seedlings may provide a pleasant surprise with new colors and flower forms. Transplant them before the expanding foliage of the original plants shades them out.

Hybrid lenten rose

Remove dead or winter-damaged leaves in late winter to make way for new growth and flowers. Once established plants seldom need division. But if you want to expand your garden, divide plants in spring; this allows time for plants to reestablish before winter. Divided plants may not bloom the following year. In Zones 4 to 5 where snow cover is not reliable, provide winter protection.

Pests include slugs, snails, and root weevils. Leaf spot can occur if soil is heavy or acid. Remove infected foliage and apply fungicide if cleaning up the plant doesn't help.

Species and cultivars: Bear's foot hellebore (*H. foetidus*) grows 32 inches by 18 inches with hanging green bells rimmed in purple. Its leaves reek when crushed. Zones 5 to 9.

Christmas rose (*H. niger*) has green-centered pinkish white blooms; it grows 12 inches by 18 inches. Zones 3 to 8.

Hybrids: 'Sunshine Hybrids' are 12 inches tall with blooms of pink, rose, white, creamy yellow, and mint green splotched with red at the base. 'Lady Hybrids' grow to 15 inches and are dark red to pale pink and white with deep red spots. 'Royal Heritage', a group of hybrids that grow 18 to 24 inches tall, have flowers ranging from white to blackish purple.

Leopard's bane *(Doronicum orientale)*

door-ON-ick-um ore-ee-en-TAL-ee
Features: Cheerful yellow flowers
Hardiness: Zones 4 to 7
Bloom time: Late spring
Size: 1½ feet tall, 1 foot wide
Shape: Rounded mound
Light: Part sun to shade
Site: Rich moist soil high in organic matter

Description: A rare daisy for shade, leopard's bane has clusters of yellow flowers covering its mound of heart-shape dark green leaves. Interplant it with ferns, which will cover up bare spots when leopard's bane goes dormant in summer.
Care: Although leopard's bane doesn't tolerate heat and goes dormant after it blooms, it is an easy

Leopard's bane

plant to grow. Give it light to medium shade in rich, moist soil high in organic matter. Space plants 12 to 15 inches apart. Mulch to conserve soil moisture. Water during dry weather.
Species and cultivars: 'Finesse' has semidouble yellow-orange flowers on 15-inch stems. 'Magnificum' forms neat, 15-inch mounds with yellow flowers on

Detail of leopard's bane flowers

2½-foot-tall stems. 'Miss Mason' (also known as 'Madame Mason') is 1 to 2 feet tall with canary yellow daisies and longer-lasting foliage than the species.

Ligularia *(Ligularia spp.)*

lig-yew-LAIR-ee-uh species
Features: Bold texture for the moist shade garden
Hardiness: Zones 4 to 8
Bloom time: Mid- to late summer
Size: 3 feet tall and wide, to 6 feet in bloom, depending on species
Shape: Coarse mound, stiff upright flower stalks
Light: Sun to shade, depending on the climate
Site: Continuously moist, fertile, well-drained soil

Description: Most ligularias stage their best performances in regions with cool nights and moist soil. Two main species are used in gardens. Bigleaf ligularia (*L. dentata*) has 12-inch-wide leathery leaves that bring a tropical flair to shady border and pondside plantings. The foliage is rounded with a deep heart-shape base, zigzag edges, and contrasting reddish stalks. It appears to be floating in horizontal layers. Orangy gold, daisylike flowers arranged in flat red-stalked clusters are a butterfly-attracting bonus.

Narrow-spiked ligularia (*L. stenocephala*) is more angular. It has large triangular leaves that are pointed at the tips and heart shape at the base. Tall, to 6 feet, narrow spikes of yellow flowers rise above the foliage in early and late summer. Like bigleaf ligularia, the foliage appears to float on a horizontal plane and the flowers attract butterflies. Both ligularias make stunning accents in moist borders and bog gardens. Plant them as specimens or grow them massed for an exotic effect.
Care: Grow ligularias in part shade or full sun (cool regions only) where soil remains moist. In hot areas it needs protection from heat and strong afternoon sunlight and must be planted in shade. Ligularia tends to wilt on hot days, even in cool regions and with moist soil. It perks up when temperatures cool down and the soil is moistened.

Ligularia

Ligularia flower stalk

Add organic matter at planting to ensure the soil holds moisture; set plants 2 to 3 feet apart. Division is rarely needed. Slugs and snails may eat the leaves.

Species and cultivars: Bigleaf ligularia: 'Desdemona' has loose, flat clusters of shaggy orange daisies that rise above the plants on 40-inch stems. Its purplish red young leaves turn bronzy green. Leaves are marked with dark maroon on their veins, undersides, and stems. 'Desdemona' has good heat tolerance. 'Othello' is similar to 'Desdemona' with orangy yellow blooms and dark purple young leaves maturing to bronzy green and maroon stems and leaf bottoms. Flowers form on 3-foot stems. 'Britt-Marie Crawford' has shiny, season-long chocolate-maroon foliage. Plants bloom in late summer on 3- to 4-foot stems. Zones 5 to 8.

Narrow-spiked ligularia: 'The Rocket' is more compact than the species, blooming on 2-foot-long stems. 'Little Rocket' has shiny green leaves and short spikes of bright yellow flowers on 2-foot-stems. Zones 5 to 8.

L. ×hessei is a hybrid ligularia with broad, 12-inch-wide, kidney-shape leaves. It bears upright conical spires of 4-inch-wide pale yellow daisylike flowers on 6-foot stems in midsummer. 'Gregynog Gold' has orange-gold daisies in late summer to early fall on 6-foot stems. 'Little Lanterns' is a miniature of the species, growing just 20 inches tall and wide, with conical spires of golden yellow blooms in mid- to late summer. Zones 4 to 8.

Lily *(Lilium spp.)*

lil-EE-um species
Features: Showy flowers, interesting foliage texture
Hardiness: Zones 3 to 9
Bloom time: Early summer to fall, depending on species
Size: Depends on species
Shape: Upright
Light: Full sun to light shade
Site: Well-drained organic soil

Description: It is difficult to imagine a summer garden without the dazzle of lilies in all their magnificence and variety. From late spring through the end of summer, lilies produce wave after showy wave of color.

Some dominate their places in the garden, others are modest in scale, and some are fragrant. One species, the Madonna lily *(L. candidum)*, has even gained the status of a religious emblem.

Detail of white lily blooms

Hybridization has increased the types, colors, and forms of lilies and made them even more adaptable, disease resistant, and easy to grow. The hybrids fall into seven general categories: Asiatic, martagon, candidum, American, longiflorum, trumpet, and oriental. Species lilies are also available.

Asiatic hybrids: These lilies bloom in early summer. They

Martagon hybrid

grow 2 to 5 feet tall and have 4- to 6-inch flowers in shades of red, pink, orange, yellow, lavender, or white. Their growth is compact, making them a good choice for growing in containers. The flowers may face up or down.

Martagon hybrids: These vigorous and beautiful lilies bloom in early summer. They grow 3 to 6 feet tall and have 2- to 4-inch flowers in white, yellow, lavender, orange, brown, lilac, tangerine, or mahogany. The flowers hang down like miniature chandeliers. Plants form roots along their stems underground.

Candidum hybrids: These also bloom in early summer. Plants grow 3 to 4 feet tall and have 4- to 5-inch flowers that typically have a heavenly fragrance.

American hybrids: These hybrids of North American native lilies bloom in late spring and early summer. They are 4 to 8 feet tall with 4- to 6-inch flowers.

Longiflorum hybrids: The familiar fragrant white Easter lily or white trumpet lily *(L. longiflorum)* and its hybrids can be grown in Zones 6 to 11. With protection they may survive in Zone 5. In the garden they grow about 3 feet tall and bloom in summer.

Trumpet lily

Trumpet hybrids: These summer-flowering lilies grow 4 to 6 feet tall and have 6- to 10-inch-long flowers. This category includes the aurelian and olympic hybrids, which have trumpet-shape blooms. Others in the group have star-shape, pendant, or flat open flowers.

Oriental hybrids: These fragrant hybrids bloom in late summer. They grow 2 to 8 feet tall with 12-inch-wide flowers. The flowers are bowl shape with petals that curve back. Colors include white, deep reds, pinks, and bicolors. Oriental hybrids can be grown in containers but may need to be staked.

Species lilies: This group includes many excellent garden lilies native to North America, Europe, and Asia. Gold-banded lily *(L. auratum)* bears up to 35 fragrant flowers per stem. Martagon lily *(L. martagon)* is a hardy species that produces dozens of dangling flowers in which the petals curl back completely. Regal lily *(L. regale)* has fragrant, trumpet-shape flowers.

Care: With few exceptions, lilies are hardy to –40°F. They grow well in most areas, although they do not like dry heat. They prefer about six hours of sun but tolerate as few as four, especially in hot climates. Plant lilies in groups in flowerbeds and perennial borders, wherever the ground over the planting area will be shaded to help keep soil cool, or apply a 2-inch-deep mulch. Water and fertilize regularly while plants are growing. Stake tall varieties, using individual supports for each stem. Take care to avoid damaging the bulb as you push the stake into the ground.

'Stargazer' lily

Lilies are available as bare bulbs and as potted plants. Plant potted lilies soon after buying them at the depth of the nursery pot, spacing large lilies 1 foot apart. Care for the plants as you would any new perennial, watering and mulching until plants become established. Don't expect your lilies to bloom again this first year.

Fall is the best time for planting bulbs, but Madonna and candidum lilies should be planted in late summer to early fall. Bulbs arrive on the market in spring; if you buy them then, go ahead and plant them.

Ensure that the bulbs you buy in fall are fresh and haven't been allowed to sit and dry out over summer. Also make sure the bulbs are neither moldy, soft, nor damaged. The healthier the bulb the healthier the plant.

Buy bulbs properly packed in ventilated bags with moist peat moss and plant them immediately. Dig the hole deep enough that the bulbs will have 2 inches of soil over them. Usually 8 inches deep is adequate. Plant Asiatic and martagon lilies up to 10 inches deep. These form roots along their stems underground, and the extra depth helps secure the plants. Plant Madonna lilies just an inch or two deep.

Species and cultivars: Asiatic: 'Connecticut King' blooms in buttercup yellow with a gold center. They grow 2 to 3 feet tall and bloom in early summer. 'Enchantment' has heavily spotted orange-red flowers and grows 3 feet tall. Flowers of 'Avignon' are red; the 40-inch plants bloom in midsummer. 'Vivaldi' blooms in clear pink on 3-foot stems in early summer. 'Sterling Star' has white flowers spotted in red. Plants grow 2 to 3 feet tall and bloom in midsummer. 'Petite Pink' has pink flowers that fade to white with darker spots; it grows 12 inches tall. 'Reinesse' is a compact 15-inch-tall lily with white flowers in midsummer.

Martagon: 'Album' has white blooms on 3- to 4-foot stems in early summer. 'Brocade' is peachy pink with butter yellow, orange, and rosy pink mixed in. Plants grow 4 to 5 feet tall and bloom in early summer. 'Mrs. R. O. Backhouse' has straw yellow blooms with red spotting and soft magenta on the backs of the petals. Plants grow 3 to 5 feet tall and bloom in midsummer.

American: Bellingham Hybrids bloom in a range of colors from yellow to reddish orange on 7-foot stems in midsummer. Flowers hang in panicles like martagon lilies. 'Boogie Woogie' has lemon yellow blooms on 3- to 4-foot stems. It resembles an oriental lily.

Longiflorum: 'Dream Catcher' has pink flowers in June and July on 4-foot stems. 'Pink Perfection' has lavender flowers and grows 6 feet tall. 'Queen's Promise' has deep pink blooms on 4- to 5-foot plants in midsummer. 'Red Alert' offers bright red blooms on 3- to 4-foot plants in midsummer.

'Connecticut King' Asiatic lily

Trumpet: 'Black Dragon' has white flowers with burgundy markings along their backs and recurved petals. Plants grow 5 to 6 feet tall. 'Copper King' has cantaloupe orange blooms on 5- to 6-foot stems. The yellow flowers of 'Golden Splendor' are backed with maroon. Plants grow 6 feet tall.

Oriental: 'Acapulco' is a late-summer bloomer with hot pink, upward-facing blooms on 3½-foot stems. 'Casablanca' offers fragrant, ruffled white flowers on 4-foot stems in midsummer. 'Stargazer' has fragrant, up-facing, red-spotted pink blooms with a deep pink center and white around their edges on 3-foot stems.

Liriope *(Liriope muscari)*

luh-rye-OH-pea MUS-care-ee
Features: Evergreen groundcover with grassy leaves
Hardiness: Zones 6 to 10
Bloom time: Late summer to fall
Size: 8 to 12 inches tall, 18 inches wide
Shape: Cascading mound
Light: Sun to shade
Site: Moist, well-drained, somewhat fertile soil

Description: Liriope grows into thick clumps of evergreen grassy leaves. In late summer through fall, it bears spikes of purple flowers followed by attractive dark blue berries. Use it as a groundcover under trees and shrubs and as an edging or a grassy covering for shady slopes. Liriope works well alone, in containers, or in mixed plantings. If using it alone consider a decorative cultivar such as 'Okina', which has broad foliage that starts out white and acquires green tips with age.

Care: Although liriope grows well in sun to shade, it prefers afternoon shade in the South. It also likes well-drained, acid, moderately fertile soil. Liriope needs regular deep watering after planting, but once established it is drought tolerant and can grow in beds with shrubs and trees. Plant it 12 to 18 inches apart in spring or fall and feed with slow-release fertilizer at planting. Water deeply when the soil feels dry about 3 inches below the surface. Deadhead faded flower spikes for tidiness. When growing liriope as a groundcover, refresh the leaves in spring

Liriope

Creeping liriope

by mowing with a lawn mower at the highest setting. Divide in spring or fall. **Species and cultivars:** 'Big Blue' has lavender flowers on 10-inch plants. 'Monroe White' provides abundant white spikes. 'Pee Dee Gold Ingot' has lavender flowers and gold-and-chartreuse leaves year-round. It's 10 inches tall. 'Samantha' grows 12 to 15 inches tall and has pink flowers. 'Variegata', another 10-incher, has lavender flowers and white-edged green leaves.

Creeping liriope (*L. spicata*) is an excellent groundcover with finer leaves than *L. muscari*. It is the same size and has the same form but blooms in lavender or white, followed by dark blue berries. Plants adapt to full sun and full shade. 'Alba' has white flowers. 'Silver Dragon' has striped silver leaves. Zones 5 to 10.

Lobelia *(See Cardinal flower)*

Lungwort *(Pulmonaria saccharata)*
pull-MUH-nair-ee-uh sack-cuh-ROT-uh
Features: Large leaves splashed with white, pink, or blue flowers
Hardiness: Zones 4 to 8
Bloom time: Early spring
Size: 1 foot tall, 1 to 2 feet wide
Shape: Low clump
Light: Partial shade to full shade
Site: Moist soil with abundant organic matter

'Bubble Gum' lungwort

Description: This enchanting early blooming shade lover has two seasons of garden interest. In spring fresh flowers clustered at the stem tips open pink and then mature to blue while new pink flowers continue to develop, to the delight of winter-weary gardeners. Yet lungwort saves its big show for summer, when a mound of huge white-splattered deep green leaves take over.

Lungwort is an eye-catching sight in shade. Its coarse foliage anchors taller, arching plants such as solomon's seal. Use it to brighten the edges of shady paths or mass it for a groundcover in woodland gardens. It looks wonderful in front of yews in a foundation planting. Other good companions include trillium, dead nettle, blue lobelias, jacob's ladder, and ferns.

Care: This easy-to-grow plant needs partial to full shade and average garden soil rich in organic matter. It tolerates drought and heat but not at the same time. Leaves of plants that get too hot or dry become brown and crispy.

Remove the flower stem after blooming for neatness and to prevent self-sowing. Volunteer seedlings, however, often have much different markings on the leaves and give you the opportunity to select your own cultivar. Plants rarely require division but are easy to divide if you desire.

'Benediction' lungwort

No need to cut plants back in fall; the foliage decomposes over winter. Lungworts are generally pest free, but they can develop powdery mildew. Deter powdery mildew by providing plants with good air circulation and adequate moisture during hot, dry spells. If mildew strikes, cutting down plants and watering them well will encourage a fresh crop of leaves to replace the old ones.

Species and cultivars: 'Excalibur' is almost completely silver. The broad, bright silver leaves have a narrow, dark green margin. It grows 10 inches tall and 20 inches wide and has rosy pink to blue flowers. Plants are mildew resistant. 'Mrs. Moon' has large silver-spotted leaves. 'Pierre's Pure Pink' has salmon-pink blooms that don't turn blue and silver-splattered foliage.

Bethlehem sage (*P. officinalis*) has smaller flowers and more elliptical, sharp-pointed, and rough leaves than lungwort. 'Sissinghurst White' grows 10 to 12 inches tall with white flowers and white-spotted leaves that are susceptible to mildew. Zones 3 to 7.

Long-leafed lungwort (*P. longifolia*) has big blue flowers and long, narrow, pointed gray-spotted leaves. Plants grow 9 to 12 inches tall and 24 inches wide. 'Bertram Anderson' has blue-green leaves with large silver-white spots. Cevenensis (*P. l. cevenensis*) has slender silver-marked leaves up to 26 inches long and broad flowers. It is an excellent choice for the South. Mature plants grow into leaf clumps up to 18 inches by 40 inches. They are extremely mildew resistant. 'Diana Clare' has narrow leaves of pure silver and violet-blue blooms that age to purple, then to pink. Blooming is a little later than other lungworts. Zones 3 to 8.

Red lungwort (*P. rubra*) is unusual in that it has blooms earlier in spring than other lungworts and has coral-red flowers. The unspotted foliage is light green and is evergreen in mild climates. It does better in areas with cool summers than in Southern ones. 'David Ward' forms a compact 12-inch clump of variegated green leaves with white margins and salmon-pink flowers in early spring. Zones 4 to 8.

Hybrids: 'Samourai', which grows 12 inches tall and 15 inches wide, has lilac-blue blooms and long, narrow silver leaves with a dark green edge. It is more sun tolerant than the species. 'Roy Davidson' has heavily spotted leaves and pale pink flowers that age to powder blue. 'Raspberry Splash' has silver-spotted leaves, raspberry pink flowers, and grows more upright than other lungworts. 'Spilled Milk' blooms in lilac-pink and has heavily splotched foliage to 9 inches tall.

Lupine *(Lupinus hybrids)*

LOO-pin-us hybrids
Features: Coarse-textured spikes in bright colors
Hardiness: Zones 4 to 6
Bloom time: Spring to early summer
Size: 3 feet tall, 2 feet wide
Shape: Upright in bloom, mounded
Light: Full sun to part sun
Site: Consistently moist, rich, well-drained soil

Description:
Lupines have fabulous showy flowers and interesting coarse-textured eight-fingered leaves. They look best massed in beds or combined with mounded perennials such as geranium or shasta daisy.

Lupine

Care: Species lupines are tough plants that survive the poorest of conditions. Hybrids are another story. They perform best in light, sandy soil and in areas with cool summers and mild winters. They will not survive in areas with hot, humid summers or wet, cold winters.

Plant lupines in fall. Buy the largest plant you can find; lupines in 1-gallon or larger containers will transplant and settle in better than smaller plants. Provide rich, moist, well-drained acid soil. Space plants 18 to 24 inches apart. Water during dry periods and mulch in summer to keep roots cool. Apply an airy mulch in winter to protect plants. They do not need staking.

Blue Russell hybrid lupine

Hybrid lupines are susceptible to powdery mildew, rust, aphids, and other insects.

Species and cultivars: Gallery Hybrids is a dwarf series to 18 inches tall. Plants bloom in blue, pink, red, and white. Minarette Hybrids are a little taller, to 20 inches, and bloom in a mix of colors. 'My Castle' has brick-red flowers on 2- to 3-foot plants. 'The Chatelaine', which is part of the Band of Nobles Series, has pink and white bicolor flowers.

Maidenhair fern *(See Ferns)*
Maltese cross *(See Campion)*
Marginal shield fern *(See Ferns)*

Masterwort *(Astrantia major)*

ass-TRAN-tee-uh MAY-jor
Features: Showy pincushion flowers in pink, rose, red, purple, and white
Hardiness: Zones 5 to 7
Bloom time: Late spring to midsummer
Size: 30 inches tall, 18 inches wide
Shape: Rounded clump
Light: Partial shade
Site: Moist soil rich in organic matter

Description:
A charming cottage garden perennial, masterwort's flowers have high, cushioned centers ringed with pointed bracts, giving them old-fashioned appeal. The white, rose, pink, and purple flowers develop in clusters on strong upright stems. Over time one planting may contain all of these colors. Plants form a dense spring clump and grow 2 to 3 feet tall in cool climates, but they struggle in the heat of the South. Flowers are attractive fresh or dried.

Masterwort

Care: Masterwort grows best in moist soil rich in organic matter. Although masterwort grows in average soil, it does best with plenty of moisture. Plants grow well in heavy clay soil and are ideal for shady stream banks and moist garden spots. They tolerate full sun where moisture is plentiful. They do not tolerate heat, drought, or hot summer nights.

Deadhead for prolonged and repeat bloom. If not deadheaded plants self-sow but not to nuisance levels. The seedlings will be different from the parents.

Cut back foliage in late fall or early spring to avoid leaf spot. Division is rarely necessary.

Species and cultivars: 'Alba' has white flowers on 2-foot-tall plants. 'Claret' blooms in deep red on blackish 22-inch stems. It forms a basal mound of palm-shape leaves. 'Ruby Cloud' grows 1½ to 3 feet tall with long-blooming, deep purplish pink flowers that are excellent for cutting. 'Ruby Wedding' has dark ruby red flowers all summer on 2- to 2½-foot-tall plants.

Detail of masterwort flowers

Meadow rue (Thalictrum rochebrunianum)

thuh-LICK-trum rosh-brun-EE-ay-num
Features: Airy clusters of dainty flowers; mound of leaves like maidenhair fern
Hardiness: Zones 4 to 9
Bloom time: Mid- to late summer
Size: 3 feet tall and wide, 6 feet tall in bloom
Shape: Airy clump, upright in bloom
Light: Full sun to partial shade
Site: Moist, rich, well-drained soil rich in organic matter

Meadow rue in bud

Description: Although this meadow rue towers above many garden plants, it is no garden bully. Its presence is magical and harmonious, like a giant lacy fern capped with sprays of blooms. Each little bud opens to reveal a lavender flower with a big tuft of yellow stamens. Both leaves and flowers are lovely in bouquets.

Before it blooms, meadow rue grows as a low, fine-textured, irregular clump that makes a graceful fine-textured accent. As the flowers develop its stems rise from the clump, so it is a splendid background for other perennials. A group of three meadow rues looks stunning in woodland gardens or combined with 'Brunette' bugbane and 'Morning Light' maiden grass. In shade grow meadow rue for height; in moist sunny sites, for its fine texture.

Care: Meadow rue prefers deep, consistently moist, fertile soil with abundant organic matter. Set plants about 2 feet apart in partial shade, except in the North where it can take full sun. However the more sun plants grow in, the more water they will need. Plants do not tolerate heat, humidity, or drought.

Although tall, meadow rue needs no staking unless soil is dry or light is strongly one-directional. Stake individual stems or use grow-through supports. There is no need to deadhead; the seedheads are as decorative as the flowers. However plants can self-sow. Cut plants back in late fall.

Divide meadow rue every five years to renew its vigor.

Columbine meadow rue

Divide sooner if plants start to bloom less or grow shorter over the years. The plants don't move easily and wilt readily afterwards. Keep an eye on recent transplants and keep soil moist around them.

Meadow rue may develop powdery mildew in dry climates. Plants are deer resistant.

Species and cultivars: 'Lavender Mist' has lavender-pink buds that open to violet with gold stamens. It is one of the best-looking and most common meadow rues on the market.

Columbine meadow rue (*T. aquilegifolium*) has leaves that resemble columbine and clouds of pink flowers in late spring to early summer. Zones 5 to 7.

Yellow meadow rue (*T. delavayi*) produces sprays of tiny lilac single blooms. It grows 3 to 5 feet tall. Because of its see-through stems, you can plant it toward the front of the border. 'Album' blooms in white. 'Hewitt's Double' has double lilac blooms. Zones 4 to 7.

Hybrids: 'Black Stockings' has lavender flower puffs on near-black stems. It is 6 feet tall in bloom and 2 feet wide.

Meadowsweet (*See Queen-of-the-prairie*)

Miscanthus (Miscanthus sinensis)

miss-CAN-thus sigh-NEN-sis
Features: Ornamental grass
Hardiness: Zones 5 to 9, depending on cultivar
Bloom time: Late summer to fall
Size: 3 to 7 feet, depending on cultivar
Shape: Cascading mound
Light: Full sun
Site: Average soil

Miscanthus

Description: Miscanthus, a Japanese native, is a versatile perennial that is probably the grass used most often in gardens. Dozens of cultivars exist, varying in foliage color, flower shape, and plant form. Starting in late summer and continuing to fall, showy pink, tan, silver, or bronze plumes rise above the leaves and persist with the foliage into winter. This sensual grass attracts birds, shimmers in strong sunlight, and quivers and rustles in wind. Use short cultivars for beds, borders, waterside plantings, and small garden spaces. Tall forms look good at the back of borders, next to ponds, and as garden specimens. You can also use them for privacy screening or to block unpleasant views. They suit informal gardens, where they harmonize with purple coneflower, black-eyed susan, and gayfeather. Plumes make attractive, long-lasting cut flowers.

Care: Miscanthus prefers moist, well-drained, fertile soil in full sun to light shade. Plants are robust and, once established, will tolerate some drought and road salt spray. In too much shade they will flop.

Cut plants back in early spring using hedge shears. Tie the foliage up out of the way before cutting. The species and some cultivars, particularly ones that bloom early in the growing season, may self-sow and become invasive. Weed out seedlings or dig them up to share with your friends.

Divide plants as they outgrow their space. A clump that is dying in the center needs to be divided. If the clump is big and old, the task requires a very sharp spade for digging, a saw to part the clump, and enough physical strength to carry out the job. Hardiness depends on the cultivar.

Species and cultivars: 'Adagio' is a 3- to 4-foot-tall cultivar with narrow green leaves marked with a white midrib.

Pink-tinted flowers begin in August, aging to white. 'Graziella' has great, fluffy white plumes in August on 5- to 6-foot stems over an arching clump of fine, graceful leaves. In late summer 'Little Kitten' has silver flowers

Zebra grass

on 30-inch stems above 15-inch foliage. 'Herkules' is a strong-growing, 5- to 6-foot cultivar with ruddy fall color.

'Silver Feather' has lavish silver flowers from September through winter. Its dense, arching 6- to 9-foot-tall form makes a terrific screen. Porcupine grass ('Strictus') is 6 to 8 feet tall with erect flowers in September above a columnar clump of green leaves with broad yellow horizontal bands. Maiden grass ('Gracillimus') grows 3 to 4 feet tall and 3 feet wide. It has narrow leaves, an arching habit, and large silvery plumes. Zebra grass ('Zebrinus') is a tall, upright cultivar with yellow horizontal bands on its leaves.

Hardier miscanthus: Flame grass (the cultivar 'Purpurascens' has red-tinged, 4-foot tall foliage that turns red-orange in fall. Fluffy white flowers appear in July and

'Variegatus' miscanthus

August on 5-foot stalks. They are earlier than many miscanthus. Plants seldom self-sow. Zones 3 to 9. 'Autumn Light' offers 7- to 9-foot deep bronze plumes in mid-September on an upright 6-foot clump of foliage that arches at the top and turns yellow in fall. Zones 4 to 9.

Less hardy miscanthus: 'Cabaret' grows 6 to 8 feet tall with wide, variegated foliage that has a large, creamy white center and deep green edges. Flowers are pink. Zones 6 to 9. 'Little Nicky' (also sold as 'Hinjo') grows 3 to 4 feet tall. It has arching, light green foliage with horizontal yellow bands and red flowers in September and October. Zones 6 to 9.

Mondo grass (Ophiopogon japonica)

oh-fee-oh-POH-gon jup-ON-ick-us
Features: Grassy clumps with small lilac flowers
Hardiness: Zones 6 to 10
Bloom time: Late summer
Size: 6 to 12 inches tall, 12 inches wide
Shape: Cascading, spreading mound
Light: Full sun to part sun
Site: Moist, organic, well-drained soil

Description: Not a true grass but resembling ornamental grasses in appearance and behavior, this unusual foliage plant is a standout, especially when contrasted with brighter colors. It spreads slowly and grows about a foot tall. It has slender, shiny, dark evergreen leaves and small tubular

flowers on spiky stalks. Blue pea-size fruits follow the blooms. Mondo grass is a good edging for beds and paths and makes a nice groundcover.
Care: Mondo grass prefers fertile, moist, humus-rich, well-drained soil and can be grown in sun or light shade. Mow or cut it back in spring before new growth begins. In full sun mondo grass needs more frequent watering.

Divide plants in spring when they become crowded. Plants are usually pest free.
Species and cultivars: Black mondo grass (*Ophiopogon planiscapus* 'Niger') is similar in form and size but has short, arched, black to violet-black leaves. Massed in shade this grassy member of the lily family creates a dark background that makes plants with bright

Mondo grass edges a raised bed

Black mondo grass

flowers or variegated leaves stand out. Black mondo grass prefers a shady site in moist, well-drained soil rich in organic matter. Zones 5 to 10.

Monkshood (Aconitum spp.)

ack-un-EYE-tum species
Features: Late-season blue flowers
Hardiness: Zones 3 to 8
Bloom time: Late summer to fall
Size: 2 feet tall, 3 to 5 feet in bloom, 1 foot wide
Shape: Mounded, upright spires
Light: Part sun to part shade
Site: Well-drained, organic-matter-enriched soil

Description: Monkshood earned its name from the hooded blooms that look like the cowl of a monk's robe. All species form clumps or mounds of coarsely lobed foliage from which tall upright flower stems begin to rise in midsummer. The purple, white, or blue flowers open late in summer or in early to midfall. All parts of monkshood are poisonous so prevent young children from accessing them.
Care: Plant monkshood in light shade or part sun. It

Azure monkshood

Monkshood detail

does well in full sun where summers are cool or plants are well watered. Heat is detrimental, especially where nighttime temperatures are above 70°F. In hot regions grow monkshood where it will receive afternoon shade. In full shade plants grow very tall, become floppy, and bloom later in fall. Amend the soil with plenty of organic matter before planting monkshood.

Stake plants that become floppy. Use individual stakes for plants that are well underway in their growth or place grow-through supports over the plants in early spring. Deadheading prolongs blooming where the season lasts long enough for the next round of blooms to form. Cut plants to the ground after frost. Remove and destroy prunings to prevent diseases. In Zones 3 to 4 mulch heavily to ensure the plants' survival. Monkshood spreads slowly; divide plants every four or five years or as needed.

Wilting in early spring is a sign of crown rot disease. Ensuring good soil drainage over winter helps to control the disease. Check for bacterial leaf spot and mildew in

'Baker's Variety' azure mokshood

midspring; remove infected leaves and apply fungicide. Cyclamen mite may be a problem.

Species and cultivars: Azure monkshood (*A. carmichelii*) is a late bloomer with deep purple flowers. Plants grow 2 to 4 feet tall and are sturdy enough not to need staking unless in too much shade. 'Arendsii' has large intense blue-purple flowers in mid- to late fall. Zones 3 to 7.

Bicolor monkshood (*A. cammarum*) has blue or violet flowers often variegated with white. Plants grow 3 to 4 feet tall, 2 feet wide, and have deeply divided leaves. Hoods of 'Bicolor' are pale lavender to violet with darker purple petals below, bordered in purple-blue. 'Bressingham Spire' has violet-blue flowers on 3-foot stems in summer. Zones 3 to 7.

Common monkshood (*A. napellus*) blooms in deep purple-blue in late summer. Plants grow 3 to 5 feet tall and 1 to 2 feet wide. Zones 3 to 6.

'Ivorine' (*A. septentrionale*) blooms in late summer, bearing creamy white flowers on compact plants to 2½ feet tall. Zones 3 to 7.

Hybrids: 'Blue Lagoon' grows just 1 foot tall and 8 to 10 inches wide. Its bright blue flowers form lower on the stem for a showier display. 'Eleanor' (or 'Eleanora') blooms in midsummer. Its white flowers edged in blue top 3½-foot stems. 'Stainless Steel' has pale lavender flowers. It too grows 3½ feet tall and blooms in midsummer. All monkshoods are hardy in Zones 3 to 7.

Mountain bluet (*Centaurea montana*)

sen-TOR-ree-uh mon-TAN-uh
Features: Blue-violet blooms
Hardiness: Zones 3 to 8
Bloom time: Midspring to early summer
Size: 1 to 1½ feet tall, 2 feet wide
Shape: Mound
Light: Full sun to part sun
Site: Well-drained soil

Mountain bluet

Description: These mounded gray-green plants grow 12 to 15 inches tall and are topped with blue-violet flowers on leafy, 18-inch-tall stems. The daisies are 2 inches across with wispy frills radiating from a darker center. Plants rebloom in midsummer if cut back.

Mountain bluet is a fast-growing clump-former that readily self-sows. Its downy foliage fills in around later-emerging, taller, and narrower plants such as balloon flower, Russian sage, and butterfly weed. The blue flowers combine well with candytuft and oriental poppy.

Care: Plants tolerate heat, drought, wind, and high-pH soil but not wet soil, especially wet soil in winter. Cut plants back hard after they bloom to promote lush new foliage and to prevent self-sowing. You might want to allow some seedlings to grow to renew the planting.

Divide mountain bluet every two to three years; they are easy to move. If plants are grown where they receive shade or if days are hot in spring, the flowering stems will stretch and require staking. Use grow-through supports.

Plants are generally pest free but occasionally are attacked by stalk borers. They will regrow from any bit of root left in the ground so take care to remove the entire root of unwanted seedlings.

There is no need to cut plants back in fall or spring. Foliage neatly self-destructs over winter.

Species and cultivars: 'Alba' has white

Mountain bluet bloom

flowers. 'Amethyst in Snow' has royal purple-centered white daisies. Chartreuse foliage provides a dazzling background for the violet-center blue flowers of 'Gold Bullion'. 'Grandiflora' has large flowers. 'Rosea' and 'Carnea' bloom in pink.

Muhly grass *(Muhlenbergia capillaris)*

mule-en-BUR-gee-uh cap-ill-AIR-iss
Features: Vibrant pink to pink-red plumes
Hardiness: Zones 6 to 10
Bloom time: Late summer
Size: 1 foot tall, 3 feet in bloom, 3 to 4 feet wide
Shape: Cascading mound, round mound in bloom
Light: Full to part sun
Site: Average to poor soil

Muhly grass

Description: This fine-textured grass is suited for beds or naturalistic settings. In late summer muhly grass sends out light purple-pink to pink-red plumes that fade to gold in the fall. Grow it as an accent or a groundcover. This well-behaved beauty is at home anywhere you would plant an ornamental grass. Its structure adds interest to the winter garden. The flowers draw butterflies.

Care: This tough native plant tolerates heat, drought, poor, wet, or sandy soil and sunny or partially shaded sites. Salt sprays do not bother it so it is good to use along a seashore or along roadsides where cities treat for ice and snow. Plants rarely need division.

Species and cultivars: Flowers of 'White Cloud' are white. Plants are 4 feet tall in bloom. 'Regal Mist' has dusky pink blooms in fall. It grows 3 feet tall and wide and grows well in the Southwest and California. Occasional watering ensures plentiful flowers.

Mullein *(Verbascum spp.)*

ver-BAS-cum species
Features: Strong vertical accent with spikes of yellow or white flowers
Hardiness: Zones 5 to 8, depending on species
Bloom time: Early to midsummer
Size: 1½ to 2 feet tall, to 4 feet in bloom, 2 feet wide
Shape: Low mound, erect in bloom
Light: Full sun
Site: Light, sandy, well-drained soil

Description: Ornamental mulleins have outstanding flower spikes that shoot up from a broad rosette of coarse leaves in early summer. In shape plants resemble a column on a broad, stable base. Flowers open from the bottom up in wonderful shades of yellow, orange, pink, and white.

Mulleins create an elegant vertical accent in shrub and perennial borders where viewers can appreciate the subtle hues of their leaves and flowers. In masses mullein looks best planted in midborder, but a random specimen (planted or self-sown) edging a cottage garden path or at the front of a raised bed has a charming effect.

The coarse gray or dark green foliage complements blue foliage plants, such as blue oat grass, and contrasts with fine-textured perennials like yarrow. Try mullein amid bigroot geranium or with the purplish blooms of 'Karley

Mullein

Rose' fountain grass.

Care: This low-maintenance but short-lived perennial needs well-drained soil to survive. Although it prefers full sun and sandy alkaline soils, it tolerates many other situations, including drought. Plants resist wind and heat but do not tolerate high humidity, wet soil, or poor drainage. Space plants about 18 inches apart.

Deadhead as seedpods begin to swell at the base of the flowering stalk. Once two-thirds of the spike has bloomed, the remaining flowers can't make up for the appearance of the spent flowers. Mulleins are short lived so leave the last flower stem to self-sow for future plants.

Fertilize only lightly. Plants should not require staking; but if stems flop cut back on fertilizer or move plants to a sunnier spot. Do not divide mulleins; take root cuttings instead.

In fall remove the last flower stalk once the seed has ripened. Leave the basal foliage.

Species and cultivars: Nettle-leaved mullein *(V. chaixii—*shay-ZEE-eye) has gray-green foliage and is 3 feet tall in bloom. The straight species has yellow flowers. 'Album' has white blooms with a purple center. 'Sixteen Candles' offers many-branched spikes of golden yellow blooms with violet stamens. Zones 5 to 8.

Olympic mullein *(V. olympicum)* has huge, branched spikes of yellow blooms on 6- to 7-foot gray stems. Zones 6 to 8.

Hybrids: 'Caribbean Crush' has many-branched salmon pink blooms on 18-inch stems and silvery foliage. 'Dark Eyes' displays peachy gold blooms with red eyes on 12-inch stems. Foliage is silvery gray. 'Jackie' has light apricot blooms on 16-inch-tall stems and big fuzzy leaves. 'Jackie in Pink' is similar but with pink blooms. 'Plum Smokey' has plum-colored blooms on 16-inch stems and blooms all summer when deadheaded. Its leaves are green. 'Raspberry Ripple' has creamy pink flowers with raspberry centers on 2-foot stems. Leaves are green. Green-leaved 'Summer Sorbet' has hot raspberry pink blooms on 2-foot stems. 'Sugar Plum' has deep plum flower spikes on 18-inch-tall stems; plants reliably rebloom. Zones 5 to 9.

'Album' nettle-leaved mullein

Nepal cinquefoil (Potentilla nepalensis)

poh-ten-TILL-uh neh-PAUL-en-sis
Features: Magenta flowers
Hardiness: Zones 5 to 8
Bloom time: Late spring to early summer
Size: 1 to 1½ feet tall, 2 feet wide
Shape: Sprawling clump
Light: Full sun
Site: Well-drained soil

Description: Valued for its slightly cupped, brightly colored blooms that look like single roses, Nepal cinquefoil's flowers appear in loose, branched clusters on wiry reddish stems. Its hairy leaves resemble the palm of a hand. Plants form sprawling clumps to about 18 inches tall. Grow Nepal cinquefoil in a container, where it will trail over the rim, or mass it in borders, near rocks, or on retaining walls, where its floppy form will soften and enhance the hard edges. It is better known for its cultivars than for the species itself. Plants can be short lived.

Nepal cinquefoil

Care: Grow Nepal cinquefoil in full sun and well-drained soil. Raised beds provide the excellent drainage the plants require. If stems look untidy after flowering, prune lightly to encourage branching and neaten the plant. Nepal cinquefoil is easy to grow and relatively untroubled by pests or diseases.

Species and cultivars: 'Miss Willmott' grows 10 to 12 inches tall. It has cherry pink flowers with a dark cherry eye. 'Rod McBeath' has deep pink flowers with a darker center from late spring through summer.

'Gibson's Scarlet Nepal cinquefoil hybrid

Spring cinquefoil (*P. neumanniana 'Nana'*) produces golden yellow flowers in spring. It grows 3 to 4 inches tall and 20 inches wide and creates a robust groundcover on dry, sunny slopes. Zones 4 to 8.

Hybrids: 'Gibson's Scarlet' is a 16-inch-tall plant with flat 1-inch-wide, dark-centered brilliant scarlet blooms all summer. 'William Rollisson', also 16 inches tall, has 1½-inch-wide vivid red-orange semidouble blooms.

New York ironweed (Vernonia noveboracensis)

ver-NOHN-yuh no-vee-bore-us-EN-sis
Features: Dark purple or red-violet flowers
Hardiness: Zones 5 to 8
Bloom time: Mid- to late summer
Size: 3 feet, 7 feet in bloom, 2 feet wide
Shape: Upright or vase-shape
Light: Full to part sun
Site: Well-drained soil with plentiful organic matter

Description: For late-season color few perennials match New York ironweed. It is a wonderful backdrop plant with large, flat-topped flower clusters that is at home in informal gardens. Plants are upright, columnar, or vase-shape and grow at a moderate pace. New York ironweed's coarse, dark green foliage complements ornamental grasses, culver's root, black-eyed susan, patrinia, hardy hibiscus, and many other perennials. The flowers attract butterflies.

New York ironweed

Care: Deadheading is unnecessary. The tallest plants may require staking; use grow-through supports or individual braces. Pinch stems several times between spring and early summer to promote density and reduce plant height.

Plants are long lived. Divide them after seven to eight years to maintain vigor and free flowering. Plants are easy to move. Cut them back in late fall or early spring.

Species and cultivars: 'Jonesboro' giant ironweed (*V. altissima*) stands up without staking, even though it grows 10 to 12 feet tall. Flowers are dark purple. Zones 5 to 8.

New Zealand flax (Phormium tenax)

FORM-eum TEN-ax
Features: Colorful foliage
Hardiness: Zones 8 to 11
Bloom time: Not grown for flowers
Size: 5 to 7 feet tall, 4 to 8 feet wide
Shape: Upright mound
Light: Full sun
Site: Deep, fertile, moist soil

Description: This broad-leaved ornamental grass has wonderfully colorful leaves that may be yellow-green, dark green, red, rust colored, or variegated in many fine stripes of any of these colors. Grown for dramatic effect and colorful foliage, New Zealand flax is perfect

'Moon Maiden' New Zealand flax

'Maori Sunset' New Zealand flax

for planting at the edge of a water garden, as a focal point in a border, or in a container, which is the solution for gardeners in cold climates.

Care: Grow New Zealand flax in a sunny, sheltered spot in deep, fertile, moist soil. Water regularly to keep soil moist. Divide plants in spring.

Species and cultivars: 'Aurora' bears leaves striped with red, pink, and yellow. 'Burgundy' is a deep wine red. 'Purpureum' has a purple-red sheen to its leaves. 'Rainbow Maiden' has glowing red leaves with gray-green margins. 'Rainbow Warrior' has purplish pink leaves streaked with green. 'Williamsii Variegated' has wide yellow-veined green leaves. 'Yellow Wave' has bright yellow leaves edged in green. Plants grow 3 to 4 feet tall and 4 to 5 feet wide.

Mountain flax *(P. cookianum)* is a smaller, 3-foot plant with pendulous flowers. It offers a number of useful varieties from which to choose, including 'Maori Chief', which has bronze leaves streaked with red and pink. It grows 6 feet tall and 10 feet wide. 'Cream Delight' has variegated creamy yellow and green leaves with red edges and yellow flowers in summer. Plants grow 2 to 6 feet tall and 4 to 8 feet wide.

Obedient plant *(Physostegia virginiana)*

fie-so-STEEJ-ee-uh ver-gin-ee-AIN-uh

Features: Dense spikes of pink, purple, or white flowers
Hardiness: Zones 3 to 9
Bloom time: Late summer to fall
Size: 2 to 4 feet tall, 3 feet wide
Shape: Spreading, upright clumps
Light: Full sun
Site: Moist, fertile, acid soil

Description: This plant brings welcome color and vertical interest to late-summer gardens and to flower arrangements. Its rampant spreading makes it ideal for naturalizing in moist meadows and wildflower gardens. During the growing season its smooth, dark green leaves are attractive backdrops for short, mounded perennials such as lady's mantle, balloon flower, and variegated Japanese sedge. The plant's name comes from the fact that you can push individual flowers on the

Obedient plant

spike and they'll remain where they're put.

Care: Obedient plant grows in most soils and conditions. It tolerates shade, but flowering is much reduced. Avoid drought and deadhead to prolong bloom. Pinching plants several times until midsummer will reduce their height at bloom.

Stake plants growing in shade using grow-through supports. Divide plants every two to three years to restrict their spread. Watch for wilting after moving plants. Cut plants to the ground in late fall or early spring.

Obedient plant is invasive, particularly in

Flower of obedient plant

moist, fertile soils high in organic matter. To control its spread in beds and borders, grow a less invasive cultivar such as 'Miss Manners' or pull out excess stems and divide plants frequently.

Species and cultivars: 'Eyeful Tower' is a 7-foot cultivar with pink flowers and shiny green leaves. 'Miss Manners' grows 2½ feet tall and has pure white flowers. It is less invasive than the species. 'Olympus Gold' is also 2½ feet tall. It blooms in pink and has variegated green leaves with wide gold margins fading to creamy yellow at maturity. 'Variegata' has pink flowers and green leaves with broad creamy margins. Plants are 2 feet tall. 'Vivid' is a bright, deep pink dwarf at 18 inches and is very invasive.

Oriental poppy *(Papaver orientale)*

pap-AY-ver ore-ee-ent-AL-ee

Features: Spectacular crepe-papery flowers in red, orange, pink, or white
Hardiness: Zones 3 to 10
Bloom time: Late spring to early summer
Size: 12 to 18 inches tall, 2 to 3 feet in bloom, 2 feet wide
Shape: Low mound, upright airy oval in bloom
Light: Full sun
Site: Moist, deep, well-drained soil rich in organic matter

Description: These fabulous flowers open in mid- to late spring but finish blooming all too soon. Surround these stars of spring beds and borders with late-blooming perennials; poppies die down by midsummer, and nearby plants will plug the hole.

Oriental poppy blooms in all shades of orange, red, pink, and white with upward-facing flowers on sturdy stems. The original species had single orange flowers, but breeding has created a wonderful range of colors on single and double blooms, many with frilly or fringed edges. The centers, which ripen into seedpods, are always a dark black, brown, or mahogany. Petals may be splotched with black or have no markings. Foliage is fairly nondescript, pale green with white bristles that make the leaves rough to the touch. Foliage disappears after seeds ripen and returns in spring.

Plants pair well with Japanese anemone, hibiscus, balloon flower, hardy ageratum, joe-pye weed, Russian sage, and butterfly weed. Grow them in large groups for an outstanding effect.

Care: Poppies need good drainage year-round and a location away from strong winds. They prefer cool climates and can't bear heat and humidity. Avoid sites with high wind or wet soil, which poppies do not tolerate. Excellent drainage is especially important over winter.

Oriental poppy

Deadhead for tidiness or let seedpods develop for dried flower arrangements. Deadheading will not prolong bloom or stimulate a second round of flowering. Flowering requires a warm-season dormancy, then a period of chilling. Hence poppies do not bloom reliably in areas with warm winters.

Once the old leaves have died, new growth begins in mid- to late summer, persists through the winter, and continues in spring. Do not cut back this growth in spring or fall.

Detail of Oriental poppy

Poppies rarely need division and are hard to move. To propagate or control the size of a planting, dig the fleshy taproots after flowering. Watch for wilting. New plants will grow from root cuttings as well as from bits of roots left behind in digging.

Plants are basically pest free but can suffer from spider mites.

Species and cultivars: 'Turkenlouis' blooms on 30-inch stems with brilliant orangy red flowers with fringed edges and a dark basal mark. 'Helen Elizabeth' has crinkled salmon pink blooms on 2-foot stems. 'Royal Wedding' has clean white petals with a black eye. 'Beauty of Livermore' blooms are oxblood red. 'Pink Ruffles' has deeply fringed, ruffled, double flowers. Flowers of 'Prince of Orange' are tangerine orange. Those of 'Patty's Plum' are reddish purple.

Ornamental allium *(Allium* spp.)

al-EE-um species
Features: Attractive flat or rounded grassy leaves with a light onion or garlicky taste and scent
Hardiness: Zones 3 to 9
Bloom time: Depends on species
Size: Depends on species
Shape: Mainly upright
Light: Full sun to partial shade
Site: Well-drained soil

Description: Valued for their flowers ornamental onions grow from a bulb to form thick clumps of green leaves that may be arching, upright, or swirled on the ground. A wide range of these cousins of edible onions, garlic, chives, and

shallots is available. All bear spherical or flat-topped clusters of flowers on top of straight, leafless stems.

Some ornamental onions are among the best flowers for cutting; their flowers last as long as three weeks in a vase. A few are delightfully fragrant; the leaves of others smell like onions when bruised. The leaves of many species die back soon after the plants bloom, but the dried flowers persist and add both texture and color to the garden. Ornamental onions look attractive at the front and in the middle of perennial beds and borders and in rock and herb gardens.

Care: Fast growing and easy to cultivate, ornamental onions prefer average, well-drained soil in full sun or partial shade. Water regularly during the growing period but avoid letting the soil become soggy.

Persian onion

Some species are available potted, meant to be planted in spring; others are available only as bulbs. Plant bulbs 5 inches deep in the fall. Leave bulbs in place so they multiply to form natural-looking clumps. Ornamental onions spread by self-sowing and by forming small bulbils (small bulbs) beside their bulbs. Divide clumps when the space becomes crowded by digging up and separating the bulbs in spring.

Species and cultivars: Blue globe onion (*A. caeruleum*) is named for its dense, bright sky blue umbels that grow about 1 inch wide in early summer. Plants are 1 to 2 feet tall. Zones 5 to 7.

Garlic chives (*A. tuberosum*) grows 9 inches tall and 6 inches wide. It has persistent foliage and in late summer has showy white blooms with a scent like that of violets. Minimize invasiveness by deadheading flowers before they set seed. Zones 4 to 8.

German garlic (*A. senescens* 'Glaucum') grows 12 inches tall by 6 inches wide. With its bluish gray-green leaves swirling around a central point, German garlic is a textural wonder at the front edge of the garden. Small, round lilac to mauve blooms rise a few inches above the foliage in mid- to late summer. 'Blue Eddy' is a miniature of 'Glaucum' with tightly swirled powder blue foliage to 4 inches tall topped with lavender pink flowers on 6-inch stems in early fall. 'Blue Twister' has brighter blue foliage and blooms all summer. Zones 4 to 8.

Giant allium (*A. giganteum*) carries 5- to 6-inch spherical umbels of purple flowers atop 3- to 5-foot-tall stems in early to midsummer. Zones 3 to 8.

Golden garlic (*A. moly*) is suitable for rock gardens, borders, and containers. It bears loose umbels of 1-inch yellow flowers on 10- to 12-inch stems in late spring. Foliage smells oniony so the flowers are not good for cutting. Zones 3 to 8.

Golden garlic

Japanese ornamental onion (*A. thunberii*) forms a tuft of slender grassy leaves up to 1 foot tall and wide and blooms in fall. The fluffy flowers of 'Album' are white. 'Ozawa' has red-violet blooms. Zones 4 to 9.

Keeled garlic (*A. carinatum pulchellum*) displays small, pendulous, rose-violet blooms on purple stems in early to midsummer. It grows 12 to 18 inches tall. The grassy tufts of foliage last all summer. Zones 5 to 9.

Nodding onion (*A. cernuum*), a North American native, has loose clusters of bright pink lily-of-the-valley-shape flowers on stems up to 2 feet tall. Zones 4 to 8.

Persian onion (*A. aflatunense*) grows 2 to 3 feet tall and has dense, 2- to 3-inch spheres of purple flowers for several weeks in late spring. The foliage starts dying back about the time the flowers open. Zones 3 to 7.

Star of Persia allium (*A. christophii*) grows 24 inches tall and 8 to 10 inches wide. It has broad, strappy leaves that often die back before the flowers are fully open. Starry, silvery purple flowers appear in late spring to early summer and grow in open spheres 8 to 10 inches in diameter. Faded blooms dry to an attractive beige and continue to give structure to the garden. Zones 4 to 8.

Tumbleweed onion (*A. schubertii*) is the "mad scientist" of the group. Its purple spheres expand to nearly 2 feet across on 2-foot-tall stems. Individual flowers shoot out from the center like stars in a galaxy. Plants are striking all summer long. Zones 5 to 9.

Yellow onion (*A. flavum*) offers fragrant yellow flowers in pendulous clusters of bell-shape blossoms in early to midsummer. Zones 4 to 8.

Turkestan onion (*A. karataviense*) produces 2- to 3-inch umbels of lilac or pink flowers on 7- to 8-inch-tall stems above wide spreading leaves. Plants bloom in late spring. Zones 4 to 8.

Hybrids: 'Mt Sinai' bears large round lavender-blue flowers from midsummer to fall and grows 12 to 14 inches tall.

Ornamental oregano (*Origanum spp.*)

oh-RIG-ain-um species
Features: Long-lasting purple to pink flowers
Hardiness: Zones 5 to 9
Bloom time: Late summer to fall
Size: 1 to 2 feet tall, 1½ to 2 feet wide
Shape: Spreading clump
Light: Full sun
Site: Average, well-drained soil

Description: A mainstay of herb gardens, oregano has some lovely, vibrant-blooming cousins. Their foliage is fragrant, but these plants are grown for their beautiful flowers and not to eat. Their pink flowers bloom from midsummer to early fall against a textural backdrop of small leaves. Some bloom all summer long.

Ornamental oregano is perfect for containers and for Mediterranean gardens. Grow it at the front of perennial borders and let its stems interlace with

'Kent Beauty' round-leaf oregano

other plants. Good companions include baby's breath, lavender, Russian sage, white and purple forms of purple coneflower, and 'Moonbeam' coreopsis.

Care: Grow ornamental oregano in full sun in average, well-drained soil, spacing plants at least a foot apart. Plants are heat and drought tolerant and do well in lean to somewhat fertile, alkaline soils. They do not tolerate wet soils where their roots can rot.

'Herrenhausen' ornamental oregano

Deadheading ornamental oreganos is not necessary; plants are self-cleaning and don't spread by seedlings. They do however spread by stems touching the ground and rooting. Oreganos have a tendency to open in the center. Keep this from happening by cutting plants back by half in early summer. This will delay the start of flowering but not by much.

Wait until early spring to clean up plants and remove the previous summer's growth. Some cultivars may need a winter mulch to ensure survival in cold climates.

Species and cultivars: 'Kent Beauty' round-leaf oregano (*O. rotundifolia*) has small hoplike light pink blooms backed with rosy pink bracts. Plants grow 6 inches tall. Zones 7 to 10.

Ornamental oregano (*O. laevigatum*) is a bushy plant with reddish woody stems and pink flowers. 'Herrenhausen' is one of the most ornamental oreganos with deep pink flowers backed with deep purple bracts and small purplish green leaves on reddish purple stems. Zones 5 to 9. Long-flowering 'Hopleys' has large, deep purple blooms. Zones 6 to 9.

Hybrids: 'Norton Gold' forms tidy 8-inch mounds of golden leaves with pinkish purple flowers in late summer. It may need afternoon shade in extremely hot climates. 'Rosenkuppel' grows 12 inches tall with bright pink to lavender-pink blooms in summer. Unlike the others it is an erect plant. 'Rotkugel' is more floriferous and has a more mounding habit while in bloom than 'Herrenhausen'. Like 'Herrenhausen' it has pink flowers backed with purple bracts.

Painters palette (*See Fleeceflower*)

Pasque flower (*Pulsatilla vulgaris*)

pulse-uh-TILL-uh vul-GARE-iss
Features: Hairy purple bells, feathery seedheads, downy foliage
Hardiness: Zones 5 to 7
Bloom time: Early spring
Size: 6 inches tall, 10 to 12 inches in bloom, 8 inches wide
Shape: Rounded clump
Light: Full sun in the North, afternoon shade in the South
Site: Well-drained, fertile soil

Description: Silky purple blooms with a yellow center on downy stems, decorative puffy silken seedheads, and ferny, hairy leaves give little pasque flower an exotic look. Up to

Pasque flower

3½ inches wide, the flowers look jumbo on the petite plant. Pasque flower is particularly charming at the front of raised beds, on top of stone retaining walls and terraces, and in rock gardens near eye level where you can appreciate its attributes.

Care: Pasque flower requires well-drained soil and average moisture to thrive. It tolerates some drought in the North. In the South it benefits from afternoon shade. Once established in the garden, it likes to stay put. If you must divide it, do so in spring after blooming.

Species and cultivars: 'Alba' offers yellow-centered white flowers. 'Papageno' blooms in pink, red, white, or blue single or semidouble flowers, with fringed tips. 'Rubra' has red bells. 'Red Clock' brings yellow-centered rosy red bells.

Dark purple pasque flower

Penstemon *(Penstemon spp.)*

pen-STIH-mun species

Features: Tubular flowers in shades of yellow, red, orange, pink, purple, blue, or white

Hardiness: Zones 2 to 10, depending on species

Bloom time: Early to late summer, depending on species

Size: 2 to 2 ½ feet tall, 1 to 2 feet wide

Shape: Airy upright, basal mound of foliage when not in bloom

Light: Full sun to partial shade

Site: Well-drained soil

Description: Depending on which species you grow, these North American natives bloom lustily beginning in late spring and continuing through summer. Plants send up numerous spires of pink, red, scarlet, orange, purple, lavender, yellow, or white flowers. The tubular blooms that form on just one side of the flower stalk may be large or small, depending on the species. No matter the size, all penstemons are showy in bloom; some also have

'Husker Red' smooth white penstemon

colorful foliage. Until plants bloom they form a neat mat of foliage.

Combine penstemons with artemisias, pearly everlasting, ornamental grasses, catmint, or geraniums. Scarlet-flowered cultivars are especially striking with 'May Night' salvia.

Care: Penstemons thrive in full sun to light shade. They tolerate heat, humidity, and wind; but a wet site in any season will be the death of them.

Most species are native to the Desert Southwest states and Mexico. A few originated in the East. This will help you determine the growing conditions your plants will need. Eastern natives do well in rich, fertile, moist soil as long it is well drained and doesn't remain wet over winter. Xeric types, the species native to the Southwest, develop poorly in such sites. Flowering is reduced, and the spires will not stand up on their own. Plants eventually die.

For all penstemons natural amounts of rainfall are plenty for the plants. During dry spells water deeply as needed. Deadhead to promote rebloom. Stake plants with floppy flower stems, especially those growing in partly shaded locations. Plants self-sow; most seedlings are variable but worth watching for. The seedheads dry well, but they have an unpleasant smell.

Cut plants back in late fall or early spring. Divide plants in spring or fall every four to five years to maintain vigor. They are easy to move. Leaf spots and nematodes may trouble older plants.

Species and cultivars: Common beard tongue (*P. barbatus*) is a western United States wildflower producing 30-inch-tall, open spikes of large red, pink, purple, blue, or white flowers in early summer. 'Coccineus' offers scarlet flowers from midspring to early summer on 12- to 18-inch-long stems. 'Schooley's Coral' is long flowering with pale orange to coral blooms. Zones 4 to 9.

Eustis Lake beard tongue (*P. australis*) is a Southeast United States native with dense 15-inch-tall spires of small pink flowers in early summer. Zones 7 to 9.

Firecracker penstemon (*P. eatonii*) is native to the Southwest and to cold desert areas in the west. It has long, striking, tubular scarlet blooms with white stamens in spring. Plants grow 2 to 3 feet tall, 2 feet wide, and have dark green foliage. 'Richfield Selection' is an improved cultivar. Zones 4 to 10.

Mexicali penstemon (*P. ×mexicali*) offers summerlong blooms in rosy red. It grows 1 to 2 feet tall. 'Red Rocks' has rose-pink flowers with white-striped throats. It reaches 36 inches tall. 'Pikes Peak Purple' has lavender to deep purple flowers. Zones 5 to 10.

Pineleaf penstemon (*P. pinifolius*) has needlelike evergreen leaves and scarlet blooms from summer to fall on 18-inch stems. It is native to Arizona and New Mexico. 'Compactum' is just 12 inches tall. 'Mersea Yellow' blooms in yellow. It originated as a seedling in an English garden, thrives in average garden soil as well as in lean soil, and needs a little more water than other penstemons. Zones 4 to 10.

Pineleaf penstemon

Rocky Mountain penstemon (*P. strictus*) provides a month of bloom in late spring to summer. The flowers, on 2- to 3-foot stems, come in shades of purple. Although native to the Rocky Mountain region, the Southwest, and California, plants tolerate typical garden conditions. They thrive in desert areas. Zones 4 to 9.

Smooth white penstemon (*P. digitalis*) is an Eastern native and one of the best choices for typical perennial gardens mixed with plants that require routine watering. They thrive in heat and humidity and do well in the South. Plants are 2 to 3 feet tall in bloom and 1½ feet wide with dark green leaves. Small white flowers flushed with pink appear in early to midsummer. 'Husker Red' is more colorful with red tints to its flowers, stems, and leaves. Leaves are a deep maroon-green in spring, turning to reddish green as the season progresses. The 2- to 3-foot-tall flower stems are also dark maroon. The tubular white flowers, which attract bees and butterflies, have a pinkish tint. Individual flowers look like bells and appear in clusters at the tips of long stems. If not deadheaded flower stems develop a rich bronze color, but seedlings will pop up all over the garden. 'Rachel's Dance' has white flowers tinted in pink on maroon 20-inch stems. Its foliage is bright purplish red. Zones 4 to 10.

Hybrids: 'Elfin Pink' grows 12 to 14 inches tall with narrow spires of rosy pink flowers and grayish green leaves. Zones 4 to 9. 'Prairie Dusk' offers rosy purple flowers from May to September on 20-inch stems. Zones 4 to 9. Plants in the Rondo Series bloom all summer in bright shades of pink, rose, lavender, purple, red, and white. Zones 3 to 9. Evergreen 'Midnight' blooms in early summer with deep purple blooms on 1½-foot stems. Zones 7 to 10. 'Apple Blossom' is another early summer-blooming evergreen species. It has coral pink flowers with white throats. Zones 7 to 10.

Peony (*Paeonia* spp.)

pay-OWN-ee-uh hybrids
Features: Pink, red, white, or cream blooms, some intensely fragrant
Hardiness: Zones 3 to 7
Bloom time: Late spring to early summer
Size: 2 to 3 feet tall
Shape: Upright, vase-shape, or round clump
Light: Full sun to light shade
Site: Moist, well-drained soil with abundant organic matter

Description: Grown for its huge, romantic flowers with an irresistible scent, peony blooms from late spring to early summer. Most have double flowers in shades of pink, purple, or white, but single- and semidouble-flowered cultivars are available as are bicolored flowers and a few yellows and corals. Often blooming around Memorial Day, these long-lived garden stalwarts provide a lifetime of bloom.

Use peonies as a low hedge or a

'Blaze' peony

backdrop for later-blooming perennials. The attractive leaves grow lush enough to cover dying spring bulb foliage. Cut the flowers for bouquets. Late-blooming double peonies pair well with early blooming double-flowered old garden roses. Although individual peonies have a relatively short flower season, you can extend blooming for five to seven weeks by planting several varieties. Peonies are a must for cottage gardens.

'Bartzella' peony

Care: Peonies tolerate a wide range of growing conditions. They do best in full sun and moist well-drained soil. The best time for planting is in fall, when root growth is greatest. Peonies won't bloom unless they have been chilled to 40°F or colder. For that reason flowering is sparse in warm climates.

Plant peonies 3 feet apart; the eyes (or pinkish buds) should be just 1 inch under ground or the peony won't bloom. When planting potted peonies keep them at the same soil level at which they were in the pot. They may take three years to flower.

Fertilize in spring when shoots appear or topdress with compost around, not on, the plant. The flowers are heavy and will drag on the ground if not staked, especially after a rain. Use grow-through supports or peony hoops in early spring, just as foliage begins to emerge. Deadhead to reduce the weight on the stems and to tidy plants.

You often see ants crawling over the unopened buds, which has led to the idea that the ants' activity is required for the flowers to open. Actually the ants are drawn to the flowers' sweet nectar and have nothing to do with the buds opening. They don't hurt the plants, but brush them off when cutting flowers to bring indoors. In late fall cut stems back to 2 to 3 inches. Divide plants every 8 to 10 years to renew the planting and the soil.

Botrytis blight is a common problem for peonies. It causes dark spots on the leaves, discolored flowers or small, dry, unopened buds, and purple-brown streaks on the stems. Sanitation is the best control. Remove and discard petals as they drop from the plants; clean up and discard foliage and stems in fall. Remove any discolored foliage as it develops. If roots are distorted or soft, remove and discard them.

Species and cultivars: Hundreds of cultivars are on the market. This is a tiny sampling. 'Bartzella' has fragrant, bright yellow double flowers. 'Coral Charm' has peachy pink blooms. 'Cheddar Charm' has a

'Sarah Bernhardt' peony

large gold center of stamen against overlapping white outer petals; it is a fragrant midseason bloomer. 'Do Tell' blooms with soft pink petals around a frilly center of rose, pink, and white. 'Festiva Maxima' offers classic large white double blooms flecked with crimson; it is very fragrant. 'Kansas' is an older cultivar with watermelon pink double flowers. 'Krinkled White' has semidouble white crepe-papery flowers with a large center of bright yellow-gold stamens. It is similar to 'Cheddar Charm' but has a smaller center. 'Pink Hawaiian Coral' has fragrant yellowish pink semidouble flowers. 'Red Charm' is an early blooming anemone-centered peony. In other words its bright scarlet flower has a ruffled central ball surrounded by flat petals. This cultivar is an American Peony Society award winner. 'Sarah Bernhardt' offers fragrant, soft pink double flowers; it is a late-season bloomer. 'Scarlet O'Hara' has single red blooms with golden stamens. It blooms well in the heat of the South. 'Vivid Rose' is a late-midseason bloomer with fragrant, deep pink double flowers.

Fernleaf peony (*P. tenuifolia*) has finely divided dark green foliage. Flowers come in only one color: red with a center of golden stamens. The species has single flowers. Foliage goes dormant by midsummer so plant fernleaf peonies where other perennials can hide the fading foliage and fill the hole. 'Rubra Plena' has double red flowers. Zones 3 to 7.

Woodland peony (*P. obovata*) is a shade lover; provide it with a site that receives two to four hours of sun in the morning and shade for the rest of the day. The single flowers are white or rose-purple with a center of yellow stamens. Plants grow 1½ to 2 feet tall and have gray-green foliage. Zones 4 to 7.

Perennial sunflower (*Helianthus* spp.)

he-lee-AN-thiss species
Features: Sunny yellow daisies, towering size
Hardiness: Zones 3 to 9
Bloom time: Late summer to fall
Size: 4 to 6 feet tall, 3 to 4 feet wide
Shape: Upright, columnar
Light: Full sun
Site: Moist, rich soil

Perennial sunflower

Description: These low-maintenance perennials feature long-lasting blooms that make excellent cut flowers. They are dependable back-of-the-border plants valued for their late-season color and statuesque size. All have large, 2- to 3-inch-wide, golden yellow flowers. Most are daisies with a bronze center, but some are fully double. Plants form sturdy columns that are half as wide as they are tall. Clumps gradually widen over time. The blooms attract butterflies, and the seedheads draw birds and other plants.

Tall and coarse, the plant makes a handsome specimen. Good pairings include tall ornamental grasses, mums, monkshood, gayfeather, asters, sneezeweed, and Russian sage. Plant shorter, mounded perennials in front of perennial sunflowers to mask the tall stems. Perennial

'Lemon Queen' hybrid perennial sunflower

sunflowers are ideal for wildflower gardens and mixed borders.
Care: Perennial sunflower likes moist, well-drained, fertile, alkaline soils but tolerates heavy clay soil and a wide range of pH. Although it thrives in full sun, it also does well in partial shade, especially in the South. For best results apply a slow-release fertilizer at planting and water during times of drought. Divide plants in spring every few years to help prevent disease and improve air circulation. To control height pinch the plant repeatedly from midspring to early summer. Deadhead to extend flowering. Support plants with tall stakes or grow-through supports.

Species and cultivars: Many-flowered perennial sunflower (*H. ×multiflorus*) is a hybrid resulting from a cross between annual sunflower and thinleaf sunflower. Plants typically grow 3 to 5 feet tall and 3 feet wide, but they sometimes reach 7 feet tall. Yellow daisies start opening in late summer and last four to six weeks. Zones 4 to 8.

Maximilian sunflower (*H. maximiliani*) is a good choice for dry gardens. It reaches 6 to 8 feet tall and 4 feet wide and blooms in early to midfall. 'Lemon Yellow' has pale yellow flowers on 6-foot plants. 'Santa Fe' has golden yellow sunflowers tightly packed on the top 3 to 4 feet of each stem. Zones 4 to 9.

Thinleaf perennial sunflower (*H. decapetalus*) grows 4 to 5 feet tall and has single yellow daisies with small tan centers. 'Capenoch Star' has light yellow flowers. 'Plenus' is 5 to 6 feet tall with double yellow pompom blooms. 'Soleil d'Or' has 3½–inch-wide yellow pompoms on branched stems all summer. Zones 5 to 9.

Willowleaf sunflower (*H. salicifolius*) has slender leaves, brown-centered yellow daisies, and the potential to grow 8 feet tall. It forms an airy mound of blooms in late summer. 'First Light' is a more manageable 4 feet tall. Its dense mass of golden yellow daisies begins its show in early fall. 'Low Down' is only 12 inches tall and covered in yellow daisies in late summer. Zones 4 to 9.
Hybrids:: 'Lemon Queen' grows 5 feet tall and has single light yellow daisies.

Phlox (*Phlox* spp.)

FLOX species
Features: Masses of pink, magenta, white, or lavender-blue flowers
Hardiness: Zones 4 to 8
Bloom time: Early to late summer, depending on species
Size: Depends on species
Shape: Upright or spreading clump
Light: Full sun to partial shade
Site: Moist, well-drained, fertile, slightly acid soil with abundant organic matter

Description: This group of heavily blooming perennials brings delightful and often brilliant color in nearly every season. Garden phlox and other tall varieties bloom in mid- to late summer in white, pink, red, magenta, purple,

Moss phlox

and all the shades between. Moss, creeping, and woodland phlox are creepers, creating a carpet of color in early to midspring. Phlox belongs in cottage gardens, meadow plantings, shade gardens, and vases. Hybrids come in a wide range of colors and have improved disease resistance. Good partners include deep pink or dark blue speedwell, repeat-blooming daylilies, shasta daisy, or fountain grass.

Care: Phlox tolerates wind and a wide range of soil pH. They do not do well in drought, especially combined with high heat and humidity. Plant woodland phlox in part to full shade; garden and moss phlox do best in full sun but can take light shade.

Water deeply and fertilize regularly. Deadheading garden phlox encourages more blooms and prevents self-sowing. (Self-sown phlox does not come true from seed.) Shear moss phlox after flowering is finished.

Stake tall varieties with grow-through supports. If stems flop thin the clumps and increase water and fertilizer the next spring.

Divide garden phlox every three or four years. Thin moss phlox whenever the planting becomes crowded.

Cut garden phlox to the ground in late fall; remove the trimmings. Moss phlox is shallow rooted; mulch lightly to protect the roots over winter.

Phlox is prone to spider mites and powdery mildew. Plant only mildew-resistant varieties such as the ones listed below. Good air circulation helps prevent mildew. Thin garden phlox to five or six stems per clump to help air them out.

Species and cultivars:
Creeping phlox *(P. stolonifera)* is another evergreen shade-loving groundcover with trailing stems and blue, pink, white, or purple flowers in spring. This plant's flowers are the most fragrant of the phloxes. Creeping phlox grows into a 6-inch-tall mat. It does best in partial shade, or at least afternoon shade, and fertile, moist, well-drained acid soil. Apply slow-release fertilizer at planting. Water when

'David' hybrid phlox

the soil feels dry 2 inches below the surface; mulch to retain moisture. Shear plants after flowering to tidy them, prevent self-sowing, and maintain compact growth. The midspring blooms of 'Bruce's White' are pure white on 8-inch stems. 'Home Fires' blooms in late spring; flowers are magenta pink. 'Pink Ridge' is a mass of hot pink in late spring. Zones 3 to 9.

Moss phlox *(P. subulata)* is a magnificent evergreen groundcover that blooms lavishly in sunny gardens from early to midspring. It makes a dense 3- to 6-inch-tall mat with blue, pink, white, or purple flowers in early to midspring. The foliage looks like moss but is prickly. Use moss phlox to edge a garden or plant it as a skirt under shrubs. Plants bloom about the same time as many spring bulbs and provide beautiful contrast or complement to their bright colors. Zones 2 to 9.

'Katherine' hybrid phlox

Woodland phlox *(P. divaricata)* is an evergreen shade perennial, lighting dark corners in late spring. It has lightly scented purple, pink, or white flowers in late spring. At 1 foot tall it is a good woodland groundcover. 'Blue Elf' grows just 3 inches tall, 4 inches in bloom, and 6 inches

Woodland phlox

wide. It has fragrant light blue flowers in midspring. Because it is so compact, keep it away from more rambunctious companions. 'Clouds of Perfume' offers ice blue fragrant flowers in mid- to late spring. 'Plum Perfect' has dark-eyed pale purple blooms from late spring to early summer and better mildew resistance than other woodland phlox. Zones 4 to 9.

Hybrids: Garden phlox type: 'David' grows 4 to 5 feet tall and has fragrant white flower clusters on strong stems. It is mildew resistant. 'Goldmine' is only 30 inches tall. It has deep magenta flowers above variegated green leaves with wide gold borders. Plants tolerate heat and humidity and are mildew resistant. 'Katherine' grows 3 to 4 feet tall with extremely mildew-resistant foliage. Flowers are lavender with a white eye. 'Shortwood', at 4 to 5 feet tall, belies its name. This extremely mildew-resistant cultivar has bright pink flowers with a deep pink eye.

Moss phlox type: 'Blue Emerald' blooms in lavender. 'Candy Stripe' has a broad pink center surrounded by white. 'Oakington Blue Eyes' has sky blue flowers. 'Red Wing' blooms are dark pink with a red eye.

Detail of phlox hybrid

Pincushion flower (Scabiosa caucasica)

SKAY-bee-oh-suh caw-CASS-ih-cuh
Features: Light blue blooms on wiry stems
Hardiness: Zones 5 to 10
Bloom time: Summer to fall
Size: 18 to 30 inches tall and wide
Shape: Round clump, long airy flower stems
Light: Full sun
Site: Fertile, well-drained soil with abundant organic matter

'Blue Butterfly' pincushion flower

Description:
Pincushion flower is grown for its attractive tufted blooms and airy habit. Delicate stamens rise above the tufts like pins stuck in a pincushion. On some species the blue-violet, pink, or creamy white flowers look like wide lace trim around a pincushion. Wiry flower stems rise as much as 30 inches above the low mound of leaves; leaves on the stem are ferny and finely cut.

Because the flowers float above their own insubstantial foliage, combine them with more solid plants, such as artemisias, mums, or Russian sage. Let the flowers weave around their neighbors at the front of a perennial border. Blooms attract bees and butterflies. They also make excellent long-lasting cut flowers and grow well in containers. Other good companions for pincushion flower are miniature hollyhocks and 'Sweet Dreams' coreopsis.

Care: Pincushion flower tolerates many types of soil but prefers fertile, well-drained, neutral to slightly alkaline soils, and cool, humid climates. High heat, high humidity, poor drainage, and wet soil are detrimental. Plants can take light frost and may bloom into December, although the typical bloom season is from June to November.

Deadheading extends the bloom season of pincushion flower. Cut first to side branches carrying flower buds; remove the entire stem when the flowers are spent. Plants readily self-sow and can become a nuisance. Seedlings vary in color.

Detail of pink pincushion flower

The wiry flower stems need no support. Cut back remaining flower stems in fall but not the basal leaves. Clean up the clump in spring. Divide plants every three to four years to maintain good flowering and overall vigor; plants move easily.

Species and cultivars: 'Fama' grows 24 to 30 inches tall and has larger and deeper blue flowers than the species. 'Kompliment' is just 18 to 24 inches tall with large lavender-blue flowers.

Compact pincushion flower (*S. columbaria*) is more compact, growing 18 to 24 inches tall in bloom. 'Butterfly Blue' has abundant lavender-blue pincushions on 12- to 18-inch-tall stems from late spring to fall. 'Misty Butterflies' offers a mix of lavender-blue and dusky pink flowers on 10-inch-tall plants. 'Pink Mist' has purple-pink flowers on 12- to 18-inch-tall stems from late spring to fall. Zones 3 to 10.

Pinks (Dianthus spp.)

dye-ANN-thus species
Features: Pink, white, rose, red, or bicolor blooms with a spicy clove scent
Hardiness: Zones 3 to 10
Bloom time: Late spring to early summer, depending on species
Size: Depends on species
Shape: Depends on species
Light: Full sun; afternoon shade in the South
Site: Well-drained, fertile, neutral to slightly alkaline soil

Description: Pinks bear profuse, often spicily fragrant blooms in late spring to summer. The frilly flowers come in all colors and combinations except blue and may be double, like carnations, semidouble, or single. The petals may be shaggy, serrated, or fringed at the tips and may have contrasting rims or eyes.

This group includes plants from tiny creepers to 2-foot-tall cut flowers. After blooming the foliage of all forms a handsome, dense, often evergreen mat of grassy grayish to bluish green leaves.

'Zing Rose' pinks

Pinks look good at the front of a border, in rock gardens, and massed along paths, where you can smell their sweet clove scent when you walk by. Flowers attract butterflies and hummingbirds. Combine pinks' grassy foliage with coarser front-of-the-border plants, such as geraniums, white sage, coral bells, dwarf bearded iris, and perennial salvia.

Care: Amend beds with lime, sand, and compost to create the light, neutral to slightly alkaline soil in which pinks like to grow. Plants do not tolerate wet soil or pH below 6. They take heat and drought but not heat and high humidity.

Deadheading extends bloom and cutting plants back after flowering keeps them compact. Apply low-nitrogen fertilizer in spring and water well throughout the growing season. Plants will often rebloom when nights cool in late summer and fall.

Divide plants every two to three years to keep the clump vigorous and prevent crowding, which promotes pests and diseases. Pinks are susceptible to leaf spot diseases, especially where soil is moist, humidity is high, and air circulation is poor. Avoid using overhead sprinklers to help prevent diseases.

Cut back foliage in early spring, leaving the leafy base of woody stems intact.

Species and cultivars: Allwood pinks (*D. ×allwoodii*) offer long-lasting fragrant double flowers in shades of pink, red, or white. The gray-green foliage grows into mounds 1 to 1½ feet tall and wide. 'Doris' is salmon-pink with a darker pink center. Dark red flowers top the blue-green foliage of 'Frosty Fire'; plants grow just 6 inches tall. 'Aqua' has white flowers and grows 10 to 12 inches tall. Zones 3 to 9.

Cheddar pinks *(D. gratianopolitanus)* are short, mat-forming plants that are more tolerant of heat and humidity than other pinks. They form tidy mounds of gray-green foliage 4 to 12 inches tall and 12 inches

Detail of pinks in flower

wide. Their fragrant flowers come in shades of pink and rose in early summer to midsummer. Deadheading keeps them in bloom nearly all summer. 'Bath's Pink' has fragrant light pink blooms with dark eyes in spring to summer and grassy light blue-green leaves. 'Firewitch' cheddar pink has fringed, fragrant magenta blooms and grows just 6 inches tall. 'Mountain Mist' has double lipstick pink blooms. 'Tiny Rubies' has fragrant deep pink double flowers with serrated edges and is 4 inches tall. Zones 3 to 8.

Maiden pinks *(D. deltoides)* form 6-inch-tall, 12-inch-wide mats of dark green foliage from which rose or pink flowers arise on 12-inch stems. Plants stand up to the heat and humidity of the South. They get their name from the fact that the flowers close partially at dusk. 'Arctic Fire' flowers are white with a pink eye ringed in red. 'Raspberry Swirl' blooms are white with a red center and edged in maroon. 'Zing Rose' has single deep rose-red blooms topping its 8-inch by 12-inch mats of dark green leaves. Zones 3 to 8.

Hybrids: 'Betty Morton' has rosy pink single flowers with a dark fuchsia eye in late spring. Plants grow 5 to 8 inches tall. Zones 5 to 8. 'Oakington' has light pink double blooms in summer above 6- to 10-inch-tall gray-green foliage. Zones 3 to 8. 'Pixie' blooms in pink with rosy splotches in the center of the single petals. The gray-green plants quickly spread in the garden to 2½ feet wide. Plants bloom from late spring to fall. Zones 3 to 8. The fragrant dark rose double flowers of 'Roshish One' are edged in white; they bloom on 10-inch-long stems. Zones 4 to 8.

Prairie dropseed *(Sporobolus heterolepis)*

spore-OB-oh-lus het-er-oh-LEP-siss
Features: Fragrant flowers, fine foliage
Hardiness: Zones 3 to 9
Bloom time: Late summer
Size: 2 to 4 feet tall, 3 feet wide
Shape: Cascading fountain
Light: Full sun
Site: Well-drained, fertile soil

Description: Prairie dropseed is a native warm-season clumping grass that looks like a fountain of emerald green hair. The leaves gradually turn tan in fall, going through several shades of orange to bronze on the way. Plants are stunning when massed. The open panicles of flowers that appear in late summer smell like cilantro; the seedheads glisten in the fall sunlight, weighing down the arching stems.

Care: Prairie dropseed grows very slowly. To make a presence as soon as possible, buy the largest clumps available. Plant it in well-drained soil of dry to average moisture Plants tolerate heat and drought; in spite of their name, they do not self-sow freely. Cut plants back in late winter before they begin growing again.

Prairie dropseed

Primrose *(Primula* spp.)

PRIM-yew-luh species
Features: Frilly pink, snow white, magenta, pale purple, or bicolor flowers
Hardiness: Depends on species
Bloom time: Early to late spring
Size: Depends on species
Shape: Ground-hugging foliage from which flowers rise
Light: Partial to full shade
Site: Moist, acid soil with abundant organic matter

Description: There are hundreds of primroses, some easy, some difficult, ranging in size from a few inches to 3 feet tall. All are favorites for their early to late spring flowers in the woodland.

Japanese primrose *(P. japonica)* is a prolific bloomer with handsome low-growing foliage. It is a candelabra-type primrose, so named for the whorls of blooms arranged around the flower stems that rise above a clump of foliage. It is a good choice for planting around a water garden. Zones 5 to 9.

Japanese primrose

Siebold primrose *(P. sieboldii)* has delightful fuzzy light green leaves growing in thick rosettes. A few weeks after emerging, clusters of delicate 1-inch-wide flowers open at the tips of erect 1-foot-tall stems rising from the leaves. Blooms can be single or double, flat, fringed, starry, or slightly cupped. With summer heat and dryness, plants go dormant. Clumps will steadily increase over the years. These late-spring lovelies look luscious under upright Japanese maples, massed around rhododendrons and azaleas, planted on the north side of your house, or tucked near a shady outcrop. Zones 3 to 8.

English primrose *(P. vulgaris)* is the best species for southern gardens. It sends up clusters of pale yellow flowers on 8-inch stems. Its basal leaves are evergreen or semi-evergreen. Many vigorous, floriferous single- and double-flowered cultivars in purple, lavender, white, pink, and bicolor are available. Easy-to-grow English primrose looks wonderful massed in woodland settings. Zones 4 to 8.

Cowslip *(P. veris)* produces clusters of scented, nodding

Double-flowering siebold primrose

yellow flowers in spring on 10-inch stems above evergreen to semi-evergreen basal leaf rosettes. Zones 3 to 8.

Care: Plant Japanese primrose in light shade in acid soil that is high in organic matter. Water abundantly during dry spells; mulch heavily to keep roots cool. Plants may go dormant in summer and reappear in fall. Divide plants every three years. Slugs and snails can be problems.

Siebold primrose thrives in cool, moist, shady acid soil with plenty of organic matter. In hot, dry summer weather, it goes dormant until the following spring. Plants prefer morning sun, afternoon shade, and they need protection in winter, either from a thick mulch or consistent snow cover. Every three years divide plants when the leaves first appear in spring or after they bloom.

English primrose tolerates full sun if soil remains constantly moist; otherwise plant it in part shade. Mulch well to keep roots cool. In areas with mild winters, plant English primrose in fall for blooms during winter.

Species and cultivars: Japanese primrose: 'Album' has white flowers and grows 16 inches tall. 'Carminea' is rose red. 'Miller's Crimson' has intense red-purple blooms on 2-foot stems. 'Redfield Strain' comes in a mix of colors, from red to white to pink as well as shades in between.

Detail of Siebold primrose

Siebold primrose: 'Lacy Snowflake' has large white flowers with fringed petals. 'Snowflakes' has 1½ inch-wide pure white flowers that open from yellow buds. 'Pink Snowflake' has pink cut-edged blooms on 12-inch stems.

English primrose: 'Blue Sapphire' has double deep blue flowers. 'Marie Crousse' has lavender purple blooms on 6-inch plants. 'Prinic', also sold as Katy McSparron cowslip, has double yellow blooms all summer.

Purple coneflower *(Echinacea purpurea)*

eck-inn-AY-cee-uh purr-purr-EE-uh
Features: Purple daisies with large rust-colored cones
Hardiness: Zones 3 to 9
Bloom time: Mid- to late summer
Size: 1 to 2 feet tall, 2 to 3 feet in bloom, 1½ feet wide
Shape: Low mound of foliage, upright flowers
Light: Full sun
Site: Average, neutral to slightly alkaline, well-drained soil

Description: Valued for its large sturdy daisies, purple coneflower is a classic of the summer border. The daisies

'Bravado' purple coneflower

have fat brownish red to orange central cones surrounded by a ring of droopy purple petals. At one time only purple and white cultivars were available, but recent breeding breakthroughs have brought new cultivars in cream, yellow, orange, and burgundy, as well as shades of purple and white. The flowers attract bees and butterflies and are excellent for cutting. Birds eat the seeds when they mature. Purple coneflower looks grand with lamb's ears, globe thistle, Russian sage, and white gaura.

Care: A low-maintenance North American native, purple coneflower's only needs are well-drained soil and full sun; it tolerates heat, humidity, drought, wind, and some shade. Staking is not necessary; however plants can be floppy in rich soil. Deadhead to prevent self-sowing; seedlings are variable in size, color, and flower size. Deadheading also extends blooming into fall. Leave some of the last blooms in the garden to provide winter interest and feed the birds.

Cut back plants in late fall or early spring. Divide plants every four to five years in fall or spring to maintain vigor. Clumps expand by creating small new plants around the base. You can transplant these offsets when you divide the clump.

Pests generally present no problems; however crowded clumps may develop stem dieback, a viral infection. If you see this in your purple coneflower, dig and discard it.

Species and cultivars: 'Fragrant Angel' has 5-inch-wide white daisies with an orange center cone. The long-lasting fragrant flowers smell of sweet clover. 'Kim's Mop Head' is a dwarf with white flowers and green cones on 12- to 15-inch stems. 'Magnus' blooms in bright rose with a brownish red cone on 2- to 3-foot stems; the petals stand out rather than droop. 'Razmatazz' has unusual "powderpuffs" of pink surrounded by pink petals. The fragrant blooms reach 3 to 4 inches wide. 'Pink Double Delight' is similar but powderpuff is a darker pink and the petals are longer and droopier. 'Ruby Giant' offers huge, 7-inch-wide flat daisies of purple-red. 'Vintage Wine' blooms

Detail of purple coneflower

are a brilliant deep purple-red. Unlike other coneflowers the petals sweep upward; a flattened dark orange center handsomely sets off the petals.

Hybrids:: The Meadowbrite Series comes out of the breeding program at the Chicago Botanic Garden, which brought some of the first unexpectedly colored coneflowers. All have semidroopy to flat daisies with slender petals. Orange Meadowbrite (also sold as 'Arts Pride') blooms in bright orange with dark cones; it grows 2½ feet tall and wide. Mango Meadowbrite offers yellow flowers with a slightly darker orange stem. Pixie Meadowbrite has flat pink, dark-eyed daisies on 1½-foot-tall, 2-foot-wide plants.

The Big Sky Series is from the breeding program at Itsaul Plants in Georgia. The semidroopy daisies display the colors of the sky at dusk and dawn, and the flowers' smell is similar to the scent of roses. Most are 2½ feet tall and 1½ to 2 feet wide; they bloom heavily from early summer on and have colorful flower stems. 'Emily Saul' (also sold as After Midnight) daisies are dark magenta-purple with black cones. The plant is just 12 inches tall and wide. 'Evan Saul' (also sold as Sundown) flowers are bright orange on 40-inch stems. The petals of 'Katie Saul' (or Summer Sky) are cherry red at their base and fade to peach at their tips. 'Matthew Saul' (or Harvest Moon) blooms in bright orangish yellow with a golden-orange cone. Flowers of 'Sunrise' are buttery yellow on 2-foot-tall and wide plants. Cones start out green and age to brown. 'Sunset' has bright orange daisies with dark orange centers on 30-inch plants. 'Twilight' blooms in brilliant rose-red with a deep red cone.

Purple moor grass *(Molinia caerulea caerulea)*

mow-LINN-ya seh-RULE-ee-uh seh-RULE-ee-uh
Features: Ornamental grass with pink flowers
Hardiness: Zones 4 to 9
Bloom time: Fall
Size: 1½ feet tall and wide
Shape: Cascading fountain
Light: Full to part sun
Site: Fertile, acid to neutral soil

Description: This graceful ornamental grass forms dense tufts of green. It is one of the most popular garden grasses because of its elegant habit. Use it as a groundcover or as a specimen plant.
Care: Grow purple moor grass in full sun and acid to neutral, moderately moist soil. In southern climates plant it in part sun to light shade. Divide plants when they outgrow their boundaries. Moor grasses are deciduous

Purple moor grass

and lose their leaves in fall, so there is no need to cut them back. Simply clean up the debris.
Species and cultivars: 'Variegata' has white-striped green leaves.

Tall purple moor grass *(M. arundinacea)* grows as a low, 2- to 3-foot-tall, fine-textured fountain of foliage. The flower

stalks rise above the clump 7 to 8 feet, swaying in the slightest breeze. The stems tend to arch out from the plant. Tall purple moor grass makes a marvelous gauzy screen in front of a window. 'Skyracer' has more erect flower stems and yellow-orange fall color. Zones 5 to 10.

Tall purple moor grass

Queen-of-the-meadow *(See Queen-of-the-prairie)*

Queen-of-the-prairie *(Filipendula rubra)*

filly-PEN-dew-luh RUBE-ruh
Features: Fluffy, fragrant plumes of cherry pink flowers; attractive seedheads
Hardiness: Zones 3 to 9
Bloom time: Early to midsummer
Size: 1 to 2 feet tall, 3 to 5 feet in bloom, 1½ to 2 feet wide
Shape: Clump of foliage from which tall flower stems rise
Light: Full sun to partial shade
Site: Moist, somewhat fertile, well-drained to boggy soil

Description: This North American native plant is a striking giant in the garden. Fluffy 6-inch-long and -wide cherry pink flower clusters rise 6 feet or more above deeply cut, three-lobed green leaves. Cultivars are shorter. The flowers turn paler as summer progresses and the seeds ripen. Queen-of-the-prairie forms dense colonies in

Queen-of-the-prairie

moist to soggy soil and full to part sun. Before the plant and your garden fill in and the plants reach their mature size, queen-of-the-prairie looks a little like a broad stick topped with cotton candy. Plant queen-of-the-prairie in moist meadows, wildflower gardens, woodland gardens, wet gardens, and at the back of the perennial border, or grow it by a pond with white astilbe and royal fern.
Care: Queen-of-the-prairie forms wide clumps in consistently moist to boggy soils high in organic matter. Plants bloom and stand tall better in full sun. Blooming plants rarely need staking; but if the weather is hot, the soil is dry, or they are growing in shade, they will be somewhat floppy. Otherwise plants require little grooming; the seedheads are appealing, so there is no need to deadhead. Cut back plants in early spring. Powdery mildew may occur. If so, cut down the plants so new leaves will form.
Species and cultivars: 'Venusta' is the most available queen-of-the-prairie on the market. It has deep pink flowers on 4-foot-stems. 'Venusta Alba' blooms in white.

Dropwort *(F. vulgaris)* has creamy white flowers that open from pinkish buds in early to midsummer. Like queen-of-the-prairie the flowers form in open panicles at the tips of 3-foot stems; however they're not quite as dense. The mound of foliage, which is more compact and finer textured than that of queen-of-the-prairie, grows 1 to 1½ feet tall and 1½ to 2 feet wide. Dropwort does well in partial shade and tolerates hot sites, if given good moisture. In cool climates

Detail pink queen-of-the-meadow

it tolerates dry soil. Plants also do well in high humidity, wind, and alkaline soil. Cut back plants in early spring. Deadhead to prolong bloom, keep the clump neat, and reduce self-sowing. Divide plants every five to six years. 'Multiplex' has double white flowers on 10- to 15-inch stems from spring to early summer. This cultivar is also sold as 'Flore Plena' and 'Plena'. Zones 3 to 9.

Queen-of-the-meadow (*F. ulmaria*) is a tidier, more compact version of queen-of-the-prairie. Clouds of white flowers hover over the plants in early summer. Plants grow 3 to 4 feet tall and 3 feet wide; they form dense colonies in moist to wet soils. Grow 'Aurea' for its foliage, which opens bright gold and then matures to yellow-green. In light to part shade, foliage is even brighter yellow when it opens. In early summer fragrant white flowers cover the plants; they don't provide quite as good a show as other cultivars. Plants grow 2 to 3 feet tall. 'Plena', also sold as 'Flore Pleno', has dense creamy white flowers in early summer. 'Variegata' has both handsome white plumes and foliage. Yellow splotches or stripes mark the dark green, coarse-textured leaves. Plants grow 3 to 4 feet tall and 1½ to 2 feet wide. Both 'Variegata' and 'Aurea' do best with some shade; their foliage will scorch in full sun in hot climates. Zones 3 to 9.

Siberian meadowsweet (*F. palmata*) is a tall coarse-textured perennial with pink plumes in early summer. It differs little from queen-of-the-prairie, except plants require staking. Like all species in this group, plants will scorch if not grown in a wet site. 'Nana' is much better, growing just 8 to 10 inches tall with pink flowers. Zones 3 to 7.

Hybrids:: 'Kakome' is a shorty, growing 12 inches tall and 10 inches wide. Its rosy pink flowers bloom from mid- to late summer. Zones 3 to 8.

Ragged robin (See Campion, page 172)
Red valerian (See Centranthus, pg. 174)

Rock soapwort (*Saponaria ocymoides*)

SAP-own-air-ee-uh oss-ee-MOY-deez
Features: Rose pink flowers
Hardiness: Zones 3 to 7
Bloom time: Mid- to late spring
Size: 6 to 9 inches tall, 18 inches wide
Shape: Ground-hugging creeper
Light: Full to part sun
Site: Well-drained soil

Description: Rock soapwort is a great perennial for softening hardscapes such as patios, sidewalks, and driveways. Let the bloom-covered trailing mat spill over walls

Pink rock soapwort

Rock soapwort

or creep over a brick pathway. It is a good companion for sedums, coral bells, lavender, and ornamental grasses, as well as many other perennials. **Care:** Plants do not tolerate wet or poorly drained soil or hot, humid summers. Shear them after they bloom to promote density, tidy the plant, and reduce self-sowing. Plants grow quickly and can overpower less competitive neighbors, especially in fertile soil. Dig out creeping stems that are overgrowing their boundaries. Divide rock soapwort in spring if desired, but self-sown seedlings are always available if your aim is to propagate the plants. Plants move easily, but watch for wilting afterwards. **Species and cultivars:** 'Rubra Compacta' has red-violet flowers and is less wide spreading. 'Snow Tip' blooms in white.

Rodgersia (*Rodgersia* spp.)

row-JERZ-ee-uh species
Features: Massive dark green leaves, fuzzy plumes of tiny pink, red, or white flowers
Hardiness: Zones 5 to 8
Bloom time: Spring or mid- to late summer, depending on species
Size: 2 feet tall, 3 to 4 feet in bloom, 3 to 4 feet wide
Shape: Rounded mound with upright flower clusters
Light: Part sun to full shade
Site: Fertile, continuously moist soil with abundant organic matter

Description: Everything about rodgersias is big. Both species have coarse leaves that can measure 3 feet across. The individual flowers, although small, come in clusters up to 2 feet long. Any plant this dramatic looks good as a specimen or as a focal point among other coarse-textured perennials, such as hosta, bugbane, fleeceflower, royal fern, astilboides (*A. tabularis*), and all species of ligularia. Rodgersias also pair well with large upright plants, such as meadow rue, solomon's seal, cardinal flower, and monkshood. Try rodgersias in groups along a water garden, in a bog garden, or in a moist, shady border. Rodgersia also makes a lovely cut flower.

Rodgersia

'Superba' featherleaf rodgersia

Care: Given proper growing conditions, rodgersias are robust plants. They thrive in constantly moist to soggy fertile, organic soil. Plants even do well in heavy clay, but they do not tolerate heat or full sun, unless you can keep the plants wet.

When growing rodgersias in groups, space plants 3 feet apart. Mulch to keep plants cool and moist. Deadheading will not stimulate rebloom but it does improve plant appearance. Cut back plants in fall once the top growth dies. Rodgersias rarely need division, and they are hard to move. If you do transplant them, keep soil moist so plants don't wilt.

Species and cultivars: Bronzeleaf rodgersia (*R. podophylla*) looks similar to featherleaf rodgersia but has bronze-green five-leaflet foliage that turns red in fall. Yellowish white flowers appear in midsummer. Zones 5 to 8.

Featherleaf rodgersia (*R. pinnata*) blooms with branched plumes of tiny pink, red, or white flowers in midsummer. The flowers are more spread out along the flower stems than they are on fingerleaf rodgersia. Foliage is compound, meaning that several leaflets make up the total leaf. In rodgersia five to nine widely spaced narrow leaflets come off a central point. This is probably the most common species on the market. 'Chocolate Wing' is a 2½-foot-tall plant with chocolate bronze foliage and red-eyed pink flowers. 'Alba' blooms in white. 'Elegans' has creamy flowers tinged with pink. 'Superba' has rosy pink blooms above attractive bronze new growth. Zones 4 to 7.

Fingerleaf rodgersia (*R. aesculifolia*) blooms with dense clusters of ivory flowers rising 4 to 5 feet above the foliage on bronze stems. This species also has compound leaves made up of seven broad leaflets arising from a central point and looking like a hand or the leaves of a horsechestnut tree. Zones 5 to 9.

Rose campion (*See Centranthus, page 174.*)

Rose turtlehead (*Chelone obliqua*)

CHEE-lone-ee OH-bleak-uh
Features: Deep rose-purple flowers
Hardiness: Zones 4 to 9
Bloom time: Late summer to fall
Size: 2 to 3 feet tall, 1 foot wide
Shape: Spreading upright
Light: Dense shade to full sun
Site: Moist, neutral to acid soil

Description: This perennial gets its name from its small flowers that resemble the heads of snapping turtles. It is a sturdy vertical plant with medium-textured deep green foliage. The flowers are interesting rather than showy; plants have a neat texture and glossy foliage that add to the shade garden.

Plant rose turtlehead as a contrast to mounded plants, finer- or coarser-textured plants, or ones with rounded

flowers. Asters, black-eyed susan, meadow rue, queen of the prairie, rodgersia, fleeceflower, daylily, and ornamental grasses make good companions.

Care: Rose turtlehead tolerates heavy clay and alkaline soils. It does as well in shade as it does in sun; but where summers are very hot or when planted in full sun, constant moisture is essential.

All turtleheads spread through the garden by shallow rhizomes and can form wide, dense colonies within a few years. To keep their growth in check, dig up the new plants that have spread beyond their boundaries each spring.

Pinch plants several times between midspring and midsummer to reduce plant height or flowering. Deadheading is not necessary.

Rose turtlehead

'Hot Lips' pink turtlehead

Cut back plants in late fall or early spring. Divide them every four to five years or topdress in late fall with 1 to 2 inches of compost to rejuvenate the clump. After being moved they'll need some pampering. Watch to keep them from wilting.

Powdery mildew is occasionally a problem, especially where soil is dry.

Species and cultivars: Pink turtlehead (*C. lyonii*) is also very similar but it has paler rose blooms. 'Hot Lips' blooms in hot pink. Zones 4 to 9.

White turtlehead (*C. glabra*) is similar to rose turtlehead but has white flowers with a red tinge. White flowers and nearly black spring foliage distinguish 'Black Ace'. Zones 4 to 9.

Rose verbena (*Verbena canadensis*)

ver-BEAN-uh can-uh-DEN-siss
Features: Summerlong bloom, mats of sturdy foliage
Hardiness: Zones 6 to 10
Bloom time: Summer
Size: 1 foot tall, 3 feet wide
Shape: Ground-hugging mat
Light: Full sun
Site: Moist well-drained soil

Description: An easy plant for all-season bloom, rose verbena forms a dark green mat carrying bright pink flowers all summer long. It looks great cascading over a rock wall or in a rock garden. Rose verbena works well as edging or as a groundcover; it is also a fine container plant.

Care: Plant rose verbena in full sun, spacing plants 1½ feet

Rose verbena

apart. A moist, well-drained soil is essential. It's not necessary to deadhead rose verbena but trim back plants in early spring to keep the planting tidy. Plants are prone to aphids, whiteflies, slugs, snails, and spider mites.
Species and cultivars: Moss verbena (*V. tenuisecta*) is similar to rose verbena but its leaves are finer cut and look fernlike. The purple or plum flowers appear in spring; blooming slows during the heat of summer and picks up when cool weather resumes. Flowers of 'Decked Out' are brilliant purple. 'Tatted Lace' blooms in white. Zones 7 to 10.
Hybrids: 'Homestead Purple' has large, dark velvety purple blossoms. Zones 6 to 10. 'Mabel's Maroon' is deep purple-red. Zones 7 to 10. 'Hot Lips' blooms in glowing red-violet. Zones 7 to 10. Flowers of 'Summer Blaze' are clear red. Zones 7 to 10.

Royal fern (See Ferns, page 185.)

Russian sage (*Perovskia atriplicifolia*)

per-OV-ski-uh at-rip-liss-ih-FOH-lee-uh
Features: Small, blue flowers, silver-green leaves.
Hardiness: Zones 3 to 9
Bloom time: Mid- to late summer
Size 4 feet tall and wide
Shape: Upright to oval, spreading
Light: Full sun
Site: Well-drained, somewhat fertile soil

Russian sage

Description: Russian sage is valued for its tiny long-lasting, bluish purple flowers and lacy gray-green foliage. Though small, the flowers cover 12 inches or more of the tips of each stem on the plant. The bruised foliage smells like sage. Plants create a silvery effect. On sunny summer days the airy foliage softens the harsh shadows of coarse-foliage flowers, such as perennial sunflower, purple coneflower, and phlox. It combines especially well with ornamental grasses and other large-scale perennials. Evening primrose, white garden phlox, and ornamental oregano are other good complements.
Care: Russian sage is easy to grow in average, well-drained garden soil, but it prefers light, alkaline, somewhat dry soils. Plants tolerate drought, heat, humidity, and wind, but not shade or poorly drained soil. Deadheading is unnecessary; the bloom period is very long without help, and plants are self-cleaning.

In rich soil or extra moist sites, Russian sage may need staking. Use grow-through supports.

Plants can become rangy if allowed to develop naturally. To keep plants in shape, treat them like the woody shrubs they are. Wait until plants start to grow in spring, then remove winter-killed stems and prune to shape the plant. Shorten stems by cutting back to a bud facing the direction in which you

Detail of Russian sage

would like the growth to head. You can also cut the branches at their base to encourage upright growth and better flowering.

In Zones 3 and 4 mulch to protect the base of the plant. Where only the roots survive the winter, cut the plant to the ground.

Plants spread by natural layering; wherever a stem touches the ground, it develops roots and a new plant grows. Dig up and discard these new plants or share them with friends. Russian sage has no serious pests or diseases if grown in full sun and well-drained soil.

Species and cultivars 'Filigran' has much finer-textured, finely dissected gray-green leaves than the species. Plants grow 3 to 4 feet tall and have airy bluish purple flowers in mid- to late summer. 'Little Spire' grows just 2 feet tall. Its lavender-blue flowers appear earlier in the summer than the species. In mild climates, plants bloom again in late fall. 'Longin' foliage is somewhat coarser than the species with the leaves less finely dissected. Plants grow to 4 feet tall and have lavender-blue flowers.
Hybrids: 'Blue Spire' has deep violet-blue flower from July to September on 12 to 15 inches of the stem tips. Plants are more upright than the species and grow 2 to 3 feet tall.

Sage (See Salvia)

Salvia (*Salvia* spp.)

SAL-vee-uh species
Features: Showy flowers in shades of blue, purple, red, white, yellow, pink, or salmon
Hardiness: Depends on species
Bloom time: Late spring to fall, depending on species
Size: Depends on species
Shape: Depends on species
Light: Full sun
Site: Average, well-drained soil

Description: This large group of showy perennials encompasses a wide variety of plants. Some have dark green foliage and blue to purple flowers. Others are large, almost shrubby plants with red flowers. Still others have gray-green foliage.

What ties the group together is their two-lipped flowers and square stems. The two top petals on the flower join to

'May Night' perennial salvia

form a hood, the top lip; the three lower petals are joined together and look like a three-lobed petal, the lower lip.

Autumn sage (*S. greggii*) blooms in scarlet red, white, and violet from midsummer to fall. In the mildest climates it can bloom from February to November. The colorful flowers attract hummingbirds. Plants grow into dense 3-foot-tall and -wide perennial shrubs and can become unruly as the season progresses. Autumn sage is extremely heat and drought tolerant. Zones 7 to 10.

Blue anise sage (*S. guaranitica*) is a shrubby woody perennial that forms a 3-foot-tall and 3- to 4-foot-wide mound of green leaves. Its 3-inch-long, intense deep blue flowers begin blooming in midsummer and last until frost. The flower stems rise 1 to 2 or more feet above the foliage. Sometimes called anise-scented sage, the crushed foliage has a mild scent but not the aroma of anise. Zones 7 to 10.

Common sage (*S. officinalis*) is the familiar culinary sage used to flavor Thanksgiving stuffing. It is an evergreen woody plant with handsome gray to gray-green foliage and racemes of blue to pink flowers in late spring. Plants grow 2 to 2½ feet tall and wide, but the long-lived plants can spread further over time. Common sage is a wonderful accent plant, complementing blue flowers and dark green foliage. Plants form an irregular rounded mound. Zones 4 to 10.

Lilac sage (*S. verticillata*) blooms in early summer with long, erect spires of lilac-blue flowers. With deadheading the show can last until early fall. Plants form clumps 1½ to 2½ feet tall and wide and have coarsely toothed grayish green spade-shape foliage. Plants are similar to perennial salvia but have coarser, lighter-colored foliage. Zones 5 to 10.

Perennial salvia (*S. nemerosa*) grows in low mounds aromatic dark green rough-textured leaves from which a dense mass of erect violet- or purple-blue flowers rises. This species is one of the showiest and longest blooming of the cold-hardy salvias. It looks stunning massed in the middle of the perennial border; small cultivars look good at the front of the border. Plant perennial salvia with light pink shrub roses, baby's breath, or Shasta daisies or combine it with the clear yellow daisies of coreopsis. Perennial salvia makes an excellent container plant or cut flower. Bees, butterflies, and hummingbirds flock to it, but rabbits and deer usually leave it alone. Zones 4 to 7.

Silver-leaf sage (*S. daghestanica*) is a pretty alpine plant with silvery blue foliage and purple-blue flowers for several weeks in late spring. Plants grow 1 foot tall and wide. They like hot, dry, full-sun sites with lean to infertile soil. Zones 5 to 8.

Yellow sage (*S. koyamae*) is a low-growing spreading plant with large arrow-shape grayish green leaves. The large pale yellow flowers rise on 2-foot-tall stems in late summer to fall. Plants spread rapidly through the garden. Unlike other salvias yellow sage grows best in shade. Zones 4 to 9.

Care: Plant autumn sage in full sun and lean to average well-drained garden soil. Plants become leggy in shade and in rich soil. Autumn sage does well in heat, drought,

and alkaline soil. Wet soil is detrimental. Cut plants back to 4 inches tall in late winter and again in late summer to keep plants tidy.

Blue anise sage does best in full sun but will tolerate light shade, although it grows taller, blooms less, and needs support in shade. Provide well-drained soil. Cut plants back about a third in early spring to make them more compact. Water and deadhead regularly during the summer. At the end of the growing season, cut plants to the ground.

Blue anise sage

Common sage grows best in full sun to light shade and slightly acid to neutral well-drained soil. Avoid highly fertile and wet soil. Water during drought. Plants will sprawl in shade. Treat common sage like a woody shrub, pruning as necessary to shape and control the size of the plants. Deadhead to remove spent flowers; deadheading won't encourage plants to rebloom.

Perennial salvia is an easy-care plant that grows in most soils and conditions but prefers moist, well-drained soil. Avoid planting it in sites that are wet in winter. Once established it will tolerate heat, humidity, and drought. Deadhead to extend blooming, cutting back flower stems to their base when flowering finishes. You can also prune back shabby clumps to encourage growth of new foliage. Divide plants every three years in early spring.

Lilac sage grows in full sun to light shade and average, dry to medium-wet, lean to moderately fertile soil. Plants become floppy in rich soil. Deadhead spent flowers to encourage rebloom, then cut the flower stems to the ground when flowering finishes. Lilac sage tolerates drought and high humidity. Feed plants with a general fertilizer in spring.

Yellow sage thrives in light to full shade and fertile, well-drained moist soil. Foliage dies back cleanly in fall so there's no need to cut plants down. Nor do you need to deadhead spent flowers. Keep plants from spreading out of bounds by simply pulling up wandering stems. Plants are shallow rooted and easy to pull. Just be diligent about keeping them in bounds.

Ccommon sage

Species and cultivars:
Autumn sage: 'Alba' has white flowers. 'Big Pink' is pink with an enlarged lower lip. 'Desert Blaze' is bright red and has variegated leaves. 'Furman's red' is a more compact, tightly branched, upright cultivar with bright red flowers. It is hardy to Zone 6. 'Purple Pastel' has clear light purple flowers and is evergreen. 'Wild Thing' blooms in pink, starting in spring.

Blue anise sage: 'Black and Blue' has deep blue flowers with black calyxes. 'Argentina Skies' blooms in pale blue.

Common sage: 'Minima' has deep lavender-blue flowers. Leaves of 'Purpurascens' are flushed with red. 'Tricolor' has gray-green leaves with irregular cream margins, some tinged red. It is hardy only to Zone 6.

Lilac salvia: 'Purple Rain' grows 2 feet tall and wide and has mauve spires from mid- to late summer.

Perennial salvia: Blue Hill (also sold as 'Blauhugel') has lilac-blue spires on 20-inch stems from late spring to fall. 'Caradonna' blooms in lavender on extra-long flower stems. The long-blooming plants can reach 3 to 5 feet tall. 'Marcus' forms a tidy 8- to 12-inch-tall, 12-inch-wide mound. Dark violet spires on 4-inch stems bloom all summer, especially when you deadhead plants. 'May Night' (also called 'Mainacht') is the king of the perennial salvias. The stiff, dark blue-violet spires open in early to midsummer; deadheading keeps plants in bloom all summer. 'May Night' grows 18 to 24 inches tall and wide. 'East Friesland' (also sold as 'Ostfriesland') has deep purple flower spikes from early to midsummer on 1½ to 3-foot plants. The pink flowers of 'Rose Wine' open from deep rose buds; plants grow 2 feet tall and wide. 'Sensation Rose' has light pink flowers on 1-foot stems. 'Snow Hill' has long-lasting white flowers from late spring through summer. Plants grow 2 feet tall.

Hybrids: 'California Sunset' is an autumn sage type with peach-orange flowers. Zones 7 to 10. 'Flare' offers hot pink blooms from early summer to frost on a compact, 2 foot-tall and wide rounded mound of foliage. It is one of a group of salvias in the Heatwave Series, which were bred for compact size, long bloom period, and heat and drought tolerance. Others in the series include 'Sizzle', which has darker hot pink flowers, 'Scorcher', whose blooms are lighter pink, and 'Blaze', which has crimson red flowers. Zones 6 to 10.

Sea holly *(Eryngium* spp.)

eh-rin-GEE-um species
Features: Thistlelike flowers in steely blue to deep purple
Hardiness: Depends on species
Bloom time: Midsummer
Size: 2 to 3 feet tall, 1½ to 2 feet wide, depending on species
Shape: Mound of foliage, upright flowers
Light: Full sun
Site: Well-drained sandy soil

Sea holly flower detail

Description: Choose sea holly for its striking flowers, prickly texture, drought tolerance, and resistance to deer, insects, and diseases. The egg-shape flowers occur in clusters and are skirted with spiky bracts at the base. Depending on the species or cultivar, the colors of the flowers, bracts, and flower stems may be deep purple to steel blue to nearly white. Best color occurs where nights are cool.

The sturdy, branched flower stems rise from low rosettes of toothy evergreen leaves. The leaves resemble the deeply cut, spiny leaves of thistles. Sea holly grows in clumps and spreads by seed. It blooms over a long period in July and August.

Stiff and prickly, this easy-care plant creates a striking effect in a garden. Its handsome form provides interesting contrast to medium-size plants, such as gray-leaved artemisias and yellow-flowered yarrows. Sea holly is excellent

Sea holly

in fresh and dried bouquets. It thrives in seaside gardens.

Care: Sea holly grows best in full sun and well-drained soil and has the best color where nights are cool. After those needs are met, plants adapt to nearly anything else you can throw at them. They do well in infertile, sandy soil as well as in soil with high salt content. Salty sea spray doesn't faze them. Plants will have trouble in rich, fertile soil, where they will fall and need staking.

Sea holly's taproot makes it difficult to transplant. Plants are pest and disease free. Cut down flowering stems after blooming to prevent excessive self-seeding. For lower maintenance grow a sterile cultivar such as 'Sapphire Blue', which does not self-sow.

Species and cultivars: Amethyst sea holly *(E. amethystinum)* grows 2 feet tall and wide. It has splendid purple-blue coloration. The most cold hardy of the species, it grows in Zones 2 to 10.

Flat sea holly *(E. planum)* has silver-blue flowers on 2- to 3-foot-tall and 3-foot-wide plants. Its leaves are scalloped rather than spiny. 'Blue Cap' (also sold as 'Blaukappe') has intense blue flowers all summer. Metallic blue flowers of 'Fluela' rise above a loose, bushy 3-foot-tall plant. 'Silverstone' has white flowers on 2½- to 3-foot-tall plants. Zones 5 to 10.

Miss Willmott's ghost *(E. giganteum)* offers large flowers on gigantic plants. The flowers can be 3 to 4 inches long while the plants grows 3 to 6 feet tall and 3 feet wide. Also called giant sea holly, Miss Wilmott's ghost is a short-lived perennial with dramatic gray-green to steel blue cylindrical flowerheads surrounded by silvery bracts. Zones 4 to 10.

Moroccan sea holly *(E. varifolium)* sports spectacular variegated dark green leaves with white veins and silver-blue stems topped with gray flowerheads. It grows 15 inches tall. Zones 5 to 10.

Hybrids: 'Sapphire Blue' (also known as 'Jos Eijking') has lavender bracts and flowers, a color similar to that of Russian sage. Plants grow 2 to 2½ feet tall and 1½ to 2 feet wide. It is a sterile nonspreading hybrid. Zones 5 to 10. 'Blue Jackpot' has showy lavender-blue flowers on 2-foot stems. Zones 4 to 10.

Sedges *(Carex* spp.)

CARE-ex species
Features: Handsome foliage
Hardiness: Depends on species
Bloom time: Grown for foliage rather than flowers
Size: 6 to 24 inches tall and wide, depending on species
Shape: Cascading to upright
Light: Part sun to full shade
Site: Moist, well-drained soil

Description: These well-known water garden plants are also excellent in perennial gardens. Most have colorful foliage that is evergreen in warm regions and semi-evergreen in cold climates. They grow in clumps and have a low, arching habit or stand upright, depending on the species. Although they look like grasses, they are not.

Sedges are excellent choices for shady gardens. In the South they supply year-round color, beauty, and interest. They make pretty accents, edging, and mass plantings.
Care: Plant in full to partial shade in hot climates, and in full

'Variegata' Japanese grass sedge

sun to full shade in cooler areas. Provide moist, well-drained soil. Avoid overwatering. Where winters are cold, placing mulch over the plants in late fall helps prevent damage to the foliage. In spring cut back any damaged foliage.
Species and cultivars: 'Beatlemania' (*C. caryophyllea*), whose official name is 'The Beatles', forms mopheads of fine-textured blue-green foliage. Clumps grow 6 inches tall and 2 feet wide. Zones 5 to 9.

Golden tufted sedge (*C. elata* 'Aurea') lights up dark corners with its yellow-edged bright green leaves. It grows

Variegated sedge

about 2 feet tall and wide in sun to partial shade, but plants in full sun require more water to flourish. Plants thrive in fertile, moist to waterlogged soil at the edge of ponds, in bogs, and in containers. 'Bowles Golden' tufted sedge has long, slender, bright golden green foliage with a thin green margin. Plants form 2- to 3-foot-tall fountains of yellow-gold. Zones 5 to 9.

'Island Brocade' broad-leaf sedge (*C. siderosticha*) grows 6 to 10 inches tall and has a spreading form with broad strappy green leaves edged in creamy yellow. It is well suited for use as a groundcover under trees, as edging, and in containers. 'Banana Boat' has broad yellow leaves edged with a broad green stripe and a thinner green stripe. Zones 6 to 9.

Japanese grass sedge (*C. morrowii*) forms 1½-foot-tall and wide clumps of ½-inch-wide glistening green leaves. Leaves of 'Goldband' have a broad white edge. It grows 1 foot tall and 2 feet wide. 'Ice Dance' is also just 12 inches tall; it has a slim white edging. 'Silk Tassel' forms wispy 12-inch-tall tufts of green and white. 'Variegata' has a broad white stripe down the center of the leaves. Zones 5 to 9.

Weeping brown sedge (*C. flagellifera*) forms an arching 18-inch clump of linear reddish bronze evergreen foliage that resembles a tuft of hair. It looks spectacular at the front of a border and in containers where it softens the edge. 'Bronzita' forms a 12-inch-tall and wide tan-bronze tuft. Zones 6 to 9.

Sensitive fern *(See Ferns)*

Shasta daisy *(Leucanthemum hybrids)*
lew-CAN-thuh-mum hybrids
Features: White daisies
Hardiness: Zones 4 to 8
Bloom time: Early summer
Size: 9 to 48 inches tall, to 3 feet in bloom, 2 feet wide
Shape: Mounded foliage, loosely columnar in bloom
Light: Full sun to partial shade
Site: Well-drained, preferably alkaline soil

Shasta daisy

Description: This timeless white daisy with a yellow center looks good in early summer borders as well as in bouquets. Flowers appear at the tips of stems emerging from a rosette of basal leaves. Individual blooms may be single or double, the latter resembling the cushion-shape flowerheads of chrysanthemum. In bloom Shasta daisy has a columnar shape; when cut back to the leaves after blooming, it makes a low mound of shiny, lancelike dark green leaves. The flowers are excellent with spiky flowers such as perennial salvia, speedwell, fleeceflower, and mullein. They blend well with other shapes, such as the flat-topped blooms of yarrow or the floating daisies of coreopsis.
Care: Grow Shasta daisies 18 to 24 inches apart in a sunny spot in well-drained, alkaline soil. Deadhead before seed sets to prevent self-sowing where you don't want the plants to

'Crazy Daisy' blossoms

spread. Some varieties will rebloom when deadheaded; others won't.

Stake taller varieties with grow-through supports. Cut plants back in fall after the foliage has died. Divide Shasta daisy in spring or fall every two or three years to keep them healthy, vigorous, and blooming. Plants are easy to move. Discard the old central portions of the plant. These are not vigorous and may harbor pests. You'll still have plenty to share.

Aphids can create problems, as can four-lined plant bugs, which damage leaves just before the flowers open. Older plantings and Shasta daisies growing in wet soils may be subject to rots, wilt, viruses, and nematodes. Stalk borers are occasional pests. Gophers avoid shasta daisy.
Species and cultivars: 'Alaska' is one of the oldest cultivars and probably one of the most widely available. Large 3-inch-wide daisies of pure white on 3-foot stems cover the plants. The long stems make the flowers especially good for cutting.

'Becky' has 2- to 3-inch-wide white single daisies on 3-foot stems. Plants bloom all summer when deadheaded. Foliage is glossy dark green. 'Brightside' is an improved 'Becky' with pure white daisies and disease resistant foliage. 'Crazy Daisy' brings semidouble to double white daisies with small butter yellow centers. The frilly blooms last all summer with deadheading. 'Silver Princess' offers pure white flowers on 9- to 12-inch-tall plants. 'Snow Lady' grows 12 to 15 inches tall and produces 2½-inch-wide, clear white daisies on short stems from June to frost. The flowers form in dense masses. 'Sonnenschein' (or 'Sunshine') has 3- to 5-inch-wide creamy white or pale lemon yellow daisies with a dark yellow center. Plants bloom from summer to fall when deadheaded. This cultivar especially tolerates drought, heat, and humidity. 'White Night' (also sold as 'White Knight') provides 4-inch-wide blooms on compact plants from late spring to frost. It does well in containers, and the flowers make good cut flowers.

Shield fern (*See Ferns*)

Showy sedum (*Sedum spectabile*)

SEE-dum spec-TAB-ill-ee
Features: Colorful broccolilike flowers, succulent foliage
Hardiness: Zones 3 to 10
Bloom time: Late summer to fall
Size: 1 to 1½ feet tall, 2 feet in bloom, 2 feet wide
Shape: Rounded clump that becomes more upright as blooms form
Light: Full sun
Site: Moderately fertile, well-drained soil

Description: This classic border perennial has four seasons of garden interest. In spring attractive, bushy succulent stems develop from a mound of blue-green fleshy nubs emerging from the soil. Summer brings flowering stems topped by dense, flat clusters of light green buds. With

Showy sedum

cooler weather in late summer to fall, pink, white, or rose flowers open, attracting bees and butterflies. In winter the now-brown blooms and tan stems maintain their form even under a blanket of snow.

All sedums have succulent, waxy, water-holding foliage and stems. Colors range from gray-green to purple- to red-tinted.

One of the most popular perennials for its foolproof nature and long-season effect, showy stonecrop is a clump-forming, fast-growing perennial. Use it as a specimen or combine it with other late-blooming or coarse-textured perennials, such as 'Chocolate' white snakeroot, purple coneflower, ornamental grasses, salvia, mullein, or yucca.

Care: Easy to grow and maintain, showy sedum thrives in well-drained soil and full sun to part sun. It does well in wind, heat, and high humidity but doesn't tolerate wet soil or poor drainage.

Staking is not needed unless plants grow in shade, in fertile soil, or are overcrowded. These conditions may cause them to fall open and need some support. You can use grow-through supports or pinch stem tips to promote density when temperatures reach 70°F in late spring. Pinching will delay flowering.

These drought-tolerant plants rarely need division, but floppy plants may benefit from dividing every five years or so to maintain vigor and shape. Keep the plant intact through the cold weather; its striking form adds winter interest to the garden.

Species and cultivars: 'Brilliant' offers large clusters of fluffy, bright rose pink flowers. 'Iceberg' blooms in white. 'Neon' sports rosy magenta flowers. 'Pink Chablis' brings bright pink flowers on top of white-edge blue-green leaves. Plants grow 14 to 18 inches tall. 'Stardust' has pale pink blooms on 18-inch-tall stems.

Goldmoss stonecrop (*S. acre*) is a creeping groundcover-type sedum with tiny round succulent leaves. Plants grow 2 to 3 inches tall and bloom in yellow in spring. Provide the same care as for showy sedum. 'Aureum' foliage is golden yellow in spring and yellow-tinged gray the rest of the season. Zones 3 to 10.

Two-row stonecrop (*S. spurium*) is another groundcover; it grows 2 to 6 inches tall. Clusters of white or rose flowers appear in midsummer. Provide the same care as for showy sedum. 'Dragon's Blood' has deep pink flowers. Foliage is bronze tinged and turns burgundy red in fall. 'Fulda Glow' offers bronze-red foliage and rose red flowers in late summer. This one may also be found as 'Fire Glow' and 'Fuldaglut'.

Kamschatka stonecrop

'Red Carpet' has red-tinted foliage that turns burgundy in fall. Plants bloom sparsely with red flowers. 'Tricolor' has variegated deep green, white, and pink foliage and pink flowers. Zones 3 to 10.

Kamschatka stonecrop (*S. kamtschaticum*) is a little taller at 4 to 9 inches, and its toothed leaves are larger than the other groundcover sedums. Clusters of flat-headed yellow flowers appear in summer. Provide the same care as for showy sedum. 'Variegatum' foliage is edged in pink and yellow; orange-yellow flowers appear in early summer. Zones 3 to 9.

Upright hybrids: 'Autumn Joy' blooms later and has denser flowers with richer color than the species. The flowers begin as a deep rose, age to bronze, and turn chocolate brown over winter. 'Autumn Fire' is an "improved" 'Autumn Joy' with bigger flowers on stronger stems to reduce flopping. 'Black Jack' has deep purple, almost black, foliage and 8-inch-wide clusters of pink flowers. 'Frosty Morn' brings white flower clusters and gray-green foliage edged in white. 'Lydia Windsor' grows to 16 inches and has deep ruby blooms in late summer to fall and very dark brownish purple leaves. 'Matrona' grows 18 to 24 inches tall with large pink blooms on polished reddish purple stems in late summer. Its gray-green leaves have rosy margins.

Creeping hybrids: 'Bertram Anderson' grows 12 inches and has intense rosy pink blooms in late summer, frosted purple leaves, and shiny purple stems.

Silver mound (*See Artemisias*)
Soft shield fern (*See Ferns*)

Spiderwort (*Tradescantia* hybrids)

trad-es-CANT-ee-uh hybrids
Features: Purple, blue, pink, or white flowers
Hardiness: Zones 3 to 9
Bloom time: Spring to fall
Size: 1 to 2 feet tall, 1 to 2 feet wide
Shape: Irregular clump
Light: Full sun to part shade
Site: Well-drained moist soil

Description: These foolproof perennials produce abundant clusters of showy three-petaled flowers in a variety of colors from spring to fall. Flowers close at night, but luckily stay open on cloudy days. The foliage is grasslike with large "joints" or nodes where the leaves attach to the stem. Foliage looks nice spilling over the edge of a path. Good companions include rose mallow, obedient plant, Japanese iris, and columbine.

Care: Spiderwort does best in full sun to light shade and moist, well-drained soil. After the first blooms in spring, the foliage becomes unattractive; cut it to the ground. New leaves will soon replace the old and plants will develop a more compact form and resume blooming. Keep plants well watered.

'Sweet Kate' spiderwort

Some species are adaptable to light, dry soil and full sun and need no special care.

Species and cultivars: 'Bilberry Ice' has white flowers splashed with soft lilac at the base of the petals and fuzzy purple stamens topped with yellow anthers. 'Blue Denim' has soft, true blue flowers. 'Blue & Gold' is outstanding with chartreuse foliage and deep blue to violet-blue flowers. You may find it also sold as 'Sweet Kate'. Flowers of

Detail of spiderwort blooms

'Concord Grape' are intense purple. 'Isis' has rich blue flowers. 'Little Doll' grows just 1 foot tall and 1½ feet wide and has light blue flowers. 'Red Grape' blooms in crimson. 'Satin Doll' has hot pink flowers. 'Zwanenburg Blue' is one of the oldest cultivars. It brings rich deep blue to violet-blue flowers to the garden.

Tharp's spiderwort (*T. tharpii*) is a native prairie plant that does well in dry sites and is adaptable to many types of soil. Rosy purple flowers appear from late spring to midsummer. Zones 4 to 8.

Spike speedwell (*Veronica spicata*)

ver-ON-ick-uh spih-CAW-tuh (or spih-CAY-tuh)
Features: Long-lasting spikes of blue, pink, or white flowers
Hardiness: Zones 3 to 8
Bloom time: Summer
Size: 8 to 18 inches tall, 12 to 24 inches in bloom, 18 inches wide
Shape: Upright clump, spiky in bloom
Light: Full sun to partial shade
Site: Moist, well-drained, somewhat fertile soil

Description: Spike speedwell brings vertical interest and bright color to container plantings and perennial gardens alike. Plants produce upright, pointed spikes of flowers in blue, pink, white, and violet. Flowers open from the bottom of the spike upward. Speedwell attracts bees and butterflies and has an informal look well suited to cottage gardens. Plant it with orange daylily, purple coneflower, and 'Goldsturm' black-eyed susan.

'Icicles' spike speedwell

Care: Spike speedwell needs good winter drainage. Plant it 18 inches apart in spring or fall in full sun to partial shade. Removing faded flower spikes encourages rebloom. Cut back spent spikes to the new growth at their base to improve the plant's appearance. Divide as necessary in spring or fall every few years.

Species and cultivars: 'Alba' has white flowers on 15-inch-tall spikes in midsummer. 'Blue Carpet' is a creeper, just 6 inches tall and 15 inches wide, with lavender-blue flower spikes. 'Blue Peter' blooms all summer in lavender-blue. 'Minuet' has reddish pink blooms on 10- to 15-inch spikes in late spring. Foliage is gray-green. 'Purpleicious' has 10-inch-long spikes of dark purple blooms above compact dark green foliage.

'Georgia Blue' creeping veronica (*V. umbrosa*) is a low, mat-forming plant 4 to 6 inches high by 12 inches wide. It produces round, bright blue blooms in late winter or spring, depending on your climate. Its dark green leaves become purple in winter. This veronica is a good choice for rock gardens. Grow it in full sun to partial shade. Zones 3 to 8.

Long-leaf veronica (*V. lonifolia*) is larger than spike speedwell but otherwise is similar. Plants grow 2 to 3 feet tall and 1½ feet wide, have gray-green foliage, and tall blue to purple spikes in midsummer. This species does not tolerate drought, wet soil, or high humidity. It does however stand up to wind. Leaf spot and mildew can be problems. The tall plants sometimes need staking; use grow-through supports. 'Eveline' has tall spikes of violet-purple flowers and grows 1½ feet tall and wide. 'Pink Shades'

Detail spike speedwell blooms

blooms in clear pink. 'Sonja' provides fuchsia-pink blooms. Zones 4 to 8.

Woolly speedwell (*V. s. incana*) grows 12 to 18 inches tall and has violet-blue flowers and furry silver foliage. Zones 3 to 7.

Hybrids: 'Baby Doll' is loaded with pink blooms on 10-inch-tall stems. 'Goodness Grows' blooms all summer with dark violet-blue spikes on 1-foot-tall and -wide plants. 'Red Fox' is a compact 15-inch-tall plant with rose red flower spikes. 'Sunny Border Blue' grows 18 to 24 inches tall and has deep violet-blue spikes and wrinkled deep green leaves. 'Waterperry Blue' is a 4- to 6-inch-tall groundcover that is good in rock gardens or on top of stone retaining walls. It has round pale blue blooms in early summer. Foliage turns purple in winter. All are Zones 4 to 8.

Stokes' aster (*Stokesia laevis*)

STOKE-see-uh LAY-vis
Features: Shaggy blue, pink, white, or yellow daisies
Hardiness: Zones 5 to 9
Bloom time: Summer to fall
Size: 12 to 18 inches tall, 1½ to 2 feet in bloom, 1½ feet wide
Shape: Round mound of flowers from low rosette of foliage
Light: Full sun to light shade
Site: Moist, well-drained, acid soil rich in organic matter

Description: Cheery 3- to 5-inch-wide flowers that last many weeks and attractive evergreen basal leaves make this native southern belle stand out in flowerbeds, borders, containers, and cottage gardens. The blooms have fringed petals and a fluffy center, and they attract butterflies. The long-lasting flowers are excellent for cutting. Grow stokes' aster with baby's breath, 'Happy Returns' daylily, and blanket flower.

Stoke's aster

Care: Stokes' aster prefers full sun and winter mulch in the North and a little afternoon shade in the South. Deadheading extends blooming; cut the flower stems to the basal foliage. Blooming clumps tend to open in the center and may need staking; use grow-through supports.

Don't cut plants back in fall; clean up the foliage in spring. Divide crowded clumps every three to five years.

Stoke's aster

Species and cultivars: 'Blue Danube' has lavender-blue flowers. The flowers of 'Colorwheel' open white, change to lavender, then to purple. 'Mary Gregory' is just 12 inches tall and has yellow flowers. 'Klaus Jelitto' blooms in light blue. 'Peachie's Pick' is 12 to 18 inches tall in bloom with blue flowers. It forms a dense mound of evergreen leaves that is less floppy than most stokes' asters.

Sundrops (*See Evening primrose*)

Sweet flag (*Acorus* spp.)

UH-core-us species
Features: Lovely colorful grassy foliage
Hardiness: Depends on species
Bloom time: Not grown for flowers
Size: Depends on species
Shape: Cascading or upright mound
Light: Full sun to part shade
Site: Moist, well-drained to wet soil

Detail sweet flag

Description: Sweet flags are not grasses, but they look like grasses, growing into arching to upright clumps of slender semi-evergreen foliage. Grow them for their leaves; flowers are not showy. Sweet flags look good in containers, massed by streams and ponds, and softening the edges of shady woodland paths. Variegated cultivars brighten shade gardens.

Care: Grow sweet flag in moist soil in partial shade to full sun; they do best with some shade. They tolerate heavy soil as well as well-drained soil. Constant moisture is key; underwatering results in burnt leaf tips. In mild climates plants are evergreen; in cold ones the foliage may or may not last through the winter. A loose mulch of pine branches or leaves will protect foliage from winter damage. Cut back any damaged leaves in spring. Sweet flags have few pests.

Species and cultivars: Dwarf sweet flag (*A. gramineus*) makes a 1-foot tuft of grassy green leaves. This slow-growing evergreen to semi-evergreen species thrives in continuously moist to wet soils and sun to partial shade. The crushed leaves are fragrant. The green leaves of 'Argenteostriatus' are striped with creamy white. 'Minimus Aureus' is 4 inches tall and 6 to 12 inches wide. It has golden leaves. 'Ogon' has

'Minimus Aureus' dwarf sweet flag

green-striped yellow foliage 6 to 12 inches tall and wide. Zones 5 to 11.

Sweet flag (*A. calamus*) can grow in several inches of water in full sun to partial shade. It forms upright plants 3 to 5 feet tall and about 2 feet wide. 'Variegatus' has striking green-and-white striped leaves. Zones 4 to 11.

Switch grass (*Panicum virgatum*)

PAN-ih-come ver-GATE-um
Features: Ornamental grass with airy, dark purple to pink flowers
Hardiness: Zones 3 to 9
Bloom time: Fall
Size: 5 feet tall, 2 feet wide
Shape: Columnar
Light: Full sun
Site: Moist, well-drained, or sandy soil

Description: Switch grass is valued for its airy flowers, narrow upright form, and multiseason interest. Some cultivars have spectacular fall color before turning tan; others change from their original color to an attractive muted tan. Switch grass may remain erect for winter interest, but it is more often crushed under the weight of heavy snow. One of the finest textured of the grasses, it is beautiful as a specimen or as a living screen.

'Shenandoah' switch grass

Care: Switch grass prefers moist, well-drained soil in full sun. It is easy to grow, and once established plants tolerate salt spray and drought. They will grow in light to part shade but may need staking. When growing in ideal conditions, plants can self-sow. Check with your extension service to see if self-sowing is a nuisance in your area. Cut them back in late winter.

Species and cultivars: 'Cloud Nine' grows 6 feet tall and forms a fine-textured clump of slender icy blue leaves and clouds of rust colored blooms in late summer and fall. 'Dallas Blues' makes a clump of drooping, pale blue leaves accented in early fall by huge rosy purple seedheads that ripen to tan. Plants are 5 feet tall. 'Haense Herms' has red to orange fall color on an arching 5-foot clump of leaves topped with open plumes. 'Heavy Metal' is a stiff, upright

'Heavy Metal' switch grass

clump of fine powder blue leaves that turn yellow in fall; plants are 3 to 4 feet tall. 'Rotstrahlbusch', also 3 to 4 feet tall, has outstanding red fall color. 'Shenandoah' forms a 3-foot clump of purple-tinged green leaves that turn deep wine red in autumn.

Swamp milkweed *(See Butterfly weed)*

Sword leaf inula (*Inula ensifolia*)

INN-yew-luh en-sih-FOH-lee-uh
Features: Long-lasting yellow blooms
Hardiness: Zones 4 to 8
Bloom time: Early summer
Size: 1½ to 2 feet tall and wide
Shape: Dense, spreading mound
Light: Full sun
Site: Well-drained soil with plentiful organic matter

Description: Sword leaf inula grows in a dense mound and spreads outward at a moderate pace. Flowers are yellow daisies with a large round center and numerous slender petals. The fine-textured foliage and flowers combine well with columnar to vase-shape plants, such as butterfly weed, yarrow, blackberry lily, bellflower, gayfeather, speedwell, and ornamental grasses.

Sword leaf inula

Care: Sword leaf inula tolerates wind but not high heat and humidity or wet, poorly drained soil. To deadhead shear plants after they bloom; this encourages repeat bloom.

Cut plants back in fall or early spring. Divide them every four to five years in spring or fall. They are easy to move. Refresh the organic matter in the soil when you replant them.

Tassel fern *(See Ferns)*

Three veined everlasting (*Anaphalis triplinervis*)

ann-AF-uh-liss trip-lyn-ER-vis
Features: White flowers, gray foliage
Hardiness: Zones 3 to 9
Bloom time: Mid- to late summer
Size: 1 to 1½ feet tall, 1 to 2 feet wide
Shape: Bushy to upright
Light: Full to part sun
Site: Well-drained soil

Description: Three veined everlasting grows into irregular clumps of gray foliage. Stem tips are topped with clusters of white pearls that open to long-lasting, yellow-centered button daisies with papery petals. The white petals are actually bracts that dry well for flower arrangements. Leaves have three veins, hence the name. Good companions include bear's breeches, speedwell, coreopsis, and penstemon.
Care: Three veined everlasting does not do well where

Three veined everlasting

summers are hot and humid. It tolerates nearly all soil conditions as long as soil is humus rich, well drained, and consistently moist. It also grows in moist to wet sites better than most gray-leaved plants. Fertilize lightly to avoid rank, weak growth. Clean up plants in early spring. Divide them every four to five years. They are easy to move. A spreading perennial, three-veined everlasting grows fast.

All everlastings are basically pest free. But they do host the larvae of butterflies, such as the American painted lady, during spring and early summer. Tolerate these leaf-eating caterpillars on well-established plants but protect new ones. The caterpillars finish feeding in time for plants to recover and bloom.

Flowers of three veined everlasting

Species and cultivars: Pearly everlasting (*A. margaritacea*) is a good choice for dry climates and, in fact, is one of the plants recommended for Colorado. It is a North American native found in dry, sandy soil and full-sun situations. The white flowers are larger than those of three-veined everlasting, and its slender, woolly foliage grows 3 feet tall. The flowers are excellent in dried flower arrangements. Zones 3 to 9.

Thrift

attractive year-round in warm climates. Use thrift as an edging; in rock gardens, troughs, and containers; tucked in stone walls; and at the front of perennial borders. Thrift spreads by seed in poor, dry, sandy soils. In small spaces it makes an effective seaside groundcover that tolerates both wind and ocean spray.

Care: Plant thrift in neutral to slightly alkaline sandy soil in full sun. It needs excellent drainage year-round. Deadheading keeps young plants in bloom and spurs occasional rebloom among older clumps. Do not cut plants back in fall. Few pests bother this plant, but it can rot in the center in humid climates or moist soils. Cultivars may be less hardy; a mulch of pine boughs helps protect them. Plants are drought tolerant and deer resistant.

Species and cultivars: 'Alba' blooms in white, as does 'Cotton Tail'. 'Bloodstone' has brilliant rose pink flowers. 'Nifty Thrifty' has pink flowers and yellow-edged evergreen leaves. 'Rubrifolia' (ruby sea thrift) grows 4 inches tall and 6 inches wide and blooms with magenta flowers in spring. New leaves open wine red in spring and turn green as summer progresses. 'Splendens' blooms in wine red (more a rosé than a merlot).

Pyrenees thrift (*A. juniperifolia*) is a dwarf, growing 2 to 4 inches tall. Its short-stemmed, pale lilac flowers are tiny too, just ⅜ inch across. Flowers are a little flatter than round. They rise from gray-green tufts of evergreen foliage. 'Bevan's Variety' has deep pink flowers. 'Rosa Stolz' flowers are pale lavender. Zones 3 to 8.

Hybrids: 'Victor Reiter' grows 2 to 6 inches tall and has light pink flowers. 'Bees Ruby' has larger, deep pink flowers on 15-inch stems. Zones 4 to 8.

Thrift *(Armeria maritima)*

are-mer-EE-uh muh-RIT-ih-muh

Features: Buttons of pink, white, or rosy purple; evergreen tufts of grassy leaves
Hardiness: Zones 4 to 8
Bloom time: Mid- to late spring
Size: 4 to 12 inches tall and wide
Shape: Rounded tuft
Light: Full sun
Site: Well-drained sandy soil

Description: Thrift's diminutive, ball-shape deep pink to white flower clusters sit on straight bare stems and are good for cutting. They open in mid- to late spring and occasionally throughout the summer. The dense grassy mounds of foliage are evergreen and look

Thrift

Thyme *(Thymus praecox)*

TIME-us PRAY-cox

Features: Evergreen foliage, bright-colored flowers
Hardiness: Zones 5 to 10
Bloom time: Late spring to early summer
Size: 1 to 8 inches tall, 1 to 2 feet wide
Shape: Ground-hugging, spreading
Light: Full sun
Site: Well-drained soil

Description: From late spring to early summer, these fragrant evergreen mats are covered in tiny but brightly colored flowers. Plants spread by layering, rooting wherever stems touch the ground and can fill large areas. They grow at a moderate to fast pace. Many cultivars are available, some with deep green foliage; others with silver or gold variegation. Foliage is

Thyme

Flowering thyme

edible, and many flavors are available.

All thymes make a fine edging or a groundcover with year-round interest. Use it as an accent petticoat for larger, vase-shape, bare-ankled perennials, such as butterfly weed or speedwell. Plants make a good foil for thrift or lamb's ears. Use golden cultivars around purple-leaf plants such as coral bell or sedum.

Care: Thyme tolerates part sun or shade from deciduous trees, as well as light foot traffic, drought, wind, and heat. They do best in full sun. Fertilize lightly to avoid rank growth. Shear or mow plants after they bloom to promote density.

Divide plantings every three to four years to renew vigor. Thyme is easy to move. Cut out sections of the plant, including the roots, fill the hole with a mixture of compost and sand, and allow plants around the hole to fill in. There's no need to cut plants back in fall.

Species and cultivars: 'Coccineus' has magenta-red flowers from early to midsummer above dark green leaves. Foliage turns bronze in fall. 'Pink Chintz' foliage is fuzzy, dark green; plants bloom in salmon pink. 'Ruby Glow' has 6-inch-long clusters of bright ruby-purple flowers that yield the scent of lemons when crushed. Woolly thyme ('Pseudolanuginosus') foliage is heavily covered in fur. It needs especially good drainage.

Lemon thyme (*T. ×citriodorus*) grows 1 foot tall and wide and also smells of lemon when crushed. Flowers are pale lilac to pink. 'Aureus' has green foliage with a broad edging of gold. 'Archer's Gold' has dark golden-yellow foliage. The foliage of 'Golden King' is variegated with gold. 'Mayfair' foliage is dark green. Zones 4 to 8.

Silver thyme

Toad lily *(Tricyrtis spp.)*

TRI-sir-tiss species

Features: Clusters of purple-spotted white flowers, interesting foliage texture
Hardiness: Zones 4 to 9
Bloom time: Late summer to fall
Size: 1 to 3 feet tall, 1½ feet wide
Shape: Upright arching
Light: Partial to full shade
Site: Moist, well-drained, humus-rich soil

Description: Toad lily is one of the most interesting perennials for the shade garden, particularly in late summer or fall. That's when the purple-dotted white flowers appear. Formosa toad lily's *(T. formosana)* up-facing 1- to 1½-inch

Toad lily

blooms look like little orchids loosely clustered at the stem tips. Hairy toad lily's *(T. hirta)* lilac blooms with purple spots form at each leaf axil where the leaves join the stem. Plants also have hairy leaves.

Until it blooms the toad lily's graceful, arching stems add an interesting textural note to the garden. Unlike hairy toad lily, which browns toward late summer, this toad lily's leaves stay relatively fresh. Long, oval, shiny dark green leaves cover upright stems that spread quickly. Grow toad lily for cutting or mass it in shady perennial borders and woodland gardens with Japanese painted fern and 'Frances Williams' hosta.

Care: Toad lily prefers part shade and moist, well-drained, acid soil rich in humus. It does poorly in high heat, drought, drying wind, and full sun. In areas with short growing seasons however, plant them where they receive part sun to ensure fast growth so it flowers before frost.

Provide more fertilizer than average perennials require. Plants need neither deadheading nor staking. Space them about 18 inches apart. Use pine needles and shredded leaves for mulch.

Divide toad lilies every three to five years to restrict their spread and renew vigor of the clump. They are easy to move. Take the time to refresh the soil at the same time. There's no need to cut toad lilies back in fall or early spring; the foliage decomposes over the winter.

Toad lilies have few pests, but leaf spots can be a serious problem on hairy toad lily, and anthracnose, a leaf-spot disease, can be especially serious on all toad lilies; choose a resistant cultivar. In hot areas or in full sun, leaf edges will scorch.

Species and cultivars:
Formosa toad lily
'Emperor' has chartreuse foliage. The midsummer flowers are speckled in deep purple. Zones 6 to 9. 'Gates of Heaven' has compact golden foliage and small dark-purple-spotted purple flowers. 'Gilt Edge' grows 2 feet tall and has striking golden-edged glossy leaves and starry white flowers with purple spots from early summer to fall. 'Samurai' has fabulous lilac-purple blooms with darker spotting. Zones 5 to 9.

Hairy toad lily 'Miyazaki' flowers are pale lavender, spotted with dark purple. 'Moonlight' has pale lavender flowers. 'Raspberry Mouse' flowers are deep red-chocolate brown. Zones 4 to 8.

Hybrids: 'Empress' blooms from midsummer to early fall. Its white flowers are heavily spotted in deep purple. The

Formosa toad lily

Toad lily

sturdy plants grow 2½ feet tall and are drought tolerant. 'Imperial Banner' is a sport of 'Empress' with creamy white leaves splotched in green. Both are hardy in Zones 5 to 8. 'Lightning Strike' blooms in lavender and has 2-foot-tall green-striped golden foliage. Zones 4 to 8. 'Moonlight Treasure' are compact 10-inch-tall plants with leathery leaves spotted in dark green. Its late summer flowers come in yellow, an unusual color for a toad lily. Zones 5 to 7. 'Sinonome' offers clustered purple-and-white spotted blooms in late summer on 3-foot-tall plants. It is drought tolerant once established in the garden. Zones 5 to 9. 'Tojen' is one of the most anthracnose-resistant cultivars. Zones 5 to 9.

Torch lily (Kniphofia hybrids)

nip-HOE-fee-uh hybrids
Features: Towering spikes of flamboyant colors
Hardiness: Zones 6 to 10
Bloom time: Summer to fall
Size: 1½ to 2 feet tall, 3 to 4 feet in bloom, 3 to 4 feet wide
Shape: Upright
Light: Full sun
Site: Moist, rich, well-drained sandy soil with abundant organic matter

Torch lily

Description: Torch lily's hot-hued spikes bring a theatrical quality to the garden. Its spikes, which narrow at the base, start out as red buds, open to orange flowers, and fade to yellow. The individual blossoms in the spike open over an extended period from the bottom upward. With this staggered opening and the changing colors, the flowers appear two-toned with red to orange tops and yellow bottoms. Long, sword-shape, blue-green leaves with toothed edges emerge from a basal rosette. The leaves are evergreen in warm climates.

The electric flower spikes, made up of 1- to 2-inch-long, down-pointing tubular flowers, stand 3 to 5 feet tall from summer through early fall. Hybrids are available from 1½ to 6 feet tall with red, yellow, orange, light green, and cream spikes.

Torch lily is a showy accent plant, and it's also a good choice for a cut flower garden. Blooms are long lasting when cut. In the garden they attract bees, butterflies, and hummingbirds.

Plant torch lily in the back of the garden. Combine it with other perennials or use it alone as an accent or specimen.

If your garden needs a cool-down, combine torch lily with blue-flowered or gray-leaved plants, such as 'Six Hills Giant' catmint.
Care: Torch lily performs best in warm climates. Plant it in full sun and moist, well-drained soil. Avoid windy spots.

You'll find torch lily available as potted plants and as bare rhizomes, or fleshy roots. Plant bare rhizomes in spring 18 inches apart and 3 inches below the surface of the soil. Set potted torch lilies at the same soil level they were in the pot.

Yellow torch lily cultivar

Remove faded flowers from the bottom of the spike to extend bloom and cut spikes to the base when flowering is finished.

Torch lily seldom needs dividing. Established plants resent disturbance and may take a couple of years to recover. Too much moisture can lead to crown rot. Tie the plant's leaves over the crown in fall to protect it in winter.
Species and cultivars: 'Alcazar' bears salmon-orange flowers on 3½- to 5-foot stems starting in early to midsummer. 'Bressingham Comet' grows 2 feet tall and 1½ feet wide with scarlet to yellow flowers from late summer to midfall. Closed flowers of 'Candlelight' are creamy yellow and open to white. 'Cobra' flowers bloom in midsummer, starting creamy at the base, changing to pale yellow-orange halfway up the spike, then to orange on top. 'Drummore Apricot' midsummer flowers are solid apricot-yellow on 2- to 3-foot stems. 'Earliest of All' blooms in rosy coral from late spring to early summer; plants are 30 inches tall. 'Shining Scepter' is 4 to 5 feet tall with solid golden yellow blooms. 'Timothy' blooms in dark salmon on 3½-foot stems.

Tree mallow (Lavatera thuringiaca)

lav-uh-TARE-uh thur-in-gee-AY-cuh
Features: Spikes of pink or white trumpet-shape flowers
Hardiness: Zones 6 to 9
Bloom time: Summer
Size: 5 to 7 feet tall, 4 feet wide
Shape: Bushy upright
Light: Full sun
Site: Well-drained soil

Description: All summer this giant perennial is big, bushy, and lush with pink, white, or purplish pink blooms. The five-petaled 3-inch-wide flowers form in loose spikes on wide branched stems. Individual blooms resemble those of hollyhocks.

Tree mallow makes an impressive show in a container. It adds

Tree mallow

Tree mallow flower detail

long-term color and stature to sunny perennial borders, where it belongs at the back, and looks good with Shasta daisies, bee balm, and coreopsis. For a flamboyant summer display, group three tree mallows, spacing them 3 feet apart. **Care:** Tree mallow grows best in continuously moist, fertile, well-drained soil, and full sun. In the South plant it in shade. Tree mallow tolerates heat and humidity and appreciates afternoon shade in hot climates. Japanese beetles can be a problem; remove them by hand. **Species and cultivars:** 'Barnsley' offers fringed white blooms with a deep pink eye on 6-foot stems from June to frost. 'Lilac Lady', also 6 feet, blooms in lavender-violet with deep purple veins. 'Red Rum' is long blooming with deep red flowers, dark stems, and bushy 3- to 4-foot growth. 'Summer Kisses' spreads 3 feet tall and wide and blooms in pink from early summer to fall. It is hardy to Zone 5. 'Sweet Dreams' has pale pink flowers with narrow petals. It is 6 feet tall and also hardy to Zone 5.

Variegated fragrant solomon's seal (Polygonatum odoratum 'Variegatum')

polly-goh-NAY-tum oh-dor-AY-tum vary-GATE-um
Features: Graceful stems of green-and-white leaves
Hardiness: Zones 4 to 9
Bloom time: Spring
Size: 2 to 2½ feet tall, 1 foot wide
Shape: Upright, arching
Light: Part to full shade
Site: Moist, well-drained soil with abundant organic matter

Variegated fragrant solomon's seal

Description: For a garden spot that's shady and a little moist, you can't do better than variegated fragrant solomon's seal. You'll love this plant for its beauty throughout the growing season. It has green-and-white patterned leaves that turn yellow in fall. In spring tiny, lightly scented, creamy bells hang from the bottom of the stem, followed by dark blue berries later in summer. The flowers are not showy but they add interest to the planting. The plants spread by shallow rhizomes and can eventually form large mass plantings. Their elegant structure of arched stems can brighten the darkness, whether grouped in a shade border with hosta and Japanese painted fern or massed with barrenwort in a grove of dogwoods or small maples.
Care: Variegated solomon's seal adapts to dry shade but

prefers partial shade and moist soil with abundant organic matter. During hot summers plants are likely to go dormant. Buy the largest container plant you can find—no smaller than a 4-inch pot. Small plants are slow to develop during the first couple of years in the garden, and it's easy to hoe them down by mistake. Space plants 1 foot apart. Don't deadhead and don't cut stems back in fall. Divide plants every five years in spring or fall. Except for the occasional slug, solomon's seal is pest free.
Species and cultivars: Small solomon's seal (P. biflorum) is 2 to 3 feet tall with arching stems of green foliage that is pubescent and silvery underneath. Plants bear greenish white flowers in late spring and dark blue berries in fall. They turn brownish yellow in fall. Zones 3 to 9.

Fragrant variegated solomon's seal foliage

Violet (Viola cornuta)

vie-OH-luh core-NEW-tuh
Features: Fragrant purple to pale purple flowers, tufted dark green leaves
Hardiness: Zones 6 to 9
Bloom time: Spring to early summer
Size: 3 inches tall, 6 inches in bloom, 12 inches wide
Shape: Mounded
Light: Full sun to partial shade
Site: Moist, well-drained, fertile soil

Description: These charming plants produce rounded, sometimes fragrant flowers lined in contrasting or darker hues. Violets grow in small, leafy tufts and have upright flower stems. They add whimsy to cottage, woodland, and rock gardens, as well as to stone walls and to the front of perennial borders. Grow them in odd-numbered groups with Lenten rose, 'Georgia Blue' speedwell, or Christmas fern. Although the species is usually a light to dark purple, cultivars are available in red, white, yellow, blue, black, apricot, and multicolor.
Care: This versatile perennial can survive in most places if it has good winter drainage. Space plants 12 inches apart in early spring. Deadheading old flowers promotes continued blooming. Clip plants back after they bloom to keep them neat and to reduce self-sowing. Violets hybridize with other violas, creating new plants. Cultivars do not come true from seed and must be propagated by division in spring or fall.
Species and cultivars: Labrador violet (V. labradorica) grows 3 inches tall and spreads indefinitely, making it an excellent groundcover. It has light bluish purple flowers

Labrador violet

White violet under tulips

through the growing season and bronzy new growth. Zones 3 to 8.

Sweet violet (*V. odorata*) is unsurpassed for fragrance and is wonderful for naturalizing in a woodland garden. It produces violet or white flowers in fall, winter, and spring in the South and spring in the North. Zones 6 to 8. 'Black Magic' and 'Painted Black' have deep purple pansylike blooms in early spring. Zones 7 to 9. 'Marie Louise' has double, ruffled lavender flowers with a powerful perfume. Zones 6 to 8.

Hybrids: 'Arkwright's Ruby' grows 6 to 8 inches tall and has red pansylike flowers. Zones 5 to 8. 'Baby Franjo' is 4 inches tall with copious pale yellow slightly fragrant flowers. Zones 4 to 8. 'Major Primrose' combines soft lilac and creamy yellow in pansylike fragrant blooms. Zones 4 to 8. 'Molly Sanderson' is 6 to 8 inches with near-black blooms all summer. Zones 5 to 9. 'Rebecca' has creamy flowers flecked with purple from spring through summer. Zones 7 to 9.

Wall germander (*Teucrium chamaedrys*)

TWO-cree-um cam-IH-driss
Features: Shiny evergreen foliage, pinky purple blooms
Hardiness: Zones 5 to 9
Bloom time: Early summer
Size: 10 to 12 inches tall, 12 to 20 inches in bloom, 1 to 1½ feet tall
Shape: Rounded clump, upright in bloom
Light: Full sun
Site: Well-drained, moderately fertile, neutral to alkaline soil

Young wall germander

Description: Wall germander has evergreen leaves and bell-shape flowers that bloom summer to fall. Grown mostly as a low hedge, its dense, lustrous, fine-textured dark green leaves make a handsome frame for other plants. The flowers attract bees and butterflies.

Use wall germander to outline a knot garden or other formal garden. Wall germander brings welcome structure and definition to the jumble of a cottage garden. Grow it in containers, as edging, or in rock gardens. Good companions include geraniums, Shasta daisy, lavender, and ornamental oregano.

Care: Wall germander grows best in any well-drained soil and full sun; but it tolerates and even thrives in sun, heat, and poor rocky soil. Once established wall germander can tolerate some drought.

Plant wall germander 12 to 18 inches apart in spring or fall. In cool climates choose a protected location for planting. Feed with slow-release granular fertilizer in spring. Water occasionally in summer but take care to not overwater.

Many gardeners routinely shear germander; however heavy pruning leaves plants weaker than ones that receive minor pruning. Clip stems to 2 to 6 inches tall in spring to remove winter damage, control legginess, and keep the shape neat and tight for hedging. Or wait until wall germander stops blooming, then remove the top third of the stems to promote plant density.

Divide wall germander in spring or fall. It is relatively free of pests and diseases, as long as you meet its cultural needs.
Species and cultivars: 'Summer Sunshine' has yellow to chartreuse leaves. It grows 6 to 8 inches tall and 15 inches wide. Its short pink flower spikes appear in late summer.

Wall germander

Wall rock cress (*Arabis caucasica*)

AIR-uh-biss caw-CASS-ih-cuh
Features: White flowers, evergreen foliage
Hardiness: Zones 4 to 9
Bloom time: Early spring
Size: 6 to 12 inches tall, 18 inches wide
Shape: Ground-hugging, spreading mat
Light: Sun to light shade
Site: Well-drained loamy soil with neutral or slightly alkaline pH

Wall rock cress

Description: Tiny white fragrant flowers cover wall rock cress in early spring. In the South plants can begin blooming as early as February and last through April. In cooler climates the show begins later but lasts just as long. This grayish green mat-forming evergreen perennial has succulent foliage and spreads by rooting wherever its stems contact moist soil. It forms colonies at a moderate to fast pace so a 6-inch plant growing in its favored location can reach 18 inches across in a single season. Rock cress looks terrific trailing over walls, scrambling through a rock garden, and at the edge of a garden. It makes a fine groundcover.
Care: Plant wall rock cress in a sunny site with well-drained,

Fringed rock cress

neutral to slightly alkaline soil. Plants thrive in cool weather and do best in the North, the cold desert, and along the coasts. They tend to open in the center in hot climates.

Wall rock cress before bloom

Deadhead plants by shearing or cut back plants after they bloom. This will help keep the centers closed and promote dense plants.

In hot, humid climates crown and stem rot diseases can hit the plants. Club root is another problem. Look for deformed, shortened roots on plants that do not thrive or that decline. Destroy infected plants; do not plant other members of the mustard family, such as basket-of-gold, in the same area. Powdery mildew may also infect rock cress. Ensure good air circulation around plants.

Species and cultivars: 'Compinkie' blooms in deep rose on 4- to 9-inch plants. 'Snowball' blooms in white from spring to early summer. 'Snowcap' offers white flowers on 6-inch-tall plants. Foliage of 'Variegata' is edged in creamy white for a striking groundcover.

Fringed rock cress (*A. blepharophylla*) is a California native with bright rose red blooms. Plants form a low tuft of evergreen foliage, 4 inches tall, from which the flowers rise on 8-inch stems. Foliage is smooth green, not hairy or gray-green. 'Spring Charm' blooms in brilliant magenta-red. 'Red Sensation' has bright crimson flowers. Zones 5 to 9.

White gaura *(Gaura lindheimeri)*

GAW-ruh lind-HIE-mer-eye
Features: Star-shape pink or white blooms on airy stems
Hardiness: Zones 5 to 10
Bloom time: Midsummer to early fall
Size: 1 to 3 feet, up to 5 feet in bloom, 3 feet wide
Shape: Upright clump
Light: Full sun
Site: Moderately fertile, well-drained soil

Description: White gaura's dainty flowers dance on wiry stems like butterflies. Its wiry wands of pink buds open to white flowers that turn pink as they age. Plants bloom continuously without deadheading, starting in late spring in the South and early to midsummer in the North. They form an airy column 3 to 5 feet tall, sometimes taller in warm climates.

White gaura looks good in the front and middle of the perennial border, where its see-through, leaning stems can intertwine with other plants in and out of bloom.

White gaura

Its clean, dark green to blue-green foliage complements spring blooming perennials, such as false indigo, gas plant, peony, and blue oat grass. Use white gaura alone in a container or mass-plant it in a bed or border. It also looks good in wildflower and prairie gardens.

Care: A low-maintenance plant, white gaura tolerates heat, partial shade, drought, and high humidity but not wet soil.

Pink flowering white gaura

Good drainage is a necessity. It does best in moderately fertile to fertile soils. The flower stems of all gauras tend to splay outward from the clump; in rich soil this trait is even more apparent. In warm climates hot summer nights shorten the lifespan of individual flowers.

Shearing plants in early summer before they bloom controls height and creates a more compact plant that blooms heavily. There's no need to deadhead white gaura; faded flowers fall from the stems without help. However occasional deadheading ensures new flower stems continue to develop.

Cut white gaura to the ground in late fall or early spring. Divide it every two or three years. White gaura tends to be short lived, but it may self-sow.

Species and cultivars: 'Bijou Butterflies' blooms in bright pink above white-edged reddish green foliage. It is hardy in Zones 6 to 8. 'Blushing Butterflies' has soft-pink blooms. 'Corrie's Gold' has gold-spotted, green variegated leaves and white flowers. Zones 5 to 9. 'Crimson Butterflies' blooms all summer with hot pink flowers above dark crimson foliage; it grows 18 inches tall. Zones 5 to 9. 'Passionate Pink' blooms in neon pink flowers and has narrow maroon leaves. Zones 6 to 9. 'Pink Cloud' has sturdy stems that never flop; it blooms in bright pink. Zones 6 to 9. 'Siskiyou Pink' grows 2 feet tall and has reddish pink flowers above reddish green leaves. Zones 5 to 8. 'So White' blooms in pure white on 15- to 18-inch stems. Zones 5 to 9. 'The Giant' reaches 5 feet tall; its white flowers are 2 inches across. Zones 5 to 8. 'Sunny Butterflies' is a 2-footer with pink flowers and white-edged grayish green foliage. Zones 5 to 9. 'Whirling Butterflies' offers lavish white blooms that fade to pink on 2 to 2½-foot-tall red stems; plants are sterile so they don't reseed. Zones 5 to 9.

Western sword fern *(See Ferns)*
White sage *(See Artemisia)*
White snakeroot *(see Joe-pye-weed)*
Wood fern *(See Ferns)*

Yarrow *(Achillea spp.)*

ACK-kill-ee-uh
Features: Red, white, pink, or yellow flowers; ferny foliage
Hardiness: Zones 3 to 10
Bloom time: Late spring to midsummer to fall
Size: Depends on species
Shape: Low mound of foliage, upright flowers
Light: Full sun
Site: Well-drained average soil and average moisture

Description: The ferny foliage and sturdy flat-topped flowers makes yarrow instantly recognizable. Some species are mounded in leaf and columnar in bloom. Others form mats of foliage with short flowers stems rising above. The foliage of all is as handsome as the flowers, and the blooms are butterfly magnets.

Yarrow's fast growth rate makes it an excellent choice to

'Moonshine' yarrow foliage

mass in beds and borders. You can also use yarrow as an edging and as a groundcover. The flat-topped flowers and ferny leaves contrast well with daylilies, beard tongue, perennial salvia, and Shasta daisies. Use the cut flowers in fresh and dried arrangements.

Care: Plant yarrow in spring or fall. Although drought tolerant it performs best planted in well-drained soil where it receives regular watering during dry spells.

The first round of blooms forms on tall stems that can be quite floppy, especially in the case of common yarrow. When the flowers fade cut the flower stem at its base, even if small, unopened flower buds are visible near the tip of the stem. Those buds will never provide much of a show. The plants will be flowerless for a few weeks and then start reblooming, this time on much tidier stems. Plants can remain in bloom until frost as long as you continue to deadhead.

Some yarrows, including sneezewort and tall forms of fern-leaf and common yarrow, flop over in humid air, rich soil, and shade. Such plants may benefit from cutting back early in the season or staking with grow-through supports.

If leaves look tatty after blooms fade, cut the plant to the ground to promote new basal foliage. Cutting back also encourages compact growth and discourages self-sowing. To take advantage of the plant's winter interest, wait until early spring to cut back dead foliage.

Yarrow is mostly pest free and resistant to rabbits and deer.

'Appleblossom' common yarrow

Species and cultivars:
Common yarrow (*A. millefolium*) is a low-growing, rapidly spreading species with white flowers and dark green foliage. Its leaves are the finest textured of the yarrows. 'Angelique' offers dark scarlet red blooms and green-gray leaves. 'Appleblossom' blooms in pale lilac and has grayish green leaves. The orange blooms of 'Fireland' fade to yellow; plants have medium green foliage. 'Heidi' has salmon pink blooms above green leaves. 'Paprika' blooms in brilliant scarlet red and has handsome gray leaves. 'Red Beauty' flowers are red-purple, and leaves are gray-green. 'Red Velvet' has fade-resistant red flowers and gray-green foliage. Flowers of 'Summerwine' are cabernet red turning pink. Zones 3 to 9.

Fern-leaf yarrow (*A. filipendulina*) reaches 3 to 5 feet tall in bloom and 2 to 3 feet wide. It has tight, flat clusters of yellow flowers from mid- to late summer and finely cut, pale green to gray-green leaves. 'Altgold' has bright yellow flowers on 3-foot stems in early summer and again in fall. Foliage is gray-green. 'Gold Coin Dwarf' offers early to midsummer blooms in mustard yellow on 3-foot stems.

'Gold Plate' grows 4 to 5 feet tall and has deep yellow flowers. Zones 3 to 8.

Greek yarrow (*A. ageratifolia*) is a suitable choice for dry mountainous regions. Clusters of white large-petaled flowers cover the 4-inch-tall, 18-inch-wide dark gray-green, evergreen to semi-evergreen mounds of gray-green foliage for several weeks in late spring to early summer. Zones 4 to 10.

Keller's yarrow (*A. ×kelleri*) thrives in the hot desert. Plants have slender ferny silver leaves and summerlong clusters of large-petaled white flowers. They grow 8 inches tall and 15 inches wide. Zones 5 to 10.

Fern-leaf yarrow

Serbian yarrow (*A. serbica*) is an evergreen gray-leaf selection for xeriscape gardens. Yellow-centered white daisies top 4-inch-tall and 15-inch-wide plants in early summer. Plants require well-drained soil and needs only occasional watering. Zones 4 to 10.

Sneezewort (*A. ptarmica*) features long, slender foliage that looks much different from other yarrows. Small, large-petaled white flowers appear in early summer. The upright plants grow 1 to 2 feet tall and 1½ feet wide. 'Angel's Breath' has small white double flowers that are good for cutting. It grows 18 inches tall and 12 inches wide. Zones 2 to 10.

Western yarrow (*A. lanulosa*) is especially well suited to western cold and hot desert regions and elevations up to 11,000 feet. It grows 6 to 12 inches tall and wide and has ferny green foliage similar to that of common yarrow. Flat-topped clusters of small white flowers appear in summer on 1- to 1½-foot stems. Plants grow in full sun to part shade, in soil with a pH of 6 to 8, and with less than 12 inches of water a year. Zones 2 to 10.

Woolly yarrow (*A. tomentosa*) is so covered in fine hairs that its finely cut foliage looks white. Plants form a tidy mound 6 to 12 inches tall and 18 inches wide. Clear yellow flat-topped flower clusters appear in early summer. Because it's so hairy, woolly yarrow does poorly in hot, humid, and wet climates. 'Aurea' blooms in golden yellow in early summer. Zones 3 to 10.

'Coronation Gold' yarrow

Hybrids: 'Coronation Gold' is a fern-leaf type with flat yellow flowers that are good for drying on 36-inch-long stems. Mounds of ferny gray foliage spread 18 inches. Zones 3 to 9. 'Moonshine', a wooly yarrow type, has lemon yellow blooms above ferny gray-green leaves and grows 24 inches by 18 to 24 inches. Zones 3 to 6. (Zone 9 in dry climates). 'Terra Cotta' is a common-yarrow type; its flowers are burnt yellow. Zones 3 to 10.

Yellow corydalis *(Corydalis lutea)*

core-ID-ill-iss loo-TEE-uh
Features: Bright yellow flowers for shade gardens
Hardiness: Zones 5 to 8
Bloom time: Midspring through fall
Size: 8 to 12 inches tall, 12 inches wide
Shape: Mound
Light: Part to full shade
Site: Moist, well-drained soil

Yellow corydalis

Description: With its bright yellow blooms and attractive leaves—green on top and frosty gray-green below—yellow corydalis looks charming at the front of a shady border or as a groundcover in lightly wooded areas, where it can naturalize by self-seeding. It's well suited for tucking into shady rock crevices and rock gardens. Although the blooms are small, they grow in eye-catching clusters. The ground-hugging foliage looks like that of bleeding heart. Yellow corydalis readily complements dark-leafed shade plants, such as heart-leaf brunnera, as well as blue or gold foliage, such as that of hostas.

Care: Grow yellow corydalis in moist, well-drained, neutral to slightly alkaline soil. Heat, humidity, and waterlogged soil can kill off this generally healthy plant. There's no need to deadhead spent flowers; plants are self-cleaning and bloom until frost anyway. They will self-sow, but seedlings are easy to remove.

Yellow corydalis rarely needs to be divided and doesn't do well when it is. Plants are easily damaged and slow to reestablish. To share plants with friends or take them to a new home, dig up seedlings instead. Plants have few pests.

'Blackberry Wine' corydalis

Species and cultivars: Blue corydalis *(C. flexuosa)*, with its finely divided bluish foliage, looks similar to yellow corydalis; but it grows more upright and has delightful blue flowers in spring. Plants do best in cool climates; they also go dormant in summer after blooming finishes. Excellent drainage is a must for their reappearance the following spring. 'Blue Panda' bears lightly fragrant blue blooms in late spring and early summer. The color is more intense in cool climates. 'China Blue' has fragrant grayish blue flowers. Zones 5 to 8.

Hybrids: 'Blackberry Wine' grows 10 to 18 inches tall and has clustered ¾-inch purple blooms from late spring to midsummer. Zones 5 to 8.

Yellow foxglove *(Digitalis grandiflora)*

DIJ-it-al-is gran-di-FLOOR-uh
Features: Spectacular spires of yellow flowers
Hardiness: Zones 3 to 8
Bloom time: Early to midsummer
Size: 1 foot tall, 2 to 4 feet in bloom, 1½ to 2 feet wide
Shape: Flat rosette of leaves from which tall flower spikes grow
Light: Partial shade
Site: Average garden soil

Description: Yellow foxglove brightens woodland landscapes with tall spikes of butter yellow flowers. It makes an impressive vertical garden accent and looks lovely in shady borders. Like all foxgloves the blooms line up on one side of the flower stalk and have a sweet nectar that attracts hummingbirds. Combine yellow foxglove with lady's

Yellow foxglove with perennial salvia

mantle, large-leaved hosta, or Bethlehem sage. It also looks charming planted among shrubs and trees. Yellow foxglove is a perennial that may self-sow in good conditions.

Care: Although yellow foxglove grows well in average garden conditions, it prefers partial shade and moist, well-drained soil high in organic matter. In warm climates it requires some afternoon shade. Yellow foxglove often blooms again if you cut off faded flower spikes before they set seed. Once the plant has rebloomed, remove the flower stalks to prevent self-seeding. Deadheaded plants may rebloom in fall. Divide the clump when the plant is not in bloom.

Species and cultivars: 'Carillon' is a 10-inch dwarf with yellow flowers through the summer. 'Temple Bells' has extra-large yellow blooms.

Common foxglove *(D. purpurea)* is a short-lived, self-sowing perennial or biennial that grows up to 6 feet tall. Its tall spikes create excitement in sunny to partly shaded borders and cottage gardens. Plants are often paired with clematis and old-fashioned shrub roses. 'Alba' has white flowers. Excelsior Hybrids develop spikes of horizontal flowers in pink, white, purple, and yellow. Foxy Hybrids bloom on 2- to 3-foot spikes of pink, cherry, cream, and white with maroon markings. 'Silver Fox' has creamy bells flushed lavender-pink on

Common foxglove

Strawberry foxglove

the outside and spotted inside. Leaves are silvery leaves. Zones 4 to 8.

Dusty foxglove (*D. obscura*) has rusty yellow flowers on 1½- to 2-foot-tall spikes in late spring to early summer. Grow it in full sun to part shade in infertile to average soil that is very well drained. Zones 4 to 9.

Strawberry foxglove (*D. ×mertonensis*) bears strawberry-colored bloom spikes up to 3 feet tall. Velvety dark green leaves up to 1 foot long are attractive all summer. Plants are short lived. Divide them every two to three years to maintain vigor. Zones 3 to 8.

Yellow patrinia (*Patrinia scabiosifolia*)

pat-REEN-uh scay-bee-OH-si-foh-lee-uh
Features: Lime-tinged yellow flowers clustered on towering stems, late-season back-of-the-border color
Hardiness: Zones 5 to 8
Bloom time: Mid- to late summer
Size: 12 to 18 inches tall, 4 to 6 feet in bloom, 2 feet wide
Shape: Mound with flowers rising above
Light: Full sun to light shade
Site: Moist, well-drained, fertile soil that has abundant organic matter

Yellow patrinia

Description: You can count on this tall perennial to bloom from summer to fall. It creates a bright greenish yellow haze at the back of borders. The airy flat-topped flower clusters cap sturdy, branched, see-through stems growing from a clump of basal leaves; they resemble a chartreuse Queen Anne's lace and indeed are sometimes called golden lace.

Patrinia is a clump-forming plant that spreads by stolons at a moderate pace. During summer heat the flowers bring the memory of cool spring greens.

Long-blooming patrinia creates a lacy effect that suits lightly shaded gardens and sunny borders. It is a long-lasting cut flower. Combine it with perennials that have dense flowers, such as ironweed or blanket flower. The chartreuse-yellow blooms also combine well with Russian sage, joe-pye weed, plume poppy (*Macleaya cordata*), and ornamental grasses.

Care: Patrinia is largely pest and disease free and adapts well to heat, drought, wind, and humidity, but not excessive wet soil in winter. During the growing season provide average to continuous moisture. Patrinia's tall stems may require staking.

Deadheading extends flowering and prevents self-sowing (plants do not bloom the first year in the garden). Cut spent blooms at the base of the flower stalk.

Species and cultivars: White patrinia (*P. villosa*) grows 2 to 3 feet tall and has white flowers in fall. It is otherwise similar to yellow patrinia. Zones 5 to 8.

Yellow waxbells (*Kirengeshoma palmata*)

ky-reng-ee-SHOW-muh palm-MAY-tuh
Features: Graceful clusters of waxy yellow flowers, broad foliage shaped like maple leaves
Hardiness: Zones 5 to 9
Bloom time: Late summer to early fall
Size: 2 to 3 feet tall, 3 to 4 feet in bloom, 2 to 3 feet wide
Shape: Rounded clump
Light: Part sun to full shade
Site: Moist, well-drained, acid soil

Yellow waxbells flowers

Description: Yellow waxbells is a woodland perennial grown as much for its foliage as it is for its flowers. The large maple-shape leaves are a textural delight in a shade garden. Their purplish stems contrast nicely with the green of the blades.

Plants form a coarse, shrubby mound of foliage. In fall large, waxy yellow flower buds develop at the tops of the stems in arched, branching clusters. The buds open to long, narrow creamy yellow bells.

Yellow waxbells is perfect for naturalizing in woodland gardens, near shrubs and small trees, or at the edge of a shady pond with Japanese iris and 'Bowles' golden sedge. It makes a good companion to fine-textured, short, or columnar plants, such as bugbane, astilbe, goatsbeard, meadow rue, corydalis, monkshood, and cardinal flower.

Care: Yellow waxbells is relatively carefree when it grows in partial to full shade and continuously moist, well-drained, acid soil that contains abundant organic matter. Plants do not take heat or drought; they will tolerate heavy soil and most other conditions if their moisture needs are met. Foliage may scorch in sun or dry soil; protect plants from harsh afternoon sun and strong winds.

Deadhead if desired. Frost usually ends the bloom season in Zones 5 and 6, so plants rarely reseed in those areas. Staking is unnecessary and plants rarely require division. They grow best when left alone.

Cut plants back in late fall or early spring. Plants take a few years to reach full size, and young plants can be mistaken for maple seedlings; take care not to weed them out. Few pests bother yellow waxbells.

Yellow waxbells foliage (background)

Yucca (*Yucca* spp.)

YUCK-uh species
Features: Architectural form, towering clusters of scented flowers
Hardiness: Zones 4 to 11
Bloom time: Early to midsummer
Size: Depends on species
Shape: Spiky rounded clump, tall branched flowers
Light: Full sun
Site: Light, sandy, well-drained soil

Description: For pure drama you can't beat yuccas, with their evergreen tufts of stiff sword-shape leaves. In summer giant, long-lasting, branched flower clusters loom as much as 5 feet above the leaves. The individual bell-shape flowers are 2 inches wide, fragrant, and creamy white. Technically yuccas are drought-tolerant, cold-hardy shrubs. Use them as specimen plants in a garden or to line a path. Grow them with roses, giant coneflowers, or ornamental grasses.

Adam's needle in bloom

Care: Yuccas require full sun and excellent soil drainage. Meet those conditions, and they are the original easy-care plants. Space them 3 feet apart. Trim off tattered leaves and remove spent flower stalks. Leaving the spent flowers, letting weeds grow through the foliage, or allowing debris to pile up in their leaves will ruin the effect of yucca plants. Yucca can be difficult to work around because of its pointed leaf tips. Wear gauntlet gloves and eye protection to avoid injury. Use a leaf blower to clean up accumulated debris.

Species and cultivars: Adam's needle (*Y. filamentosa*) grows 3 feet tall and wide, has dark green leaves with long curly hairs along the edges, and flowers that rise 5 feet above the foliage. Adam's needle can take light shade. 'Bright Edge' makes a 20-inch mound of slender dark green leaves edged in creamy gold. Flowers rise just 3 feet tall. 'Color Guard' is a 20-inch-tall, 3-foot-wide tuft of bold yellow-centered leaves with deep green edges. White flowers rise 6 feet above the foliage, which flushes coral in winter. 'Hairy' has grayish green leaves and lots of curly hairs coming off the edges. It grows just 1½ feet tall and 3 feet wide. 'Ivory Tower' blooms in greenish white; foliage is blue-green and 3 to 4 feet tall and wide. 'Variegata' has bluish green leaves edged in

'Bright Edge' adam's needle

white. Plants grow 3 to 4 feet tall and wide; flowers rise 6 feet above the foliage. Zones 5 to 9.

Banana yucca (*Y. baccata*) is a small, 1½-foot-tall, compact plant composed of thick, stiff dark green leaves. The dense spike of large purple-tinged white flowers barely rises above the top of the foliage. Although it is native to New Mexico, plants are hardy in Zones 4 to 10.

Blue-beaked yucca (*Y. rostrata*) has 2-foot clusters of white flowers in late spring and early summer. Its powder blue foliage radiates from a short central stalk. Leaves are sharp tipped and remain on the trunk when they die. Beaked yucca grows slowly, reaching 4 feet tall in 10 years. It potentially can grow to 10 feet tall. 'Sapphire Skies' is even bluer than the species. Zones 5 to 10.

Curve-leaf yucca (*Y. recurvifolia*) develops a single, unbranched 6- to 10-foot-tall trunk over time. In late spring or early summer, large white flowers appear in loose, open clusters on 3- to 5-foot-tall stems. Curve-leaf yucca spreads by offsets and can form large colonies. Its blue-green leaves grow 2 to 3 feet long and have a sharp bend. The spiny leaf tips bend to the touch. 'Monca' (sold as Banana Split) has arching yellow leaves edged in gray-green. Flowers occur in 4-foot spikes. The evergreen plants eventually reach 6 feet tall, 4 feet wide, and have a trunk. Zones 7 to 10.

Small soapweed (*Y. glauca*) forms low rosettes of slender leaves that grow 2½ feet long and often trail whitish threads. Flowers are similar to those of adam's needle. Does best in the desert. Zones 4 to 10.

Spanish dagger (*Y. gloriosa*) has 1½- to 2-foot-long, stiff, straight leaves with soft points that won't penetrate skin. Eventually plants can grow into an 8- to 10-foot-tall multitrunked evergreen shrub. Creamy white 4-inch-wide flowers appear in late summer. The blue-green leaves of 'Variegata' are edged with a slim line of yellow. The fragrant white flowers have a purple blush and grow on a 6- to 8-foot spike. Plants are 4 to 5 feet tall and wide; they eventually form a trunk and reach 6 to 8 feet tall. Zones 6 to 11.

Weakleaf yucca (*Y. flaccida*) looks like adam's needle, but its evergreen leaves are less rigid and its flower stalks are somewhat shorter. The 1½- to 2-foot-long leaves arch downward from their midpoints. Plants bloom in early summer on 3- to 5-foot branched stalks. 'Gold Garland' forms a 3-foot-tall and -wide clump of green-and-yellow leaves with fragrant white flowers. Over time plants develop a short trunk. 'Golden Sword' has green-edged yellow leaves. Zones 6 to 10.

'Variegata' adam's needle

'Ivory' weakleaf yucca

Index

A

Acanthus spp. (bear's breeches), 164
Achillea spp. (yarrow), 243–244
Acid-loving plants, fertilizing, 117
Aconitum spp. (monkshood), 213–214
Acorus spp. (sweet flag), 236–237
Actaea simplex (bugbane), 170–171
Agapanthus (Agapanthus hybrids), 158
Agastache spp. (hyssop), 201
Aggressive plants, 75
Alcea rosea (hollyhock), 199
Alchemilla mollis (lady's mantle), 204–205
Allium spp. (ornamental allium), 218–219
Amendments. See Fertilizer; Soil, amendments; specific amendments.
Amsonia (Amsonia spp.), 158
Analogous color, 50, 68
Anaphalis triplinervis (three veined everlasting), 237–238
Anemone (Anemone ×hybrida), 159
Annual color, planting for, 107
Anthemis tinctoria (golden marguerite), 195
Aphidiid wasps, 141
Aphids, 142
Aquilegia spp. (columbine), 177
Arabis caucasica (wall rock cress), 242–243
Armeria maritima (thrift), 238
Artemisias (Artemisia spp.), 159–160
Aruncus dioicus (goatsbeard), 194
Asclepias tuberosa (butterfly weed), 171
Asters (Aster spp.), 160–161
Astilbe (Astilbe spp.), 161
Astrantia major (masterwort), 211
Asymmetric vs. symmetric, 40–41
Aurinia saxatilis (basket-of-gold), 164–165
Automated watering systems, 113
Autumn fern. See Ferns.
Avens (Geum species), 161–162

B

Baby's breath (Gypsophila paniculata), 162
Bacteria, soil amendment, 93
Balance, design guidelines, 40–41
Balling shovel, 94
Balloon flower (Platycodon grandiflorus), 163
Baptisia australis (false indigo), 184
Bare root plants, 102, 105
Bark mulch, 98
Barrenwort (Epimedium spp.), 163–164
Basket-of-gold (Aurinia saxatilis), 164–165
Beach wormwood. See Artemisias.
Bear's breeches (Acanthus spp.), 164
Beat test, 141
Bed shaping, 35–36, 64–65
Bee balm (Monarda didyma), 165
Begonia grandis (hardy begonia), 196
Belamcanda chinens (blackberry lily), 166–167
Bellflower (Campanula spp.), 165–166
Bergenia cordifolia (heart-leaf bergenia), 197–198
Big betony (Stachys grandiflora), 166
Biological control, pests and diseases, 141, 154–155
Black, design guidelines, 52
Blackberry lily (Belamcanda chinens), 166–167
Black-eyed susan (Rudbeckia fulgida), 167
Black snakeroot. See Bugbane.
Black sooty mold on foliage, 142
Blanket flower (Gaillardia hybrids), 168
Bleeding heart (Dicentra species), 168–169
Blooms. See also specific plants.
  design guidelines, 61
  encouraging large flowers, 124
  flowering window, 14–15
  spent, removing, 123–125
  symptoms
    distortion, 143
    gray mold, 149
    large holes, 145
    unexpected color, 152
    white powder, 150
    white streaks, 142
  year-round progression, 8–9
Bloom time. See also specific plants.

description, 157
matching, 72
by season, 76–79
Blue fescue (Festuca glauca), 169
Blue oat grass (Helictotrichon sempervirens), 169–170
Blue star. See Amsonia.
Boltonia (Boltonia asteroides), 170
Borders, 64–65
Borers, 143–144
Botanical plant names, 29
Botyritis blight, 149
Branching, encouraging, 118–119
Brunnera macrophylla (heart-leaf brunnera), 198
Buds, propagation from, 130–131
Bugbane (Actaea simplex), 170–171
Bugs controlling bugs, 141, 154–155
Bulbs, propagation, 135
Burning, from excess fertilizer, 117
Butterfly weed (Asclepias tuberosa), 171
Buying plants. See Sources for perennials.

C

Calamagrostis acutiflora (feather reed grass), 185
California fuchsia (Zauschneria californica), 171–172
Campanula spp. (bellflower), 165–166
Campion (Lychnis spp.), 172
Cardinal flower (Lobelia cardinalis), 172–173
Care. See also specific activities.
  branching, encouraging, 118–119
  calendar for, 136–137
  challenges, 15
  container gardens, 119
  definition, 157
  discipline, 139
  disease. See Disease control.
  dormancy, 127
  fall and early winter, 134–135
  feeding plants. See Fertilizer; Soil, amendments; Soil, nutrients.
  grooming, 126–127
  hail damage, 127
  large flowers, encouraging, 124
  myths, 15
  pests. See Pest control.
  postplanting, 106–107
  pre-planting, 99

problems. See Symptoms; Troubleshooting; specific problems.
pruning
  deadheading, 123–125
  disbudding, 124
  pinching, 118–119
  unhealthy plants, 126
  spent blooms, removing, 123–125
  spring, 135
  staking, 120–122
  storm damage recovery, 127
  unhealthy plants, 126
  winter preparation, 134–135
Carex spp. (sedges), 232–233
Caryopteris (Caryopteris ×clandonensis), 173
Catananche caerulea (cupid's dart), 180–181
Caterpillars, 144–145
Catmint (Nepeta racemosa), 173–174
Celandine poppy (Stylophorum diphyllum), 174
Centaurea montana (mountain bluet), 214
Centranthus (Centranthus ruber), 174
  chart of solutions, 11
  maintenance, 15
  myths, 15
  poor drainage, 10
  shade (shadow), 11
  short flowering window, 14–15
  soil, 11
  space requirements, 15
  steep slopes, 10
  sunlight, 11
  tough locations, 10
Checkerbloom (Sidalcea malviflora), 175
Chelone obliqua (rose turtlehead), 229
Christmas fern. See Ferns.
Chrysanthemum (Chrysanthemum hybrids), 175–176
Chrysogonum virginianum (goldenstar), 196
Cinnamon fern. See Ferns.
Cinquefoil. See Nepal cinquefoil.
Clay soil, 22–23, 82–83
Clematis (Clematis spp.), 176–177
Climate. See also specific plants.
  hardiness zones, 17, 157
  summer care, 9, 69
  temperature extremes. See also Care, calendar.
    cold, 9, 134–135
    container gardens, 119
    hot, 9, 69
  winter care, 9, 134–135

USDA Hardiness Zone Map

Range of Average Annual Minimum Temperatures for Each Zone

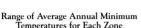

Zone 1: Below -50 F (below -45.6 C)
Zone 2: -50 to -40 F (-45.5 to -40 C)
Zone 3: -40 to -30 F (-39.9 to -34.5 C)
Zone 4: -30 to -20 F (-34.4 to -28.9 C)
Zone 5: -20 to -10 F (-28.8 to -23.4 C)
Zone 6: -10 to 0 F (-23.3 to -17.8 C)
Zone 7: 0 to 10 F (-17.7 to -12.3 C)
Zone 8: 10 to 20 F (-12.2 to -6.7 C)
Zone 9: 20 to 30 F (-6.6 to -1.2 C)
Zone 10: 30 to 40 F (-1.1 to 4.4 C)
Zone 11: Above 40 F (above 4.5 C)

This map of climate zones helps you select plants for your garden that will survive a typical winter in your region. The United States Department of Agriculture (USDA) developed the map, basing the zones on the lowest recorded temperatures across North America. Zone 1 is the coldest area and Zone 11 is the warmest.

Plants are classified by the coldest temperature and zone they can endure. For example, plants hardy to Zone 6 survive where winter temperatures drop to -10° F. Those hardy to Zone 8 die long before it's that cold. These plants may grow in colder regions but must be replaced each year. Plants rated for a range of hardiness zones can usually survive winter in the coldest region as well as tolerate the summer heat of the warmest one.

To find your hardiness zone, note the approximate location of your community on the map, then match the color band marking that area to the key.

METRIC CONVERSIONS

U.S. UNITS TO METRIC EQUIVALENTS			METRIC EQUIVALENTS TO U.S. UNITS		
To convert from	**Multiply by**	**To get**	**To convert from**	**Multiply by**	**To get**
Inches	25.4	Millimeters	Millimeters	0.0394	Inches
Inches	2.54	Centimeters	Centimeters	0.3937	Inches
Feet	30.48	Centimeters	Centimeters	0.0328	Feet
Feet	0.3048	Meters	Meters	3.2808	Feet
Yards	0.9144	Meters	Meters	1.0936	Yards
Square inches	6.4516	Square centimeters	Square centimeters	0.1550	Square inches
Square feet	0.0929	Square meters	Square meters	10.764	Square feet
Square yards	0.8361	Square meters	Square meters	1.1960	Square yards
Acres	0.4047	Hectares	Hectares	2.4711	Acres
Cubic inches	16.387	Cubic centimeters	Cubic centimeters	0.0610	Cubic inches
Cubic feet	0.0283	Cubic meters	Cubic meters	35.315	Cubic feet
Cubic feet	28.316	Liters	Liters	0.0353	Cubic feet
Cubic yards	0.7646	Cubic meters	Cubic meters	1.308	Cubic yards
Cubic yards	764.55	Liters	Liters	0.0013	Cubic yards

To convert from degrees Fahrenheit (F) to degrees Celsius (C), first subtract 32, then multiply by ⁵⁄₉.

To convert from degrees Celsius (C) to degrees Fahrenheit (F), multiply by ⁹⁄₅, then add 32.